If I Did It . . .
I Don't Remember

Salisbury's Edwardian Murder Mystery
or
Who killed Teddy Haskell?

JEREMY B MOODY

and

BRUCE S PURVIS

2008

For George Fleming,
in friendship and admiration

First published in the United Kingdom in 2008 by

The Hobnob Press,
PO Box 1838, East Knoyle, Salisbury SP3 6FA

British Library Cataloguing in Publication Data
A catalogue record for this book is available from the British Library.

ISBN: 978-0-946418-78-7

Typeset in 10.5/12.5 pt Octavian
Typesetting and origination by John Chandler
Printed in Great Britain by Salisbury Printing Company Ltd, Salisbury

Contents

Acknowledgements

OUR FIRST and most long-standing debt is to the shades of those who were caught up in the horrific death of Teddy Haskell on the night of 31 October 1908, and the drama of the police investigations and legal proceedings, culminating in the two trials of Teddy's mother, Flora, indicted for murder, early in the spring of 1909. The only way we have been able to attempt to repay that debt has been to try to solve the mystery, to this day, of who it was that slew Teddy. In doing so, we have entered upon what his mother's defending counsel, Rayner Goddard, described as 'dangerous realms of speculation' in trying to ascribe a motive for the killing, to shed light on who might have been guilty.

Amongst the living, we have been sustained by the interest and forbearance of our publisher, John Chandler, and our friends and families. We are especially grateful to John, to Petrina and to George Fleming, whose enthusiasm and insights in our regular meetings have contributed immeasurably to our deliberations. A special word of thanks is due to Petrina for her support during the research process, her advice during many an evening talking over the Haskell case and her help with proof reading. To George, also, we owe the mapping, plotting minute-by-minute the movements of all those involved on the evening of 31 October. He would surely have been a robust and insightful expert witness a century ago. We are grateful, too, to Robin Odell, the doyen of Jack the Ripper studies and of murder studies generally, for his introduction to our work.

We have been more fortunate than we could possibly have imagined as a result of the generosity of Mr Patrick and Mrs Betty Thomas, present owners of 40 Meadow Road for allowing access to their home; of Mr Timothy Walker and Mrs Ann Whittle who have furnished us with the photographs of the crime scene and of Meadow Road from the papers of their grandfather Frank Richardson; and of Mr Brock Trethowan, who has provided access to the case notes and briefs to counsel of his great-grandfather, William Trethowan.

Our thanks go to the staffs of Salisbury Reference Library and of the Wiltshire and Swindon History Centre for guidance and access to a range of resources, including most importantly the press reports on the case; likewise to the staffs of the British Library Newspaper Library and of The National Archives, to Dr Lorna Haycock, Librarian at the Wiltshire Archaeological and Natural History Society, to the librarian of Southampton University Library, and also to John Pothecary for allowing us access to his collection of newspapers. We wish to thank the Chief Executive of The National Archives, and Mr Trethowan for their permission to reproduce the text of the police and medical reports to the DPP and the defence counsel's briefs and case notes of William James Trethowan respectively. Similarly, we thank the Chief Executive of The National Archives, the Director-General of the Ordnance Survey, the Registrar General, Mr Walker and Mrs Whittle, Nicholas Connell, Andy Nicklen, Messrs Chambers Harrap and the Editor of the Salisbury Journal for permission to reproduce illustrative material as individually credited. If there are any rights-holders whom, despite our best efforts we have failed to acknowledge, we apologise and will make good the omission in any future edition of this book.

On more specific matters, we wish to thank George Fleming, Jane Howells, David Purvis and Brock Trethowan for kindly reading and commenting on drafts of the text, Ann Ireland for lending us contemporary house furnishing bills, Charles Ranaboldo for his illuminating advice on the treatments for and prognosis of tuberculosis, Peter Gillham, Archivist at Salisbury District Hospital for helping with our research into Edwin Haskell's amputation and details of the operation, Charles Byrne, Senior Clinical Engineer at Salisbury District Hospital for his advice on prosthetics, and to George Harris, for his memories of father-in-law who was a playmate of 'Teddy' Haskell. And so, as we have tried for the centenary of this sad and shocking case, to shed some little light on the continuing mystery, we hope the spirits of Flora Haskell and her 'dear little Teddy', and of all who were touched by the affair, may rest in peace.

Foreword

ROBIN ODELL

(author of The Murderer's Who's Who, Jack the Ripper in Fact and Fiction, Exhumation of a Murder, *and many other books in the field of criminology and forensic science)*

T WELVE YEAR OLD TEDDY HASKELL was a popular boy in Fisherton, the suburb of Salisbury, Wiltshire, where he lived with his widowed mother. Six years earlier he had contracted tuberculosis, which resulted in his leg being amputated above the knee. Everyone admired the pluck of this cheerful lad who got around on his crutches and even managed to play football with his pals.

The shock and sadness that followed news of Teddy's tragic death in his own home in 1908 was palpable. The manner of his death was particularly brutal; his throat was cut while he lay in bed. Suspicion soon fell on his mother, Flora Fanny Haskell, whose early statements contradicted those of other witnesses. Her blood-stained clothing, like her bewildered denials, would be subjected to intensive forensic scrutiny in two trials for murder when her own life was at stake.

This story which shook the local community to its roots and gripped the nation is admirably set out in all its forensic and social detail by the authors. They paint a graphic picture of suburban Edwardian life and revisit a crime that the passage of time had relegated to a backwater. In setting the scene, they show that the murder of Teddy Haskell and its investigation and prosecution drew in an impressive assembly of *dramatis personae*.

Chief Inspector Walter Dew, approaching his moment of fame in the arrest of Dr Crippen, was called in from Scotland Yard to boost the police investigation of the crime scene. Dr Augustus Pepper, consultant surgeon of considerable distinction and a Home Office expert, would defend his deductive skills in court against the incisive examination of Rayner Goddard, a future Lord Chief Justice of England. And Flora Haskell's second trial for murder would be presided over by Mr Justice Darling, a judge whose reputation for wit endeared him to court reporters.

The progress of the Haskell Case was comprehensively reported in the newspapers of the day. The essential elements of a lone woman in a state of obvious distress accused over the death of her crippled boy tugged at the heartstrings of the nation. In an age when newspapers were the only media, all the comings and goings at the trial proceedings were reported in great detail.

This fund of reportage has been used to good advantage by the authors to convey the essence of the contemporary scene and to infuse their telling of the story with refreshing interpretation. They have sieved through all the evidence available, ranging from Chief Inspector Dew's reports on the progress of his enquiries and questioning of Flora Haskell to the trial transcripts of Rayner Goddard's compelling performance in her defence.

At the heart of the story is the dedication of a hard-working mother to her handicapped son. In court, a witness described her as ,'Everything a mother ought to be, she was.' Flora Haskell's own words, spoken to a prison wardress, '. . . if I did it, I don't remember,' eloquently echo her distress and are tellingly used by the authors as the title of their account.

Robin Odell
Oxfordshire, September 2008

1
Prologue

SALISBURY, SATURDAY 31 October 1908; Allhallows' Eve. At about 6.50 in the evening in the neighbourhood of the County Gaol at Fisherton, Teddy Haskell, a disabled lad, just turned twelve, calls on his cousin and next-door neighbour Walter Noble to ask how his school football team had fared in the match with the Dean Village Eleven, and is delighted with the news of a five-nil victory. Before he leaves to take a stroll, Walter promises to take Teddy to the match with Downton the following week. Later that evening the post arrives at Teddy's home, No. 40 Meadow Road, including a letter for him with some picture postcards from another of his cousins, living in Plymouth, which Teddy reads and re-reads. He has a chat with his other cousin, Walter's younger brother Percy, who decides likewise to go out for a while.

'What time will you be back?' asks Teddy. 'Soon after 10 o'clock' is the reply. 'All right, don't be late'.

At about 9.00, his mother Flora, four years widowed, gives Teddy a bath and puts him to bed. She steps out to buy some groceries, and is gone some time. But by 9.45, Flora has returned, for her neighbour Gertrude Steer, who lives next door but one, at No. 36, calls at the back door to bring round a coat she has made for Flora. Pleased with the coat, Flora exclaims it is just what she wanted, and that tomorrow she would be a 'toff'. Flora offers to pay, but Gertrude has to be on her way, for she is due to meet her sister at the Railway Station at 10.00. Flora's mood is 'bright and cheerful'. At about 10.20, Flora has locked up for the night, when John Wyatt,

a Co-op delivery boy, knocks on the door. Perhaps she doesn't hear the first time he knocks; perhaps she is at the back of the house, for only after John has knocked again does Flora come to the door. John asks after Flora's neighbour Mrs Manning, at No. 42, and learns that she is out, but Flora takes her neighbour's parcel in to give to her the next morning – a simple act of neighbourliness.

Shortly afterwards, no later than 10.30, Percy Noble returns, to call upon his aunt. He depresses the back-door latch and presses hard against the

40 MEADOW ROAD, FROM A SKETCH PUBLISHED IN
LLOYD'S WEEKLY NEWS SHORTLY AFTER THE CRIME
HAD BEEN COMMITTED

door with his knee, but it is locked. From within he hears a commotion, then the door is opened by a terror-stricken Flora, with the words, 'Oh Percy! Go and stop that man; he has been and murdered my Teddy!' Percy turns and runs out of the back yard, into the passage behind the houses and along into York Road: he looks up and down the street, but there is no-one. He sprints along York Road and into Wilton Road, there to summon the help of the local doctor, Herbert Wilks.

At the door of her house Flora is screaming. Her neighbour Walter Steer rushes from the passage into Meadow Road, where he meets the distraught mother. She gasps 'That man!' and Steer runs to the corner of York Road. But all he sees are two men standing in the middle of the road outside the *Duke of York* public house, and they have seen no-one. Steer returns, climbs the stairs of no. 40, and looks in the front bedroom, where the light of the street lamp reveals nothing untoward: the rooms at the back of the house are in darkness, so he leaves to fetch a lamp. Flora runs from her house to the corner of York Road, and screams again, 'Someone has killed my boy,' and Sarah Butt, of 40 York Road comes out: back inside No. 40. Flora sobs 'Somebody, go and see my son,' but they vainly search in the kitchen for a candle. Steer returns with the lamp, Mrs Butt asks Flora 'Shall I go up?' – 'Do', begs Flora, and the pair climb the stairs to Teddy's room. There they come upon a sight no parent should face. Tucked up in bed is Teddy, with a hand outside the coverlet; his eyes are closed as if peacefully slumbering. Nearby is his packet of sweets; beneath his pillow is his watch. But from a gash in his throat blood has seeped, drenching the undisturbed bedclothes. Steer touches the little boy's face, and the realisation dawns, which he then has to share with the neighbours crowding into the little house, that the child is dead.

Soon afterwards, Wilks arrives, and confirms that Teddy is beyond all hope; so does Police Sergeant William Golding, of the City Police Force. He learns from Flora that a man had rushed down the stairs past her, dropping a bloodstained kitchen knife. In the darkness of her hall she could only see that the man was in his thirties, medium height, clean-shaven, and wearing a dark suit but no collar or tie, wearing

EDWIN 'TEDDY' HASKELL
© *SALISBURY NEWSPAPERS*

a light cap and possibly carrying a light overcoat. Golding recovers the knife. The city's Chief Constable, Frank Richardson, summoned by telephone, arrives on the scene, and calls up all his off-duty constables to scour the area, and Superintendent Stephens, in charge of the Salisbury Division of the County force, despatches his men on bicycles to check all the exit routes from the city, and to extend searches into the hinterland.

Shops had remained open late that Saturday evening, and even at 10.30 the streets of the Gaol Ground neighbourhood are busy with shoppers returning home, and word soon spreads of the outrage which has happened right on the doorstep. Crowds gather: those already asleep are awakened, and throw up their windows to ask what is happening, why the disturbance? When they are told, many will dress and come down to the street. The police on the scene are beseiged with offers of help to look for the murderer. Search parties form up, with people carrying lanterns and every kind of weapon.

Every street, every alleyway, every passage is searched: groups fan out over the fields and the water meadows; out as far as the Butts, between the railway line and Victoria Park, and as far as Elm Grove, beyond the historic city centre. The search continues practically until daybreak, and even then there are still crowds in and around Meadow Road. Throughout Sunday, more and more people come to visit the area, some to find out what has happened, others simply to gaze at the house where the murder took place. At the crossroads of York Road and Meadow Road it is difficult to get through the crowds, whose faces all are turned in one direction.

By Sunday morning, the police, despite having searched through the night, many after a day's duty, and having followed up various reports of unfamiliar men, are no further forward. Richardson, meanwhile, has contacted Scotland Yard, and Chief Inspector Walter Dew of the CID arrives to bring his expertise to bear, as does Hoel Llewellyn, Chief Constable of the Wiltshire Constabulary in his car, a 14/20-h.p. Siddeley with a tonneau body, resplendent in pansy purple with white coachlining, to examine the crime scene. There even arrives the celebrated pack of bloodhounds belonging to Mr Oliphant of Elston Hill, Shrewton – though in the event they are not deployed.

Throughout Monday, inquiries continue, and on into Tuesday, 3 November, in preparation for the inquest scheduled for 3.00 p.m. At the inquest, the jury view the body, and the Coroner takes formal evidence of identification, when the Chief Constable applies for and is granted an adjournment until Wednesday 11 November, starting at 10.00 a.m.

By Tuesday evening, things have quietened down somewhat, and no-one pays much attention to a car which has been much in evidence in the vicinity of the Gaol Ground for the past three days. It is this car which, at about 10.30 stops outside No. 40. From it emerge Richardson, Stephens, Dew and another inspector of the City Force, Herbert Stroud, they call at the house, and are invited in. There, Richardson takes out and reads a warrant for Flora's arrest on a charge of murdering her son. She says 'No, no', but is taken to the car where she is driven to the Police Station. Few in Salisbury are aware of this dramatic development.

THE POLICE STATION, ENDLESS STREET, SALISBURY. CHIEF INSPECTOR DEW STAYED HERE DURING THE INVESTIGATION.
© *J.B. MOODY COLLECTION*

The story thus far is what the man or woman in the street would have learned from reading two of the local newspapers, *The Wiltshire County Mirror and Express*, published on Tuesday 3 November and *The Salisbury and Winchester Journal*, published on Saturday 7 November. If we are to get behind these accounts and learn what really happened, we need to take ourselves back to Edwardian Fisherton and see what sort of a place it was; and that is where our story begins.

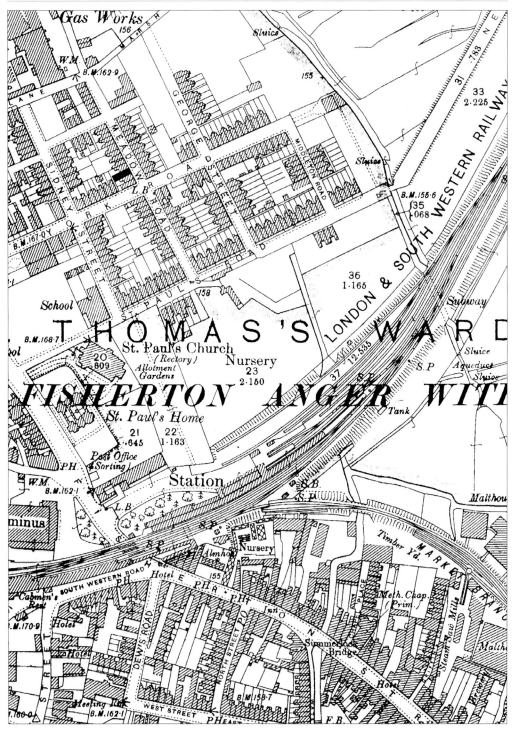

PART OF FISHERTON IN 1900. MEADOW ROAD LIES NEAR THE TOP OF THIS EXTRACT, AND FISHERTON STREET, LEADING TO SALISBURY CITY CENTRE, RUNS AWAY BOTTOM RIGHT. ST PAUL'S CHURCH, TEDDY'S SCHOOL AND THE TWO RAILWAY STATIONS ARE SHOWN (THE GWR TERMINUS IS ON THE LEFT. 40 MEADOW ROAD, WHERE THE MURDER WAS COMMITTED, IS BLOCKED IN BLACK (SEE ALSO MAPS AT END OF BOOK).

2
Edwardian Fisherton

S ALISBURY IN 1908 was the quintessential English city. Although by the turn of the twentieth century most people lived in large conurbations, such as Birmingham or Liverpool, it was towns like Salisbury – at once a market town and a cathedral city – that signified the life and spirit of England. With a population of about 22,000, Salisbury was the same size as nearby Winchester or Poole and rather less than half of its present-day size. Even at the time, Salisbury had long been outstripped in Wiltshire by Swindon, which had grown from a population of 1580 in 1821 to nearly 45,000 by 1901, and by other boom towns elsewhere, such as Aldershot and Gosport. Salisbury, by contrast had barely more than doubled in size, from just over 10,000 in 1821, and by 1908 it was about the same size then as Melksham, Romsey or Warminster today. In earlier times, Salisbury had been among the major English cities, its pre-eminence built upon the cloth trade, but in subsequent centuries it depended on speciality trades, such as cutlery and bone-lace, the development of transport, including tourism, and its continued importance as a market centre.

Edwardian Salisbury was recognisably the city we have today. But there were significant differences. The arrival of the railways between 1847 and 1857 was followed by development of suburbs in the surrounding areas, particularly to the west of the city, along either side of Fisherton Street, near the stations, and in a second phase along the Wilton and Devizes Roads. As Fisherton developed, so it was taken into the city, by extensions to the boundary in 1835 and 1904. And it was here, among Fisherton's people and businesses, its working-class quarters around the railway stations, gas works and the new milk-processing factory, its young communities spreading out along and between the main roads, from the Church Fields to the Coldharbour, that the drama of All Hallows' Eve 1908 was played out.

Until around 1600 Fisherton Anger had been a separate community, with its main street running north–south from its mill, on the Nadder, to the east of the church and on towards Devizes. Just north of the church was the junction with the road from Salisbury to Wilton. It was this latter road which by the seventeenth century if not earlier had become Fisherton's main thoroughfare, with ribbon development westwards from Salisbury visible on Speed's bird's-eye view of 1612. Before 1835 the River Avon, flowing two hundred yards west of the Poultry Cross, was the boundary between the city and Fisherton Anger. Legislation in that year extended the boundary to a point on the Wilton Road just east of the Lunatic Asylum, thence almost due north to the Devizes Road just west of Fisherton Farm house, then eastwards across the Avon's northern water meadows to the junction of the Stratford and Castle Roads, three quarters of a mile north of the Market Place. This split Fisherton Anger into two; the 1904 extension brought the whole of the ancient parish into Salisbury.

Before the railways Fisherton's businesses were a small proportion of the city's. In 1848, of some 350 businesses in Salisbury, 50 were located in Fisherton, and of these – alongside five general shopkeepers, seven public houses and a beer retailer – only seven lent any kind of industrial character to Salisbury's western suburb. These were two blacksmiths, a coach-smith, a wheelwright, a wire-maker, the gasworks and a brick-maker. A similar situation prevailed in 1907. Then some 900 businesses were listed in Salisbury, of which 209 – a higher proportion than sixty years earlier – were based in Fisherton. Of these, no more than 30 were engaged in manufacture or in any kind of engineering, a proportion similar to that noted for the city as a whole, but it is the character of the largest of these enterprises which gave Fisherton its distinctive atmosphere.

These firms comprised firstly the maltings built in the last quarter of the nineteenth century on land to the north of Fisherton Street by Messrs Williams Brothers. Alfred Williams was trading in Churchfields by 1865, but the brothers had moved to Fisherton by 1867. Five great square buildings and a sixth, L-shaped by the river Avon, most of them over 100 feet square, covered an area of about 1¼ acres. Between them, from the downside of the station to the city's Market House, ran the country's shortest standard-gauge railway. From these premises Williams produced 'pale, brown, patent, crystal & amber malts'.

Then there were the three utilities, of which the largest employer was the gasworks. This was enormously labour-intensive, more akin to a chemical works since, as well as producing gas, and its major by-product coke, other by-products included tar, used in making tar macadam for road surfacing, and ammoniacal liquor, which, when combined with sulphuric acid yielded sulphate of ammonia, a potent and widely-used agricultural fertiliser. From every ton of coal, about 13,000 cubic feet of gas was produced, but every ton of coal had to be brought by horse-drawn cart a quarter of a mile up the Devizes Road and into Gas Lane to the coal store in the works. The gas works had arrived in 1833, occupying a site of just over half an acre to the north-west of the Devizes Road, in the angle between Gas Lane and Coldharbour lane. The business developed apace in the last quarter of the nineteenth century, with the

purchase of additional land adjacent the original site in 1868 and of two acres beyond Coldharbour Lane in 1878. The second purchase allowed for the removal of two smaller gasholders, and the expansion of production capacity, and the erection of the company's largest gasholder in the angle between Coldharbour Lane and Marsh Lane, with the works occupying about an acre by the turn of the century. By contrast, electricity supply was in its infancy, with the power station having been in operation only since 1898, and at the time generating power only for lighting.

Another major manufacturer in Fisherton in the second half of the nineteenth century had been Robert Harding, proprietor of the brick, lime and whiting works to the south west of the Devizes Road. His works had provided much of the raw materials for Fisherton's rapid housing growth up to 1900, and occupied about six acres. By 1907 the firm had ceased trading, and bricks for Salisbury's continued expansion came from brickworks outside the city. The site of Harding's brickworks was then being developed for residential and industrial use, and the centrepiece of the scheme was a milk-processing factory which opened in April 1908. The milk company claimed to supply milk, 'from the best farms in the district, to householders in sealed bottles only of pint and quart size, and to Royalty.' Apart from these proud claims, one which attracted a less enthusiastic response from some quarters was that their factory siren would sound at 6.30 am and throughout the day.[1]

The largest single employment sector was that of the railways, which had come to Fisherton in the space of three years from mid-1856. There was no engineering or manufacture as there was at Swindon, Ashford or Eastleigh, so unlike them Fisherton never became a railway town. Nevertheless, there was an enormous amount of passenger rail traffic to from and through Fisherton. The Great Western Railway had a terminus at Salisbury, with trains travelling to and from Trowbridge, Bath, Bristol and Cardiff. On weekdays there were eleven arrivals and eleven departures. For the London and South Western Railway, Salisbury was a hub, with trains eastward to and from London and Basingstoke, and westward to and from Exeter, Yeovil and Templecombe, near

Wincanton. On this spine of routes there were thirty-three arrivals and thirty-four departures daily on weekdays. Even Sunday services accounted for nine arrivals and eleven departures.[2] But this was by no means all, for there was a service to Bournemouth and Weymouth, to Eastleigh, Southampton and Portsmouth, with eleven services from Portsmouth and one service from Eastleigh only, and by 1908 a very recently opened service to Amesbury and Bulford. Taking into account rail freight traffic as well – the presence of Milford Station as a goods depot notwithstanding – one can readily appreciate why there were so many railway workers in Fisherton's more recent housing developments. Indeed one telling example of the station's increasing busyness was the demolition of a row of fourteen artisans' cottages known as Railway Terrace opposite the up side of the L&SWR station to make way for the Post Office Sorting Office. These dwellings were built sometime between 1860 and 1879, and were gone by 1899.

Finally there was the *Salisbury Times and South Wilts Gazette*, whose office and printing works were by 1908 in Dews Road. Salisbury had had in the *Journal* one of the earliest provincial newspapers, first published in 1729 and continuously since 1736. It was rivalled from the early nineteenth century by *Simpson's Salisbury Gazette*, which relocated in 1819, after three years in New Canal, to Devizes, where it became the *Devizes and Wiltshire Gazette*. The *Salisbury Herald* was more ephemeral, published from about 1837 to 1842. The *Wiltshire County Mirror*, established in 1833 was by 1907 published twice a week and boasted 'The largest circulation of any paper printed in South Wilts, consequently the best medium for advertisements of all kinds'. Its handsome head office still stands on New Canal, with the lettering 'Steam Printing Works' on the front façade. Liberal opinion was catered for from 1860 by the *Salisbury Examiner and South Western Gazette*, and from 14 March 1868 by the *Salisbury Times*, which within six months had subsumed the *Examiner*.

In the inaugural edition the editor had this to say: 'The cheap press has now become an established fact; and its use in disseminating information on all important questions of the day, and in duly catering for the reading public, is appreciated in every quarter of the kingdom. … Without adopting the views of any sect or party, *The Salisbury Times* will steadily uphold the principles of justice, progress and utility. Public topics will ever be treated with candour and honesty. It will be a close and observant recorder of public events, a fearless exponent of public abuses, and a straitforward exponent of public claims. . . *The Salisbury Times* will strive to reflect the sound view of deep-thinking minds, seeking to use the vast machinery of the Reform Bill for the promotion of no mere class interest, but for the common good of all. . . That such an organ of public intelligence and opinion was much needed and greatly desired amongst us is evidenced by the satisfaction with which the announcement of its appearance was hailed.'[3] The *Salisbury Times* was initially printed and published in St John's Street, later moving to 98 Fisherton Street, and, from 19 May 1899, from new premises in Dews Road. And while the lion's share of local printing seems to have been by the rival Bennett Brothers from the *Salisbury Journal* offices, the *Times* also undertook some jobbing printing, ranging from auctioneers' sale catalogues to local bye-laws. Apart from brickmaking and brewing, these enterprises are represented amongst the occupations of residents of the Gaol Ground, to which our attention will shortly turn.

Fisherton's growth in the early modern period had been by way of ribbon development, along what is now Fisherton Street, and this continued along the Devizes and Wilton Roads during the early nineteenth century. But there were also three areas of new building of 'bye-law housing', characteristic of the later nineteenth century. The earliest were the four blocks of houses facing onto North, East, West and South Streets, south of the western end of Fisherton Street and bounded on the east by Water Lane, on the south by Harcourt Terrace and on the west by Dews Road. Then there was the area directly north of the Great Western Railway terminus known as Milton Place and Egerton Place. Its northern boundary was the western extremity of Fisherton Street and the first four hundred yards or so of Wilton Road. Its southern boundary was a street originally

FISHERTON BRIDGE, WHICH LINKS SALISBURY TO ITS SUBURB OF FISHERTON, EARLY 20TH CENTURY. SALISBURY INFIRMARY STANDS BEHIND AND TO THE RIGHT OF THE VICTORIAN CLOCK TOWER.

named Great Western Terrace, and by the turn of the century as Windsor Road. Its western boundary was formed by the side of 47 Wilton Road and, to its south, the backs of the properties in Windsor Street.

Somewhat later than these were the properties either side of the Devizes Road as far out as Nelson Terrace and Ashley Road, off the west side and on the east side respectively of Devizes Road. The properties on the left (west) side of the road comprised little groups and terraces of houses, some in pairs or groups of three or four, others in terraces never more than eight, and with names like Lawn Terrace and Model Row. Even when one of the access roads was graced with a name – Hartington Road – nothing could disguise the ad-hoc nature of its development. By contrast, the terraces of houses on the eastern side of the Devizes Road and the hinterland beyond were as crisply demarcated as the chequers within the historic city centre. Away from the Devizes Road down towards the water meadows by the River Avon ran St Paul's Road, York Road, Gas Lane, Clifton Road and Ashley Road. Parallel to the Devizes Road and as far as the gas works ran Sidney Street. Beyond that was Church Road, of which the extension beyond Gas Lane was named Coldharbour Lane. Church Road, so named

by the late 1870s, became Meadow Road by 1891. Beyond Meadow Road, and parallel to it were George Street and Middleton Road, built in the last decade of Victoria's reign.

The area between the Devizes Road and the water meadows had a quite distinct character. One might almost describe it as the St Paul's village, and in the late nineteenth century it was known colloquially as 'the Railway Town'. That village atmosphere derived partly from topography: the propinquity of the parish church, the school and the allotments either side of St Paul's Road; and partly from the looming presence of the gas works, which separated the linear developments of Ashley Road and Clifton Road to the north from the grid-pattern development to the south. And, like rural villages the Railway Town had its own shops, such as Saunders' in York Road and Cox's, later Slade's in Meadow Road, both grocers and provision dealers, and by 1907 a branch of the Co-op on the corner of York Road. By 1908 there was also a public house, the *Duke of York*, which began life as a beer house under the proprietorship of Miss Beatrice Newman, and which was to feature at the inquest and trials of Flora Haskell.

The area owed its character in great part to the vision and energy of its rector for 41 years from 1873 to 1914, Edgar Nembhard Thwaites. He raised

THE ONLY PORTION OF THE FORMER GAOL TO SURVIVE IN 1908, WHEN IT WAS IN USE BY THE WAR DEPARTMENT. IT STOOD ON THE CORNER OF YORK ROAD AND DEVIZES ROAD AND HAS SUBSEQUENTLY BEEN DEMOLISHED.

£2,500 for a north aisle in 1876 for a church built only some twenty years before, and further funds for a new organ. His chief contribution, in hindsight, was his provision of schooling in the parish. His obituary states that 'the characteristic energy of Canon Thwaites soon made itself felt as a real force in the parish. Infant day schools being required, funds were soon collected, and the schools built at a considerable cost. . . Subsequently funds were collected for new day schools, which were erected at a cost of over £4,500.' The total of his fundraising, which also provided for the building of the Maundrel Hall, was over £13,000, and Bishop Wordsworth awarded him the prebendal stall of Woodford and Wilsford in 1908 in recognition of his services to education and foreign missions. His obituarist described him as 'a born evangelist, an enthusiastic missionary, who was never tired of urging the claims of the Church Missionary Society, and a genial, kindly and sympathising friend'.[4] His personal qualities would be a source of strength to Flora Haskell in the dark days of the autumn of 1908, whilst his spirit lives on in the life of St Paul's Church to this day.

Not simply a residential area, the township was home to a number of distinctive craft trades, such as Ernest Say, a cabinetmaker at 22 St Paul's Road, William Chalke, rug maker in Meadow Road and Thomas Jacobs, pianoforte maker, repairer and tuner. There were other historical factors, of a somewhat doleful nature, perhaps leaving their stamp on the vicinity. In the mists of time, almost three centuries earlier, the area around Coldharbour Lane had been the site of a pesthouse, built on the orders of John Ivie, mayor of Salisbury, in the late 1620s. Title deeds of properties built two hundred and fifty years later still record the location as 'the Pesthouse Ground field'.

More recently, the south-eastern quarter of the area which included St Paul's School and which was bisected by Sidney Street and York Road, had been the County Gaol. Built between 1818 and 1822, it was closed in 1870, and all but the central administrative block and the chapel were demolished in 1875. The central block became the headquarters of the Second Army Corps, later the Southern Command. Whilst the Gaol had been the site of

executions earlier in the century,[5] the city's gallows, for public executions in earlier times, had been at the junction of the Devizes and Wilton Roads, right opposite the site of the prison, which was known locally as the Gaol Ground Area.[6]

The name of Scamell, which we shall encounter again on the fourth day of the inquest into Teddy Haskell's death, is the clue to the importance of this little area, and Thomas Scamell deserves more than a footnote in Salisbury's history. Born on 5 January 1840 in Gigant Street, the son of George and Mary Scamell, Thomas was originally a brickmaker, shown as such on the 1861 Census, aged 21. As he lived on the Wilton Road he may well have worked for Robert Curtis Harding whose home and office was in Nelson Terrace, set back from the Wilton Road and hard by the Brick, Lime and Whiting Works marked on the first two editions of the 1:2500 Ordnance Survey of the area. A man of enterprise and talent, he appears on the 1871 Census as a baker and grocer in Culver Street; by 1881 he is a master builder, living in 'The House on the Meadow', Fisherton Anger, and in 1891 as living on his own means at Avon House, York Road. Rather oddly, his career as a builder is not noticed in any trade directory, although it is in this area of activity for which he is remembered today. He is referred to in 1875 as a furniture broker in 28 Milford Street; then in 1889 as 'Scamell and Son, brokers, 13 Fisherton Street', and again in 1895 as 'Scamell and Sons, furniture brokers, 13 Fisherton Street.' By 1897 the business has evidently passed to his second son, Charles, as it is referred to as 'Scamell, Charles, and Son, furniture dealers.'[7] Despite the references to him as a furniture broker in 1875 and later, Scamell senior was by then involved in a property deal that would set him up for life.

When the Old Gaol became available for purchase in 1875, Scamell joined forces with Thomas Leach, a grocer at 22 Oatmeal Row and Stephen Hill, a solicitor at 26 Endless Street, to purchase it for £6,305 for residential development, with St Paul's Road being built and starting to be developed the following year. Leach did well enough out of the deal to be able to move to 1 Phoenix Cottages, Church Street (now Mill Road) in the historic quarter of Fisherton and to have retired by 1881, while Hill

A VIEW LOOKING DOWN YORK ROAD. TAKEN SHORTLY AFTER THE CRIME, 1908. THE HOUSE THAT THOMAS
SCAMELL BUILT FOR HIMSELF CLOSES OFF THE FAR END OF THE ROAD
© *Timothy W. Frank Walker and Ann Richardson Whittle, grandchildren of Frank Richardson, Chief Constable*

founded the legal partnership of Hill and Sladen in Bridge Street. Scamell, meanwhile, had built himself 'the house on the meadow', by 1881, at which time Church Road had been renamed Meadow Road, and comprised 24 properties, of which six were in course of construction and two were unoccupied. From its position in the schedule, it seems likely that Scamell's house was on the corner of Coldharbour Lane and Marsh Lane. Ten years later, he had repeated the exercise, with his new property Avon House terminating York Road.

Most famously Scamell drained the water meadows and built a 600-metre road across them to link Castle Road with the western (station) end of Fisherton Street via St Paul's Road. There were obstacles, legal and practical, which Scamell surmounted. The trustees of Hayter's Almshouses owned the land over which the road would pass, and took some persuading to relinquish it; then Scamell tried unsuccessfully to get the town council to agree to build it, so resolved to undertake the work himself. It involved the purchase and re-siting across the Avon in 1898 of the old Castle Street railway bridge, 'without the aid of any machinery',[8] and allegedly cost of over £30,000. Having built the road, Scamell

was able to charge a toll of 1d. – later reduced to ½d. – for pedestrians. The toll cannot have been popular, for while 'It was recognised that the work would be of great advantage to the neighbourhood . . . it was not generally understood at first that he intended to charge a toll for crossing the bridge.'[9] Tolls were levied until 1931, when the road was bought by the council. And that, of course, was not Scamell's main source of income. There were over 230 households on the Gaol Ground, and while a few properties were in multiple occupancy,[10] the vast majority were not, and as we shall learn, a typical small house would earn Scamell 5s. 6d. (£0.27½) per week in rent. Scamell also owned the houses in Nelson Road, so derived a rental income from some 250 properties altogether: about £65 per week, possibly more, or just under £3,400 a year, equivalent to £200,000 in today's money on the most conservative of estimates. Scamell had six children, and it would seem that Charles Street and Sidney Street were named after two of them, and George Street after his father, with Nelson Road (from whence the toll was levied) being named after Nelson Terrace. Another son, Edwin Richard, is listed in local directories from 1903 at 5 Nelson Road, first as a carpenter, later as a builder. A staunch Wesleyan, Thomas Scamell was also active in politics, initially a Liberal and then a Conservative, serving on the town council from 1879 to 1882 and from 1893 to 1902, and chairing the Fisherton Conservative Club from 1901 to 1903. He was also a member of the Board of Guardians. He died, tragically and inexplicably on 20 May 1903 on the railway line not far from his home. The family insisted that Scamell 'had no worry whatever on his mind', but the death was by decapitation, which implies a degree of deliberation, and the inquest jury returned an open verdict.

There were close ties of family and friendship networks within the Railway Town, but it was distinctly a new estate in the Edwardian era, with none of the houses much, if any, older than thirty years and many only about ten years old. The first phase, built after the demolition of the Gaol in 1875, by 1879 included York House and York Terrace, later known as 2-20 Devizes Road. Houses on the Devizes Road continued with the County Police Station (home to three officers), and seven tiny cottages in front of the two rows off Gas Lane and Alma Cottage. There were four properties on the north side of York Road known as Belgrave Villas, opposite Radnor House, and eight more houses to the west, seven of them between Sidney Street and Church (later Meadow) Road, and properties on the north side of St Paul's Road, then numbered 1-8, but later as 9-23. Most of the houses on the east side of Sidney Street were in place, but few on the west side, as was also true of the south side of York Road. Church Road formed the eastern boundary of this first phase of the Railway Town, and it was developed only, and then not completely, on its east side. Between York Road and Gas Lane west of Sidney Street was an unnamed street having just three houses on either side: this would from about 1891 be known as James Street. There were no houses on the south side of Gas Lane, and on the north side there were two terraces of eight and seven minute cottages, Merom Row and Park View Row, and a terrace of three houses next to the Gas Works. North of the Gas Works there were only the 27 south-facing houses of Clifton Terrace (later Clifton Road) with work beginning on the houses

over Coldharbour Lane in what would become Avon Terrace, with the house on that corner, over the lane from 27 Clifton Terrace, having the reference to the Pesthouse field in its title deeds.

By 1891 the two gaps on the east side of Sidney Street between York Road and St Paul's Road had been filled in, and the west side had gained an extra five houses, and a courtyard-style development names Charles Street. Gas Lane had gained nine new houses on its south side. There was further development along the east side of Devizes Road, north of Gas Lane; a total of 42 houses, including the redevelopment of the houses in front of those on Gas Lane, and the building of terraces of four and six houses, such as Avon Bourne Terrace, Palmal Cottages, Virginia Terrace and one called Ashley Terrace, which name would be taken to name the street to the north of Clifton Road in due course. That street had begun life as New Road, and had four houses by 1891. But the major area of development was east of Church Road, which had now become Meadow Road. In Meadow Road itself, the 22 houses on the west side had become 28, and on the east side there were fifteen new houses running north from St Paul's Road and over York Road. In York Road, the major addition was the eight houses on the south side. Continuing development on the north side was heralded with the building of Thomas Scamell's new house, Avon House on the extension east of Meadow Road. Likewise St Paul's Road gained an extra unnumbered house on its north side.

Development continued through the 1890s, with a new street to the west of Meadow Road called George Street, running north from St Paul's Road and over York Road. It eventually reached the southern perimeter road of the extended gas works site, which ran east from Gas Lane and was marked as Marsh Lane on the Ordnance Survey of 1899. George Street only had seven houses on its west side and eleven on its east side, increasing to 16 two years later. The westward extension of York Road resulted in 14 new houses on the north side, and on the south side five more houses between 1897 and 1899 to add to the five – four of them from infilling as Gloucester Terrace – over the previous six years. Likewise, St Paul's Road underwent a considerable expansion between 1891 and 1897, on the north side, firstly with the ten houses between Meadow Road and George Street known as Prospect Terrace, and then with the 14 named but unnumbered properties up to the corner of a new street, Middleton Road, linking the eastern ends of York Road and St Paul's Road. Finally, the two years to 1899 saw the building of a further six houses on the north side of St Paul's Road, east of the junction with Middleton Road, and nine houses on the south side. Middleton Road was at the same time colonised with five houses on its west side and six on its east. Away to the north, Ashley Road was developed on both sides, with 18 dwellings on the north side and 22 on the south side. By 1899 another three houses had been added on the south side. Clifton Terrace, meanwhile, remained apparently unaltered until 1897 when 18 houses in three groups were added on the south side. With that the terrace was renamed Clifton Road. However, there was between 1891 and 1897 an extension of Clifton Terrace/Road, known as Avon Terrace, and this comprised 23 houses in a single long terrace beyond Coldharbour Lane plus two more completely separate semi-detached properties. The Railway Town continued to develop over succeeding years with, for example, southward extensions of Meadow Road and George Street beyond St Paul's Road, and the extension northward to Marsh Lane of Middleton Street. But the description above is one of a community in flux, at the time when Flora Haskell was taking in washing and Teddy was playing about the streets.

The houses were, with rare exceptions all bye-law houses, with frontages of about 18 feet, and extending backwards between forty and fifty feet. There were some smaller that this: some houses in Gas Lane were only about 10 ft wide and 32 ft deep, and those in Merom Row were even smaller. A typical bye-law house – like those on the Wyndham Park estate, for example – had an enormous back garden, up to 130 ft long, but because of the chequer-style plan of the streets in the Railway Town, there were substantial numbers of houses that did not. Most properties opened straight on to the street. The minority possessed what is now referred to as a palisade, *i.e.* an enclosed area of between two and ten feet between the front of the house and the road,

demarcated by a low wall of stone or brick, on top of which there might also have been a wrought-iron fence, taking the overall height of the undertaking to about six feet. The palisaded properties tended to be on the outer streets of an estate; in this instance St Paul's Road, and some on the Devizes Road. The exception in Railway Town was Ashley Road, Clifton Road and Avon Terrace, in which all the properties were palisaded save the very few that were set well back in their own grounds.

The people who lived here were respectable working-class, very much like the denizens of Lambeth surveyed by the Fabian Women's Group between 1909 and 1913, and described in Maud Pember Reeves's *Round about a pound a week*:

> They are not the poorest people of the district. Far from it! They are ... some of the more enviable and settled inhabitants of this part of the world. The poorest people – the river-side casual, the workhouse in-and-out, the bar-room loafer – are anxiously avoided by these respectable persons whose work is permanent, as permanency goes in Lambeth, and whose wages range from 18s. to 30s. a week. They generally are somebody's labourer, mate or handyman. Painters' labourers, plumbers' labourers, builders' handymen, dustmen's mates, printers' labourers, potters' labourers, trouncers for carmen, are common amongst them. Or they may be fish-fryers, tailors' pressers, feather-cleaners' assistants, railway-carriage washers, employees of dust contractors, carmen for Borough Council contractors, or packers of various descriptions. They are respectable men in full work, at a more or less top wage, young, with families still increasing, and they will be lucky if they are never worse off than they now are. Their wives are quiet, decent, 'keep themselves-to-themselves' kind of women, and the children are the most punctual and regular scholars, the most clean-headed children of the poorer schools in Kennington and Lambeth.[11]

The mix of occupations above is echoed in the Railway Town, though there were at least as many skilled craft and white-collar workers as there were unskilled. So, in 1897 in York Road, there were a waiter, a bricklayer's labourer, a compositor, two carpenters, two cabinet makers, a tailor, a baker, a coachman and a carter, and four small businessmen. Of these latter probably the most substantial was

40 MEADOW ROAD AS IT APPEARED IN THE LOCAL
PRESS IN 1908.
© *SALISBURY NEWSPAPERS*

William Chalke the hearth rug manufacturer. In St Paul's Road there was a clerk and church sexton, a grocer's traveller and a grocer's porter, a gardener, a postman, a brickmaker, a jeweller's assistant, a painter and decorator, an RSPCA inspector, a butcher, two printers, a photographic printer, a currier, a carpenter, two divers, a commercial traveller, a bricklayer and a cabinet maker. But by far the largest employment sector was that of the railways. Of the 277 main householders in the Railway Town in 1897, 88 (32%) were railway employees; 30 were engine drivers, 16 were firemen, 10 were guards and 10 were porters. There was a coal trimmer and a carriage examiner, there was a platelayer and a parcel clerk, there was an inspector and a Railway Clearing House number taker. There was a signal fitter and the Foreman of the G.W.R. Coal Stage. There were others, such as telegraph clerks, maybe not employed by the railways, but dependent on the railways for their livelihoods: these included the manager of the local W.H. Smith's which was in the station complex, not in the city, and a railway constable. The 27 houses of Clifton Terrace had a striking concentration of railwaymen: over half the householders, comprising seven engine drivers, two guards, two firemen, two signalmen, a porter and a ticket collector.

From the kinds of occupations noted above, we can infer that householders in the Railway Town were able to make a good enough living to be able to afford to live there with some assurance of stability: these were not 'the workhouse in-and-out' of society. The salaries of such people can be deduced from a number of sources. The Fabian Women's Group survey gives as approximations the annual salaries of a middle-class well-to-do man, of £2,000, a middle-class comfortable man, of £500 and a poor man, of £62 8s od annually, from 24s per week.[12] Examples are then given of specific amounts given by individuals as housekeeping money, and one has to approach such figures with care as they exclude what the wage earners retain for their out-of-pocket expenses. That said, from references elsewhere in the book, the sums allowed would seem to be about 90% of the husband's take-home pay, and they range from 28s. and 21s. 9d. from two printer's labourers to 27s. from a policeman, 24s. and 18s. from two plumber's mates, 19s. 6d. from a railway-carriage washer, 19s. and 20s. from two carters, 23s. for a fish-fryer, 24s. for a carman's trouncer, 22s. for a labourer, 20s. for a shop assistant, 24s. for a stoker and 20s. for a gas worker, and so on.[13] The average wage in 1908-1908 of Salisbury's Police Force – comprising two inspectors, three sergeants and 22 constables – was around 25s per week.[14] Two examples, one fictional, will suffice to give an indication of the top wages for skilled craftsmen: the 31s. 3d. earned per week by the Burdens' most skilled workers[15], and the 38s. per week earned in 1905 by the workers in Andrew Undershaft's munitions factory in Shaw's *Major Barbara* (1905).

Flora and Teddy Haskell's immediate neighbourhood lay within the Railway Town. At the inquest witnesses included several neighbours, some of whom were close relatives of Flora's. Her mother, Mary Carter, was an almswoman by 1908, but was in 1901 head of the household which included Flora and Teddy. Their home was then numbered 20 Meadow Road, but by 1908 was No. 40, the houses having been renumbered from the other end of the street. Flora's nearest neighbours were the Mannings at No. 42 and the Nobles, Flora's widowed brother-in-law and his two boys at No. 38. Her neighbours at 36 Meadow Road were Walter and Alice Steer, their daughter Gertrude and Alice's mother Emma Chivers. Slightly further away was Thomas Rawlins at No. 26, and in the opposite direction William Eccott at No. 48 and Edwin Daniels at No. 54. Across the road at No. 23 lived the Skutts. At No. 27 were the Houses, at No. 31 their relations the Hayneses.

The three witnesses who lived on York Road, Matilda Cooper at No. 27, Sarah Butt at No. 40 and Emily Sweetman at No. 42 all lived on corners of York Road and Meadow Road[16], while Gertrude Skutt's mother lived at 17 York Road. One block east of Meadow Road is George Street, where lived Lily Stretch at No. 32 and Edward Butt at No. 27. One block west of Meadow Road is Sidney Street, where at No. 24 lived Emily Hayden. And at 'Glenbrook', 14 St Paul's Road, one block south of 40 Meadow Road, lived Matilda Cooper's son John Moxham Cooper. Emma Lodge, a new witness at the magistrates' hearing, lived at 20 Meadow Road. The shops and the public house cited at the inquest were those of William Saunders, grocer, provision dealer and wheelwright, for whom evidently Mrs Sweetman kept shop at 42 York Road, Edgar Slade, greengrocer at 53 Meadow Road and the *Duke of York* Inn at 34 York Road, whose licensee Miss Beatrice Newman had but recently been granted the full licence from one only to retail beer. Alfred Uphill's grocery, at 36 Sidney Street, was mentioned at the magistrates' hearing.

They all lived within an area identified on the 1901 Census in the following terms: 'All the houses on the Old Gaol Ground, including St Paul's Road, Sidney Street, Charles Street, Meadow Road, James Street, George Street, York Road, Middleton Road; also Mr Scamell's house in the meadows.' The boundary was set as 'On the north, by Gas Lane, on the East, by the River Avon, on the south, by St Paul's Road and the South Western Railway and on the west, by the Wilton Road [*sic, i.e.* the Devizes Road].' Of these streets, St Paul's Road and York Road ran east-west, St Paul's Road being the southern of the pair. These two streets were cut into four by three roads running north-south. From west to east, these were Sidney Street, Meadow Road and George Street. Finally, York Road and St Paul's Road were bounded in the east by Middleton Road. In other words, the area — the Old Gaol Ground — comprised the realisation of Thomas Scamell's housing project of 1875. The great majority of these properties were simple bye-law houses opening onto the street, with the exceptions being the two houses which Thomas Scamell had built for himself, and many of the houses in St Paul's

Road, which hinted at their higher status and better accommodation by having names rather than numbers, and all being palisaded, as were a few in Sidney Street and York Street.

In 1901 the district had just over 1,040 residents — many more than in the Cathedral Close and more than Alderbury, comparable in number with Amesbury and around half as populous as Downton or Wilton, and had a village-like character, with Scamell in the big house perhaps as the lord of the manor, and the church, school and beer-house, later to become the *Duke of York*, close at hand. What was it like? The suburbs of Kennington and Lambeth, surveyed by the Fabian Women's Group are described as follows:

The streets they live in are monotonously and drearily decent, lying back from the main arteries, and with little traffic other than a stray barrel-organ, a coal-lorry selling by the hundredweight sack, or a taxi-cab going to or from its driver's dinner at home. At certain hours of the day — before morning school, at midday, and after four o'clock — these narrow streets become full of screaming, running shouting children. Early in the morning men come from every door and pass out of sight. At different times during the evening the same men straggle home again. At all other times the street is quiet and desperately dull. Less ultra-respectable neighbourhoods may have a certain picturesqueness, or give a sense of community of interest or of careless comradeship, with their untidy women chatting in doorways and their unoccupied men lounging at the street corners; but in these superior streets a kind of dull aloofness seems to be the order of the day.[17]

One suspects, however, that the Gaol Ground was a little livelier. The range of occupations suggests this was the case, for in 1901, there were just over 420 people with obviously wage-earning occupations, plus eight 'living on their own means' or of 'independent means', six who are stated to be retired — railway workers, a postman, a policeman, a carman and an army pensioner. Far and away the largest employment sector was the railway, with 100 manual workers from engine drivers to porters, and 15 clerical and administrative workers — ticket inspectors, carriage examiners, clerks, etc. The next largest sector was of the building and allied trades —

builders, carpenters, plumbers, bricklayers, paperhangers, decorators, etc., numbering 74. Next came dressmaking and tailoring, including one each of mantle maker, sewing machinist and milliner, total 31, and then the only solely feminine occupations of housekeepers, domestic servants, mothers' helps, nursemaids and parlourmaids, total 19. Smaller numbers worked as general labourers; porters and errand boys; and in retail trades.

From the range and diversity of occupations one can infer a sense of liveliness about the Gaol Ground. The railwaymen – two out of every seven workers – would have been coming and going at all hours, as they were shift workers, and very likely those in the building trades – two out of every eleven workers – would have been out and about. Many of the occupations – laundresses and the piano tuner spring to mind – would have involved some to-ing and fro-ing. The four local shops and the alehouse would have served throughout the day and (as will be discovered at the inquest) until late in the evening for the exchange of information as well as goods. At lunchtime children and workers would have been returning to eat.

In the Gaol Ground were 235 householders, almost one-third with railway workers as their heads, most of whom were born outside Wiltshire. Indeed, inward migration was characteristic. Of its heads of households 50 had been born in Salisbury and 62 elsewhere in the county, so the majority, of 123, came from elsewhere in the United Kingdom, predominantly from England. This characteristic is reflected amongst the female adult population also. Of the 212 wives and female heads of household, 116 came from Wiltshire and 96 from outside the county. Nearly two-thirds of households included two parents with children, and only thirteen people lived on their own – of these four were in Belgrave Villas, York Road.

The striking difference between then and now is that 61 of the 235 households took lodgers, including 36 of the 146 two-parent families. This was one source of family income: the other was having wage-earning children, and of 41 large households 26 had wage-earning children, and of these 26 six took in boarders as well. The vast majority of people in the Gaol Ground, with the chief exception of Mr Scamell, can have had no concept of personal space, and for many if not most, there was no security of employment. The Fabian Women's Group routinely encountered families in which people had to sleep four in a bed, for example,[18] and this must have been common in the Gaol Ground. There were variations within and exceptions to these family structures. Parents and grandchildren feature quite frequently, but there are also a handful of adopted children and one nurse child, a couple whose dependants were their nephew and niece, a brother, sister and cousin and two households with a servant apiece.

So the Gaol Ground was in many ways a microcosm of Fisherton and in many respects of Salisbury: busy, crowded, multifarious and multi-talented. The people who lived there mostly worked with their hands. There were only fifteen white-collar railway workers and some twenty others engaged in clerical, administrative or information-handling. About a quarter were in service industries and an eighth were in manufacture, mostly dressmaking or similar. The rest, almost a half of the workforce, were traditional manual workers ranging from the highly skilled – the engine drivers and electricians – to basic labourers. But above all the Gaol Ground was full of children and young people, for there were well over 200 schoolchildren listed in 1901.

Of those who appeared at Flora's legal proceedings, thirteen can be readily identified in 1901 as living within the Gaol Ground. John Moxham Cooper was a house decorator and an employer, living at 'Glenbrook', St Paul's Road, with his wife and five children aged from two to ten, and two boarders, including his nineteen year-old brother, a house painter. His mother, Matilda Cooper, was in 1901 already widowed and living with her daughter and son-in-law the Langmeads of Milford. The Haskells' next-door neighbours and relations the Nobles were an all-male household, the widowed father Alfred a whip-thong maker, self-employed and working from home,[19] and the elder son, another Alfred, a compositor. Next door to them were Walter and Alice Steer and their four sons and three daughters, who included a dressmaker and a nursemaid, and a harness maker. Gertrude, Flora's dressmaker, was still at school. The dairyman up the road from the Haskells, Thomas Rawlins, and his wife Elizabeth had in 1901 a three year-old daughter and a one year-old son. Three doors further along from the Rawlinses were Harry Lodge, a soldier, and his wife Emma, as yet with no family, having been married less than four years, and a boarder employed at the Gas Works. In Sidney Street were William Hayden, a railway engine fireman and his wife Emily and their three young sons and a daughter, and John, William's younger brother, also a locomotive fireman. Living in Meadow Road in 1908, but seven years earlier at 15 Sidney Street was Edwin Daniels, a carpenter, with his wife and a daughter who worked in a laundry and two sons of whom the elder was a junior clerk to a builder's merchant. The household also included a boarder, another carpenter. Lily Stretch, the nursemaid of 32 George Street, was in 1901 still at school and living with her parents – her father, Frederick Stretch, a gardener – in Water Lane, off Fisherton Street.

By and large they were all local folk. Alfred Noble came from West Harnham and his sons were Salisbury-born, as were Thomas Rawlins and his children, with his wife from Lyndhurst. William and John Hayden were born in Winterslow, Emily and their children all born in Salisbury, as was Lily Stretch. The Coopers all came from Romsey, although John's wife was from St Pancras, London, but they had been established in Salisbury long enough for all their children to have been born there. Those who had travelled around somewhat were not the railwaymen but the Steers and the Danielses. Walter Steer was born in Exeter and Alice in Trowbridge, their eldest daughter in Exeter and their eldest son in Taunton. Even so, they had by 1908 been living in Salisbury many years, for their younger children of whom the eldest was 14 in 1901 had all been born in Salisbury. Likewise, Edwin Daniels came from Wilton and his wife from Bodenham, while their two eldest children had been born in Poole, but, again, the age of their younger son, born in Salisbury, shows they had been settled in Salisbury for around 20 years by 1908. Walter Haynes and Ernest House were more recent arrivals. Walter Haynes, born in Bristol like his parents and nearly all his siblings, had come to Salisbury by 1901 with the return of his father, an engine driver, to the city. In 1901 they lived at 15 Clifton Terrace. Ernest House hailed from Chilton Polden in Somerset, and in 1901 was a lodger in Kew Villas, Bemerton. From their neighbours in the Gaol Ground we turn to the Haskells of 40 Meadow Road.

3
Flora

THE 1901 CENSUS portrays the Haskells of Meadow Road; an unremarkable family comprising a youngish couple – the husband aged 33, the wife, 26, with an only child, a son aged four, and with the wife's widowed mother.[1] Although in Salisbury the name Haskell today calls to mind the son, Edwin Richard, the murdered amputee, it is his mother, Flora Fanny, who is at the heart of our story.

Flora Haskell was born in 1874, the second daughter and fifth of the seven children of Richard Carter and Mary Ann Yeats. Richard Carter was born in Warminster in 1824 to John and Ann Carter; his father was a wheelwright, but Richard Carter was as a young man an agricultural labourer. While still in his teens he married Arabella Waters, from nearby Heytesbury and the young couple settled in Longbridge Deverill, where their first son George was born in 1844. By 1855, when their second son, John, was born, the Carters had moved back to Warminster, where Richard gained a position with James Lush, a corn merchant,[2] but by 1859 the family had moved to Winterbourne Earls, in the Bourne Valley three miles north of Salisbury, whither Lush had relocated. For Lush had moved to Winterbourne Earls by March or April 1859, to farm 75 acres, bringing the Carters with him. And by about 1863 Arabella was dead, and Richard Carter was about to embark on his second relationship. He met Mary Ann Yeats in Winterbourne Earls, when he was not far short of 40 and she was still a teenager, and their eldest child, Emma, was born in Winterbourne Earls in the summer of 1864; Richard and Mary were not to marry until the spring of 1868. Around 1869 or 1870 the family moved to Salisbury, where their next two children, both boys, were born only about a year apart. In 1871 the family were living at 3 Crane Bridge Road: Lush had relocated to Salisbury to become a sack dealer, living in nearby Bowling Green Road, and had taken Richard Carter on as a groom and gardener.[3] By 1881, and with two more boys and two more girls, the Carters were living in Hurst's Terrace, a row of ten cottages, off Great Western Terrace, now Windsor Road, in Fisherton's earliest railway quarter. Richard was now a coal haulier, and his wife and eldest daughter added to the family income by working as laundresses. By 1891, however, Richard had died, and Mary had moved with her four younger children to Meadow Road. At the Census she is shown continuing her work as a laundress, joined therein by her middle daughter, Flora, by then sixteen. Her two brothers were a clerk in a printing works – presumably the *Salisbury Times* offices, then at 98 Fisherton Street – and a whip maker. There was also a boarder, recorded as Thomas Jefferies, who may have been a relative, perhaps the younger brother, of Mary Carter. By 1901, with Mary Carter working as a laundress still, in her fifties, with Flora no longer recorded with an occupation but presumably running the household while her mother and her husband – by then working as a house-painter – were at work.

Flora and Edwin were married at the parish church of St Paul, Fisherton Anger, on 11 May 1896, when she was 21, and already pregnant, and her

HASKELL FAMILY PORTAIT WITH 'TEDDY' STANDING IN
FRONT OF HIS FATHER
© *LLOYD'S WEEKLY NEWS*

husband was 27, and then employed as an orderly at the Fisherton House Lunatic Asylum. Edwin Haskell was born in 1868 at Verwood, Dorset, the middle of five children of Henry and Emma Haskell. He enlisted in the Wiltshire Regiment, being promoted to corporal, and served in India. When he left the Army he remained on the Reserve list, and served in the Veterans' Corps on garrison duty in the United Kingdom during the Boer War. Edwin junior, 'little Teddy', was born on 19 October 1896. A family portrait, taken in 1900, when Teddy was three, shows Flora standing at the left, resting her hand on the back of the upright chair on which her husband is seated, in his regimental uniform with Teddy standing in front of his father. Flora is slim, and about 5ft 2in, while Teddy has blond curls and wears a sailor suit. The portrait captures an atmosphere of connubial contentment, and all three gaze steadily out, with a suggestion of confidence in the future. However, a photograph may often do no more than capture an evanescent moment; never more so than in the case of the Haskells, for Edwin senior's health was already compromised, possibly as a result of

his Indian military service. Edwin succumbed to pulmonary tuberculosis, cared for by Flora, and with a spell in Ventnor on the Isle of Wight. He was just thirty-six when he died on 19 February 1904, and Flora and he had been married less than eight years; young Teddy was just seven years and four months old at the time. On Edwin's death certificate it is stated that he had been ill from tuberculosis for three years, and by then his son had fallen victim to the same illness; except that in Teddy's case it had affected his hip-joint, and he had had to have his right leg amputated. His mother, whom one imagines to have been aching in her bereavement, spared no effort in bringing Teddy back to health, including taking on a trained nurse for a time to care for him.

More than that, Flora strove to ensure that Teddy wanted for nothing, while at the same time raising him to be a bright and happy child. She took pleasure in him making friends at school, and in his evident prowess on the football field. It is possible, indeed probable, that for a working mother, Teddy could be at times a 'handful'. Such is the handed-down recollection amongst the older residents of the Meadow Road area, and it is corroborated in evidence gathered by Chief Inspector Dew of an incident when Teddy had been caught chalking swear-words on a neighbour's fence and Flora had threatened him with severe punishment. After his death, however, whether in tributes at his funeral or in memorial services, and both at the inquest and the trials, the portrait of Teddy which is painted is of a bright, lively lad, popular with all who came across him; perhaps even a little cheeky. Of the two portraits of Teddy as an older child, he appears in one looking as though butter would not melt in his mouth, and in the other, possessed of a knowing confidence and an easy charm. He certainly was not weighed down by a sense of fate's injustice, but instead had the same sorts of concerns and interests that any other Edwardian twelve-year old would have had. He loved football, both playing it and discussing it. The *Salisbury Times* reported that 'Poor little Teddy Haskell, whose untimely death the city is mourning, was one of the youngest contributors to this [*i.e.* the sports] page, and many are the reports of the doughty deeds of "St Paul's Rangers" that have been received at this office signed "Teddy Haskell, 40 Meadow Road, Fisherton".[4] He collected foreign stamps, he could make toys for his own amusement (a tip-cat was mentioned at the trial), he enjoyed reading comics, and he was happy enough to receive odd coppers from people who admired his pluck in going about his life. What also seems clear is that, although his hip had not been cured by the amputation (for his cousin Alfred Noble was only one of those who testified that it continued to discharge), it is uncertain how much distress it caused him. It had not reached the stage of bringing about a serious and generalised debilitation. It was an ongoing irritation, and maybe painful enough for his mother to sleep with him routinely in order to comfort him or to be on hand to administer some aspirin or other painkiller.

One suspects that Teddy inherited his winning ways from his father, and from his mother, a happy-go-lucky temperament. Flora, as was her privilege, was not called to give evidence when on trial, so we have only the words of others to gain an insight into her character; apart from a generous and impulsive nature to be inferred from her condition when she was married. Gertrude Steer, her young neighbour two doors along, and a dressmaker, recounted at the magistrates' hearing and at the trial, how Flora, trying on a little jacket Gertrude had made for her said 'I *shall* be a toff tomorrow!' And again, when rumours of re-marriage were in the air, Flora's response was light-hearted: she said she was going to get married, but with a laugh echoed by everyone else present at the time. But the quality which shines through from evidence at the trials is Flora's steadfast and unwavering devotion to her child. Witness after witness, asked about their relationship under cross-examination, said that Flora was a good and affectionate mother, or that she always treated Teddy kindly and well, or that there was great affection between the two: the Noble boys, the Steers, Thomas Rawlins the dairyman. When they said this they usually prefixed their comments by saying that they had known Flora 'twenty years', or 'all my life.' Some of them – including Walter Steer, and Percy Noble at the inquest – added that Teddy was 'always nicely dressed and cared for'; and this, when other witnesses were ready to testify that Flora was not lavish in

spending on her own clothes: specifically, that the dark skirt she wore on the night of the murder had seen a good deal of wear. But when she had to, she looked smart; as when she was photographed with her husband and son at the turn of the century, or when she appeared in court, dressed in black and sporting a black feather boa.

Then there was the question of Flora's matrimonial intentions. Richard Carter had been firm friends with Alfred Mold, a steward on the White Star Line whose mother lived only four doors away from the Haskells in 1901. As a result, Flora and Teddy had got to know him very well, and Teddy could rely on a few pennies from Mold every time he came ashore to visit his mother. Mold was keen to marry Flora, and had said as much in the summer of 1908. Flora, at 34, was an attractive woman who at the same time bore herself with modesty. Flora was not so certain about remarrying, not because she did not care for Mold: it is evident from her remarks that she did at some level, and maybe without the events of 31 October their friendship would have developed. But the key point was that her first loyalty was as a mother. Whenever marriage came into the conversation, Flora was careful to say that if she did remarry, she would always carry on working, to support Teddy.

Just how successful Flora was, not simply and solely as a mother, can be gauged from her business and financial affairs. Like her mother, who had worked as a laundress even when her husband was alive, in 1881, Flora had made a career out of laundry work, assisting, and no doubt learning her craft from, her mother after her father had died, in 1881. Mary Carter, identified on the 1901 Census as head of her household at the then 20 Meadow Road[5] was still working as a laundress, which Flora was to take up when her husband died and her mother was to move into Hayter's Almshouses. At the Magistrates' hearing, the prosecuting counsel T.H. Parr, discounting the possibility of burglary as a motive for the murder, would remark on Flora being an unlikely candidate as she was known to be making a 'precarious living' as a laundress. Yet, surely, Rayner Goddard, defending barrister at Flora's jury trials, was closer to the mark when, in his closing speech, he referred to her earnings as 'a very nice income for a woman in that position'. Flora was a woman who kept a close eye on her incomings and outgoings, as is evinced by the fact that she called upon her nephew Alfred Walter Noble to make up her books for her on occasion. He was able to testify that she earned 22s. per week in winter and more in the summer, when a greater need for clean, fresh blouses would result in greater demand for her services. She also had £1 in the Co-op – the equivalent of a week's wage, and a large enough sum to provide her with a dividend for the purchase of odd extras from time to time. Flora's regular outgoings were 5s. 6d. in rent, plus the cost of the prerequisites of her work (soap, starch, blue, soda, etc.) This was, Goddard pointed out, 'an ample sum.' A great many people in the Gaol Ground and in Salisbury earned about a pound a week, as we have seen, and in some instances a little more – the railwaymen averaging 25s., the police likewise and the employees of the Scout Motor Company whose highest earners managed just over 30s. per week. Many of these were men supporting a wife and family, whose situations must have been comparable with those of the people of Lambeth and Kennington studied by the Fabian Women's Group. A typical budget spent approximately one-third on food, one-third on rent, and one-third on everything else, including fuel, clothing and insurance.[6] Flora's earnings and expenditure must have been roughly equivalent. Admittedly she had to take her business expenses out of her wage, but her weekly rent, at 5s. 6d. was less than the above examples, and she had two mouths to feed, not six or eight. Even so, the cost of keeping Teddy as well turned out as witnesses testified could lead to temporary difficulties. Thus Richard Carter, reported in *Lloyd's Weekly News,*[7] explained that his mother had given to her daughter £10 some time before the murder, to give Teddy 'a start in life', and Flora had recently taken £2 to buy Teddy some new clothes.

Her home, too, was decently furnished, if somewhat sparsely by modern standards. Horace Messer's photographs of the crime scene show the usual accoutrements of a late Victorian household – the framed homilies on the wall, the stuffed bird in a glass case, and so on. We know that to furnish a

smaller house on the Gaol Ground – as, doubtless Lily Stretch and Herbert Primmer did when they married in the autumn of 1915 – would have cost about £50 – then, the best part of a year's wage, now, around £3,000. Contemporary bills from Moody and Sons in Fisherton Street show the cost of fitting out a house in Ashley Road in May and June 1908. A bedstead, spring mattress and woollen mattress cost £3 7s.; a four-foot kitchen table 14s. 6d. and the four chairs to go with it 18s. A front room suite in velvet was 13 guineas, an Albert armchair 10s. A bedroom toilet set – ewer, basin and chamber pot – cost 10s. 6d., a hearth rug 15s. 6d., 26-inch stair rods 5s. each, a 3 by 4 yard Brussels carpet £3 7s. 6d . . . and so on. Flora would have had some of these things, possibly inherited from when she took over the lease of her house on her mother's admission to the almshouses, and other items acquired when there were two wage-earners at 40 Meadow Road. At any rate, Flora was a world removed from the some subjects of the Fabian Women's Group survey, three of whom used banana crates as cots for their infants.

One of the odder conclusions drawn by Chief Inspector Dew, in his efforts to discredit Flora's income from her living, was that her trade was not enough to furnish her with a living. Dew reported to the Director of Public Prosecutions on 7 January 1909 that he had elicited from the nurses' home that they gave Flora no more than £2 worth of work per year: nevertheless that is still two weeks' worth of work for which Flora would have to have travelled a tidy step, when there was work closer at hand. Another lead was Mrs Sarah Atkins, wife of a railway porter and mother (in 1901) of two, who lived at 28 Meadow Road: she said she occasionally used Flora to 'get up' a collar. In the address book Dew commented on there were eight other clients, housewives and an adult daughter living in sheltered accommodation – Katharine Mitchell, of 5 St Paul's Homes. Two of the others were Mrs Jemima Clissold, mother (in 1901) of two and wife of a commercial traveller in coal, who lived at 8 York Terrace, and Mrs Kate Kite, mother (in 1901) of two, and wife of a carpenter, living on Devizes Road, whom Flora would have known from when they lived in Meadow Road. The others all lived on or just south of the Wilton Road, on the Devizes Road and on South Western Road, opposite the station. Then there is the question of competition. Kelly's Directory records only six laundries in Salisbury, including Laverstock, and only one of these, the Salisbury Steam Laundry in St Edmund's Church Street was an industrial-scale business. All the others were women operating as sole traders, and the nearest to the Gaol Ground was Miss Newman at 119 Devizes Road. Of the nine working in laundries in the Gaol Ground at the 1901 Census, three were daughters of the house employed in various capacities in laundries. It is, then, arguable that Flora had plenty of custom, with the scores of railway workers and builders, and some, but not a great deal, of competition. Dew's other notion, from an address which turned out to be that of a brother, though of a different surname, was that Flora could have been making a living from prostitution. Given her spare room, that is a possibility, and the obvious cover for such activity would have been for Flora to take lodgers. But she never did: the night before the murder she was approached by a man seeking lodgings who had been recommended to her, and she robustly rebuffed his entreaty. The rare instance of her allowing in a man not related to her was of Alfred Mold, and that happened only because his mother's rooms were taken up with lodgers. Besides, lodgers stay, while punters come and go. The Gaol Ground was a busy quarter, and someone would have seen something; yet in all the witnesses' depositions there is no hint of Flora leading anything other than a life of the utmost probity. As Emma Chivers put it, she was a quiet woman, who kept herself to herself, and was respected by all her neighbours. Her statements and her prison letter attest to someone who both orally and in writing was intelligent and articulate.

We have seen Flora's background, how she earned her living, the kind of house she kept and the way she seemed to her family, friends and neighbours. What of her mental condition at the time of the murder and afterwards? The testimonies of her state before the murder give no clue to any sense of foreboding, except for the worry about the stranger calling for lodgings, which she voiced to Alfred Walter Noble on the evening of the murder. In the immediate aftermath of the attack, she was distraught and incoherent, but by the time she came to make her police statement she was calm and self-possessed – until the murder weapon was produced, when she became agitated. During her time in custody, Flora, whether in writing to her mother or in her conversations with the Rector, Canon Thwaites, holds fast to her declared innocence of the act, in conjunction with her faith in the Heavenly Judge. However, it is in the course of such conversations, between 30 November and 5 December that Flora made a number of admissions to Thwaites, the last of which he had mentioned to a duty officer that he could not divulge, 'but that it looked very black against her'; and then there was the famous admission to more than one person that if she did kill Teddy, she didn't remember it.[8] ' It is not to be wondered at that during the inquest and the magistrates' hearing Flora was constantly in a state of collapse. The possibility was mooted at the inquest that Flora was temporarily insane, and killed her son in some kind of fit of madness. But while in Devizes Prison she was examined by the Prison Medical Officer, Henry John Mackay, who found her to be 'an intelligent, self possessed and fairly well educated woman [who] converses readily on the subject of the charge against her and discusses it in an intelligent and reasonable manner.' He continued 'Whilst recognising fully the gravity of her position, she exhibits no violent or unreasonable manifestation of grief. On the contrary, she appears on all occasions to have her emotions well under control.' Mackay went on to record that there was neither personal history nor family background of mental instability, and to discuss the possibility of an epileptic attack. He concluded that even if Flora had suffered such a seizure – for which there had never been any precedent – it would not have manifested itself in a murderous attack. He concluded 'I am of the opinion that the prisoner is in no sense insane, that she is in complete possession of her faculties, and that she is fit to plead to the indictment'. But to remark on Flora's distress at the inquest and before the magistrates, and her generally calm demeanour at the jury trials is to move ahead to those events; to which we now turn.

4
'Here is a horrible affair'
The Inquest, Tuesday 3 November – Wednesday 11 November

IN THE IMMEDIATE AFTERMATH of the murder, and even before Flora's sensational arrest, events were moving rapidly. The scene for both the inquest and the subsequent magistrates' hearing was Salisbury's Guildhall, the gift to the city of the second earl of Radnor in 1795. Standing in the south-west corner of the city's market place, its front façade, a doric portico of six columns faces onto the market square, providing a backdrop for real-life drama and spectacle for thousands of observers. The building had ceremonial functions as it does today, and has provided the setting for events as diverse as an international exhibition of arts and trades in October 1852, following the Great Exhibition of 1851, and the opening of the public inquiry into the feasibility of road improvements near Stonehenge in February 2004. But in 1908 the Guildhall was also the city's administrative hub,[1] and its functions included the delivery of justice through weekly petty sessions and a monthly County court as well as coroners' inquests.

That on Teddy Haskell was opened at 3 o'clock on the afternoon of Tuesday 3 November, before Sidney Buchanan Smith,[2] the City Coroner, accompanied by the Mayor, Robert Michael Hall, Chief Constable Richardson and Chief Inspector Dew. Few observers attended the proceedings, but outside the Guildhall there was a huge crowd, running into thousands by one account, waiting to see the jurors and the witnesses. The fifteen-strong jury was made up of the following: James Miles, foreman, and James Asbridge, Thomas Bowden Bennett, William Bingham, Walter Cripps, George Henry Davis, James John Gater, Howard Lapham, John Sidney Rambridge, George Herbert Rawlings, Henry Simmonds, Elisha Sims, Leonard John Sly, Edwin James Summers and Edward Montague Whaley. All were pillars of the Salisbury business community and many were or would become prime movers in the city's governance. Four (Asbridge, Gater, Rambridge and Sly) were watchmakers and/or jewellers, and the panel also included two grocers, an ironmonger, a bookseller, a hosier, a milliner and draper, an auctioneer and estate-agent and the proprietor of the *Salisbury and Winchester Journal*. Two-thirds of the panel had less than a quarter of a mile to walk to the courtroom, another two lived and worked only in Fisherton Street.

The first day of the inquest was taken up with formalities. The jurors were all present on the stroke of three when the coroner called out their names, and they were sworn. At once they were driven off with the coroner, Richardson and Dew to view Teddy's body at Meadow Road. The *Salisbury Times* recorded that the policemen "carried away with them and brought back with them when they returned two big Gladstone bags." Twenty minutes later, the party returned and the proceedings were reconvened, and a few minutes later the day's only witness was called, an elderly lady, dressed in black, in considerable distress and helped into court by a man who turned out to be her son.

HAYTERS ALMSHOUSES, FISHERTON STREET – HOME OF
MRS CARTER, FLORA HASKELL'S MOTHER
© J.B. MOODY COLLECTION

Once she was sworn the coroner asked her, 'Is your name Mary Carter, and do you live at Hayter's Home, Fisherton Street?' – 'Yes.'

'Are you a widow?' – 'Yes.'

'Have you been to 40, Meadow Road?' – 'Yes.'

'And did you see there the body of a boy?' – 'Yes.'

'And did you recognise him?' – 'Yes. Edwin Richard Haskell, my grandson.'

'What is his mother's name?' – 'Flora Fanny Haskell.'

'Is she a widow?' – 'Yes.'

'And does she reside at 40, Meadow Road, Fisherton?' – 'Yes.'

'How old was the boy?' – 'Twelve.'

The jury had no questions, and Mrs Carter's evidence was read back to her for signature. Richardson stood up beside the coroner, and said that that was all the evidence he proposed to offer, and that he would ask that the enquiry be adjourned until Wednesday 11 November. The coroner asked 'Is there any likelihood of getting through it [the hearing] then? If so we will sit early and get through it then.'

'I think it would be advisable to sit early', replied Richardson.

'Then we will sit at ten o'clock. Very well, gentlemen, I will bind you over until tomorrow week at ten o'clock.' With that, the day's proceedings ended; in the event it would take a very great deal longer than one day for the inquest to be concluded.

Outside the court, where a cab was waiting in the Market Place to take Mrs Carter away, the crowd had become larger, and surged forward to catch sight of her as she was helped aboard. A quarter of an hour later, the police car drove away, and the sense of disquiet was only heightened by the abrupt adjournment of the inquest. But mystery was to be compounded with sensation when it was learned that at 10.30 on that Tuesday evening, quite in secret, Flora had been arrested on suspicion of murder and taken at once by car to spend the night in the police cells. Word got round on Wednesday that the Magistrates' hearing would begin at 11.00, and from that time on a crowd began to build in the Market Place. The cloak of secrecy continued up to the start of the hearing, at 1.00, which was attended by few individuals, among them the wives of the present and immediate past mayors, one of the latter accompanied by her young son.

Flora had been remanded at the Police Station and it was from there that she had been brought in a cab. Accompanied – indeed practically held up – by a female warder and by P.S. Golding in plain clothes, Flora was guided along a narrow passage and up steps to take her place in the dock. The *Salisbury Times* gives a pen-portrait of her as "a woman of slight build and medium height, … [with] rather a gentle, pleasant face, but …[looking] terribly worn and wan" and "Dressed in mourning". As she took her place she hung her head, and when seated she was almost in a stupor, and closed her eyes during the hearing. Behind Flora came the policemen Richardson, Dew and Superintendent Stephens, and they sat alongside W.J. Trethowan, who was appearing for Flora, and his son Frank. William James Trethowan was the senior partner in the firm of Nodder and Trethowan, whose offices were at Crown Chambers, Bridge Street. There also he acted as deputy city coroner, and as an agent for the Scottish Equitable, Alliance, Atlas and Ocean Accident insurance companies, while his son Frank Henry Trethowan was a solicitor in the same firm.

Upon the entry of the magistrates the court rose. The bench comprised the Mayor, Robert Michael Hall, himself a solicitor with an office at 39 New Canal, Samuel Grove, the former mayor and a pork butcher and bacon curer with shops in Butcher Row and the High Street, Samuel Ralph Atkins, of the firm of Atkins and Son, chemists and photographic dealers at 37 Blue Boar Row, William Maxwell Hammick

SALISBURY COURTROOM WHERE THE INQUEST WAS CONDUCTED.
© *J.B. MOODY COLLECTION*

of The Close, John Alfred Folliott, proprietor of a brewery and firm of wine and spirit merchants with premises in Winchester Street and Rollestone Street, and Charles Haskins, a dealer in china, glass and clothing, with two shops looking out onto the Poultry Cross.[3]

Before the hearing began, Richardson, W.J. Trethowan and Arthur Charlton Jonas, clerk to the magistrates and senior partner in the firm of Powning, Jonas and Parker had a brief discussion, for Flora was clearly not fit to take part in the proceedings. During this exchange, two of Flora's brothers slipped in and sat down behind the defence team. Trethowan then beckoned Flora over to relay the outcome of the conversation, and she nodded dumbly. Richardson stood up, glanced across to Flora and said 'This woman is brought here, your worships, on a charge of murdering Edwin Richard Haskell. She was arrested late last night, and I should be glad if you would remand her until next Wednesday.' Hall replied, 'Until eleven o'clock?'

'Yes, until eleven o'clock.' Trethowan concurred: 'I consent to that remand. I don't know what evidence you are going to take now; that is for the Bench to decide.' Flora was brought to the bar of the dock, a pitiable figure supported by the wardress and the policeman. Jonas, clearly mindful of the impact of his words, quietly read out the charge, "in a kindly, conversational voice", according to the *Salisbury Times*. 'Flora Fanny Haskell, you are charged with that you did feloniously and of your malice aforethought kill and murder Edwin Richard Haskell aged twelve years at forty, Meadow Road, on Saturday thirty-first October, by cutting his throat.' Flora could not speak. Hall turned to the wardress at Flora's side and, in a kind tone of voice, said, 'Let her sit down.'

After another brief consultation between Richardson and Jonas, the Mayor advised that the court should have evidence of arrest, and Richardson entered the witness box. His testimony, given in brief sentences to facilitate recording, was as follows:

'Last night, at ten thirty, accompanied by Inspector Dew of Scotland Yard and Superintendent Stephens of the County Police, I arrested the defendant at 40 Meadow Road, and charged her with murdering her son, Edwin Richard Haskell on October thirty-first, by cutting his throat with a knife. I cautioned her and she replied "No, no." I took her to the Police Station." Trethowan had no questions to ask, but requested permission for Fanny's brothers to be allowed to visit her at the Police Station. Richardson chipped in 'In the presence of an officer.'; Trethowan retorted 'Why in the presence of an officer?'

'We must have somebody there.' — 'You will be outside.'

'Outside where?' — 'Outside the cell.'

Grudgingly, Richardson responded 'Yes, as long as we do not lose sight of the woman.' — 'You can look through the keyhole if you like.'
The magistrates granted the application, and with that the hearing finished for the day.

Outside the Guildhall, a large crowd had gathered round the cab which was waiting to take Flora back to the Police Station. When she emerged she was, as before, dependent on the support of her escort, and, openly grieving, buried her face in her handkerchief as she made her way to the cab. The atmosphere was one of concern, even anxiety, for the accused, as the crowd looked on in sombre silence. Another facet of the public's interest was the comment given by one of the Carter brothers to the press that the family had received many letters of sympathy and offers of assistance to provide for Flora's defence, for which he wished to convey the family's grateful thanks. Meanwhile Flora, now a prisoner on remand, had been taken to the County Gaol in Devizes, where she was to remain for another five months. This grim edifice on the Bath Road was built in 1810 at a cost of about £30,000. The "monstrous building", in Cobbett's phrase, was fronted by a lodge of massive ashlared and rusticated blocks, every bit as severe as the Lion Gate at Mycenae — more so, when it was recalled that until 1860, executions took place in public at the top of this lodge. The death sentence was still exacted here, and had last taken place in 1903. Were Flora to be found guilty, it was here that she would spend her last days.

That same afternoon, on Wednesday 4 November, Teddy's funeral took place. Long before the appointed hour of three o'clock, crowds of sympathisers gathered around the house, along the route to the Devizes Road Cemetery and at its entrance. When the time came for the cortege to leave the house, Meadow Road was closed by a police cordon directed by Inspector Stroud. A dozen of Teddy's schoolmates,[4] drawn from the senior classes at Fisherton Boys' School and accompanied by the headmaster, Martin Winterton, marched from the school to rendezvous with the cortege. At the head was a glass hearse containing Teddy's coffin, of elm with white facings, covered with floral tributes; next was a closed carriage with the chief mourners — the Carter brothers, Flora's brother-in-law Alfred John Noble and his elder son. Behind them, led by Winterton, walked the schoolboys, two by two, each holding a bunch of white chrysanthemums and a sprig of spirea. Along the route, window-blinds had been drawn as a mark of respect. The family had wanted to keep the funeral a private affair, but although there was no admittance to the public, there were about a hundred people around the grave.

The coffin was borne from the cemetery gates to the grave "on the shoulders of strong men", to be met at the head of the grave by the Rector of St Paul's, Canon Edgar Nembhard Thwaites. Close at hand were the Mayor and Frank Baker, one of the

SCHOOL FRIENDS OF 'TEDDY' ATTENDING THE FUNERAL AT DEVIZES ROAD CEMETERY.
© *LLOYD'S WEEKLY NEWS*

councillors for the St Paul Ward and George Frederic Henbest, doubtless representing the coroner.[5] Sadder yet by their absence, neither Flora nor her mother were among the mourners. After the service of committal and the recital of the Grace, Teddy's schoolfellows filed past the grave, bare-headed, and, one by one, dropped their flowers on to the coffin in farewell to their dead comrade. Thwaites delivered an address, as touching as it was brief:

'There is nowhere where this dear lad will be missed more than in our school. He was loved by everyone who knew him, and it is a real pleasure to me to see so many dear, loving, sympathising friends here. Many of you are in tears, and I feel fit to cry myself. A dear, bright little boy and, as far as one can judge, a dear, sweet little Christian lad, going to bed a little before ten o'clock is found at ten thirty, lifeless. I am sure the friends are grateful for your kind sympathy and for coming here in such large numbers.'

The floral tributes came from the gamut of Salisbury society – 'To darling little Teddy from his loving mother and grandma'; 'In loving sympathy' – this, in the shape of a football, from the directors of the Salisbury Football Club; 'With deepest sympathy from Pamela Tennant'; 'With loving thoughts of Teddy from children and teachers of Fisherton School'; 'Poor little Teddy, from Sir Walter and Lady Palmer'; 'From all his dear little friends and playmates'; 'From Mr and Mrs Locker Lampson'; 'from St Paul's Wardens of the Primrose League'; 'From St Martin's Boys' School'; and from 'Bob and Milly'.

The city's final public valediction was expressed through two services staged by the Salisbury Corps of the Salvation Army, on Sunday 8 November, at the County Hall, a public meeting room on the corner between the south side of Chipper Lane and the west side of Endless Street. According to the *Salisbury Journal*, "Both gatherings were largely attended, and the proceedings were of a most impressive character", doubtless owing much to the efforts of the band and the corps' songsters. The afternoon service opened with prayers, the hymns "Above the waves of earthly strife" and " When the trumpet of the Lord shall sound" and a reading from the Book of Daniel, chapter 12. In his address, Vincent James Blew, the Secretary of the corps, said 'We are met together to sympathise with those who are in trouble and sorrow, in consequence of the sad calamity

THE FUNERAL PROCESSION OF 'TEDDY' HASKELL IN DEVIZES ROAD, SALISBURY. 1908.
© *THE DAILY GRAPHIC*

which has occurred in the city. The tragedy is the outcome of evil, the result of sin. We, who belong to the Salvation Army, and go about, know that, although everything in our city might seem fair and bright on the surface, yet underneath it all there is a seething amount of iniquity. If the people of Salisbury loved and served God, they would not hear tales of immorality and sin culminating in murder. You who have gathered here in this hall this afternoon are here to show your sympathy, not only with regard to the sad termination of the lad's life, but also with his relatives, who have to suffer because of the sin of someone. We, the people of this city must not judge as to who committed this awful crime, because we do not know. We must have mercy as well as justice, and until we know who is guilty of the deed we must not judge. But we do know that it is the result of sin. There is no getting away from that fact, and it must be a warning to us all to seek salvation and to try and live a life free from sin and wrong-doing.'

Adjutant Greasley dwelt upon the Army's motives in staging the services. 'The officers of the Salvation Army in Salisbury, recognising the public character of the sad event which has occurred in the city and how it has got hold of the people, feel that as the Salvation Army belongs to the people, and is of the people, a public memorial service in a public building would be appreciated. To this end we have ventured to take the County Hall for today's services in memory of the little boy, Teddy Haskell. Some people may think that the Salvation Army are going to try and make some money out of this occurrence, but I can assure you that nothing is further from our thoughts. The services are purely and simply being held in memory of the little boy, the tragic nature of whose death the whole community keenly feels and regrets. Of course, considerable expense is attached to our services today, and, as is usual in all Salvation Army meetings a collection will be made, but simply and solely in order to defray the expenses of securing the hall and advertising the services.' Sergeant-Major Chalk mentioned a visit to Salisbury Infirmary when he met Teddy, and recalled how Mr and Mrs Haskell sat either side of Teddy, 'and the scene was a very touching one, but the boy himself was very bright

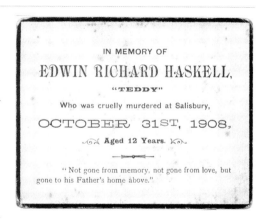

EDWIN RICHARD HASKELL FUNERAL CARD OWNED BY
PC WILLIAM CUTLER, 1908.
© ANDY NICKLEN COLLECTION

and merry.' He then sang 'Safe in the Arms of Jesus'. Mrs Pepper, wife of the Colonel, told her audience 'I am quite sure that the awful thing which has happened in our city is a call from God. It is a warning to us from God to flee from the wrath to come, and to seek salvation.' The service closed with the hymn "I'm but a stranger here", and a blessing by Adjutant Greasley. The audience were furnished with a song sheet printed for the occasion, with a portrait of Teddy.

In the evening there were many children and young people attending, and the hall was almost full. After opening prayers, Adjutant Greasley addressed his audience in the following words: 'We are met together under very sad circumstances. We are holding a service in memory of dear little Teddy Haskell, who met his death so sadly the other night. The Salvation Army thought it would hardly be proper to allow such a sad thing to happen and pass away without a little notice on our part. It is true that we can do nothing for the dear little chap who has gone, but we can hold a service in his memory, and I think the people will appreciate such a service. I thank all who have attended to show their sympathy, and pray that God will bless the bereaved friends, and be to them all that they need in this dark hour.' Then, with the audience standing, the band played the Dead March from Handel's *Saul*. After further addresses and a rendition of "We shall meet our loved one there" by the songsters, Sergeant-Major Chalk again recalled how he had met Teddy in the Infirmary some years before, and allowed him to try to play his cornet. 'The little lad's face lit up with smiles when it was suggested that when he grew up he would be able to play in the band. However, God has allowed it otherwise. We would not say God sent the calamity, but He has allowed it, and instead of playing in the Salvation Army band, Teddy is in the Golden City with those who have washed their robes.'

Adjutant Greasley then announced the collection, and again referred to the fact that some few people had questioned the Army's motives in hiring the hall for the memorial service. 'Some think that the Salvation Army is trying to make money out of it. I am very pleased to tell them the Salvation Army is above that. We thought people would appreciate a service of this kind, and by holding it in a public hall we thought that many who do not usually attend a place of worship would come.' Then Greasley spoke on Genesis chapter 42 verse 22: "Spake I not unto thee, saying, 'Do not sin against the child?'" 'The dear little lad in whose memory we are holding this service seems to have been very popular with every body. I don't think I have seen a city or town so moved as Salisbury has been moved during the past week. All of us have had our hearts drawn out to the little chap who has been taken from us so suddenly. I suppose one reason for the sympathy is the lad's affliction – having only one leg, and also because he was a fatherless little boy. He was a bright little chap, and always had a smiling face, although, no doubt, he was weak in body. . . I think that what has happened is a call to us from Almighty God.

'It is a call to men and women not to sin against their children. People do it by taking them into the public-house and giving them intoxicants. Many sin against their children by overlaying them, between five and six hundred dying in this way annually. Most of these deaths occur on Saturday nights, when the fathers and mothers get their money and take it to the public house. I thank God for what is being done at the present time by legislation for the protection of little children. But there is something higher than legislation, and that is for the parents to have their hearts changed by divine grace.' The adjutant instanced the wisdom of using fireguards, and not allowing children to wear flannelette nightdresses, and urged that 'children should not be taught to deceive or gamble, and they should not be allowed to smoke. I urge, in conclusion, that greater care should be taken of the children than is often taken now, and I believe that farmers think more of preserving their rabbits, or their fields of turnips than some people think of preserving their children.' And so the service was brought to a close, with a prayer meeting afterwards. As if in support of the Adjutant's denial of mercenary motives, the takings from the collection were some two pounds less than the Army's expenses in staging the events.

Already Flora's plight had caught the public's attention, and the first call to her aid had come from her own sex in an anonymous letter to the *Salisbury Times* on 6 November, under the heading "A suggestion":

DEAR SIR, - No doubt there are many in Salisbury who, like ourselves, take no personal interest in Mrs Haskell's case, yet for the sake of fair play, feel that she should have such legal help as would be secured by the friends of a richer woman.

Should not a subscription list be started?

A donation to such a fund as we suggest would not in any way be an expression of opinion as to character, innocence or guilt. We are merely asking that the woman, probably already dazed by the ordinary, but to her, unusual procedure of the law, should not be penalised by her poverty and ignorance.

Will not some of the citizens volunteer to organise a defence fund?

Faithfully yours, THREE WOMEN.

This was at once replied to by Frank Baker, Flora's councillor, in a letter to the *Salisbury Journal*, published the day after the *Times*:

SIR, - I have seen a letter in the *Salisbury Times* of today's date, signed by "Three Women", suggesting that a subscription list be started to supply funds for Mrs Haskell's defence. I have known Mrs Haskell for many years, and as senior representative for the Ward of St Paul's, in which she resided, I shall be glad to receive and duly acknowledge all sums which may be sent to me for this purpose.

Yours faithfully,

FRANK BAKER

Sturminster, Victoria Road, Salisbury, Nov. 6 1908.

Baker's appeal was echoed throughout the land on the Sunday, with the publication of letters from the Mayor and Canon Thwaites in *Lloyd's Weekly News*:

SIR, - The murder of a crippled boy and the arrest of his mother involve a great sensation in our quiet and well-conducted city. As chief magistrate for the time being, it is impossible for me to express an opinion on the merits of the case; but there is a feeling here that the prisoner, a poor widow woman, fighting for her life, should be supplied with adequate funds to conduct her defence.

ROBERT HALL
(MAYOR)
Salisbury.

SIR, - Mrs Haskell is a poor woman, who has supported herself and her murdered boy by laundry work. She has no power of finding money properly to defend herself. I have no judgment of my own as to who murdered the boy, but certainly the poor woman ought to be properly defended.

EDGAR N. THWAITES,
Rector of St Paul's, Fisherton.

And with that, *Lloyd's Weekly News* opened the account by launching "The Mrs Haskell Defence Fund" with ten guineas, adding by way of instruction:

"Subscriptions should be addressed, Editor, 'Lloyd's News', Salisbury Square, E.C., and envelopes marked on the outside 'Mrs Haskell'. It should be remembered that the smallest sums can be received, and that money should be sent in either stamps, postal orders, or cheques." Elsewhere, it said, "It should be distinctly understood that no reflection on the action of the police is implied. It is not at all because we think she has been treated unfairly that we take up the matter, and ask our readers to contribute to the fund which will enable her to get the best legal advice and advocacy. It is because of the desperate straits in which the poor woman is."

Lloyd's Weekly News was at the forefront of the campaign to secure justice for Flora, for it drew attention to her plight in two ways. The first and most graphic was a facsimile of a three-page letter written to her mother, written from the gaol on 5 November, and published on the front page on Sunday 8 November. In it Flora wrote: "My dearest Mother, I hardly know how to write to you and my dear brothers and all kind friends to thank them and you for all the kindness an[d] loving sympathy shewn to me in every way. I am praying constantly and I am sure you and many others are doing the same –

LETTER SENT BY FLORA HASKELL TO HER MOTHER FROM DEVIZES PRISON.
© *LLOYD'S WEEKLY NEWS*

that the 'God of all Grace' may order all things aright in the terrible trouble we are all now under-going. One thing dear Mother there is One over all before Whom I can say I have a clear conscience for you and every-one knew I loved my precious little Teddy with a love only a mother could do. My one hope is that you will be given the strength to bear up under it and I know you and my dear brothers will do whatever you can. God bless you dear Mother – pray for me constantly – and with my love to you and all loving friends I am your ever loving daughter Flo." The facsimile was reproduced in the *Salisbury Times* of the following Friday, and the text in the *Salisbury Journal* on 14 November. Secondly, *Lloyd's* published an interview with Richard Carter the eldest of Flora's three brothers, again reprinted with some abridgement in the *Salisbury Times*, in which he said, "My sister, I am convinced, is absolutely innocent of this charge. As she says in her letter, she loved Teddy too dearly to think for a moment of taking his life . . . I saw my sister at the police station on Wednesday [6 November]. After the proceedings at the police court I asked her, point blank, "Do you know anything about this?' She replied, 'Oh, Dick, you know I didn't do it. I would not hurt a hair of his head. Won't they let me see him before they take him away?'" *Lloyd's* reported that Carter was "now busily engaged with his brothers, William and Albert, in assisting to prepare the defence of his accused sister", and elsewhere reports on statements made to him by various people who would be called to give evidence on Flora's behalf.

As if to reinforce the sense of locally-felt concern for Flora's circumstances, both the *Salisbury Times* of 13 and the *Salisbury Journal* of 14 November reported Robert Hall's last pronouncement from the bench in his Mayoral capacity. He was replying to a vote of thanks for his services as Chair of the Bench over the previous year, and considered some of the cases he had heard. He said 'We have had at the finish a great tragedy – a very sad and terrible thing – and I am sure the sympathies of everyone must go out to the bereaved family in the loss of that poor little cripple boy. I think it right to say that whether the prisoner be innocent or guilty of the charge that is brought against her, I do hope that nothing will be

done by people in the town to increase that suffering one way or the other. We must recognise that until a person is proved guilty by due course of law, the law naturally assumes that he or she is innocent, and it would be very sad if any ebullition of feeling one way or the other were shown either against the police or for the police, in the conduct of their important and responsible duties, or for or against the woman in the very sad charge under which she is now labouring.'

And with that the scene was set for the substantive business of the inquest, which resumed on Wednesday 11 November at 10 o'clock. Word had got round of the continuing investigations at 40 Meadow Road. The previous Sunday, 8 November, Dr Augustus Pepper had arrived from London on the 11.28 train, to be met by Stephens and Dew. The three of them drove quickly round to Meadow Road, and while Dew and Pepper entered No. 40, Richardson drove round to the Wilton Road to collect Drs Wilks and Row. They were followed at the house by Gilbert Kempe, surgeon both to the city and county police, and then by Charles Notley, the Assistant City Surveyor, who arrived laden with plans and drawings. At the time little notice was taken: *two* motor cars outside the property had, after an eventful week, almost become a commonplace, and on that Sunday morning, with few people about, the famous Home Office pathologist went about his business unnoticed. Even so, the investigation took four hours, and the external manifestations of this – a constable emerging to borrow a candle from one of the neighbours, Stephens departing and returning with a large lamp, and finally one of the car headlamps being brought in – only served to heighten the atmosphere of mystery and intrigue. Two of those involved in the events of 31 October, Walter Steer and Thomas Alfred Rawlins, were called in to assist the investigation for some considerable time, and one of the Gladstone bags which were remarked upon on the first day of the inquest was brought in. So well before the proceedings started the court was crowded, with the gallery reserved for women, and, as it seemed to the *Salisbury Times* reporter, almost as many pressmen in the front seats of the well as there were members of the public behind. Following the arrival of the coroner and the swearing of the jury, H.J. Sims, the Treasury Solicitor arrived, followed by Captain Llewellyn and Superintendent Stephens. The Trethowans, father and son, took their place next to Sims, while, as St Thomas's was striking ten, Richardson and Dew strode into the court to take seats in the front row of the court, alongside Dr J.E. Gordon, and with Flora's family in the row behind.

Opening the proceedings, Buchanan Smith said 'Gentlemen of the jury, you are re-assembled here today to make further enquiry into the circumstances attending the death of a cripple boy named Edwin Richard Haskell, aged twelve, who was found dead in bed at No. 40 Meadow Road, in this city, on the night of October thirty-first, with his throat cut. After hearing the evidence it will be your duty to find out when, where and how, and if necessary by whose hand, the said Edwin Richard Haskell came by his death. I am sure I need hardly ask you to erase from your minds any rumours you may have heard outside the court, or anything you may have read in the papers, and give a verdict according to your oaths.'

The first witness was John Stanley Wyatt, an apprentice draper at the Salisbury Co-operative stores, who lived at 2 Beulah Place, Skew Bridge Road, Bemerton. He testified that on Saturday 31 October, at five minutes past ten, he was sent by the manager to deliver a parcel addressed to Mrs Manning, Meadow Road.

The coroner asked, 'On arriving at Meadow Road, did you ask anyone where Mrs Manning lived?' – 'Yes, I asked a woman.'

'What did she say?' – 'She said she did not know.'

'What did you do then?' – 'I enquired at a shop close by, and was told it was No. 42.'

'Did you go to No. 42 Meadow Road?' – 'Yes.'

'Did you get any answer to your knock?' – 'No.'

'What did you do then?' – 'I enquired at No. 40, which is next door.'

'Did you knock?' – 'Yes.'

'Did you hear anything then?' – 'I heard the door unlocked inside.'

'Was it opened by a woman?' – 'Yes.'

'What did you say?' – 'I asked if Mrs Manning lived next door.'

'What was the reply?' – '"Yes"'.

'Anything else?' – 'Yes: she thought she [Mrs Manning] was out.'

'Did you then ask her to take in the parcel?' – 'Yes.'

'And deliver it to Mrs Manning in the morning?' – 'Yes, and I asked her to say it was from the Co-operative Stores.'

'What time was it when you knocked at the door of No. 40?' – 'About twenty past ten.'

'Did you notice any person in Meadow Road other than the woman of whom you asked the way?' – 'No, sir.'

The coroner then asked, 'Do you wish to ask any question, Mr Sims?' – 'Yes, with your permission', and, turning to Wyatt, 'Where are the Co-operative Stores?' – 'Winchester Street.'

'Meadow Road is quite at the other end of the city is it not?' – 'Yes.'

'And what is the name of the manager who sent you on the errand?' – 'Mr Sladen.'

'And how did you go?' – 'On a bicycle.'

'Were the streets pretty crowded at that time?' – 'No, sir.'

'There were people about, I suppose?' – 'One person.'

'I am not speaking of Meadow Road, I mean the streets of the town. You had to ride with care: you couldn't dash through the streets?' – 'No.'

'Had you to go back to the stores that night?' – 'No.'

'What time did the stores close?' – 'Ten o'clock.'

'Were they commencing to close when you came away?' – 'No, they had shut up.'

'You say you enquired in a shop for Mrs Manning?' – 'Yes.'

'What sort of a shop was it?' – 'A little general shop.'

'When you knocked at No. 42, did you knock more than once before you got an answer?' – 'Several times.'

'How many times did you knock at No. 40?' – 'Several times.'

'When the woman came to the door and answered it, did you see her face?' To this question Wyatt had no answer, and Sims pressed the point:

'Do you see her here today?' At that point Trethowan interjected 'I don't think you had better ask him that.'

Almost as if on cue, there was a slight disturbance in the court, as Flora, accompanied by a warder and a wardress, was brought in to take a seat near to Trethowan, just below what was normally the dock. For a moment, she had the attention of everyone in the court, a slight figure, her pale complexion contrasting with her black dress, black feather boa, black straw hat trimmed with black ribbon, and black hair. No longer haggard as she was before the magistrates, she had an air of quiet self-possession, even when Wyatt was questioned about her and she was pointed out to him. Sims continued: 'Just look at the woman you see there: did you see her?' — 'I don't know.'

'When you gave her the parcel and thanked her, what did she do?' — 'I don't know.'

'Did she shut the door?' — 'I can't say.'

'You got on your bicycle and rode away?' — 'Yes.'

'Which way did you go home?' — 'Up York Road and Wilton Road.'

'Did you see anyone in the street as you rode away?' — 'I didn't notice anyone.'

Trethowan then introduced himself: 'I appear for Mrs Haskell who is under arrest for the murder of this poor boy. Turning to Wyatt, he asked, 'Fisherton Street, just after ten o'clock on a Saturday night is usually crowded, is it not?' — 'Not particularly crowded.'

'Did you not meet lots of people from the railway bridge . . . past Fisherton Church . . . up to York Road?' — 'Not very many.'

'What do you mean by "many"? Forty? Twenty? Ten?' — 'Not many.'

'When you went to 40, Meadow Road, are you quite sure you knocked several times?' — 'Yes, two or three.'

'Can you tell whether it was two or three?' — 'Not for certain.'

'Can you say you knocked more than once?' — 'Yes.'

'Did the woman come to the door almost immediately?' — 'I am not sure.'

'Perhaps you were pretty impatient, were you? When the woman, whoever she was, came to the door, did you see anything unusual in her appearance?' — 'No, sir.'

'She took the parcel from you, and if there had been anything unusual in her appearance, you must have noticed it?' — 'Yes, I should have noticed it, but I didn't.'

'She spoke to you in a calm, collected way, did she not?' — 'She spoke like an ordinary woman would speak.'

'Now what time did you say it was when you knocked at 40, Meadow Road?' — 'About twenty past ten.'

'How did you fix that time?' — 'I don't know, I'm not certain, but I should think it was about that time.'

'Did you see this gentleman, Mr Steer, in Meadow Road?' — 'No.'

'Or in York Road?' — 'No.'

'You went home after that as fast as you could?' — 'I went home at an ordinary pace.'

'Did you see anything of a political meeting at the corner of York Road?' — 'No.'

'Did you see anyone outside the *Duke of York* Hotel?' — 'No.'

Sims had a few more questions: 'You say you noticed nothing unusual about the woman's appearance?' — 'No.'

'You had never seen her before?' — 'No.'

'And you didn't know what her usual appearance was?' — 'No.'

'How long were you at the door talking to her?' — 'I didn't talk to her at all . . . [I just] handed the parcel in.'

'You must have spoken to her to do that. Was it a few seconds?' — 'Yes.'

Trethowan and Flora conferred briefly. The foreman of the jury asked, 'Did you knock at the front door or the back door?' — 'Front door.'

'And was there sufficient light in the passage for you to distinguish the woman when she opened the door?' — 'No, sir.'

Trethowan asked, 'Is there not a lamp on the opposite side of the road, almost opposite No. 40?' — 'I don't know.'

While Wyatt's testimony, which had been taken down in longhand, was read back to him by J.T.

Jarratt, the coroner's clerk, four of the city magistrates – Atkins and Haskins, and Robert Curtis Harding and Edwin John Orchard – came into the court.

Next to testify was Gertrude Steer, Flora's neighbour who had made her the coat. She lived at 36 Meadow Road, with her parents Walter and Alice Steer. Aged 20, she was a dressmaker by profession, and described by the *Salisbury Times* as "a nice-looking young woman". Sims asked 'Had you been doing any work for Mrs Haskell?' – 'Yes, sir.'

'Was it before October thirty-first?' – 'Yes, sir.'

'What was it?' – 'I was making a little coat.'

'On October thirty-first did you take it to her home at 40, Meadow Road?'- 'Yes, sir.'

'At what time?' – 'At about a quarter to ten.'

'Who opened the door?' – 'Mrs Haskell.'

'Did she ask you in?' – 'Yes, sir.'

'And you went in?' – 'Yes.'

'To which room?' – 'The kitchen.'

'Did she try the jacket on?' – 'Yes.'

'Was it for herself?' – 'Yes.'

'And she tried it on herself?' – 'Yes.'

'And said she was pleased with it?' – 'Yes, sir.'

'Did she make any further remark?' – 'She said it was just what she wanted, and said she would be a "toff" tomorrow.'

'Did she say anything else?' – 'She asked what she was in my debt.'

'Did she pay you?' – 'No.'

'Did you then leave?' – 'Yes, I went out the back way.'

'And did you join your mother in York Road?' – 'Yes, sir.'

'How long were you with Mrs Haskell?' – 'I should think about five minutes.'

'Did she seem in her usual manner?' – 'Quite.'

'On your going out at the back door, did you see anyone?' – 'Only my mother.'

James Miles, the foreman of the jury, then asked which way she had gone to No. 40. – 'By the back door.' Sims continued 'Your house is next door but one to Mrs Haskell's, is it not?' – 'Yes.'

'The front door, of course is in Meadow Road?' – 'Yes.'

'Is there a back entrance to Mrs Haskell's house from a back passage leading into York Road?' – 'Yes.'

'And it was to the back door that you went on this Saturday night?' – 'Yes.'

'On that Saturday night had you to meet someone at the railway station?' – 'Yes.'

'At what time?'- 'Ten o'clock.'

'Was it on your way to the station that you called at Mrs Haskell's with the little coat?' – 'Yes.'

'You told me you were there about five minutes. Were you in time at the station to meet your friend?' – 'Plenty of time.'

'You knew the little boy Teddy Haskell?' – 'Yes.'

At the mention of her son's name, Flora burst into tears.

'Did you see him that night or hear him?'- 'No.'

'When Mrs Haskell let you in the back door, can you say whether it was locked or not?' – 'I couldn't say.'

'You told us you went into the kitchen and Mrs Haskell tried the little coat on. Tell me, what was she wearing that night?' – 'A light cotton blouse, I think.'

'Did you notice what her skirt was, what colour?' – 'I believe it was a dark skirt.'

'Any apron?' – 'I can't say whether she had one on or not.'

'What was the appearance of the kitchen? Was the tablecloth on?' – 'Yes.'

'Had she been having supper? Were the supper things on the table?' – 'Yes, as far as I remember.'

'What had she been doing?' – 'Having supper, I think.'

'It is a small kitchen, is it not?' – 'I think it is the ordinary type.'

'And lit with a gas jet – a naked burner?' – 'Yes.'

'Did you see a foot bath, washing tub or towels in the kitchen?' – 'No, sir.'

'I didn't ask you, when I asked you about the blouse, had it long sleeves or short sleeves?' – 'Long sleeves.'

'How much had she to pay you for the little coat?' – 'I hadn't decided.'

'Did she say anything about paying you?' – 'She said she would pay me then, but I said I was in a hurry.'

'Did she say anything about money?' – 'Yes.'

'What did she say?' — 'She said "My purse is upstairs, or I could give it to you now."'

Trethowan then asked 'I believe you have known Mrs Haskell and Teddy all your life?' — 'Yes.'

'That being so would you know whether there was great affection between mother and child?' — 'Yes.'

Again, Flora broke down.

'Was there great affection?' — 'Yes.'

'The boy was always bright and happy when you saw him?' — 'Yes.'

'For a boy in his position in life, always nicely dressed and cared for?' — 'Yes.'

'When you knocked at the back door, did she come immediately?' — 'Yes.'

'Was she bright and cheerful when you saw her?' — 'Yes.'

'I believe she joked with you?' — 'Yes.'

'You said you stayed with her about five minutes. Mightn't it have been more?' — 'I don't think it was.'

'How long would it take you to go from this house to the railway station?' — 'About five minutes.'

'So you might have stayed there ten minutes and still have been in time to catch the train?' — 'I don't think so.'

'You might have stayed there ten minutes, and still had time to meet the train at the station?' — 'I might have.'

'She couldn't pay you for the coat because you didn't state the price?' — 'No.'

'When you left Mrs Haskell, what was she doing?' — 'She had the coat in front of her.'

'Was she doing anything to the coat when you left?' — 'Wrapping it up in the brown paper.'

'When you parted with her, you parted in the usual way, exchanged good nights, and she was still bright and cheerful?' — 'Yes.'

'You were asked about this blouse, whether it had long sleeves.' — 'I think it had.'

'You are not at all certain?' — 'I am not certain.'

Smith interjected 'She said in her evidence it had long sleeves.' Trethowan retorted 'I can't help that; I want you to put down what she says in cross-examination.' Gertrude repeated that she was uncertain whether or not the blouse had long sleeves.

Next to be called was Gertrude's father, Walter Steer, a compositor.

'What time did you arrive home on October thirty-first last?' — 'At about a quarter past ten.'

'Where did you go when you arrived home?' — 'Into the kitchen.'

'Was your back door open?' — 'Not when I arrived.'

'While you were in the kitchen did you hear anything?' — 'Yes.'

'What?' — 'I heard a scream.'

'Did you go out into your back garden?' — 'Yes, sir.'

'Did you then find where the screams were coming from?' — 'Yes, I found they were proceeding from Meadow Road.'

'Did you at once go to Meadow Road?' — 'Yes, sir.'

'How did you go there?' — 'I ran down the passage by the side of the house into Meadow Road.'

'Did you there see anybody?' — 'Yes, I saw Mrs Haskell.'

'Where was she?' — 'Between her own door and mine.'

'Did she come towards you?' — 'She was coming towards me.'

'And when she got to you did she say anything?' — 'She said "Man round the corner."'

'What did you do?' — 'I ran to the corner of Meadow Road and several yards up York Road.'

'Did you see anything?' — 'I saw two men outside the *Duke of York Hotel.*'

'Did you go to them?' — 'Yes, sir.'

'And did one go into the yard?' — 'Yes.'

'Is that the yard of the *Duke of York?*' — 'Yes.'

'Did you follow him in?' — 'Yes, sir.'

'What did he say?' — 'I followed him in and pushed the gate against him and apologised. He said "What's up?"'

'What did you do?' — 'I made no reply, but stepped back onto the path again.'

'When the man came out of the doorway of the yard did you do anything?' — 'I said to the man whom I recognised as a Salisbury man, "Do you know that man?"'

'What did he say?' — '"No."'

'Did the other man walk away?' — 'Yes, without

speaking.'

'Did you follow him?' – 'Yes.'

'How far?' – 'Almost to the corner of Meadow Road.'

'Then did you return to the house on hearing Mrs Haskell still screaming?' – 'Yes.'

'When you got back to the house, what did you do?' – 'I ran upstairs into the front bedroom, and seeing no-one there I went into the back bedroom.'

'Did you see anything there?' – 'No, sir, it was too dark.'

'Did you call for a light?' – 'Yes, sir.'

'Was one brought?' – 'No, sir. I went down into the passage and said to the people who were downstairs, "Go and get my lamp."'

'Who brought you your lamp?' – 'My boy.'

'Did you then go upstairs again?' – 'Yes.'

'Into the back bedroom?' – 'Into the middle back bedroom.'

'What did you find there?' – 'I saw that a terrible murder had been committed.'

'Ah! What did you see?' – 'I saw Teddy Haskell lying in bed with his throat cut.'

'In what state were the bedclothes?' – 'Saturated with blood.'

At this most graphic point in the narrative, Flora was seized with uncontrollable sobbing, and Frank Trethowan suggested she be allowed to leave the court. The sight of her being led, crying, down the steps, reduced to tears many of her onlookers, including, unsurprisingly, her family and the hapless depictor of that awful scene.

Sims pressed on with his interrogation. 'Did you go up to him?' – 'Yes, sir, I went to the side of the bed.'

'Did you feel his face?' – 'Yes, stooping down I felt his little face and saw that he was dead.'

'Did anyone follow you upstairs? – 'Yes, Mrs Butt.'

'Did you say anything to her?' – 'I said, "Here is a horrible affair." She suggested sending for a doctor.'

'And what did you say then?' – 'I came out on the landing and called out "Send for a doctor and the police." Soon afterwards Dr Wilks and Dr Row came running up the stairs, and I followed them into the room.'

'Had the police arrived then?' – 'No, sir, and after a short while I went down into the kitchen and said "Who could have done it?" Mrs Haskell said "I heard a man coming down the stairs and as I went to the door he threw a knife at me." I went back into the bedroom, and shortly afterwards P.S. Golding arrived. He looked round for a moment and said "I must get on the telephone somewhere." He then came downstairs and I followed him. At the foot of the stairs was my mother-in-law, who said "There is the knife that was thrown at Mrs Haskell." P.S. Golding said "Don't touch it!", and he picked it up himself from the foot of the stairs in a piece of paper. I then went out into Meadow Road and looked among the crowd to see if I could identify the man whom I had seen in the yard of the *Duke of York*.'

'Did you see him?' – 'No, I went out with P.S. Golding and gave a description to several people of the man I had seen. I went with P.S. Golding as he was going into Mr Slade's shop[6] in Meadow Road, where he despatched his message on the telephone. We then went into York Road and back to the gateway of the *Duke of York*, where I lit a match to see if I could see any bloodstains.'

'Could you?' – 'I saw one or two damp spots, but I could not say whether they were bloodstains or not. Returning to the house I stood at the foot of the stairs. Soon afterwards Mrs Carter came in. She said "Is Teddy dead? Oh, let me see him." I said "Don't come up now," and she went out into the kitchen and was missed for some time afterwards. I went upstairs again, and a watch was found under the pillow. Then I went downstairs and asked Mrs Haskell whose the watch was. She did not answer the question, but said "Is my Teddy all right?" I did not answer, but repeated my question, and she said "Yes, it was Teddy's, and there was some money in the drawer." I went back and told the police what she had said. I remained in the room some time and on [my] going downstairs Mrs Carter and Mrs Haskell came and asked if they could see Teddy. I said "Don't", but Dr Wilks, who was in the kitchen, said they could presently if they wanted to.'

'Did the doctor ask you to give him some water and towels?' – 'Yes.'

'Did you take the water and towels to the doctor?'

– 'Yes, sir, Mrs Carter gave me the towels.'

'Did you assist the doctor?' – 'Yes.'

'Did the doctor require anything else?' – 'Yes, two clean handkerchiefs, which I got for him.'

'Did you afterwards throw away the water and wash the towels?' – 'I threw away the water and wrang out the towels.'

'Where did you place them?' – 'On the window sill.'

The foreman of the jury asked exactly when it was that Steer heard the screams; he replied 'It was five minutes after I got home that I heard the screams.'

Some forty minutes after she had been led away, Flora came back into the court. The coroner then asked 'I don't know whether your examination will take long, Mr Sims, or whether we shall adjourn.'

'With your permission it will take a considerable time.'

'I think, perhaps, it would be better to adjourn now.'

'You know Mrs Haskell has to appear in another place; perhaps it would be convenient to adjourn now. Do you propose going on again?'

'Shall we adjourn until half-past one or two o'clock?'

'Do you propose to go on again?'

'If you like, we will leave it where it is.'

Sims then explained 'I would much rather leave it where it is. There is reason for it. It is impossible to finish the examination today or on any one day. There is a large amount of testimony to be put before the court.

For his client Trethowan countered 'One would like to know the reason. One would like to get it through as soon as possible. This poor woman is hanging about and will have to come before the magistrates today. We ought to go on and finish before the case commences before the magistrates.'

Sims replied 'The usual practice is to wait until the inquest is finished. It is not settled yet whether we shall adopt that course in this case or not. Probably not.'

'What is the objection', Trethowan asked, 'to proceeding with the inquest this afternoon?'

'I could go on with Mr Steer at one-thirty, but then his cross-examination would have to follow.'

The coroner turned to Trethowan: 'I have no further evidence to offer the jury.'

'Then you must adjourn it.'

'This day week.'

Sims asked 'Can you arrange to sit on this day week and the following day, and long days?'

Tetchily, Smith replied 'I am not going to sit for twelve hours.'

Sims conceded 'Anything in reason under that.'

With that the inquest was adjourned until Wednesday 18 November, at 10 a.m.

After a night in the cells in Salisbury, Flora appeared before the magistrates; not, as widely expected, in the Guildhall, but in the Police Station itself. So the crowds gathering outside the Guildhall and the Police station were disappointed, and the camera set up and trained on the front door of the Police Station to catch a glimpse of Flora on her way to the court was in vain. For the hearing in the chief constable's office, Atkins took the chair and was joined by Harding and Folliott, while Richardson was represented by his inspector, Herbert Stroud, and Arthur Jonas was in attendance. Flora, looking drawn from her experience at the inquest was brought in by a warder and wardress and seated on a stool in front of the chief's desk. Jonas turned to Stroud and said 'I believe you are making an application for a formal remand?' – 'Yes, sir, until the twentieth.'

'The enquiries are still proceeding and the inquest is not over?' – 'That is so.'

'Then', asked Jonas of the chairman of the bench, 'will you remand her, sir?'

Atkins replied, addressing Flora, 'Flora Fanny Haskell, you are remanded until Friday the twentieth at eleven o'clock.' – 'Yes, sir.' And with that, Flora was escorted to a "covered motor-car" at the front of the police station, where a few of the crowd caught a glimpse of her, before speeding away along Endless Street, into Queen Street and onwards to Devizes.

5

Dodge the policeman: The Inquest, Wednesday 18 November to Thursday 19 November

THE INQUEST WAS RESUMED on the morning of Wednesday, 18 November. Once again the gallery filled with women spectators, and many more were turned away. Buchanan Smith again presided, and Dew, Richardson and Stephens were in attendance as before. Trethowan was first to arrive, and opposite him from now onwards was Thomas Parr, instructed by William Lewis for the Treasury, as Sims was no longer able to be present. Last to arrive, and a little after the proceedings had begun, was Flora, escorted by a warder and wardress from Devizes Gaol.

Walter Steer was recalled to conclude his evidence, and Parr's examination began with events before the discovery of the murder.

'I want to know the route you took before you came home on the Saturday night. You had been to the G.W.R. Station?' – 'Yes.'

'To meet a train coming from Warminster?' – 'Yes.'

'Did you there meet your daughter Alice, your wife, Mrs Chivers and your daughter Gertrude?' – 'Yes.'

'About what time was it when you met them?' – 'I couldn't tell, as the train had arrived when I met them. I should think about three or four minutes past ten.'

'Did you talk with them for a short time . . . how long?' – 'Probably about a minute.'

'And then did you and your wife and Mrs Chivers go towards your home?' – 'Yes.'

'Did you walk slowly or fast?' – 'Slowly.'

'Which direction did you follow? – 'Fisherton Street, across to the drinking fountain at the junction of the Wilton and Devizes Roads.'

'Did you then go down York Road?' – 'Yes.'

'Which side of York Road did you walk down? – 'On the left-hand side.'

'And did you then turn down Meadow Road to your house?' – 'Yes.'

'How long did it take you to walk from the station to your house?' – 'About ten minutes.'

'From the time you got to York Road to the time you got to your house, did you see anyone?' – 'I did not notice anyone.'

'When you came out of your house after hearing the screams, did you see anyone in Meadow Road, except Mrs Haskell?' – 'No sir.'

'Were you able to see in both directions, up and down Meadow Road?' – 'I did not look to the left.'

'You have told us Mrs Haskell said "Man round the corner". Did you hear anything about Teddy having been killed?' – 'No, sir.'

'And hearing her saying "Man round the corner" you rushed round the corner to York Road and Meadow Road?' – 'Yes, sir.'

'Passing Mrs Haskell as you went?' – 'Yes.'

'Did she say anything as you passed?' – 'Man round the corner.'

'You told the coroner on the last occasion that you saw two men outside the *Duke of York*?' – 'Yes.'

'Have you seen them since?' – 'One of them.'

WALTER STEER GIVING EVIDENCE AT THE INQUEST AS
DEPICTED IN THE MORNING LEADER, 1908.

Parr called 'Fetch the man Butt!' and a tall young man stepped forward. He asked 'Is that the man you saw?' — 'That is about the stamp of the man I saw.'

'How was this man dressed? Had he an overcoat on?' — 'No, sir, I think not.'

'As to the other man, are you able to say what he was wearing?' — 'A square cut coat.'

'Were you able to notice whether he had anything round his neck, any collar or scarf?' — 'No, he had nothing round his neck.'

'Are you able to say that the man here named Eccott was one of the men you saw?' — 'Undoubtedly.'

'When you went back to No. 40 did you go to the back or front door?' — 'The front door.'

'When you went in did you see Mrs Haskell?' — 'I noticed no-one when I went in, only some woman at the kitchen door.'

'Did Mrs Haskell come out at all before you went upstairs or say anything further?' — 'No, sir.'

'I understand you rushed upstairs at once?' — 'Yes.'

'Why did you rush upstairs?' — 'Because I thought there might be a man or burglar up there.'

'I understand that when you got into the room you touched the little boy's face. What was it like?' — 'Just warm, like a child asleep.'

'With regard to the condition of the clothes on the bed, were they disarranged?' — 'No, sir, [they were] as if the bed had just been made.'

'How were the upper clothes?' — 'They were lying just up underneath the little boy's neck, and folded back.'

'Was the little boy lying peacefully?' — 'Quite.'

'With regard to the other things in the bedroom – the articles of furniture – were they in position or disarranged?' — 'In order, sir'

'Did you notice the lamp there at all that night?' — 'No.'

'You remained on the landing until the doctors arrived?' — 'Yes.'

'How long would that be?' — 'About five minutes.'

'Did you, after you had been in the bedroom with them, go downstairs?' — 'Yes.'

'Was it after, or before, the arrival of the police sergeant, that Mrs Haskell said a man had thrown a knife at her?' — 'Before.'

'Where were you standing when she said this?' — 'In the kitchen.'

'Will you please tell me the exact words she used about the man throwing the knife?' — '"I heard someone coming down the stairs and as I went towards the door a man threw a knife at me."'

'Did she say where the man was when he threw the knife at her?' — 'No.'

'Or anything about him as to the direction in which he was going?' — 'No.'

With that, Parr's examination finished, and it was time for Trethowan to cross-examine.

'How long have you known Mrs Haskell, the prisoner?' — 'For the last twenty years.' At this point Buchanan Smith interjected 'She is not a prisoner here', at which Trethowan pointed at the wardress at Flora's side, and drily remarked 'She *is* a prisoner.' The coroner smiled and said 'We have no prisoners here.' Trethowan resumed. 'How long have you known Teddy?' — 'Ever since he was born.'

'And have you and Mrs Haskell lived close

together during the whole of this time?' – 'Yes.'

'Was there great affection between Mrs Haskell and the boy?' – 'The greatest affection.'

'Did you know Mrs Haskell's late husband?' – 'Yes.' At this point Flora buried her face in her handkerchief and sobbed uncontrollably.

'Since his death has Mrs Haskell worked to maintain Teddy?' – 'Yes.'

'Since you have known them have you ever heard of any quarrel or squabble between them?' – 'No.'

'Has the boy always seemed well cared-for, well dressed and happy?' – 'Yes.'

'On the thirty-first October, you left the G.W.R. station sometime after ten oclock?' – 'Yes.'

'At that time, I think, as a rule, it is a busy time in Devizes Road?' – 'There were lots of people about, but it was not crowded. We were not inconvenienced.'

'When you got to York Road were there any people there?' – 'I didn't notice them.'

'Might there have been twenty or thirty?' – 'I might have noticed them if there were so many as that.'

'If there were fifteen or sixteen would you have noticed them?' – 'I don't think I passed a dozen people that I noticed.'

'Which direction were they going?' – 'There might be some crossing Sidney Street.'

'When you heard the screams you were in your kitchen?' – 'Yes.'

'You went into Meadow Road by means of a passage?' – 'Yes.'

'To do that you had to go out of the kitchen into the scullery, through the scullery door into the yard, from the yard through another doorway into the passage, and still be at the back of your house?' – 'Yes.'

'You would then have had to come the whole length of the passage to get into Meadow Road?' – 'Yes.'

'Supposing a man started out of the front passage of No. 40 when you first heard the screams, wouldn't he get into York Road before you could get from the back of your premises into Meadow Road?' – 'Doubtful.'

'If you didn't hear the first scream there would be no doubt that he could?' – 'No doubt.'

'The first scream you heard came from the direction of Meadow Road?' – 'No.'

'"Whilst I was in the kitchen I heard a woman scream. I went out to the back garden, but found it came from Meadow Road." That is what you said last time. Where did the first scream come from?' – 'I think it came from the back of Mrs Haskell's house, but I am not certain.'

'What do you mean by the back?' – 'I mean from her back kitchen door.'

'Your door doesn't open towards Mrs Haskell's house, but the other way?' – 'No, my back door opens towards Mrs Haskell's house.' Dew then produced a plan of the house, and Steer was forced to concede that in fact his back door opened in the opposite direction to Flora's. Trethowan continued.

'When you heard a scream, whether it was the first, second or third, you went out and met Mrs Haskell coming towards you?' – 'Yes.'

'Be careful how you answer this: did she then say "Man round the corner who came down my stairs"?' – 'No, sir.'

'She gave you no intimation as to which corner the man had gone round?' – 'No, sir.'

'And it was at your own initiative you ran to York Road, the opposite direction [to that] in which she had been going?' – 'Yes.'

'Did you stop in your running to speak to Mrs Haskell?' – 'No, sir, it was said as I was running.'

'So she might have said "Man down my stairs", and as you were running you did not hear it?' – 'She might have said anything.'

'Then you went to the *Duke of York* and saw these two men and came back?' – 'After watching the two men.'

'How long?' – 'Until they came out of the yard.'

'Almost as soon as you came back did you see Alfred Thomas Rawlins?' – 'No, sir.'

'How long was it?' – 'Several minutes.'

'Did he ask you whether you saw anybody about when he came in?' – 'He may have.'

'Did you tell him you had seen two men outside the *Duke of York*?' – 'I might have; I don't recollect.'

'If he says you did you wouldn't dispute it?' – 'No.'

'Did you tell Rawlins that you could neither identify [n]or describe these men?' – 'I don't recollect.'

'Try to recollect.' – 'I may have said it but I don't recollect it.'

'When you went upstairs with the lamp, did Mrs Haskell follow you up three of the stairs?' – 'No.'

'Did you tell her not to come up?' – 'Not then, later.'

'How long later?' – 'An hour.'

'It was an hour after you got to No. 40 that you refused to let Mrs Carter or Mrs Haskell come upstairs -?' – 'It might have been an hour or more. I had no means of telling how long.'

'You refused to let them go up?' – 'I told them not to.'

'Listen to this: this is what Mrs Haskell says: "When the light was brought, I tried to go upstairs, but Mr Steer met me on the stairs and made me go down. At the same time, I said 'Somebody go for the police.'" Did that take place?' – 'No, sir.'

'It didn't take place at all?' – 'No, sir.'

'Did you say somebody was to go for the police?' – 'I called out from the landing.'

'And did you say that Mrs Haskell was not there at the bottom of the stairs at that time?' – 'No.'

'Were there many people there?' – 'Three or four women.'

'I think you were a little confused at the time.' – 'Very likely.'

'And you have been ever since.' – 'No.'

'You felt this very badly?' – 'Yes.'

'Having an affection for the little boy yourself.' – 'Yes.'

'May I put it to you that when you shouted out for the light you were a little bit confused?' – 'Yes.'

'May I go further and say Mrs Haskell might have been at the bottom of the stairs at the time?' – 'She may have been.'

'At the time were you preventing people [from] going up?' – 'Nobody was anxious [to do so]. Nobody passed me.'

'Didn't you say something horrible had happened?' – 'Yes.'

'You found the body in the middle room?' – 'Yes.'

'The bed was right in the corner of the room, on the same side as the door, but at the opposite end?' – 'Yes.'

'The boy was lying on the outside of the bed, which was opposite the fireplace and a chest of drawers?' – 'Yes.'

'At the side of the bed there was oilcloth?' – 'I didn't notice.'

'Did you look on the chest of drawers and see there was blood on the coverlet?' – 'No.'

'Did you see that there was blood on the paper between the bed and the chest of drawers?' – 'No.'

'Did you look on the oilcloth to see whether there were any bloodstains?' – 'No.'

'Did you see any drops of blood on the floor leading from the bed to the staircase?' – 'No.'

'What were you doing there if you didn't see these things?' – 'I saw the child.'

'May I take it you were too dazed to notice anything else?' – 'I didn't notice anything else.'

'Were you dazed?' – 'No, sir.'

'You were there when the doctors arrived?' – 'Yes, sir.'

'Was there blood on the hands of Dr Row?' – 'There must have been.'

'Did you see him washing his hands?' – 'No.'

'Did you hear Mrs Haskell constantly ask for permission to go upstairs and see her dear Teddy?' – 'No.'

'Not when the doctors were there?' – 'No.'

'Were you there when the doctors were downstairs?' – 'Once, I think.'

'Did you go into the front room at all when Mrs Haskell was there with the doctor?' – 'Not that I can remember.'

'Did you hear Dr Wilks say "Whoever did this, it must be the work of a maniac?"' – 'I heard him say that.'

The playing-out of the events of that night was too much for Flora, and, with a gentle cry, she fainted, and had to be carried out of the court. Once the court had settled, Trethowan's questioning resumed. 'I think you saw the wound in the throat?' – 'Yes.'

'And you saw a lot of blood in the room?' – 'Yes.'

'Was Mrs Haskell covered with blood when you saw her first?' – 'I noticed some blood on her sleeve.'

'The right sleeve, was it?' – 'I think it was the left sleeve.'

'Did you see any marks on her in the street?' –

'No.'

'But when you came back you saw these spots on the sleeve, I suppose?' – 'Yes.'

'Did you hear [her] tell people that it was that that frightened her?' – 'I never heard her.'

'Did you notice that Mrs Haskell's nose was cut?' – 'I couldn't say for certain.'

'You think you did?' – 'I think I saw a scratch of some sort.'

'On the bridge of the nose?' – 'I would not be certain.'

'Did you notice that week, from Tuesday until the Saturday, that the little boy's ear was bleeding?' – 'No, sir.'

'Have you heard so since, that his ear had been bleeding that week?' – 'Yes.'

Parr had a few further questions: 'If Mrs Haskell's back door and your back door were open, would the sound of a scream reach you easily?' – 'Yes.'

'I understand that you didn't prevent Mrs Haskell going upstairs, but told her not to go?' – 'Yes.'

'Was that from motives of kindness?' – 'Yes.'

'Only the word *refused* was used. Are you quite certain that it was not for some time after you got into the house that you told her not to go up?' – 'Yes, some time.'

'Was it after Mrs Carter had come?' – 'Yes.'

'How long?' – 'I don't know, but Dr Wilks would know.' With that, Steer's testimony was concluded.

Charles Notley, who was next to testify, was the Assistant City Surveyor. He was also, like the medical and legal witnesses, a man of many parts, being the headmaster of the Collegiate School in St Thomas's Square and Secretary to the Salisbury and South Wilts Provident Dispensary, and thus a close associate of both Kempe and Wilks, the Haskells' family doctor. His appearance was brief, being to explain to the coroner how he had made plans of No. 40 Meadow Road, a block plan of the neighbourhood and a diagram of witnesses' routes plotted on an Ordnance Survey map of the area.

Next was Alice, Walter Steer's wife and the mother of Gertrude. The coroner asked 'Were you at home on the evening of October thirty-first?' – 'Yes, sir.'

'At what time?' – 'About a quarter past ten.'

'Were you sitting in your kitchen with anyone?' – 'Yes, sir, with my mother.'

'Did your husband come home about that time?' – 'Yes, sir.'

'Whilst there did you hear anything?' – 'No, sir. I heard nothing whilst sitting in the kitchen'

'Did you go out of the kitchen?' – 'Yes.'

'Why?' – 'I followed my husband into the garden and heard someone screaming.'

'Did you go into Meadow Road?' – 'Yes, sir.'

'Whom did you meet?' – 'Mrs Haskell.'

'Did you hear what she said?' – 'Yes. She said to me, "Someone has murdered my Teddy".'

'Did she say anything else?' – 'Yes, she asked me to go for a policeman and her mother.'

'Did you go for her mother?' – 'Yes, sir.'

'And on your return did you go back to Mrs Haskell's house?' – 'Yes, sir.'

'Did you see Mrs Haskell?' – 'Yes, she was sitting in an easy chair in the front room.'

'Was anyone else there?' – 'There were two or three people beside Dr Wilks.'

'Did she say anything?' – 'I heard her say a man came for lodgings on the preceding night.'

'Did you notice anything?' – 'No, sir.'

James Miles, the jury foreman, asked her 'Was your husband present when Mrs Haskell made that remark?' – 'No, he had gone round the corner.' She was then asked about her exchange with Flora: 'It was immediately I met her that she told me someone had murdered her Teddy.'

It was then Parr's turn to examine Alice. 'You had come from the G.W.R. station and walked home with your husband that evening?' – 'Yes.'

'And you had come, had you not, from the junction of Wilton and Devizes Roads along York Road to Meadow Road?' – 'Yes.'

'Did you notice anybody walking about along York Road or Meadow Road to your door?' – 'No, sir.'

'On hearing the scream you and your husband went out to the front door?' – 'Yes.'

'Did your husband go out first?' – 'Yes.'

'Did you follow immediately after him? Was it a question of minutes or seconds?' – 'About a minute.'

'At any rate, was Mrs Haskell still out when you got into Meadow Road?' – 'She was by the doorstep of her front door.'

'And then when you got to her front door had she got into the passage?' – 'Yes.'

'Are you quite clear it was before Mrs Haskell had got back to her house that she made use of the words "Somebody has murdered my Teddy?"' – 'Yes.'

'Did your mother come to the house afterwards?' – 'I left her in my own kitchen.'

'Did you notice anything on Mrs Haskell's clothes?' – 'I noticed one or two spots of blood on the right sleeve of her blouse.'

'Was it a light-coloured blouse?' – 'Yes.'

'Where was she when you noticed those spots?' – 'In the front room.'

'Was that immediately after you got into the house or sometime afterwards?' – 'Soon after.'

'From the time you got into the house to the time you noticed this on the blouse had Mrs Haskell gone upstairs?' – 'I don't know.'

'Were you present with Mrs Haskell all the time you were in the house?' – 'No, sir. I was only there about five minutes.'

'Mrs Haskell was in the passage when you first went to the house. Did you see her go into the front room?' – 'No, sir, I did not.'

Over to Trethowan. 'You have known Mrs Haskell for a great many years and the boy all his life?' – 'Yes.'

'Were you in court when your husband gave evidence about the affection between the mother and the boy?' – 'Yes.'

'Do you corroborate that?' – 'Entirely.'

'Mrs Haskell has always been a quiet and good neighbour?' – 'Yes, sir.'

'And since her husband's death has supported herself and her boy?' – 'Yes.'

'And to your knowledge she has never been about with men at night?' – 'No.'

'You said in your evidence, when you were in York Road you didn't notice people. You don't mean to say there weren't any?' – 'I was in too much of a hurry.'

'Do you say you didn't meet any?' – 'I didn't notice any.'

'When you got back you and your husband went into the kitchen together?' – 'Yes.'

'Did you hear any screams?' – 'No.'

'Therefore when your husband said "I was in the kitchen when I heard the screams," do you think he is incorrect?' – 'Yes.'

'When you went into the passage, what did your husband do?' – 'He went to wedge the window.'

'And then for the first time you heard a scream?' – 'Yes.'

'What direction did you think the scream came from?' – 'The road.'

'Did you speak to your husband or did he speak to you?' – 'We didn't speak at all.'

'When you saw Mrs Haskell did she appear frightened?' – 'Yes, sir.'

'You are quite sure she used the term "*murdered my Teddy?*"' – 'Yes.'

'Did she mention the spots of blood on her sleeve?' – 'When I came back and got in the front room I saw some spots on her sleeve.'

'Did she point them out to anybody?' – 'I didn't hear her.'

'Did you know Mrs Haskell had a cut on the bridge of her nose?' – 'I didn't notice it.'

'Do you know that during that week Teddy's ear had been bleeding?' – 'I have only heard since.'

'You went for the policeman?' – 'Yes.'

With that, Alice's testimony was concluded, and the court rose for lunch, resuming at 2 p.m. The first witness after the break was Gertrude Skutt, of 23 Meadow Road, the wife of Jesse Frank Skutt, an engineer. She testified that 'On Saturday October thirty-first I was at my mother's house, 17 York Road, and left at twenty past ten in the evening. I went down York Road towards Meadow Road and passed the passage leading to the back of Mrs Haskell's house.' The coroner asked 'When you got there, what did you see?' – 'I saw a lad named Percy Noble run from the passage.'

'Where did he go?' – 'Towards York Road.'

'Did you hear anything?' – 'I heard some screams.'

'Where did they seem to come from?' – 'From the front of Mrs Haskell's house.'

'Did you go to the corner of Meadow Road?' – 'No, sir, I went and looked down the passage.'

ALLEYWAY LEADING FROM THE BACKYARD OF MEADOW ROAD ONTO YORK ROAD, 1908.
© *Timothy W. Frank Walker and Ann Richardson Whittle, grandchildren of Frank Richardson, Chief Constable*

'Did you see anything?' – 'No, sir.'

'What did you do then?' – 'I went to the corner of Meadow Road.'

'Did you see anybody there?' – 'I saw Miss Stretch and her young man.'

'Did you speak to them?' – 'Yes, I said "Oh dear, whatever is the matter?"'

'Did you see anyone else?' – 'Yes, I saw Mrs Haskell standing on her doorstep.'

'Did she say anything?' – 'She said "Oh dear, someone has murdered my Teddy."'

'Did you see anybody else?' – 'No, sir.'

Parr began his examination. 'You were only up the passage a moment or so?' – 'Yes, sir, I stood at the top a few seconds looking up the passage.'

'Did you hear more than one scream?' – 'I heard two.'

'Did you hear any scream while you were looking up the passage?' – 'Yes, the second scream, and it sounded from the front of the house.'

'Did you immediately turn towards Meadow Road?' – 'Yes, sir.'

'Were the streets quiet that evening?' – 'Yes, sir.'

'You told me you did not see anyone. Did you hear a noise, as if someone was running?' – 'No, sir, except Percy Noble.'

Then Trethowan cross-examined. 'You saw nothing of a political meeting in Devizes Road?' – 'No.'

'You heard two screams. When did you hear the first?' – 'When I was outside the passage, and I saw Percy Noble run out.'

'Had you got to Meadow Road when you heard the second scream?' – 'No.'

'Nearly?' – 'Yes.'

'When you saw Miss Stretch and her young man, did you speak to them?' – 'Yes.'

'Therefore you stopped?' – 'Yes.'

'How long?' – 'About a minute.'

'Did you see Mr and Mrs Steer at this time?' – 'No.'

'Do you know them?' – 'Yes.'

'They weren't there?' – 'No.'

'Did you go towards Mrs Haskell's house?' – 'No, the opposite direction.'

Mrs Skutt went on to explain that she had walked past the Steers' house but had not seen the Steers, although she did see Mrs Haskell at her doorstep shouting – she said – 'Oh dear! Someone has murdered my Teddy!' To this Trethowan suggested 'Miss Stretch and her young man must have heard the screams too?' – 'Yes.'

'And do you mean to say that neither made any move towards Mrs Haskell?' – 'No.'

'You heard her scream, all three of you, but took no notice?' – 'No.'

'And you even walked on the other side of the road?' – 'Yes, to see how my own baby was.' There was laughter at Mrs Skutt's answer.

'Did you go straight home?' – 'Yes.'

'And was your baby all right?' – 'Yes.' More laughter in the court.

'When you passed Mrs Haskell you must have seen her clearly?' – 'When I was at the corner.'

'When you got opposite her, where was she?' – 'In the front passage.'

'There is a lamp just opposite the house –?' – 'Nearly.'

'Couldn't you see Mrs Haskell clearly?' – 'No.'

'How do you fix the time?' – 'By the time I left my mother's house.'

The next witness was Walter Ernest Haynes, a young clerk at the firm of Taunton and Co., who lived at 31 Meadow Road. On the evening of 31 October he had been out with his brother-in-law Ernest House, who lived two doors along at No. 27. He had been indoors five or ten minutes when he heard a scream and went back out into the street. There he saw Flora. The coroner asked 'Where was she?' – 'Standing on her doorstep.'

'Did she say anything?' – 'She said "Someone has killed my Teddy."'

'Did you see anybody else?' – 'I saw Mr Steer.'

'Where was he?' – 'By Mrs Haskell's.'

'Did he go into Mrs Haskell's house?' – 'I could not swear to that.'

'What did you do?' – 'I crossed the road.'

'Where was Mrs Haskell all this time?' – 'On the doorstep.'

'Did you see anyone else about?' – 'No.'

Parr began his examination. 'Had you been at a Mr Beresford's shop¹ in Fisherton?' – 'Yes.'

'Did you go along St Paul's Road, Sidney Street, by York Road into Meadow Road?' – 'Yes.'

'Did you cross to Meadow Road?' – 'Yes, in York Road by the *Duke of York* Hotel.'

'Were those streets quiet at the time you went home?' – 'Yes.'

'Did you notice anyone about there?' – 'No.'

'On hearing the scream did you go at once to your front door, or was it some time afterwards?' – 'At once.'

'Did you see anyone running?' – 'No.'

'Or walking hurriedly?' – 'No.'

'Did you hear any sounds of anyone running or walking hurriedly?' – 'No.'

Trethowan cross-examined. 'You didn't see the last witness, Mrs Skutt?' – 'I can't remember.'

'Do you remember seeing a young man and a young woman together at the corner of Meadow Road?' – 'No.'

'You saw Mr Steer there. Did you see Mrs Steer?' – 'No.'

'Did you see anybody in the road you didn't know?' – 'No.'

'You saw nobody but Mrs Haskell and Mr Steer?' – 'No.'

'Did you look down the road?' – 'No.'

'How long did you wait?' – 'About a minute.'

'There may have been other people there –?' – 'The people were beginning to collect by that time.'

'Have you ever played "Dodge the policeman" there?' The court laughed as Haynes, evidently ruffled by the suggestion, answered 'No.' Trethowan pressed his point.

'But is it not a usual bit of fun on a Saturday night, dodging the policeman round these streets?' – 'Well, I have never noticed it.'

'Don't you know the fences of the gardens in these streets are usually something like four feet high?' – 'Our's is about three feet.'

'Anybody could pop down your passage and jump over the garden fence without any difficulty?' – 'Yes.'

'Have you ever done that?' – 'No.' There was

more laughter as Trethowan retorted 'Well, you don't seem to know as much about it up there as I do.'

'How long was Mrs Haskell standing on her doorstep?' – 'About two or three minutes.'

'Did you see Mr Steer go back across to the *Duke of York* Inn at all, and come back again?' – 'No.'

Next was Haynes's brother-in-law, Ernest James House, a boot and shoe repairer, of 27 Meadow Road. Smith began by asking 'On October thirty-first were you with your brother-in-law, the last witness?' – 'Yes.'

'What time did you reach home that evening?' – 'Between a quarter and twenty past ten.'

'When did you come out again?' – 'About a minute afterwards.'

'Where did you go?' – 'To Slade's, a greengrocer's shop.'

'How long were you in the shop?' – 'Between five and seven minutes.'

'Did you remain at the shop?' – 'I was walking to Mr Slade's and I heard a woman scream.'

'What did you do?' – '[I] came back to opposite Mrs Haskell's'

'Did you see anything?' – 'I saw Mrs Haskell at her door.'

'Did she say anything?' – 'I couldn't catch exactly what she said: it was either "my poor boy or "my poor Teddy".'

'At this time there were several other people there?' – 'Several round the door.'

'Did you recognise any of these?' – 'Not then, I went in[to] my own house next and came out again.'

SLADE'S SHOP IN MEADOW ROAD PHOTOGRAPHED SHORTLY AFTER THE MURDER, 1908.
© *Timothy W. Frank Walker and Ann Richardson Whittle, grandchildren of Frank Richardson, Chief Constable*

'Where did you go?' – 'Opposite Mrs Haskell's'

'Did you see anybody then?' – 'I looked in the front door and saw Mr Steer going upstairs.'

'When you left Mr Slade's shop was there anybody in Meadow Road?' – 'I couldn't swear to anybody. There might have been two or thereabout.'

'Did you notice anybody at the corner of Meadow Road and York Road?' – 'There was somebody there, but I couldn't swear as to who it was.'

Mr Parr then questioned House. 'You came back with Haynes. On your way back did you notice anybody about there?' – 'No.'

'Your house is very little farther up the street?' – 'Yes.'

'I understand you were in your house not quite five minutes?' – 'Yes.'

'To get to Slade's shop you would pass Mrs Haskell's house?' – 'Yes.'

'When you went to Mr Slade's shop did you notice anyone about? – 'I didn't notice anyone.'

'Was that at about twenty past ten?' – 'As near as I can tell.'

'Did you hear a clock strike half-past ten?' – 'Yes, when I was standing by Slade's door.'

'Was it before or after you heard the clock strike that you heard the scream?' – 'Directly after.'

'On hearing the scream did you look in the direction of Mrs Haskell's house?' – 'Yes.'

'And immediately walked up. Did you at that time see anyone running or walking hurriedly?' – 'No.'

'From the direction of Mrs Haskell's house?' – 'No, I saw nobody.'

Trethowan continued. 'In going to Slade's you say you didn't notice anyone about. Do you suggest there was no-one in the streets?' – 'I didn't notice anyone.'

Asked how he was able to fix the time, House testified that at the greengrocer's, Slade had asked him the time, and he had replied "You need not ask me: the clock has just struck."

'Did you say you didn't see anyone until you got up to Mrs Haskell?' – 'I didn't notice anyone.'

'How long would it take you to get from Slade's shop to No. 40?' – 'I should think I could get there in a minute.'

Except for Steer, the witnesses to this point had given evidence mainly to determine or to check timings, and to set the scene in the immediate aftermath of the discovery of the crime. That of the next witness, Percy Noble, was key to establishing the precise chronology of events surrounding the murder. Percy was the youngest son of Alfred and Emma Noble,[2] and Teddy's cousin. Living at 38 Meadow Road, the Nobles were Flora's and Teddy's next door neighbours, and although Percy was four years older than Teddy, the two boys were in and out of each other's houses. He testified that on 31 October he had gone into Salisbury and was back in Meadow Road around 10.30, calling on Flora to repay a shilling he had borrowed. The coroner asked 'Did you try to open the back door?' – 'Yes, sir.'

'Could you do it?' – 'No, sir, it was locked.'

'Did you knock at the door?' – 'Yes, sir, twice – with my knee.'

'Did you hear anything?' – 'Mrs Haskell said "All right".'

'Did she come to the door?' – 'Not immediately.'

'Did you hear anything further?' – 'I heard a chair pushed back.'

'Then did she come to the door?' – 'Yes, but not immediately. I just heard a thump, as though somebody had jumped.'

'Did she then come to the door?' – 'Yes, sir.'

'What was she doing?' – 'She was screaming.'

'What did she say?' – 'Go and see if you can see that man, he's killed my poor Teddy!'

'Did she say anything else?' ‴Go for the doctor, quick!‴'

'What did you do?' – 'I ran up the passage into York Road.'

'Did you see anyone?' – 'No, sir.'

'Where did you go next?' – 'Down to the corner of York Road and Meadow Road.'

'Did you see anyone then?' – 'No, sir.'

'Did you go for the doctor?' – 'Yes, I went straight for Dr Wilks.'

Parr then questioned the lad. 'You had started, I think, from the *County Hotel*[3] to come home?' – 'Yes, sir.'

'About what time did you start?' – 'I think I heard the clock strike ten.'

'A boy was with you?' – 'Yes, a boy named Archie Waters.'

'Did you walk back by St Paul's Road and Sidney Street into York Road?' – 'Yes.'

'And did you once or twice stand talking with him on the way?' – 'Yes, sir.'

'How long were you stopping and talking?' – 'About a quarter of an hour.'

'Then you left your friend and went up the passage?' – 'Yes.'

'And you think you got to your aunt's door by ten thirty?' – 'Yes.'

'When you got outside the back door did everything seem quite quiet?' – 'Yes, sir.'

'To get to the back of your aunt's house have you to go through a wicket gate?' – 'Yes, sir.'

'That is a little way up the passage?' – 'Yes, sir.'

'Was that open or shut?' – 'Open.'

'You knocked at the door?' – 'Yes.'

'Was there a light burning there?' – 'Yes.'

'Did it appear to be a large light, or turned down?' – 'It was the usual light.'

'Enough to see to read by ‑?' – 'Yes.'

'Had you arranged to go back? – 'No, my aunt did not know I was coming back.'

'Mrs Haskell is your aunt?' – 'Yes, and I went back to pay her back a shilling.'

'It was not till after you had knocked twice that you heard the first noise?' – 'No, sir.'

'I understand you heard two noises – a chair moving, and something like a thump. Was it the thump of a foot?' – 'Yes, sir.'

'But it might have been caused by something else?' – 'Yes.'

'Did you tell the coroner anything about your aunt's shadow?' – 'No.'

'Did you see the shadow of a person in the kitchen?' – 'Yes, I saw the shadow of a person coming towards me.'

'Was that shadow on the blind of the kitchen window, or in the wash-house?' – 'It was in the wash-house.'

'Then you saw the shadow through the window of the scullery?' – 'Yes, sir.'

'Was it immediately after that, that your aunt came to the back door?' – 'Yes.'

'Did she say anything about the way you were to go?' – 'No, sir.'

PERCY NOBLE, THE BOY WHOM Mrs HASKELL FIRST INFORMED OF THE MURDER

SKETCH OF PERCY NOBLE PUBLISHED IN LLOYD'S WEEKLY NEWS

'As far as you recollect, did your aunt say anything about the passage?' – 'No.'

'Before she said that, she had unlocked and opened the back door?' – 'Yes, sir.'

It was then Trethowan's turn, to cross-examine the boy. 'You had been playing in a football match that afternoon at Dean?'[4]

'Did the deceased boy come into your father's house just before seven to talk about the football match?' – 'Yes.'

'How long did he stay?' – 'About five minutes.'

'Did you and Teddy go into Mrs Haskell's house?' – 'Yes.'

'I believe Mrs Haskell was out of the house at the time, but Miss Lawrence was there with your brother Walter?' – 'Yes.'

'When you got into Mrs Haskell's house, there was a letter for Teddy -?' – 'Yes, sir.'

'And he read her that letter?' – 'Yes, sir.'

'Before you went to dress before you went down town, did you not say you would be back at half-past ten?' – 'I told Teddy that.'

'Weren't you to come back at half-past ten to pay back that shilling?' – 'I did come back. I told Teddy I was coming back at ten thirty.'

'When you found the door locked, didn't you

knock it twice? – the second knock following immediately on the first?' – 'Yes.'

'And didn't you hear Mrs Haskell say at once "All right?"' – 'Yes.'

'No waiting about?' – 'No.'

'And did she say that in her usual calm voice?' – 'Yes.'

'No excitement?' – 'No, sir.'

'When you heard that, was it then that you heard the chair pushed back?' – 'Yes.'

'From the sound of the chair you could tell where the chair was moved from?' – 'Yes.'

'Where?' – 'From between the fireplace and the table.'

'And was it almost immediately after that, that you heard the thumping noise?' – 'Yes.'

'From the sound, could you tell where that came from?' – 'Yes: from the further end of the kitchen, at the bottom of the stairs.'

'Did it sound like a jump from the stairs?' – 'Yes.'

'Directly you heard that thumping sound, what did you hear?' – 'Mrs Haskell screamed.'

'What sort of a scream was it?' – 'It was not like her usual voice.'

'What happened then?' – 'She came to me.'

'What condition was she in when she opened the door?' – 'Some of her hair was coming down'

'Did she seem frightened?' – 'Yes.'

'Then she told you to go for the doctor?' – 'Yes.'

'Did you go straight up York Road?' – 'No, I went as far as Mrs Cooper's corner[5] and then went up to the doctor.'

'You and your father and brothers are constantly in the habit of going into Mrs Haskell's at all times of the day and evening?' – 'Yes.'

'On Saturday there was nearly always a football match in which you and Teddy would be interested?' – 'Yes.'

'And you would run in and out of each other's houses more especially then?' – 'Yes.'

'Are the fences that separate the gardens very high?' – 'Not very.'

'There would be no difficulty in anybody getting over them?' – 'No, sir.'

'And to anyone who knew the neighbourhood, there would be no difficulty in getting away from Mrs

Haskell's house without going into any open street?' – 'No, sir.' With this line of enquiry, as with his cross-examination of Haynes, Trethowan established the hypothesis that were anyone else to have been in the house beside Flora and Teddy, they could make good their escape without having to spend much time in the streets.[6] Parr then took the opportunity to re-examine Percy. 'You and the Haskells would be in and out of each other's houses all day?' – 'Yes.'

'The front door would be locked and the back door open?' – 'Our front door was locked.'

'Did you keep your back door open?' – 'Yes.'

'Was Mrs Haskell's back door generally unlocked?' – 'Yes.'

Then Miles asked 'Was there any sound heard at the front door when he was waiting at the back of Mrs Haskell's?' – 'No, sir', replied Percy.

'Was it unusual to find the back door locked at ten thirty at night?' the foreman continued. – 'Sometimes it was locked, and sometimes it was open.' At that point the inquest was adjourned until the morrow.

The inquest resumed at 10.00 a.m. on Thursday, 19 November. As before, the court was crowded, and shortly after the coroner took his seat, Flora was brought in, looking somewhat better than before, but nevertheless pale and drawn. The first witness was Lily Stretch, a nursemaid living a block over from Meadow Road at 32 George Street. Her striking attire of a long overcoat with a fur collar and a large green straw hat was slightly at odds with her bashful demeanour when in her opening words she divulged she was being escorted by Herbert Primmer on the night of the murder. The coroner asked 'Did you see anybody in York Road?' – 'No, sir, except a little boy named Noble.'

'Did you then go to Meadow Road?' – 'Yes, I was going up York Road to Meadow Road.'

'When you got to Meadow Road did you hear anything?' – 'No.'

'Did you see anybody?' – 'No.'

'Did anybody pass you in Meadow Road?' – 'No.'

'And you saw nobody but the lad Noble?' – 'No.'

'Where did he come from?' – 'I couldn't see whether he came from Meadow Road or from the back of the houses into York Road.'

Parr took over from Smith. 'You had come from George Street?' – 'Yes.'

'You heard nothing when you passed Meadow Road?' – 'No.'

'Did you hear anything afterwards?' – 'Yes, I had just got round the corner of Meadow Road when I heard screams from Meadow Road.'

'You would then be only two or three yards round the corner?' – 'Yes.'

'Did you turn round at once?' – 'Yes.'

'And did you then go round Meadow Road?' – 'No, sir, I went to the corner and stood up there.'

'Did you then see anyone running or walking hurriedly?' – 'No.'

'Were you able to see up Meadow Road, past the Haskells house?' – 'Yes.'

'Did you hear anyone running?' – 'No, sir.'

'Did you see Mrs Haskell?' – 'Yes, she was standing on her doorstep.'

'Do you know Mr Steer?' – 'Yes.'

'Where was he when you first saw him?' – 'Coming from his home towards Mrs Haskell.'

'Did you hear Mrs Haskell say anything?' – 'Yes.'

'What was it?' – '"Somebody has killed my little Teddy."'

'Did you hear her say that once, or more than once?' – 'More than once.'

'What did Mr Steer do?' – 'He came running round into York Road.'

'Was it before or after you heard the scream that you saw the little boy Noble run across York Road?' – 'After.'

Then it was Trethowan's turn to cross-examine, and to have a little sport with his witness. 'When you saw young Noble come into York Road, where did he go?' – 'I can't say: he went towards the *Duke of York* Hotel.'

He didn't come down toward you?' – 'No.'

'And if he didn't go into the *Duke of York* he must have gone towards Wilton Road?' – 'I don't know.'

'Are you the young lady who is said to have a sweetheart?' – 'Yes.'

'You had something much more pleasant to do than to watch the streets -?' – 'I don't know.'

'I think I should under the circumstances. You

were talking to each other?' – 'Yes.'

'You may be even more affectionate than that, mayn't you?' – 'I cannot say.'

'If that were so, people may have been in the street and you would not see them?' – 'I didn't see anybody.'

'I know, but if you were otherwise engaged there may have been other people in Meadow Road and York Road and you would not have seen them?' – 'I don't think so.'

'Before you heard the scream you had crossed Meadow Road?' – 'Yes, I had got to the door of No. 27 in York Road.'

'So you could not look either up or down Meadow Road?' – 'No.'

'Why did you stop opposite Mrs Cooper's front door?' – 'Because I heard the scream.'

'Then you came back into Meadow Road?' – 'Yes.'

'You only heard one scream?' – 'Oh, more than one!'

'They were coming from the front of Meadow Road?' – 'Yes.'

'Did you see Mr Steer come back?' – 'Yes.'

'He was only gone a moment?' – 'Yes.'

'You have talked about this case a good deal, haven't you?' – 'Not much.'

'Every day?' – 'I can't say.'

'Was Mrs Haskell inside when you heard her say the words you told the coroner?' – 'She was on her doorstep.'

Mr Parr resumed his examination. 'On what day was it you made your first statement to the police?' – 'On the Monday [2 November].'

Then it was the turn of her companion, Herbert Primmer, a gardener from Quidhampton. He testified that on that Saturday night in October he was walking with Miss Stretch. Smith asked him 'Did you call at her mother's house?' – 'Yes.'

'What time?' – 'We got to her mother's house at about ten oclock.'

'How long did you stay there?' – 'A quarter of an hour or twenty minutes.'

The rest of his testimony corroborated Lily's evidence, and Parr had no questions to ask. Trethowan asked 'When you left George Street and were coming up York Road, you did not watch the street?' – 'No.'

'And when crossing Meadow Road, there might have been people at either end and you would not have seen them?' – 'I did not see them.'

'Unless you looked down Meadow Road, you would not have known whether any people were there or not?' – 'No.'

'Were you talking with Miss Stretch as you walked along?' – 'I expect I was', replied the hapless Primmer, amid the laughter of the court.

'And when you talk to her, don't you look at her? I should be a funny fellow if I did not.' Amidst more laughter, Trethowan continued 'I don't mean to be funny . . . answer me "Yes" or "No."' Covered in confusion, Primmer had no answer.

'That being so', said Trethowan, 'it would hardly be likely for you to see people if they were there?' Perhaps with a degree of exasperation, Primmer replied 'I should have seen them if there had been any there.'

Doggedly pursuing his quarry until he had him cornered, Trethowan asked, finally, 'Could you have seen them if you had looked up?' – 'I don't think I looked up or down the road as I was crossing it.'

After this exchange Parr had only one question: 'Did you, after the scream, look up the road and see some people?' – 'Yes.'

Edward Butt, the next witness, lived, like Lily Stretch in George Street. He was a gas worker, and his testimony was that on 31 October at 10.15 p.m. he was by the side gate of the *Duke of York* Hotel when he saw Walter Steer coming towards him. Smith asked him 'At that time did any other man come?' – 'No, sir, I had only just got there.'

'Did you see a man come out of the *Duke of York* gate?' – 'Yes, I saw a man come out when Mr Steer was there.'

'Did Mr Steer say anything to you?' – 'Yes, he asked me if I knew the man.'

'What did you say?' – '"Yes, I knew him."'

At this point William Eccott, the next witness, stood forward, and Butt agreed that this was the man Steer had seen coming out of the gate at the *Duke of York*. Smith continued: 'Did Mr Steer then leave you?' – 'Yes, he went back towards Meadow Road.'

'Did you follow?' – 'Down towards the corner.'

'Did you go down Meadow Road?' – 'Yes, up towards Mrs Haskell's house.'

'Did you go as far as the house?' – 'Yes.'

'Did you see Mrs Haskell?' – 'Yes, she was stood at the doorway.'

'Did you hear her say anything?' – 'Yes: "Do go up and see what is the matter with my poor Teddy." There were two women with her.'

'Were you there when the police sergeant arrived?' – 'Yes, and I then left and went into my own place.'

Parr continued where the coroner had left off. 'Had you known Eccott before?' – 'Yes.'

'Did you know where he lived?' – 'Yes – in Meadow Road.'

'After this [incident at the public house] was he shown to you on the Monday afterwards?' – 'Yes.'

'And you identified him?' – 'Yes.'

Trethowan then asked 'You and Steer got to the *Duke of York* gateway about the same time?' – 'Yes, about the same time.'

'And from what direction did you come?' – 'From Sidney Street.'

'You didn't see Percy Noble, did you?' – 'I did not.'

William Eccott, Butt's acquaintance at the *Duke of York* spoke next. He was a builder's labourer, who worked for Edwin Scamell,[7] and he lived at 48 Meadow Road, in the terrace beyond York Road. His account was that on the night of October 31 he went to the *Duke of York* at about 7.45 p.m., and left at 10.25. He went out to the gateway on the east side of the pub, and as he left he saw Walter Steer. The coroner asked 'Did he speak to you?' – 'No, sir.'

'Did he go away?' – 'I did not see him go?'

'When you got into Meadow Road, did you hear anything?' – 'Yes, I heard some screams.'

'Did you go down Meadow Road?' – 'Yes, a little way.'

'Did you see a woman standing at the door of No. 40?' – 'There were several women standing round the doorway.'

'Did you hear anyone say anything?' – 'I heard a woman inside, screaming.'

'What did she say?' – '"Someone has killed my Teddy," or words of that description.'

'You then went away?' – 'I stayed about a minute

and went home.'

Then Parr continued the enquiry. 'You are in the employment of Mr Scamell, the builder?' – 'Yes.'

'On the night in question, how were you dressed?' – 'As a labourer in working clothes. I had nothing round my neck – no collar nor scarf.'

'What sort of coat?' – 'Square-cut coat.'

'Did you subsequently that evening take part in a search?' – 'Yes.'

'After seeing Sergeant Golding, and at his request?' – 'Yes.'

'For what purpose?' – 'To see if we could find a man.'

Trethowan cross-examined. 'You saw Mr Steer, and he said nothing to you or you to him?' – 'I said "What's up?"'

'Did he follow you, or you him?' – 'He went off towards Sidney Street.'

'Then you went to Meadow Road and you saw the women round the door -?' – 'Yes.'

'You didn't see Mrs Haskell?' – 'No.'

'How many women were there round the door?' – 'About a dozen.'

'You heard a sound of somebody saying something, and she may have said "Somebody has hurt my Teddy"?' – 'Yes.'

James Miles, jury foreman, sought to clarify a point: 'The jury would like to know whether the witness is quite sure Steer went up York Road towards Sidney Street.' – 'He went in that direction.'

Next to speak was Emma Chivers, the widowed mother of Alice Steer, who lived with her daughter and son-in-law at 36 Meadow Road. She testified that on the night of October 31, she was in the kitchen of No. 36 when she heard screams. She went out into the street to see Mrs Haskell standing at her door and crying out "Someone has killed my Teddy!" Mrs Chivers said to her, "Oh, don't think that." The coroner asked her 'Did she reply?' – 'She said she thought someone had killed him, because he was so quiet, she could not hear him.'

'Did she say anything else?' – 'She pointed to the knife at the foot of the stairs.'

'Did you see the knife?' – 'Yes, sir.'

'Did she say anything about footsteps?' – 'She said she fancied she heard footsteps upstairs.'

'Did she say anything about the back door?' – 'No, sir.'

Miles had a question about the knife, and Mrs Chivers replied 'Mrs Haskell pointed to the knife and said "There's the knife".'

Parr then asked 'Did she say how the knife was there?' – 'She said the knife was thrown at her by someone coming down the stairs.'

'Did she say who the someone was, whether it was a man or woman?' – 'No.'

'Did she say where she was?' – 'In the kitchen.'

'Did she say anything more about the knife?' – 'She pointed to it at the foot of the stairs, and it was lying crossways.'

Trethowan asked her 'You have known Mrs Haskell for a good many years, and Teddy all his life, and you know the great affection there was between the mother and the son?' – 'Yes.'

'Even up to the day of his death?' – 'Yes.'

'Had you seen Mrs Haskell or Teddy on that day, October thirty-first?' – 'Yes, I saw them both.'

'Where?' – 'I saw Mrs Haskell in her own home and the boy on the Gaol Ground.'

'What time did you see Mrs Haskell?' – 'Somewhere about nine oclock in the evening.'

'Was she then in her usual spirits?' – 'Yes, she was quite bright, and in her usual spirits.'

'No undue excitement about her?' – 'Not at all.'

'Did you have a conversation?' – 'Spoke and passed the time of day in the usual way.'

'Did she say anything about Teddy?' – 'No, his name was not brought forward.'

'What time did you see Teddy?' – 'About nine o'clock on the Gaol Ground. He was going home.'

'Was he alone?' – 'Yes.'

'Was he as usual?' – 'Yes, happy and cheerful as he always was.'

'Did you speak to him?' – 'I wished him good night and asked him if he was just going home, and he said "Yes"'.

'Your daughter said when she was in the kitchen she heard no screams?' – 'No, she wouldnt if the middle door was shut.'

'Until Mr Steer and your daughter went into the scullery you heard no screams?' – 'No.'

'The scream you heard came from the direction of Meadow Road in front of the house?' – 'Yes.'

'You went to the front?' – 'Yes.'

'When you got to Mrs Haskell's you didn't see Mr Steer?' – 'No.'

'Therefore you might have been there first?' – 'I couldn't say.'

'Mrs Haskell seemed very frightened, didn't she?' – 'Yes.'

'Did she make you come inside the passage?' – 'She asked me to come in and I went inside.'

'She said "Somebody has killed my Teddy," and she pointed at something?' – 'At the knife.'

'Did she point and say "There?"' – 'She said "Look! There is the knife".'

'And you thought it frightened her, and that that accounted for her being frightened and made her think Teddy was dead?' – 'That was what I thought.'

'Did she point to the blood on her blouse?' – 'Yes.'

'Did she do that then?' – 'A few minutes after.'

'And when you looked at her blouse you saw a few spots of blood?' – 'Yes.'

'Wasn't that sufficient to frighten any woman?' – 'I should think so.'

'And [that] would, in your opinion, account for her saying "My Teddy is killed?"' – 'Yes.'

'After that, did she tell you she heard footsteps upstairs?' – 'Yes.'

'And did she say "I thought it was the Noble boys?"' – 'No.'

'Did she tell you a man came the previous evening?' – 'No.'

'Did she tell you about anybody asking Teddy for his name and address, and giving him twopence?' – 'No, she didn't say that to me.'

'How long were you there?' – 'About ten minutes.'

'During the whole of that time Mrs Haskell was in a terrible condition?' – 'Yes.'

'When you looked at the sleeve of her blouse you saw the spots of blood, but no other blood on her?' – 'No.'

'Was that on the left sleeve or the right?' – 'The right.'

'Mrs Haskell has always been a very quiet woman?' – 'Oh, yes.'

'Kept herself pretty much to herself?' – 'Yes.'

'And respected by all the neighbours?' – 'Yes.'

'Saturday night after ten o'clock, Wilton Road and Devizes Road are pretty busy?' – 'I don't know, I am not out at that time.'

'Devizes Road is a busy road?' – 'Yes.'

Parr had some further questions for Mrs Chivers. 'Is it usually a quiet neighbourhood?' – 'Yes.'

'And did it appear as usual that night?' – 'Yes.'

'You told us that amongst other things Mrs Haskell said she fancied she heard footsteps upstairs. Did she say "I fancied I *heard* footsteps," or "I fancy I *hear* footsteps"?' – 'She said "I fancied I *heard* footsteps".'

Miles then asked 'When Mrs Haskell said she thought someone had murdered Teddy and pointed to the knife, did she make any attempt to go upstairs to see if anything had happened?' – 'I don't know. Not in my presence.'

'Did Mrs Haskell say anything to account for the blood on her sleeve?' – 'From the knife, she said it was. She said the knife was thrown at her and that it hit her on the wrist.'

Parr interjected 'Did she say by whom it was thrown?' – 'Yes, by a man who came downstairs.'

Miles asked 'Did you notice any wound or anything?' – 'No.'

The last question came from the coroner, who wanted to clarify where Emma had seen Flora at 9 p.m., and Emma realised and admitted that the encounter took place in town.

The next witness was Mrs Matilda Cooper, a widow who lived at 27 York Road. Her testimony was that on the night of October 31, while sitting in her dining room with her daughter, Edith Langmead, some time after 10 p.m. she heard a scream. She went out to her front door, from where she saw a young couple at the corner of York Road and Meadow Road. She did not know them, nor did she notice anyone else in the street. She walked into Meadow Road and saw Flora standing at her door. As Mrs Cooper approached, Flora said "Someone has murdered my little Teddy," and she seemed deeply distressed. The coroner asked 'Did she say anything further to you?' – 'I went into her sitting room, and as I was trying to comfort her, I said "Who could have done such a thing?", and she said "A man who had been for lodgings".'

'Did she say what day that was?' – 'On the day before.'

Parr then asked 'After you got to your front door did you see or hear anyone running away?' – 'No, sir.'

'You asked her who could have done it, and it was in reply to your question that she said something about the man who had been for lodgings. While you were there did she make any attempt to go upstairs?' – 'No.'

'Did you see anything in the room whilst you were in the front room – anything produced?' – 'A pocket handkerchief.'

'Do you remember where it was when you saw it?' – 'Somebody was going to use some eau-de-Cologne, and she asked Mrs Haskell for her handkerchief.'

'On that [occasion] did you see the handkerchief?' – 'Yes.'

'Who had the handkerchief?' – 'Mrs Sweetman.'

'Did you notice anything about it?' – 'I noticed that it had some blood on it.'

Trethowan then cross-examined Mrs Cooper. 'Have you known Mrs Haskell for long?' – 'I don't think I had ever spoken to her before.'

'You have known her by sight -?' – 'Ever since I have lived there.'

'Did you know Teddy?' – 'Yes, I had seen him play. He would throw his ball over.'

'When you arrived, was Mr Steer there?' – 'I can't remember.'

'Were there some other people there?' – 'One or two, I can't be certain.'

'And were they talking to Mrs Haskell?' – 'Yes.'

'It was then that you heard her say "Someone has murdered my Teddy?"' – 'No, she was screaming "Someone has murdered my Teddy" at the door.'

'When you got there was she very frightened?' – 'Yes, and she was sobbing very much.'

'What else did she say about the man?' – 'She thought it was a man who had come for lodgings.'

'Didn't she say "I couldn't say who the man was?"' – 'No, she didn't say that.'

'Did she also say anything about another man and Teddy?' – 'No.'

'Nothing?' – 'No.'

'Did she show you the bloodstains on the blouse?' — 'I noticed them.'

'You can't remember whether you noticed them first or whether she showed them to you?' — 'No.'

'Did you see any other bloodstains about Mrs Haskell?' — 'No.'

'Did you notice whether the bridge of her nose was cut?' — 'No, I didn't notice.'

'You didn't see the knife, because you didn't go farther than the front room -?' — 'No.'

'How long were you there?' — 'I expect I was there half an hour.'

'In the front room all the time?' — 'Yes.'

'What were you doing?' — 'Trying to comfort her. I spent all my time at that, and didn't notice anything else'

'When you asked her who could have done it, she mentioned about the lodger?' — 'Yes.'

'You don't suggest that she said to you that the man who came for lodgings was the man who murdered Teddy?' — 'No.'

'Your recollection isn't very clear -?' — 'I think it is.'

'Do you remember that a few days ago you said it was not very clear, and that all you could remember was what Mrs Haskell said, and those words were "Someone has murdered my Teddy?"' — 'Yes.'

Parr now had some further questions of Mrs Cooper, which he prefaced by saying 'She made her statement to the police on the Monday after the murder.' Turning to Mrs Cooper he asked 'There were other people in the room, and there was other conversation going on, and that you don't remember?' — 'No.'

'All you remember is what Mrs Haskell said?' — 'Yes.'

'They were all talking together, but you were quite close to Mrs Haskell?' — 'Yes.'

Trethowan cleared a final point with Mrs Cooper, and she answered that Flora might have been answering questions put to her by others in the room, but she was not certain.

At that point, wearing a long black coat with a big sable collar, in came Dr Pepper, and sat down next to Parr, just in time for the lunch-time adjournment.

The first witness after lunch was Mrs Cooper's daughter Edith, wife of Oliver Langmead, sometime City Librarian.[8] On the night of the murder she was staying with her mother, the previous witness, and was sitting with her in the dining room at 27 York Road when, at about 10.30 p.m. she heard someone scream, and went with her mother to the front door. She spotted a young couple at the corner of Meadow Road, and asked the young man what was going on. She didn't understand what the young man — Herbert Primmer — said, but thought he was talking about someone being drunk. The coroner then asked her 'Did you go to Meadow Road?' — 'Yes.'

'Did you see Mrs Haskell?' — 'Yes, and heard her shout "Someone has murdered my little Teddy." She was standing outside her front door.'

'When you got to the door did you hear anything [else]?' — 'I heard a man shout "Get a light!", and I ran indoors.'

'Did you hand some candles to the man?' — 'I lit them, and put them in the sitting room in Mrs Haskell's house.'

'When you left the house the first time, did you see anyone in the street except the young man and young woman to whom you have referred?' — 'No-one.'

Questioned by Parr, Mrs Langmead said she neither saw nor heard anyone running or walking hurriedly away. Afterwards, she went into the house with Mrs Sweetman, and pointed out the knife, which was lying on the floor, near the kitchen door.

Next was Sarah Butt, the wife of Frank Butt, a cashier with Whitehead's, a legal practice at 35 New Canal. The couple lived at 40 York Road, less than ninety feet from 40 Meadow Road, and Mrs Butt was among the first to arrive on the scene after hearing Flora's screams at, by her own estimate, about 10.25 on the evening of October 31. She testified that she then went to 40 Meadow Road, and, at Flora's request, went upstairs behind Walter Steer and followed him into the bedroom, where they came upon the dead child lying in his bed. The room was in perfect order, and the bedclothes were quite undisturbed. Mrs Butt waited in the room until Dr Wilks arrived, and held the lamp aloft while Wilks was examining the floor for bloodstains. These they traced from inside the bedroom to the top of the stairs.

She also poured water out for Dr Wilks to wash his hands, and gave him an underslip on which to dry his hands as she couldn't find a towel. Afterwards she saw Mrs Haskell, and noticed bloodstains on her blouse, and she also saw Mrs Haskell's handkerchief, stained with blood. She didn't touch it, and could not say if the bloodstain was fresh.

Trethowan asked how long Mrs Butt had known Flora, and she replied 'I have known Mrs Haskell for five years, but I have never spoken to her. I knew Teddy very well, as he was always throwing his ball into our yard. I often saw the boy and his mother together, and they were very affectionate, and the lad well cared for and very happy indeed.'

'When you first got into No. 40, Mrs Haskell seemed frightened -?' – 'Yes.'

'And you offered to go and see what was the matter with Teddy?'

'But you didn't come back to tell her?' – 'No – because she knew.'

'Oh, no, no! You must answer my questions! You didn't come back to tell her?' – 'No, because I think somebody had told her already.'

Mrs Butt continued with her testimony, that she did not think that the body was moved before the police came: only the clothes were moved back. She did not hear Flora say, "Oh, do tell me, doctor, what is the matter with my Teddy." She also did not hear the doctor say, "Has not anyone told her yet" nor "Whoever did it, it is the work of a maniac." Answering Parr, she testified that when she first went into the house, there was no light burning upstairs, but then Steer came with the lamp. Miles then asked about the little brass lamp, and Mrs Butt said she did not notice any bloodstains on it.

The next witness was Mrs Emily Sweetman, a widow who worked for Mrs Saunders, the shopkeeper at 42 York Road.[9] She recounted to the coroner that as she was having supper, Eccott came into her shop, and said that Mrs Haskell was crying out that someone had killed her little boy. Mrs Sweetman then went round to 40 Meadow Road, where she saw Mrs Haskell, with several people around her. As she was standing in her passage, Mrs Haskell said that little Teddy was killed. Mrs Sweetman was also present when Dr Wilks came

into the room, and bore witness that Flora had asked him to say whether her little Teddy was all right. The coroner asked 'What did the doctor say?' – 'He turned to us, who were standing round her, and asked us if she knew the truth.'

'Then did the doctor tell her?' – 'Yes, the doctor told her Teddy was dead.'

'Did she say anything?' – 'I can't remember; she was very much upset. I was then called into the passage by Mrs Langmead and shown the knife which was lying on the floor. The blade of the knife was pointing towards the kitchen. I saw some bloodstains on Mrs Haskell's sleeve, and I understood from her that the man coming down the stairs threw the knife, and that that caused the blood[stain]. I washed her face with eau-de-Cologne, and I noticed a scar on her face.'

'Was it bleeding?' – 'No, it was not.'

'Was it an old scar?' – 'No, it was not an old scar.'

'What did you use to wash her face with?' – 'My handkerchief.'

'Did you see any other handkerchief?' – 'Yes. I took a handkerchief from Mrs Haskell's hand. There were bloodstains upon it. I put it on the mantelpiece.'

Parr then examined Mrs Sweetman. 'Did you take the handkerchief and feel it?' – 'Yes.'

'Did it feel dry or damp?' – 'It felt a little damp.'

'Did Mrs Haskell say anything as to how she got the mark on her nose?' – 'I understood from Mrs Haskell that the knife must have cut her face, and that that caused the blood on the handkerchief.'

Trethowan's cross-examination of Mrs Sweetman began, as had his others, with an acknowledgement on her part of the great affection between mother and son. She added that although the doctor had broken the news as kindly as he could, Flora was terribly upset, so much so that he left to fetch a soothing draught for her, returning with it half an hour later. The doctor also said "Whoever did it, it must have been the work of a maniac". She (Mrs Sweetman) did not recall Flora pointing out the bloodstains on her sleeve to the others present. From what she saw of the scar on Flora's nose, it would bleed easily if it were rubbed with a handkerchief, and Flora had been crying bitterly before Mrs

Sweetman took the handkerchief from her, and that might account for it being damp.

Miles asked if the handkerchief could be produced, and Parr agreed: 'Yes, it will be produced. I think it desirable that it should be produced now, in order that the witness can identify it.' Mrs Sweetman was then recalled, and Dew handed it to her: she agreed that it was the one she had taken from Flora. Parr asked 'Was it the only bloodstained handkerchief shown to you in the police station?' – 'There were two more, and I picked this one out. There is a mark on it, which was placed there by me.' Trethowan had no further questions, but showed Flora the handkerchief.

The next witness was John Moxham Cooper, a house decorator, the son of Matilda Cooper and brother of Edith Langmead, who lived at 'Glenbrook', 14 St Paul's Road. He testified that word had got round of a murder near his mother's home on the evening of October 31, and he called on his mother at about 10.30 to see if she knew anything about it. The house was empty so he went round to 40 Meadow Road. As he was in the passage, Wilks came down the stairs, saying he had to go, and Flora was saying "No, don't go, doctor." While there Mrs Carter was found to be missing, and Cooper joined in the search, Wilks exclaiming "For God's sake, where can the woman be?" The coroner asked 'Whilst you were in the house, did you hear Mrs Haskell say anything about a man?' – 'Yes: she said that a man offered her Teddy twopence.' He added 'I had a good look round the back of the house, and tried to find Mrs Carter', and that Mrs Carter came back eventually, and that he, Cooper, noticed the blood on Mrs Haskell's sleeve, and had the knife pointed out to him. Parr interjected 'Someone in Mrs Haskell's presence said something about the knife being thrown at her?' – 'Yes, by a man coming downstairs.' He further testified to examining the back of No. 40, and, after midnight, to taking part in the seach for a man. Under cross-examination, Cooper conceded that while Mrs Haskell was in a pitiable condition, she neverless knew, in Cooper's opinion, what was being said by the people in the front room. He added, in answer to Trethowan's question, that Mrs Haskell showed him the spots of blood on her sleeve; he thought the suggestion was that it came from the knife thrown by the man when he came downstairs. Trethowan remarked, somewhat drily 'I think most of your time was spent in valuing the back[s of] buildings and going round looking for Mrs Carter?' – 'Yes.'

Next to speak was Emily Hayden, the wife of William Hayden, a railway fireman, who lived at 24 Sidney Street, on the corner of York Road. On the night of 31 October, she testified, she was on her way to Mrs Saunders's shop, at 42 York Road, hearing the clock strike a quarter past ten as she passed the *Duke of York*. Whilst in the shop she spent a few minutes talking to Mrs Saunders, and then a man opened the door and said someone had murdered the one-legged little boy. She then went home. Mrs Hayden added that she was sure she saw no-one about from Sidney Street to Meadow Road, nor passing the shop. However, Trethowan challenged her on the point, and she admitted that while she was in the shop it was too dark outside for her to see along Meadow Road. And with Mrs Hayden's testimony complete, all of the witnesses to Flora's immediate reaction to Teddy's death, and to whether anyone else was around at the time, had spoken. All but one, that is, and he was perhaps the key witness.

6

'He could not have cried out or shouted': The Inquest, Thursday 19 and Friday 20 November: Medical and Forensic Evidence.

THE INQUEST THEN MOVED into a new phase with the depositions of the medical experts, their evidence shifting from the narrative to the forensic. The first such witness was Herbert Lorraine Earle Wilks, Licenciate of the Royal College of Physicians of London and Member of the Royal College of Surgeons of England. In general practice in Salisbury since at least 1897, he had, on the night of the Boat Train Disaster in July 1906, been the first doctor to enter the wrecked carriages to tend the wounded, and many hours later had been seen staggering home exhausted, his clothes stiff with blood. He had a surgery for general practice at Grove House, at the bottom end of Wilton Road, just past the Methodist Chapel. The Haskells had long been patients of his. He was also on the panel of medical officers of the Salisbury and South Wilts Provident Dispensary. On the night of 31 October, he had as his house guest Dr F.Everard Row, and when at about 10.30 p.m. a boy called to ask him to come down to 40 Meadow Road, because someone had murdered Teddy Haskell, the pair of them left at once, cycling down.

Parr asked him 'Did you first go into the kitchen?' — 'I went into the kitchen for one moment. I did not speak to Mrs Haskell. I was told to go upstairs at once, and went with Dr Row and a man with a light.' 'Did you go into a bedroom at the top of the stairs?'

— 'Yes.'

'What did you see there?' — 'I saw the boy lying in bed on his back. His head was slightly turned to the left. He looked quite peaceful. His arms were away from his sides and slightly flexed. The fingers extended, there was no clenching of the hands. The left leg was half-flexed and abducted. There was a wound on the right side of the neck, about two and a half inches in length, beginning at the left side of the windpipe, and continuing in a transverse and slightly downward direction. The wound was covered in a mass of blood and hair. On removing this I found that the upper part of the windpipe and the main artery of the neck had been divided. There was a slight wound on the fourth finger of the left hand.'

'Will you just tell us what kind of wound it was in the neck?' — 'It was a clean incised wound with a small jag about halfway across.'

'Was it of a uniform depth, or not?' — 'Shallower on the left side of the windpipe, but deepened towards the right side of the neck.'

'Were the bedclothes disturbed?' — 'No.'

'How far up the boy were they?' — 'Up to the beginning of the neck.'

'As to the position of the arms?' — 'The left arm was lying outside the bed.'

'And the right was in the inside?' — 'Yes.'

'Was the wound of such a nature that death would

be instantaneous?' – 'Death would have taken place within a minute, I should say, of the inflicting of the wound.'

'What would be the immediate effect of the wound?' – ' 'There would be a large spurt of blood to begin with, and blood would be sucked into the lungs at once by the breathing. There might have been a momentary movement, but for all practical purposes death would have been instantaneous.'

'And power of speech and articulation cease?' – 'Yes, because the wound was below the vocal chords.'

'What would the immediate effect be?' – 'A very large quantity of blood would spurt out from the artery.'

'How far would that blood travel?' – 'Three or four feet, but that depends whether the artery is obstructed by any tissue.'

'In this particular instance, how far would the blood spurt from the wound? Was there any tissue to prevent it?' – 'There was evidence of the artery having spurted about a yard on one side, and there was a large quantity of blood underneath the boy's head on the other side. In the first instance the blood must have spurted, and the position of the head must have slightly changed, because the second part of the blood, after the first spurt, took place inside the wound, that is to say it went under the wound and had not free access of the air.'

'In a case of this kind would there be a spray of blood?' – 'Yes, there would be a certain amount of air mixed with blood coming out.'

'With regard to that, the air bubbles through and carries the blood?' – 'Yes.'

'In this case, was there a spray thrown to the right of the boy?' – 'Yes.'

'You examined the room to see where the blood marks were?' – 'Yes.'

'Was there, on the pillow to the left of the boy's head, a large quantity of blood?' – 'Yes, on the left pillow there was blood, and the right pillow was saturated with blood. The top portion of the under-sheet was also saturated with blood. There were several spots of blood by the right side of the bed, and there was a spot of blood on the floor close to the foot of the bed. Those were all the blood marks I noticed in the room.'

'Did the blood on the top of the undersheet correspond in position with the right pillow?' – 'Yes.'

'That would show that nothing had been moved since the wound was inflicted?' – 'Yes, it would.'

'Had the wound been inflicted with force?' – 'Yes, with considerable force.'

'With a sharp instrument?' – 'Yes, a sharp instrument.'

'Was there anything to show it was inflicted with one hand or the other?' – 'In my opinion it was inflicted with the right hand.'

'Did you form any conclusion as to the position of the person who inflicted the wound?' – 'I should say it was done by a person standing at the head of the boy, using the right hand, cutting from left to right. I should say the assailant was between the bed and the chest of drawers, opposite to the boy's head.'

'How long had death taken place before you arrived there?' – 'I should say within a quarter of an hour.'

'As far as you can fix it, can you tell us what time you got to the house?' – 'Five and twenty minutes to eleven, I should say – as near as possible.'

'What was your reason for saying death had taken place within a quarter of an hour?' – 'Because when I got into the room air was still escaping through the blood.'

'Any other reason? Would that be more or less conclusive as to time?' – 'In my opinion.'

'Did you then go downstairs?' – 'Yes.'

'Did you leave the house to go back home?' – 'I went back to my house with Dr Row to get some medicine for Mrs Haskell.'

'Did you see Mrs Haskell and talk to her before you left?' – 'Yes, I did.'

'What did you say?' – 'I don't remember any conversation. She was in a hysterical state and incoherent, and I tried to soothe her and told her I would get a draught.'

'About what time was it you left to go home?' – 'I can't remember with any accuracy. I should think I was in the house a quarter of an hour.'

'It would be five minutes to eleven -?' – 'About.'

'Were you away a long time?' – 'About half an hour.'

'Did you then come back?' – 'Yes.'

'Did you see Mrs Haskell?' – 'I did. She was in the front room then.'

'I want you to tell the jury what she said.' – 'She asked me whether it was really true that her Teddy was dead, and I told her that he was. She then wanted to see him, and I told her I would take her upstairs after we had made the bed presentable.'

'Did you and Dr Row go upstairs?' – 'Yes.'

'Anyone else?' – 'Yes, a woman came up.'

'Did you partially wash the body?' – 'Yes, I put a handkerchief round the neck where the wound showed, and covered up traces of blood. I covered the body with a clean covering. We rolled up the blood-marked bedclothes and put them at the foot of the bed, inside the bed. We then went downstairs and brought up Mrs Carter, and she kissed the boy's face.'

'Did you then bring up Mrs Haskell?' – 'I did.'

'What did Mrs Haskell say when she got in the room?' – 'She burst out crying, and then kissed the boy.'

'Did she touch anything in the room?' – 'No, she stepped forward and kissed the boy's face.'

'You then took her downstairs?' – 'Yes, to the front room.'

'Did she say anything to you?' – 'A statement was made to me in her presence – I am almost positive she made it herself – that a man had come to her the previous night and wanted a lodging. She had refused him. He appeared to be very much annoyed, was very persistent, and she thought she recognised the same man in her house that night.'

'Did you notice blood on Mrs Haskell?' – 'Yes, on the right sleeve and also on the front.'

'Was a knife shown to you that night?' – 'It was.'

'By a constable?' – 'By one of the police.'

'Did you examine the edge of the knife with your finger?' – 'Yes, I felt the edge with my finger.'

'Were you able to say whether it had been recently sharpened?' – 'Recently sharpened, but roughly sharpened.'

'Was the wound in the boy's neck such that it could have been inflicted with that knife?' – 'Yes, it was.'

'Was there blood on the knife at the time you examined it?' – 'Yes, on the blade of the knife; I didn't examine the handle.'

UPSTAIRS LANDING OF 40 MEADOW ROAD.
PHOTOGRAPH TAKEN SHORTLY AFTER THE CRIME,
1908
© *Timothy W. Frank Walker and Ann Richardson Whittle,*
grandchildren of Frank Richardson, Chief Constable

'Was the blood dry or not, at the time?' – 'It was partially dry.'

'Were you shown a mark on the floor by the kitchen door?' – 'Yes.'

'Was there a mark of blood?' – 'Yes, a lineal mark of blood.'

'How did it compare in length with the blade of the knife?' – 'The mark I saw was less than the length of this knife.'

'Is it your opinion that that mark could have been caused by the knife lying on the floor?' – 'Yes.'

'Is that opinion based on the amount of blood you found on the blade of the knife?' – 'Yes.'

'This mark on the floor by the kitchen door was on the linoleum?' – 'Yes.'

'Was there any other mark of blood corresponding with the blade of the knife close by?' – 'No.'

'Either on the wall or on the floor?' – 'I found no other blood downstairs, but I did not make a careful examination.'

'Assuming that the knife, covered with the amount of blood you found on the blade had been brought down by someone, and had been thrown at a person standing in the dooway of the kitchen, would you have expected to find more than one mark on the floor?' – 'Certainly I should.'

'What was the cause of the boy's death?' – 'Haemorrhage.'

Trethowan reserved his cross-examination at that point, saying 'I am not prepared to go on with the cross-examination of the doctor tonight. I think you can quite understand.' – 'Oh, yes, certainly', said the coroner. With that the court rose for tea.

After the interval Wilks's friend Frederick Everard Row went into the witness box. He testified that whilst he was staying with Wilks, on the night of the murder he and Wilks cycled down to Meadow Road, arriving at No. 40 at about 10.30; also that he was present with Wilks upstairs. Having heard his friend's testimony as to the state of the bedroom, the nature of the wound and the account of how it had been inflicted with a sharp instrument, by someone standing behind the boy and using considerable force, he agreed with the evidence and the hypothesis. Parr then asked 'What was the position of the left hand?' – 'It was outside the bedclothes, and there was a small cut on the back of the ring finger.'

'Will you explain how that wound could have been caused?' – 'The edges of the wound were pointing towards the nail, and it could have been caused by the hand being put in front of the throat at the time of the original injury to the throat.'

'Were there any signs of a struggle at all?' – 'No.'

'Are you able to form any opinion as to whether the boy was asleep or not when the wound was inflicted?' – 'I can't form an opinion.'

'Was the incised wound on the fourth finger consistent with the boy having been asleep at the time of the infliction of the sound in the throat?' – 'Yes.'

'Were there any signs at all of the little boy having been drugged, or a narcotic having been given to him?' – 'None that I could find.'

'Did you notice the condition of the pupils of the eyes?' – 'I did: they were dilated.'

'If a drug had been administered would they have been dilated?' – 'No, they would have been contracted.'

'By "drug", you mean an opiate -?' – 'Yes.'

Continuing his testimony, Row recounted how he came downstairs and noticed a blood mark inside the kitchen door, between three and four inches long and quite straight. The mark on the floor corresponded in length with the blade of the knife, which, when he saw it, was covered with blood, on the handle as well as the blade. The edge of the knife appeared to have been recently sharpened. Parr then asked 'If the knife is the one which inflicted the wound on the murdered boy's throat, do you think it had been used since it was sharpened?' – 'No.'

'The wound could have been caused by it?' – 'Yes.'

'The mark on the kitchen floor was wet?' – 'Yes.'

'You did not see any other marks of blood on the floor near that mark, nor on the wall near, nor on any part of the door or doorway?' – 'No: I saw no other marks of blood downstairs except the one on the floor which corresponded with the knife.'

'If the knife had been carried downstairs, having been first used for inflicting that wound on the boy's throat, and thrown at a person standing in the kitchen doorway, would you have expected to find more marks of blood?' – 'Yes.'

'If the knife, covered with blood, had been thrown at such a height as to reach the right sleeve – just below the yoke – of a person standing up, where would you have expected to find other marks?' – 'I should have expected to find more marks of blood on the clothes of the person, on the floor, and on the side of the door.'

'Had you any conversation at all with Mrs Haskell?' – 'No.'

Row further testified that he and Dr Wilks had subsequently rearranged the bedroom in the condition in which they found it 'in order that Dr Pepper might see it.'

As with Wilks, Trethowan reserved his cross-examination until the next day.

The final witness on the Thursday was Gilbert Kempe of 17 Endless Street, Doctor of Medicine and Bachelor of Surgery of the University of Durham and a member of the English Royal Colleges. A surgeon at the Infirmary and Medical Officer of

Health to the Salisbury Rural District Council and consultant to the Great Western Railway, it was in his capacity as Police Surgeon to the City and to the Salisbury Division of the County Constabulary that he was now called to give evidence. He had examined the body of the murdered boy on Tuesday November 3 at 40 Meadow Road, as police surgeon, and at the request of the police, and his description of the injuries corroborated the testimony of Drs Wilks and Row. He said he thought the murderer stood, when committing the act, facing the foot of the bed, on the right-hand side, and somewhat behind the lad's head. He imagined that the boy's hand was raised in response to some comparatively slight stimulus, such as disarranging the clothes around his neck, and that the wound on the finger and that on the throat were caused almost simultaneously. There was also an abrasion of some days' duration on the boy's left ear, covered with a dry scab which, when removed, showed signs of healing at the edges. Kempe was later shown the blouse and skirt which Flora had worn on the night of the murder. The skirt was black, and was bloodstained down the front and down the right-hand side. Parr asked 'Of what shape and size?' – 'They might roughly be grouped into two types of spots. Those on the upper part of the skirt were irregularly rounded, and those on the lower part appear as splashes, arranged vertically, and with the larger end of the splash downwards.'

'Now, with regard to the blouse?' – 'It was a light one, and was spotted with blood over the right sleeve pretty well up to the shoulder.'

'As to the shape and character of the spots?' – 'They were rounded, and not grouped in any particular pattern.'

'Was there any mark on the right sleeve consistent with the knife produced being covered with blood and striking it?' – 'I saw none.'

'If the knife produced, when so covered with blood, had been thrown at a person standing up wearing the blouse and skirt, would it have caused the number of spots which you found on the blouse and skirt?' – 'Not in my opinion.'

'If the knife had been so thrown, would you expect to find more than one mark on the floor?' – 'Yes, I should.'

'If the person had been standing at the doorway when the knife was flung, would you have expected to find marks of blood on the doorposts?' – 'It is not certain, but it is possible.'

'If the knife had been carried down, dripping, from the bedroom above, and thrown, would it have been possible for so many spots of blood to be caused?' – 'No.'

'Having regard to the position of the body at the time of the infliction of the wound in the throat, the efforts of breathing would have projected a spray of blood to the boy's right?' – 'Yes.'

'In the direction, therefore, of a person standing as you have described.' – 'Yes.'

'Were any of the bloodmarks on the skirt and blouse consistent with having been caused by a spray of blood so blown out?' – 'Yes: those on the blouse and some on the upper part of the skirt.'

'Could they have been caused by blood falling from a knife held near the skirt and just outside it?' – 'Yes.'

'You have examined the knife carefully?' – 'Yes.'

'Had it been recently sharpened?' – 'Yes.'

'Had it been used since it had been sharpened till it was used for this purpose?' – 'I think it is impossible to form an opinion.'

'You were able to see whether the knife was bright?' – 'At the time I examined it there were sharp, bright scratches showing through the film of blood.'

'Could the knife, after it had been sharpened, have lain out exposed to the damp? Were there any signs of rust?' – 'No.'

'There were spots of blood at the foot of the bed and on the landing outside?' – 'Yes, I examined them casually.'

'In your opinion, how could they have been caused?' – 'They were rounded spots of blood such as would be caused by drops of blood falling.'

'Did you form any opinion as to whether an opiate had been administered?' – 'I made a special examination on Tuesday morning with the special view of clearing up the point from external appearances, and I formed the opinion that no opiate had been administered.' Trethowan again reserved his cross-examination, and with that, just before eight o'clock, the inquest was again adjourned until the following morning at 11 a.m.

At that same time, however, Flora was in the dock of the Police Court, and, looking 'very pale and worn',[1] between a warder and a wardress, again before Samuel Atkins and John Folliott, but, chairing the bench, Tom Perkins, the new mayor and a councillor for Fisherton. Perkins was the manager of the South Wilts Dairy Company in Fisherton Street and, a resident of York Road at No. 14, doubtless with a close interest in the case. Parr advised that he had been instructed by the Director of Public Prosecutions to prosecute in this case, but as the inquest was ongoing, he had to apply for the prisoner to be remanded until Monday 30 November, when it was understood that the magistrates would be able to hear the case. Trethowan consented on Flora's behalf to that arrangement, and with that the inquest resumed.

The first witness to appear was Professor Augustus Joseph Pepper, Master of Surgery of the University of London and Fellow of the Royal College of Surgeons. He was senior surgeon at St Mary's Hospital, London, but it was in his capacity of Consultant Adviser to the Home Office and the Treasury that he now appeared. He began his testimony by recounting that Dew and Richardson had brought a collection of items to his home in Wimpole Street, London, on 6 November, for examination. These items, which he now produced in court, comprised the knife with which Teddy had been slain, the whetstone on which it had been sharpened, three handkerchiefs, two aprons, a pair of drawers, a chemise, a black skirt and a blouse.

Parr asked him 'On Sunday, the eighth of November, did you visit 40 Meadow Road?' – 'Yes, and certain articles were selected and handed to me by the police.'

'What were those articles?' – 'A white toilet cover from the top of the chest of drawers in the bedroom; a cushion cover from a chair near the head of the bed; two pieces of linoleum, one from the passage floor and the other from the kitchen floor next to the passage; two pieces of linoleum from the bedroom floor; one piece of linoleum from the landing at the top of the stairs; a piece of wallpaper from behind the chair near the head of the bed; and a piece of

AUGUSTUS PEPPER, CONSULTANT ADVISER TO THE HOME OFFICE AND KEY WITNESS FOR THE PROSECUTION.
© NICHOLAS CONNELL

wallpaper from the left-hand side of the staircase going up. All of these I produce. They were in position on the occasion of my visit to the house in Meadow Road.'

'Did you examine on November eighth the scullery downstairs?' – 'Yes: hanging behind the door leading to the back yard were the following articles: a clean white bag with a comb and brush in it; a clean sponge cloth; and a towel. There were no visible marks of blood on any of them. There were no blood marks on the inside of the scullery door leading to the back door, nor on the key, nor the latch, nor the handle of the bolt. There were no blood marks on the scullery sink, nor [on] the tap above it. In a clothes basket in the scullery were a number of articles, chiefly soiled linen, which call for no special mention. There were no blood marks on the inside of the front door, nor on its lock.'

'Did you also examine a small brass lamp?' – 'Yes: there were no blood marks on it.'

'Will you, please, come to the other blood marks you found in the house?' – 'Yes. The bedclothes were placed for my inspection in the position in which Dr Wilks and Dr Row said they first saw them. There was blood upon them, and I found blood marks also at the doorway leading from the passage to the kitchen. These were on the floor; there were none on the door or adjacent woodwork. There were blood marks on the staircase paper on the left-hand side going up; there were no bloodstains on the right-hand wall of the staircase, nor on the rails at the top of the stairs. I also found a large drop, like a blood mark, on the landing at the top of the stairs, on the left of the stair head coming down. In the bedroom there were several spots on the wall between the head of the bed and the chest of drawers, and similar spots on the knob and woodwork of the top right-hand drawer of the chest of drawers, also on the toilet cover on the chest of drawers, and on the cushion cover of the chair which stood between the head of the bed and the chest of drawers. A few blood spots were on the linoleum by the side of the bed, and several spots on the linoleum at the foot of the bed.' 'Will you also look at that top left-hand drawer from the chest of drawers?'

'Yes: there are no marks on the top left-hand drawer whatever.'

'Was there any mark in the bedroom consistent with a knife having been placed or laid down there?' — 'No. To be quite exact, a knife might have been placed on the bed where the blood was.'

Pepper then took the two pieces of linoleum and pointed out the blood marks, as he continued his testimony: 'All the blood I found in the house was a few days old: it might have been some weeks or some months. After a week the change takes place very slowly. They were obviously of comparatively recent date, but all the marks were of the same age. I examined the marks microscopically, chemically and with a spectroscope.'

'Are you able to say of what origin they are?' — 'I can only say they are mammalian: I cannot say they are human.'

'Does that apply to the bloodstains on the articles of clothing and the knife?' — 'Yes.'

Turning his attention to the blouse, Pepper said 'There are twenty-eight spots of blood on the right side of the body and about fifty on the sleeve. The spots on the body of the blouse are widely scattered over at least ten inches. The marks on the sleeve are also widely scattered and extend from the hook which fastens at the wrist to within an inch of the yoke. Generally speaking, some of the spots were small rounded ones, and others irregular. The irregularity is chiefly caused by the blood soaking into the textile unevenly.'

'Are there any marks to which you wish to draw particular attention?' — 'There is one at the top of the sleeve which is tailed in an upward direction, and there are two linear blood marks above it. These were caused by the blood going upwards. That is the only distinctive mark as regards direction. The densest mark is where the hook is fixed at the wrist.' 'Did you form an opinion, Dr Pepper, as to the direction of the blood which caused those stains?' — 'Yes, they were obviously either sprinkled or sprayed on.'

'Assuming that a spray of blood was projected by breathing from the neck of the boy in bed, might they have been so caused?' — 'Yes, by air escaping through the open windpipe.'

'Does a spray of that kind carry some considerable distance?' — 'Yes, it might carry two yards.'

'If that knife covered with blood had been thrown at a person wearing the blouse, would it account for the marks you found?' — 'No, they are too widely distributed, and are too uniform in character to be caused by blood from such a knife as this striking the blouse or passing it in its fall.'

'Did you form any opinion as to whether the knife could have struck any portion of the person or clothing?' — 'No, there is no evidence of its having struck either the blouse or skirt. If it had, the blood would have been aggregated where the impact of the knife took place.'

'If the knife had hit the nose of a person, would it have accounted for the spots on the blouse and skirt?' — 'Not these spots. They would not have been so widely distributed. The remark I made with regard to the knife hitting a person's nose applies also to the wrist.'

'Now take the skirt.' — 'Yes, there were about nineteen blood marks on it. The skirt being of black or dark blue material, the spots show only faintly, and can only be seen with difficulty. The rounded marks on the upper part are similar to those on the blouse. Others are elongated and one is an inch and a half long.'

'With regard to the elongated ones, in what way would they have been caused?' — 'By blood dropping down the front of the skirt.'

'Are they consistent with a knife having been held parallel with the skirt?' — 'Yes, quite. There are other marks which look as if they have been smudged or smeared. In my opinion it is impossible for the knife covered with blood to be projected at the person wearing the skirt, and to account for all the blood marks on the skirt, taken collectively.'

'Taking the skirt and blouse together, what is your opinion?' – 'The inference is still stronger.'

The examination then moved on to the bloodstains in the house. Pepper recalled his findings there: 'On the occasion of my visit to 40, Meadow Road, I examined the kitchen door, the woodwork and the wall adjacent, and I found no marks of blood there at all. If people walked on the blood on the linoleum by the kitchen door before it was dry, it would be smeared, but there was no smearing. However, if the spots were very small, they might have been obliterated, but if they were large they certainly would have been smeared.'

'If the linoleum had been wiped over with a wet cloth at, say, six o'clock the next morning, would the blood have been removed?' – 'Some of the blood would have been removed, but not the stains.'

'If there was more than simple wiping, what would happen?' – 'If there was scrubbing with a view to removing the bloodstains, they could have been so removed.'

'Having examined the linoleum by the kitchen door, have you come to any conclusion as to whether it had been wiped or scrubbed?' – 'I don't think it could have been rubbed much because the marks are very distinct. Of course the glazed surface would allow the marks to come away more easily when rubbed.'

'What is your opinion as to [the] blood marks there on the linoleum?' – 'The spots remaining are perfectly distinct, and as thick as ever they were. No blood has been removed from the small spots.'

'As to the chemise, were there any blood marks?' – 'Yes, a few on the right sleeve, due to their soaking through the blouse. There was no blood on either of the aprons. It is quite impossible for them to have been worn when the blood marks were produced on the skirt.'

'Will you deal with the handkerchiefs now?' – 'Yes. I examined them, and on one with a pink border there are separate blood marks and others mixed with mucus from the nose. Some of the blood may have come from an abrasion of the ear. Some of the blood certainly did come from the nose. The blood on a second handkerchief might have come from the ear, or when the scab was rubbed off. A third handkerchief contained more blood than I should expect from such an abrasion of the ear as was described by Dr Kempe yesterday. I understand it was no bigger than a pea.'

'On the toilet cover of the chest of drawers and on the cushion cover you found spots of blood?' – 'Yes, and there were also marks on the wall between the bed and the chest of drawers.'

'In your opinion how were those spots caused?' – 'I think they were caused by blood being sprayed out by the air from the open windpipe. The blood marks on the wall going down the stairs looked as if they had been swished onto the wall, and could have been caused by a knife being carried downstairs. There were four blood marks on the floor at the side of the bed. Two were round and were spots of blood which had fallen on the floor. The other two were much smaller, and were probably splashes from the larger one. I also found nine round spots at the end of the bed.'

At this point Flora again collapsed in a dead faint and had to be carried out of the court, and her mother, 'overcome with grief' in the *Salisbury Journal*'s words, had to take her leave of the inquest. As for Flora, she would not return to the inquest that day.

Pepper continued with his account of the bloodstains. 'There was one large round spot on the landing at the top of the stairs and another small one close to it. All these spots, in my opinion, were caused by blood dropping from some object.'

'Will you come to the knife? Had that recently been sharpened?' – 'Yes. Since it had been sharpened, in my opinion, it could not have been exposed to the moisture of damp atmosphere. There are still bright sharpening marks showing on the knife. It is impossible to form an opinion as to whether the knife had been used since it was sharpened, and before inflicting such a wound as the boy had received in the throat. There are several blood marks on the handle, evidently caused by a hand gripping it. Some of the blood has been scraped off in a spiral direction. It may have been done by a finger- or thumb-nail, but I cannot say, as there are other ways in which it might have been done. This might have been caused by a person picking up the knife and putting it in paper. It had been handled a good deal before I saw it. The blood marks on the blade of the knife are of four kinds – a general smearing, some round spots, a local smearing near the handle and some marks running vertically near the back of the blade, where the blood had spurted out. There were no marks of blood on the whetstone.'

'You heard the evidence of the doctors as to the position in which the boy was found in bed, and the position of his left hand. Have you formed an opinion as to how that wound on the boy's fourth finger of his left hand was caused?' – 'Yes. I think the bedclothes were slightly disturbed about the neck; that the boy involuntarily carried the left hand to the neck; that the knife notched the finger, which would be immediately withdrawn, and at that moment the throat was cut. That accounts for the mark on the finger. If he had struggled to defend himself, there would have been more marks. The carrying of the hand to the throat was involuntary, I think, and I believe he was asleep at the time.'

'Have you formed any conclusion as to his waking up before death?' – 'My belief is that directly his finger was withdrawn in consequence of its touching the knife, his throat was cut, and he would know nothing and could do nothing. The jag in the wound was caused, I believe, by the skin moving, and not by any movement of the child, nor does it mean more than one stroke of the knife. The assailant, in my opinion, stood on the right side, and probably at the boy's head. In my opinion, the left hand of the assailant was placed on the right temple of the boy, pressing the head towards the left side. The head and neck of the boy were turned towards the left, and the blood gushed towards the left side, as shown by the marks on the pillow and sheets. The head then fell over towards the right side, and the blood being blown out from the right side of the neck, formed the spray, or shower, before mentioned. The blood from the carotid artery did not spurt onto the floor by the side of the bed. None of the blood from the carotid artery could have found its way onto the lower part of the assailant, but the spray of blood projected

by the air would have done so.'

'Were the blood marks on the blouse and the round ones on the upper portion of the skirt consistent with them having been caused by a spray of blood so projected to the right?' – 'Yes.'

'If that knife had been carried down from the bedroom dripping with blood and thrown at a person at the foot of the stairs, what is your opinion as to whether it would have caused the blood marks on the blouse and the skirt?' – 'If all the marks on the blouse and the skirt had been so caused, I should have expected to find much more blood on the floor, the woodwork of the doorway and the adjacent wall.' Pepper finished by adding that there was a large, irregular, smear-like mark of blood four inches long, on the right side of the front of the skirt.

Wilks was then recalled for a cross-examination by Trethowan which opened with enquiries about the family doctor's relationship with Flora and Teddy. He replied 'I have known both Mrs Haskell and the murdered boy for twelve years. I have attended the mother professionally, and I am in a position to say that there was great affection between them. I believe the woman's husband died about six years ago, and since that time she has worked for and provided for the lad. Teddy Haskell always appeared to be well dressed and well looked after. I attended the boy both before and after the operation, when his leg was amputated.

'What was your first impression when you saw the wound in the boy's neck?' – 'That his throat had been cut, and that he had died from the effects.'

'Cut with deliberation?' – 'Yes.'

'Would you say, knowing the woman as you do, that she would, about ten minutes to ten, have been trying on a new coat and joking with Miss Steer, and at ten twenty be murdering her boy?' – 'No, judging from her nature.'

'If she had murdered her boy at ten twenty, could she have answered the door to a boy named Wyatt about that time and spoken to him in a calm and collected way?' – 'Not, as I knew her, judging from her nature.'

'To have inflicted this wound on this boy would have required great force and great presence of mind?' – 'Yes.'

'Did you express any opinion as to who could have committed the crime, and said something to the effect that it must have been a maniac?' – 'I think I made the remark to Dr Row downstairs.'

'And do you still think so?' – 'I think that anyone who commits a diabolical act of that sort cannot be sane at the moment of doing it.'

'Did you see Mrs Haskell almost immediately afterwards?' – 'Yes, I saw her three times.'

'When you first saw her, did she look like a maniac?' – 'She was hysterical and crying.'

'I think she was asking you and others about Teddy -?' – 'Yes, she was asking what was the matter.'

'Have you ever found any indication of insanity in Mrs Haskell?' – 'No, never.'

'When you examined the boy, could you see whether he had been washed previous to death? There were no marks of mud about his leg -?' – 'No. The boy was perfectly clean.'

'I believe later on you did take Mrs Haskell to the room where the boy was?' – 'Yes.'

'And I think she went into the room and kissed him?' – 'Yes.'

'Do you think it probable that any woman would have gone into the room and kissed a child she had murdered?' – 'No.'

'And if she had seen a man drop something with blood on it at the foot of her stairs, do you think she would have been frightened?' – 'Yes.'

'And there would be quite sufficient reason for her rushing out into the street to get help?' – 'Yes, certainly.'

'What area do you think would be likely to be affected by the spray of blood to the right from the boy's neck?' – 'I don't think there would have been a spray at all on that side.'

'I think you said that, in your opinion, the assailant at the time of the murder was standing between the boy's head and the chest of drawers?' – 'Yes. In my opinion he was standing opposite the boy's head.'

'Do you say that in that position no blood would be sprinkled over the assailant?' – 'There would not.'

'I think there was blood close to the bed. How do you account for that?' – 'Whoever cut the boy's throat, I think, walked down by the side of the bed,

and the spots we saw dropped to the floor.'

'Under those circumstances, would you expect to find blood on the boots of the assailant?' – 'That would be a matter of chance, and [would] depend an the position in which the knife was held.'

'Who first showed you the knife which has been produced?' – 'Some policeman.'

'Did you see whether it was wrapped in blotting paper?' – 'Brown paper, I think. I only saw the blade of the knife; I did not examine the handle.'

'If the handle of the knife was covered with blood, as was suggested, the hand must also be covered with blood?' – 'Yes.'

'Judging from the position and condition of the wound, as you saw it, and [the condition of] the blade and handle of the knife, the hand of the person who used the knife would necessarily have had blood on them as far as the wrist?' – 'In my opinion, yes.'

'If the assailant's hand was clasped as he came downstairs, and there was no blood on the stairs, the blood in his hand would be retained until he got downstairs.' – 'Yes.'

'Do you know that before the knife was taken up there had been lots of people in and out of the house?' – 'The knife had been taken up before I went there.'

'If there were spots of blood on the linoleum and anyone walked over them, they might be taken up on their boot?' – 'Yes, if anyone walked over them a second or so afterwards, and continual walking over the blood spots would tend to obliterate them.'

'If the murder had been premeditated and committed by Mrs Haskell, would not the first thing she would do be to remove the traces of her guilt?' – 'I suppose anyone would.'

'You would not expect her to leave a bloodstained knife in the passage?' – 'No.'

'Supposing blood did spurt out over her skirt, would not she have known it?' – 'I don't think it did on that side of the bed.'

'At any rate, if she had on clothes covered with blood, you would have expected her to take them off?' – 'Of course I should.'

'Did you see whether a drawer in the chest of drawers had been broken open?' – 'I saw it subsequently.'

'Did you see the lock had been broken off?' – 'I

was shown it on the Tuesday afternoon.'

'Could the crime more easily have been committed by a man than a woman?' – 'Yes.'

Trethowan's final questions concerned the cut on Teddy's finger, and his death a second or so later. Wilks replied that 'The wound on the lad's hand might be due to his being disturbed, and raising his hand at the first moment of waking. Death would have been almost instantaneous, so that there would have been no time for any severe physical struggle. He could not have cried out or shouted. There might have been a gurgling noise, and probably there was. It would not be sufficient for anyone in the kitchen to hear.'

At that point in the proceedings, Trethowan declared that, as his client would soon have to appear before a magisterial hearing, he proposed not to spend any further time examining the medical evidence. He said 'this case must soon go to the other court, and the prisoner will, there, be more ably represented than she is at the present time. Under these circumstances I do not propose to go fully into all the questions raised by the doctors' evidence. I think it would be better for me not to raise all the questions which I had intended to raise, because I [would] prefer that they should be gone into before the magistrates. I do not want my friend Mr Parr to think that I have any other reason for not going into many other controversial points in the evidence.' He turned to the coroner and said 'You have got evidence as to the cause of death sufficient for the jury's purpose. If the jury are going to bring in an open verdict, then I don't propose to call evidence or cross-examine all these doctors, but if they are determined to go on with it, then I must bring the whole of my evidence and we must be here for another week. I thought there might be some expression from you, sir, or the jury, as to whether . . .' He never finished his sentence, because Parr interjected 'I don't want to stop Mr Trethowan, but it is unusual at a coroner's inquest, that anyone representing any party should make anything in the shape of a speech – with comments! – in the presence of the jury. I don't want to stop my friend Mr Trethowan, but we must be guided by the ordinary practice in these matters.

Trethowan retorted 'I thought that the ordinary practice was that when a jury have found the evidence of death their duty is ended. The other court[2] has the prisoner before it. I won't say anything more. I have thrown out the hint, and if we can save time I shall be glad.' Parr parried, 'Appearing, as I am, in the interests of the Treasury and the administration of justice, I am bound under my instructions from the Crown to place before you and the jury all the evidence available and material with regard to the clearing up of this case.' Trethowan replied 'If I don't cross-examine all the medical witnesses I have stated my reasons for not doing so.' Buchanan Smith disposed 'It is the duty of the jury to find the cause of death, but, if there is sufficient evidence, to say also by whose hand death was caused.'

Wilks was then recalled by Parr, to clarify his testimony as to the initial flow of blood from Teddy's wound. He said 'I have no doubt whatever that there was a spurting of blood from the main artery to the left of the but none to the right. I have no doubt the blood on the chest of drawers and the cushion, and to the right of the boy, was caused by blood being projected as a spray, and not by spurting. The character of the two fluids would be entirely different. The assailant was, in my opinion, in a direct line with the spraying of the blood.' Discussing the carrying of blood on people's feet, he said that if people trod on wet bloodspots with boots, some of the blood would be taken up, and some remain. If the blood had dried at all, less would be taken up, and in any case a stain would be left. He declared 'I do not pledge my opinion in any way to the effect that it was impossible for this crime to have been committed by Mrs Haskell.' Miles had one last question, and the doctor replied that the boy's body was lying on the right side of the bed as he went into the room. If the boy had been fully awake when he was murdered his face would not have been so peaceful. He turned to Saunders and said 'Then you are discharged.' The case had taken just two and a half hours. Fresh from this success, Goddard would, after the weekend, face his sternest test to date in the role of defending counsel; indeed, as it turned out, his sternest case ever in such a role.

7
'This wretched case': The Inquest, Friday 20, Saturday 21 and Thursday 26 November: Police Evidence.

THE INQUEST WAS THEN adjourned for tea, and the jury reconvened at 5.30 to hear the testimony of Sergeant William Golding, the first of the police witnesses, who had been the earliest on the scene of the crime and who had remained on duty for the whole of the night. He began by testifying that 'On October thirty-first I was called to 40 Meadow Road, and arrived there at ten thirty-five p.m. I met Mr Steer in the passage of the house and was informed by him that a boy had been hurt and "the man [responsible]" had gone round into York Road. I went with him into York Road, but did not see a man. We looked through a crowd in Meadow Road, but saw no-one answering the description of the man given [to] me by Steer. I then went back to the house and saw Mrs Haskell in the front room. In the kitchen I saw a knife by the jamb of the door by the stairs. Both the handle and blade were covered with blood. I placed the knife in some brown paper, and afterwards handed it to the Chief Constable. I went into the middle bedroom upstairs and there found Dr Wilks, Dr Row, Mrs Butt and Mrs Steer. I saw the boy Teddy Haskell with his throat cut: the doctors were attending to him. We afterwards came downstairs, and I went into the front room, where Mrs Haskell was. She was wearing a light blouse and dark skirt. On the right sleeve of the blouse I noticed several spots of blood. I remained in the front room a minute or two, and then went into the kitchen where I stayed until three thirty a.m. on Sunday. At three thirty Mrs Haskell asked me if I knew whether the money was all right, and I replied that I didn't know. Both Mrs Carter and Mrs Haskell asked me several times to go up in the bedroom to see if the money was all right.'

Smith asked 'Did they say where it was?' – 'Yes: they said it was in the top drawer [of the chest of drawers] near the fireplace, and if the drawer was locked, the key would be in a basket on the chest of drawers.'

'Did they say how much money there was?' – 'Yes: that there should be eight pounds there. I went up to the room and found the drawer open. I brought the drawer down and placed it on the kitchen table in front of Mrs Haskell. Both Mrs Haskell and I looked in the drawer at the same time. I saw three sovereigns and one half-sovereign. Mrs Haskell said "There should be eight pounds, or eight pounds [and] two shillings." I turned over the cloth in the drawer but I saw no more money. I then took the drawer back to its place in the bedroom. I remained in the house until about nine thirty a.m., and during that time Mrs Haskell appeared very much upset.'

'Did the lock appear to have been forced off?' – 'It was off, sir, and was lying inside.'

Miles, the jury foreman, then asked 'Did Mrs Haskell pass any remark as to where the money had gone?' – 'Oh, no, sir.'

SERGEANT WILLIAM GOLDING WHO ALLOWED VITAL
EVIDENCE TO BE WASHED AWAY.
© *J.B. MOODY COLLECTION*

'Did you notice any blood on or about Mrs Haskell's hands?' – 'No.'

'Did you notice any blood on the drawer you brought downstairs?' – 'No,'

'Did you examine the drawer sufficiently to see if the lock had been lately forced off?' – 'No, I did not.'

Parr's examination then began with questions about Eccott and the knife. Golding replied 'The man described by Steer was Eccott, whom I had seen outside the *Duke of York* Hotel.' On the knife, 'When I picked up the knife I noticed the stain on the linoleum. The blade of the knife was over the stain, [and] at the time I first saw the bloodstain I should say it was dry.' Questioning then moved on to the state of the hallway at No. 40, and Golding's astonishing revelation that forensic evidence, at the very least of great significance, if not crucial, to the inquest, had been destroyed on his watch.

'Was anything done to the passage on the Sunday morning?' – 'Yes, the passage was brushed up.'

'Who by?' – 'By a woman [at] about six o''clock in the morning.'

'Did she do anything further?' – 'Yes, she washed over the floor in the passage, the floor in the doorway of the kitchen and the kitchen floor with a damp cloth.'

'We want to know exactly how she did it.' – 'She washed it in the usual way, on her knees, moving backwards as she did it.'

'Did she use any scrubbing brush or soap?' – 'No. She did not touch the sides of the doorway, the door itself, nor the wall near. It was Mrs Haskell's mother, Mrs Carter, who washed up the place.' Golding added that he 'noticed a speck' on Flora's nose that night.

The drawer was then produced, and Golding placed the money and broken lock as he had discovered it.

Trethowan then cross-examined, and Golding testified that mother and daughter were together when the money was being discussed. Mrs Carter had first asked him to go up and see if the money was all right, but both women had asked him to do so.

'Didn't she say "The key is in a basket on top of the [chest of] drawers"?' – 'Yes, "if the drawer is locked."'

'Didn't you come downstairs and say there was no necessity to look for the key, adding as you brought the drawer "Look at this"?' – 'No, I didn't.'

Questioning then turned to Golding's arrival on the scene, with the sergeant testifying that Steer told him that the boy had been hurt, and that the man who did it had gone round the corner. He and Steer then searched for this man, who turned out to be Eccott, who was also involved in the search . . . for himself, to the amusement of the court. Questioning turned to the knife, with Golding stating that the knife was not pointed out to him by Mrs Carter. Trethowan continued 'You wrapped the knife in brown paper?' – 'Yes.'

'Have you got it?' – 'No, I cannot produce it.' – because the knife had already been produced in court, wrapped in blotting paper. Golding's subsequent evidence included the facts that Mrs Carter did not point out the blood mark left by the knife on the linoleum, nor the bloodstains on her daughter's blouse, of which the Chief Constable had asked her to divest herself. As for the hallway, a good many people had walked up and down it on the fatal night. When Mrs Carter washed it down she did so with a bucketful of water, and she did not have to use much effort, because the bloodstains came out without rubbing. Miles then asked 'Did Mrs Carter take the flannel and dip it in the water and wash the passage?' – 'Yes.'

Parr had some questions about the knife, and Golding explained that he took the knife, wrapped up in brown and white paper, in a bag to Scotland Yard, and, on its return in the same paper he had handed it to his Chief Constable. In a final, faintly damning revelation, Golding stated that no description was given by him of the man the search parties were looking for. And with that, the inquest was adjourned until 10.30 the next day.

The only witness on Saturday 21 November was the Chief Constable of the City, Frank Richardson. As on previous occasions, the hearing had a large audience; Flora, meanwhile, still looked very ill, and was not to last the morning. Speaking in answer to the Coroner, Richardson testified that 'On Saturday, October thirty-first, I received a message at my office at about ten forty p.m., to the effect that a boy had been found at a house in Meadow Road with his throat cut. I at once went to 40 Meadow Road, with Superintendent Stephens of the County Constabulary. On entering the front room I saw Mrs Haskell with several women round her. She appeared distressed, and it was some little time before I could get anything out of her. She eventually said there was some money upstairs in a bedroom – eight pounds in gold and two shillings: seven sovereigns, two half-sovereigns and a two-shilling piece. She afterwards said "Is it all right?" I went upstairs and could not find it at first, so Mr Stephens went down again, and enquired where it was. On his return he said it was in the top drawer [of the chest] near the fireplace. On opening the drawer I found three pounds ten shillings in a fold of a table cover. There were several folds of the cloth over the money. I examined the drawer and found no mark of force. The lock was hanging by one tack at the bottom, and the bolt was thrown. There were two other tin-tacks in the drawer with the head of the one by which the lock was hanging. The fourth

tack was still in the wood in position.' The drawer with its lock and tacks was on display, and Parr took it to show to Trethowan and the jury. In response to a question from Parr, Richardson testified, confusingly, 'The eyelet of the lock would not go over the tin-tack which was in position: I saw the two tacks lying in the drawer and the head of the other when I first opened it.'

As for the murdered child, Richardson testified to being in court to hear the evidence of Drs Wilks and Row, and he corroborated their evidence of the position of the body and the state and placing of the bedclothes. 'The doctors had been into the room before me, and had put the body right. There were bloodstains on the oilcloth near the chair and at the foot of the bed. I saw a spot on the landing just outside the bedroom door and then went downstairs. I examined the kitchen door, and saw a streak of what appeared to be blood on the floor. I examined the passage and the front door, but did not find any other bloodstains. [On] going into the front room, Mrs Haskell gave me a description of a man who had called the previous evening for lodgings.'

At this point, about half an hour into the proceedings, Flora collapsed in a dead faint, and had to be carried by her gaolers into the magistrates' retiring room. She was not to reappear that day. Richardson continued giving evidence. 'Mrs Haskell told me that the man said he had left his luggage at the station. I then gave instructions to my constables to search the neighbourhood and make enquiries. I returned shortly after one o'clock on Sunday morning. Mrs Haskell then told me about a man asking Teddy on the previous Wednesday for his name and address, what his mother did, and whether he had any brothers or sisters. She also said that a man gave Teddy twopence, and said that she had seen Teddy writing his name on a piece of paper. Mrs Carter gave Mr Stephens a handkerchief, which she had found in the sitting room. I asked Mrs Haskell if that was the blouse she was wearing when the man rushed downstairs and threw something at her, and she said it was. I asked if she would mind me having it, and she said "No", took it off and handed it to me. In the front room Sergeant Golding showed me the knife, which he had picked up, and I took possession of it a little later. I went back into the kitchen and asked Mrs Haskell and Mrs Carter for a description of Mrs Haskell's knives. Mrs Carter pulled out the drawer of the dresser where the knives were, and showed them to me. I asked if any knife was missing, and after looking through them they said that the knife Teddy used was missing. Mrs Carter said it was a brown-handled one.' Parr then asked 'On Sunday November first, did you make another examination of the house?' – 'I did.'

'And was anybody with you on that occasion?' – 'Yes, Inspector Dew of Scotland Yard and Superintendent Stephens.'

'On that occasion did you find anything further?' – 'We found spots of blood by the bedside.'

'Was it on the floor?' – 'No, on the paper on the wall.'

'Did you hear Dr Pepper's evidence as to the bloodstains found?' – 'Yes.'

'Do you corroborate his evidence?' – 'Yes.'

'You heard Dr Pepper say he had certain articles handed to him -?' – 'Yes.'

'Do you corroborate that?' – 'Yes.'

Miles then asked 'Was any money found on Mrs Haskell, or in the house, in addition to the money found in the drawer?' – 'Ten shillings in the front room. Eight pounds was found on Mrs Haskell some days later, but that was Mrs Carter's.'

Trethowan interjected 'You have cleared that up?' – 'Yes, and it was in Mrs Carter's purse, and I handed it to her son.'

'Was there any blood on the drawer in which the money was found?' – 'No.'

'Was the drawer closed when you first found it?' – 'Yes.'

'Were there signs inside the drawer of it having been forced?' – 'It was a little bit rough, as if it had been pulled out.'

'Some of the jury are not quite clear whether Mrs Haskell asked the Chief Constable to see if the money was safe, and also at a later hour asked Sergeant Golding to see.' – 'She asked me as soon as I came into the house, and told me the money was gone. I didn't tell her whether the money was gone.' Parr then asked 'On the following day did you see Mrs Haskell in the presence of the Chief Constable

of Wiltshire and Chief Inspector Dew?' – 'I did.'

'Did Detective Dew make certain statements to her?' – 'Yes.'

Trethowan interjected 'Will you say "ask some questions"?'

Parr stuck to his line: 'He made certain statements -?' – 'Yes.'

'What was it [sic]?' – 'He simply asked her if she could give an account of what happened.'

'Did she then make a statement?' – 'Yes.'

'Did you write it down?' – 'I did.'

'Was it afterwards read over to her?' – 'It was.'

'And did she initial it?' – 'She did – initialled every page.'

'On Monday the second, did she make a further statement in the presence of yourself and Chief Inspector Dew?' – 'She did.'

'Was anyone else present?' – 'I don't think so.'

'Was that taken down in writing by you at the time?' – 'It was.'

'Later in the day did she make a second statement to yourself and Chief Inspector Dew?' – 'Yes.'

'Did you take it down in writing?' – 'I did.'

'On the following day, November third, did she make another statement?' – 'She did.'

'In the presence of yourself and Inspector Dew?' – 'And Superintendent Stephens.'

'Were all those statements taken down at the time in writing by you?' – 'They were.'

'Read over at the time to her?' – 'Yes.'

'And each page initialled by her?' – 'That is so.'

'You produce these statements?' – 'I do.'

'Will you hand them to the coroner?' – 'Yes.'

'You got there between five and ten minutes to eleven?' – 'Yes.'

'What time did you first get to the house?' – 'Between five and ten minutes to eleven.'

'Were P.S. Golding and P.C. Cutler then in the house?' – 'Yes.'

'Where was Cutler?' – 'He was in the passage at the bottom of the stairs.'

'Was there any light upstairs when you first went in?' – 'No.'

'Did you take a lamp upstairs?' – 'Yes.'

'In what position was the bedroom door? – 'It was ajar.'

FRANK RICHARDSON, CHIEF CONSTABLE OF
SALISBURY CITY POLICE.
© J.B. MOODY COLLECTION

'Did Mrs Haskell say anything to you before you went upstairs about going upstairs herself?' – 'No.'

'Did she ask to go upstairs?' – 'Not in my presence.'

'Did you examine the passage from the foot of the stair to the front door?' – 'I did.'

'And also, did you examine the doorway into the kitchen?' – 'I did.'

'Did you examine the kitchen door and the adjacent wall?' – 'Yes; [but] I did not at that time examine further into the kitchen than where the knife had lain.'

'You knew something very terrible had happened?' – 'Yes.'

'And did you make a very careful examination of all those parts?' – 'I did.'

'Was Superintendent Stephens with you?' – 'Yes.'

'Had you with a lamp with you in your hand?' – 'I had.'

'When you first went in you heard the conversation about the money, and at that time you hadn't been upstairs at all. You then went up and saw that the boy had been murdered. Was it then you made a careful examination of the bedroom with regard to the marks of blood?' – 'Yes.' Richardson added 'After making the examination of the house I went to the police station to circulate information of the murder, and that accounted for my not telling Mrs Haskell how much money I found in the drawer. Sergeant Golding afterwards told me that Mrs Haskell had said that some of the money was missing.'

'While you were in the house did you notice a mark on Mrs Haskell's nose?' – 'Yes.'

'What sort of a mark?' – 'A little scratch.' The chief constable further testified that it was because of what Mrs Carter had reported to him what her daughter had said to her, that he asked Flora if the blouse she was wearing was the same one she wore when she alleged the knife was thrown at her. 'Sergeant Golding', he continued, 'handed me the knife between two and three o'clock on Sunday morning. We were in the sitting room then.'

'Was it on Tuesday, November third, that you and Chief Inspector Dew showed the skirt and blouse to Dr Kempe?' – 'It was, sir.'

'Did you subsequently on that day get Dr Kempe's report?' – 'I did.'

'Was it after about half-past ten that you, Detective Dew and Superintendent Stephens arrested Mrs Haskell?' – 'It was.'

It was then time for Trethowan's cross-examination, but as Flora's statements would not be read out to the court until Dew was called, he proposed to defer cross-examining Richardson on them until that point in the proceedings, and to that the coroner assented. He began his questioning. 'Were there several people in the house when you first got there?' – 'Yes, and the street was full of people.' There was then a brief pause as Trethowan, on receipt of a sickness certificate signed by Dr Levi Luckham, advised the coroner Flora would not be present that day. He continued: 'I believe you found the doctors had been into the bedroom before you, and that the body had been moved -?' – 'I found that the doctors had been there.'

'It was a very common lock on the drawer -?' – 'Yes.'

'And very little force would be necessary to pull it

out locked.' – 'Very little.'

'There is nothing inconsistent with that having been done?' – 'No.'

'Did you ask certain questions of Mrs Haskell soon after entering the room?' – 'I could not get anything out of her.'

'But you did ask certain questions? I am not trying to catch you.' – 'Yes.'

'And quite right too. Considering the distress of mind she was in, she rendered you all the assistance she could -?' – 'Yes, she did.'

'I think you have given in the time when Mrs Haskell handed the blouse to you, but you haven't told us when the skirt was handed to you?' – 'On Sunday afternoon, when the statement was taken.'

'When Golding produced this knife to you …'

Trethowan never finished the sentence, because at that point Kempe came in and after a few words, Parr asked the coroner whether the chief constable might agree to Flora being returned to Devizes. It turned out that she was so ill that she had two doctors in attendance. To this request the coroner said 'Oh, certainly.' During the exchange the chest of drawers was brought into the court, where both jury and coroner had a good look at it. Trethowan's cross-examination resumed. 'When the knife was shown you, you went from the front room into the kitchen?' – 'Yes.'

'And both Mrs Haskell and Mrs Carter opened the drawer and showed you the knives?' – 'No, Mrs Carter did it; [but] Mrs Haskell was there.'

'And did Mrs Carter look through the knives with you?' – 'Yes.'

'And did she afterwards confer with Mrs Haskell about a knife which might be missing?' – 'No, they said a knife was missing.'

'Practically, what I said was correct, that both Mrs Carter and Mrs Haskell were looking through the knives together?' – 'Yes.'

'Mrs Haskell told you that Teddy's knife was missing?' – 'Mrs Carter said it.'

'And Mrs Haskell was there?' – 'I know from both of them that the knife was missing.'

'Did they not tell you this was a knife Teddy used for rough purposes?' – 'Not then, but later. It is in her statement.'

'Did Mrs Haskell tell you where she last had seen that knife?' – 'Yes, in the statement.'

'What did she say?' – 'I want to refer to the statement.'

'I want your impression of what took place. When did she say she had seen it?' – 'On the Thursday before.'

'Did she tell you then what Teddy was doing with it?' – 'Something about sharpening. It is all down in the statement.' At this point, Richardson, clearly at something of a loss otherwise, was handed the statement.

'Did you ask whether the knife had been sharpened?' – 'No, sir.'

'Did she tell you it had been sharpened on his father's whetstone?' – 'She said in her statement "I did not see him sharpen it, but I believe he sharpened it on his father's whetstone, which was in a tool bag."' Richardson continued, reading from the statement 'Teddy was sharpening some wood making a tip-cat, I think. I have not seen it since. It was a brown-handled knife. . . . On Thursday my son was using it to cut wood with. I should think it was rusty or dirty. It was sharpened, because my little boy said "This knife won't cut much", and I believe he sharpened it on a stone which his dad had in the coal shed.'

Trethowan then turned to the subject of Flora's friendship with Alfred Mold, the ship's steward employed by the White Star Line.

'I believe you, or Mr Dew, asked Mrs Haskell about her proposed marriage.' – 'Mr Dew asked her that. He didn't ask Mrs Haskell that; he asked Mrs Carter that.

'She was asked that question?' – 'The question was whether she had got a young man, or words to that effect.'

'Where he was?' – 'No.'

'When he was last there?' – 'No.'

'No question asked about it?' – 'No, I asked her mother.'

At this point Parr interjected 'It is in the statement: "The shirt, collar, waistcoat, and white cricketing trousers belonged to a Mr Alfred Mold, a steward on the Adriatic, which sails between New York and Southampton. He has slept in this house twice within the last three months. I do his laundry work, which he leaves behind when he goes on a voyage. He left a fortnight ago. He slept here on those occasions because his mother was full up." Therefore I was right in saying there was nothing in this statement about Mrs Haskell's proposed marriage to the man.' Trethowan continued. 'Did you ask her whether she had a young man on the *Adriatic*?' — 'No.'

'What was said about courting?' — '[I] simply asked whether she had a young man.'

'Then you went to Mrs Carter?' — 'No, I asked Mrs Carter previous to the statement because a communication was made to me when I came out into the street.'

'What did you ask Mrs Carter?' — 'I asked her whether her daughter was courting a young man — whether there was any truth in it. She said "No, she wasn't."'

Parr asked 'Did she say she was not, or that she did not know?' — 'She said she was not.' Trethowan continued. 'Did you ask Mrs Carter anything about this man Mold?' — 'No.'

'Nor Chief Inspector Dew?' — 'What I am talking about happened before Inspector Dew arrived.'

'What was it that made you and Chief Inspector Dew go down to Plymouth on Wednesday November eleventh to meet the *Adriatic*?' — 'In the course of enquiries.'

'What did you ascertain, or think you ascertained?' — 'I obtained a statement from Mold.'

'That isn't what you ascertained. You said you made enquiries. What did you go there for?' — 'To interview Mold.'

'And you boarded the *Adriatic* to see Mold?' — 'I did.'

'I think it was late at night when you got on board?' — 'Yes.'

'You got him out of his berth.' — 'We didn't get him out.'

'You asked that he should be got up.' — 'The petty officer got him out.'

'You got him out?' — 'No, we asked to see him.'

'It was late at night?' — 'Yes.'

'He came out to you?' — 'Yes.'

'Did you then ask him whether he knew of this murder?' — 'I didn't ask him anything. Mr Dew questioned him.'

'What did he say?' — 'He asked him if he had heard anything about a serious matter that had happened at Salisbury. Nothing was said about a murder.'

'What did he say? What is that you have in your hand?' — 'It is his statement. I took it down in writing.'

'What was the answer you got when Chief Inspector Dew asked him whether he knew anything of a serious matter that had happened in Salisbury? What did he say?'

At that point Parr rose from his seat and declared 'I think the best evidence should be called before the coroner.' Trethowan responded 'In all probability Mold will be back in time and I will call him. . . . The suggestion was that this man had something to do with the murder.' And then, with Parr's response, a serious, potentially crucial flaw in what would be the Crown's case against Flora came to light: 'I know nothing at all about it. The suggestion hasn't been made on behalf of the police or the Treasury.' The coroner added 'I don't see anything in the statement: he simply says he was on friendly terms.' Trethowan resumed his cross-examination; 'Did you then tell him of the murder?' — 'We told him what had happened.'

'Did you or Inspector Dew tell him he must have seen it in the New York papers?' — 'That is absolutely untrue.'

'Did you tell him that he ought to come forward and help the poor woman?' — 'Nothing at all of the sort was said.'

'And did you ask him how intimate he had been with this woman?' — 'No.'

'Nothing of the kind?' — 'No.'

'Did Mr Dew ask him?' — 'Not in my presence.'

'Nothing to that effect?' — 'Nothing to that effect at all.'

'Did you go with him to Cherbourg?' — 'The boat called at Cherbourg: we couldn't get off.'

'You could have got off!' — 'Oh, no, we could not!'

Trethowan laughed and retorted 'I know why the boat went off very well!' He continued his questioning: 'Did you interview him more than once?' — 'No, only on one occasion.'

'Did he, after the first occasion, ask you whether he could sign on for the next voyage or not?' — 'He didn't ask in my presence.'

'Do you know whether there was such a question asked?' – 'No.'

'Don't you know, as a matter of fact, [that] he didn't sign on without the permission of the police?' – 'No, I don't. It is the first time I have heard of it.'

'At all events you raised no objection to his signing?' – 'No.'

'And you didn't take him into custody?' – 'No.'

Trethowan then turned to the interviews resulting in Flora's statements. 'You had a room to yourselves – the three of you?' – 'Yes.'

'And you examined her.' – 'She was not examined at all. She was asked to state in her own words exactly what had occurred.'

'You did not caution her?' – 'There was no occasion.'

'Were any questions put to her while that statement was being put down?' – 'There were a few questions, but very few.'

'Who put them?' – 'Mr Dew.'

'Did he put them all?' – 'Yes.'

'How long were you in that room, three policemen with that poor woman?' – 'Three or four hours.'

'Do you mean to tell me it took three or four hours to put down that statement?' – 'Yes, sir, as she made it.'

'At what time was the second statement taken?' – 'During our visit there on Monday morning.'

'What time?' – 'I can't tell exactly, but between ten and eleven o'clock.'

'A further statement was obtained from her?' – 'Yes, I took it down.'

'Who was there beside?' – 'Mr Dew.'

'Who else?' – 'No-one.'

'Was the Chief Constable of Wilts there?' – 'He was there on Sunday afternoon.'

'Oh! You did not tell us that!' Parr remonstrated 'It was only a slip!' Trethowan replied, suavely 'I don't suggest it was anything else. I know Mr Richardson too well to think he would mislead me.'

Richardson enlarged on his admission: 'Captain Llewellyn, having received information of what had happened, motored over from Devizes on Sunday for the purpose of rendering me any assistance he could.' Parr added 'Mr Richardson's jurisdiction does not

go outside the city.' Trethowan returned to his task: 'How long did the second interview of Mrs Haskell and yourselves take?' – 'Not more than an hour.'

'Oh, just consider a moment!' – 'It was not very long.'

'Was it under two hours?' – 'Oh, yes.'

'Were questions then asked [of] Mrs Haskell?' – 'No, she asked questions of us.'

Prompting laughter, Trethowan enquired 'Oh, she examined you, then?' – 'Well, she began "There is something I forgot to tell you yesterday."'

'She approached you and not you her?' – 'Yes.'

'Do you honestly tell me you did not ask her questions?' – 'I do.'

'Neither did Mr Dew?' – 'No, Mr Dew did not on this occasion.'

'When was the third statement taken?' – 'About mid-day, shortly after the other.'

'How long did that interview last?' – 'Not very long.'

'Now, how long?' – 'Not more than half an hour, or three quarters.'

'Did you ask any questions then?' – 'No, Mr Dew did.'

'You arrested her on the following day?' – 'Yes, on the Tuesday at ten thirty at night.'

'There was another statement taken? – 'Yes, on November third, at ten o'clock in the morning.'

'When I get the statements I will consider them, and [I] will not ask any questions if I can help it.' – 'The statement speaks for itself.'

'Oh, don't be too anxious. Was she questioned then?' – 'Yes, by Chief Inspector Dew.'

'Did you suggest any questions he should put?' – 'No. She said she would like to speak to the police officers alone, and then I took it down.'

'Who were there?' – 'Mr Dew and myself.'

'How long were you there then?' – 'About an hour.'

The jury asked about Wyatt's parcel and Richardson answered 'I did not see a parcel in the house on the night of October thirty-first. I saw it the following day: there were no marks of blood on it.' They then asked whether there were any traces of anyone having washed their hands, and whether there were any bloodstains on the towel: 'No' replied the Chief Constable. Parr asked 'Was there not a sink in the scullery?' – 'Yes, close to the outside scullery door.'

'Is there a tap of water there?' – 'Yes.'

'That tap was in working order?' – 'Yes.'

'Did you, from the time you first went into the house, ever see any towels in any part of the house?' – 'No.'

'Did you ever see any wet towels or towel that had been used?' – 'No, there was a basket of dirty clothes there.'

'Were there any towels amongst them which had any blood marks on them?' – 'No.'

'Did you hear Mr Steer's evidence that he brought down the towels used by the doctors and left them on the window sill of the washhouse?' – 'I did.'

'Were any of those towels ever seen by you?' – 'No.'

'Nor have they since been seen?' – 'No.'

Explaining the presence of the Chief Constable of the county force, Richardson said 'Captain Llewellyn came for the purpose of assisting me in tracing the man described, who might be in the county.'[1]

'Were you present at all those interviews with Mrs Haskell?' – 'Yes, sir.'

'During those four interviews there was no thought in your mind or in the minds of responsible police officers to arrest her?' – 'Not at all'.

'It was not till after Dr Kempe's examinations of the skirt and blouse that any intention was formed of arresting her?' – 'No.'

'During the whole of those four interviews, was every possible consideration shown to Mrs Haskell by the police officers?' – 'This is so.'

In response to a question by the jury, Richardson said 'Mrs Carter did not come into the house till after I arrived.' At that point the inquest was adjourned until 10.30 on Thursday morning, 26 November.

At the resumption of the inquest, now into its seventh day, the court was, as on previous occasions, full of spectators. Upon Flora's entrance, just before the proceedings began, a hush fell on the court. Looking ill, she smiled sadly across to her brother who was sitting next to Trethowan. Among others present were the police officers Richardson, Stephens and Dew, all of whom were due to testify, and whose

appearance thus was probably anticipated as highlights of the inquest. For poor Flora it was once more all too much, and within a quarter of an hour, perhaps as her statements were being read out by Richardson, that she collapsed and had to be removed from the court for the duration. The proceedings began with a reading of Flora's four statements by Chief Constable Richardson, followed by cross-examination by Trethowan, who began by recalling the police's treatment of Flora in the immediate aftermath of the murder. 'I believe you know Mrs Haskell fainted immediately after the first statement was taken?' – 'Yes, in the kitchen.'

'Do you know Dr Wilks was sent for?' – 'That is within my knowledge.'

'And that she was ordered to lie down?'

'Did the police refuse to let her go upstairs?' – 'No, sir, not to my knowledge.'

'Or refuse to let her have a mattress, or any other bedclothes brought downstairs?' – 'Not to my knowledge. This is the first I have heard of it.'

'Did you know she had to get a mattress and bedding next door?' – 'I know she borrowed some, but I don't know where from.'

'And that she lay on the bedding in the front room?' – 'Yes.'

'On the floor?' – 'Yes.'

'Now, Mr Richardson, from the very first time when you entered the house and saw Mrs Haskell, did you not keep her under close observation?' – 'Absolutely untrue. I might add that I suggested to Mrs Carter and Mrs Haskell that they should go out of the house, and let the place stop as it was, and go and sleep with some friends. I was not in charge of the house myself, but several officers were. I told them that they should leave a police officer in the bedroom, and they approved of it. They said they would be very glad. On Saturday last [21 November], I called on Mrs Carter twice, and she told me she had handed over two towels. She said she found them on the window sill of the scullery.'

'After they had been used by the doctor, and were wet, or damp?' – 'No, I don't think she said so. She gave Mrs Steer the kitchen towels, for the use of the doctors.'

'She went further than that. Didn't she say she

had told you or Mr Dew that she had put them in a basket standing on the stove in the back kitchen?' – 'No.'

'Did you go up and find them?' – 'I found them in the basket.'

'You remember when you were searching the kitchen on Sunday, that Mrs Carter said "Those two towels I have thrown in the basket."?' – 'No.'

'You won't swear that she didn't?' – 'No.'

'Did you afterwards go to 40 Meadow Road and find the towels where Mrs Carter said they were?' – 'I found them in the basket.'

'I don't say you are misleading anybody, but it was suggested last Saturday that these towels had not been seen since. These are the towels?' – 'Yes.'

'Did you afterwards go back to Mrs Carter's?' – 'Yes.'

'And did you produce two towels to her?' – 'Yes.'

'Did she not tell you those were the towels she handed to Mr Steer, and that she found them on the window-sill and threw them into the basket?' – 'She said those were the towels.'

'You are still in possession of the house?' – 'Yes.'

'Who is going to pay the rent?' – 'That is a matter for after consideration.'

'We are not there, you know. We cannot get in.' – 'You can if you come to us.'

'It is a question that will crop up by and bye, you know. We must give notice.'

Parr added helpfully 'There will be no difficulty about that.'

Trethowan retorted testily 'I get questions from all over the world about this wretched case, and I must answer them if I can.' Returning to his cross-examination, he asked 'Do you know, Mr Richardson, what Sergeant Golding did with the knife when he went to Slade's to communicate with you on the telephone?' – 'Yes, I have heard something about it.'

'Tell me about it.' – 'I have heard that Golding got a bag.'

'No, tell me about the knife.' – 'That he took it to Mr Slade's.'

Parr interjected 'That is what he heard.' Trethowan snapped 'I am going to prove that that is what he did.' Turning back to Richardson for

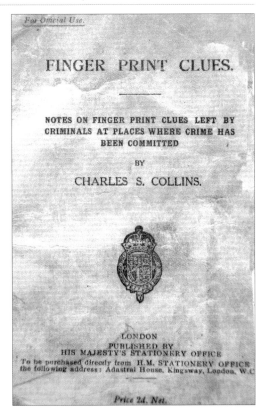

FINGERPRINT CLUES BOOKLET ISSUED TO THE SALISBURY POLICE (BUT NOT APPARENTLY REFERRED TO BY SERGEANT GOLDING)
© *ANDY NICKLEN COLLECTION*

confirmation he added 'That he took the knife in his open hand, without anything round it -?' – 'Yes.'

'And put it on the slab on Mrs Slade's counter?' – 'Yes.'

'And asked Mrs Slade for a bag or paper to wrap it in?' – 'That is quite untrue. I have enquired into it. The blood was from some rabbits.'

'But is it true about asking for the paper?' – 'No, none of it is true as far as I can ascertain.'

'Do you know whether Golding had found the knife when he went to Slade's?' – 'No, he hadn't. That is my information.'

'Have you searched for the brown paper the knife was wrapped up in?' – 'I have.'

'Have you found it?' – 'No, sir.'

'Golding said he gave you the brown paper, what did you do with it?' – 'I put it on my desk, and unfortunately it was mislaid. There were no marks of blood on it.'

'Any name on the paper?' – 'I did not notice any, but I won't be certain.'

'Did not you recognise then, or don't you recognise now, that it was very important that the paper should have been kept!?' – 'It would have been better if it had been kept.'

Parr then asked 'You told us on Saturday that before her arrest you treated Mrs Haskell with every possible consideration -?' – 'Yes, sir, as a matter of fact Mrs Haskell, her mother and her brothers have thanked us for the consideration the police have shown.'

'As regards the police taking possession of the house: that was obliged to be done?' – 'Yes, sir.'

Trethowan interjected 'That question was only asked in order to be able to answer enquiries as to the rent. I now understand the police will pay it.'

Parr continued. 'After hearing Steer's evidence, had you in your mind the question of the towels?' – 'I had.' Richardson explained 'No towels were found up to last Saturday, and for that reason I made further enquires after the adjournment and showed those cloths to Mrs Carter, and she told me what I said. Until Saturday Mrs Carter had not told me about these cloths, and at the time I saw Mrs Carter I had not got Steer's statement. It was [only] yesterday that I received a statement from Mrs Daniels with regard to Golding being in Slade's shop with the knife. I had not heard of it before. I saw Golding about it and was satisfied that none of it was true.'

The jury then asked 'Were any proper towels found in the house beside the cloths?' – 'There was a round towel behind the door.' Trethowan added 'There were other towels upstairs in the front room.'

Next to testify was Superintendent Stephens, who recounted how he visited No. 40 with Richardson on the night of the murder, and corroborated the Chief Constable's testimony of what he saw there. He continued 'I had a conversation with Mrs Haskell about a scratch on her nose. She put up her hand and said "I cut it with my ring a day or two ago." That was all that was said about it. There was a conversation about a handkerchief, and to the best of my belief Mrs Haskell heard it, because she was sitting nearer Mrs Carter than I was. Mrs Carter said "I picked up little Teddy's handkerchief in the front room." She then produced a bloodstained handkerchief from her pocket and handed it to me. This', said Stephens, producing the exhibit, 'is the handkerchief. I said "How do you know this is Teddy's handkerchief?" She replied "I gave it to him for a present; in fact I gave him two." A little later I showed her another handkerchief which I found in the boy's jacket pocket and said "Is this the other one which you gave him?" She replied "No." I said "Is it Teddy's?" and she said "I can't say, as they have so many with different borders upstairs." It is the one I found in the left-hand pocket. I found another in the right-hand pocket. I was present when Mr Richardson asked Mrs Haskell to take off her blouse. She handed it to me and I handed it to Mr Richardson. Mrs Haskell did not say anything to me about being allowed to go upstairs that night. On Sunday at noon I again visited the house, and there were present the Chief Constable of Wilts, Mr Richardson and Mr Dew. I made a close examination of the bedrooms, stairs, passage and kitchen, and found marks of blood in the same place which Mr Pepper has already spoken to. On Tuesday November third I went again to the house and removed the pillows and bedclothes to the City Police Station. On the fifth I removed the floor cloth from the bedroom floor and landing, two pieces of floor cloth from the floor leading from the passage to the kitchen and also the chest of drawers from the bedroom. I replaced those articles for the purpose of Mr Pepper's examination on the eighth. Before I removed the articles Mr Notley had taken accurate measurements as to the position of the bed and various articles in the bedroom. These were replaced in accordance with Mr Notley's measurements. I noticed at one a.m. on Sunday [1 November] there was a white tablecloth on the kitchen table. Mrs Haskell, Mrs Carter and others were there. There were several cups and saucers on the table. My attention was not called at any time to a mark on the kitchen [table]cloth, neither on that night nor on the days immediately following. I did not examine the back door when I first went into the house, so I was not able to tell whether it was locked or not. I examined it later at about one fifteen on Sunday morning, and it was not locked then. I did not see Alfred Walter Noble come into the house that night. When I first went in Mrs Haskell was not wearing an apron. While Mrs Haskell was making her statement on the first, I went into the kitchen with Mrs Carter and asked her for the apron she, Mrs Carter, was wearing, and she gave it to me. I took it back to Mrs Haskell and she said it was the one [she had been wearing the previous night].'

Parr then asked 'Did you on your way to the house stop at the *Duke of York?*' – 'Yes, and I heard someone say there were bloodstains on the gates. There were several men there. There were several wet marks on the outside of the gate. On the lower end of one was a drop. I removed it with the tip of my finger and found it clear water.' Laughter echoed round the courtroom. Parr continued, 'Did Mrs Haskell on Saturday night give you a description of a man?' – 'Yes, she spoke of a man calling the previous night for lodgings, and said she told him she could not accommodate him, when he replied "That's strange, as I have been recommended to you."'

'Did she describe him?' – 'Yes, she described him as being dressed in dark clothes and wearing a bowler hat. She said he was about such a build as the young man next door.'

'Were instructions given to the police to search for a man answering to that description?' – 'Yes, sir.'

'Has any such man been found?' – 'No, sir.'

'Did you see a roller towel hanging on the outside door of the scullery?' – 'Yes, on the Sunday morning.'

'Did you notice whether the blind of the kitchen window was up or down?' – 'It was down on the Sunday morning, at ten o''clock, when I first noticed it'

'On the Sunday night did you find in the house a letter?' – 'Yes, sir.'

'Where was it?' – 'On the mantel shelf in the kitchen.'

'Did you take possession of it?' – 'Yes.'

'Why?' – 'I noticed the flag on the back of the envelope, and took it down and read it.'

Trethowan interjected '*Adriatic?*', which raised more laughter around the court.

Parr explained 'It was addressed to Mrs Haskell,

and there is a postmark which looks like Southampton.'

Smith, the coroner, read the letter out:

'R.M.S. *Adriatic*, Southampton. Dear Flo, Thanks very much for your letter. I am very sorry to hear Mother is so poorly. I hope the pain will soon pass. I think a doctor ought to be seen right away. Nothing is gained by delay. Thanks very much, dear, for looking after her. It is very kind of you. I am scribbling this before I go out. With love, yours sincerely, Alf.'

Parr, keen to stress the warmth of the relationship, corrected 'With *much* love.'

Smith conceded 'Yes, "With much love."'

Parr added 'The postmark is five p.m., October 20th, 1908.'

Then came Trethowan's opportunity for cross-examination. Instead, however, of subjecting Stephens to the kind of interrogation Richardson had undergone, he merely inquired banteringly 'Just for curiosity I should like to ask Mr Stephens if he took off the gates of the *Duke of York* and sent them to Professor Pepper.' Amid more laughter, Stephens replied simply 'No, sir.'

'All right', said Trethowan, 'I won't bother you.' Well might he not, for his real quarry was the next witness.

On enquiry from the jury as to whether Mrs Carter accounted for the bloodstains which were on the handkerchief which she picked up in the front room, Stephens replied that she did not. Then, at one o'clock, the court adjourned for lunch.

After lunch the first witness, and the last of the police witnesses, was Walter Dew, Chief Inspector of the Criminal Investigation Department at Scotland Yard. He gave to the coroner an account of his arrival in Salisbury and gathering of evidence including Flora's statements. 'I arrived at eleven twenty-eight on Sunday morning, [1 November] and was met by the Chief Constable, who gave me a brief outline of the case. I went with Mr Richardson to the bedroom and in company with Superintendent Stephens I examined the room. I agree with Dr Pepper's evidence as to the blood spots that were found there. I went out into the washhouse and found two handkerchiefs with blood spots. Mrs Carter,

FLORA HASKELL'S KITCHEN WHERE SHE CLAIMS TO HAVE HEARD A MAN RUNNING DOWN HER STAIRS. 1908.
© *Timothy W. Frank Walker and Ann Richardson Whittle, grandchildren of Frank Richardson, Chief Constable.*

who was present, said they belonged to Teddy and that he had hurt his ear the other day, and that the blood on the handkerchief was caused through that. I subsequently made enquiries and found that he had hurt his ear at school. I afterwards saw Mrs Haskell in the presence of the Chief Constable of Wiltshire, the Chief Constable of Salisbury and Superintendent Stephens. I told her who I was and said that I desired to do everything I possibly could to detect the person who committed the crime. I asked her to tell me what had happened in her own way and that it would be taken down in writing. She said "I will tell you all I know, sir", and she sat down in the front room with us and told us the story in No. 1 statement.' Dew then related how Flora came to make her subsequent statements and also his gathering of material for Pepper's attention.

Parr began his examination. 'Did Mrs Haskell tell you how she was standing when the man came downstairs?' – 'Yes. She said the kitchen door was about three parts open and she was standing in the doorway immediately at the foot of the stairs. She stood in the position to show me, and her body was fully exposed to anyone running downstairs, both her right arm and her left arm being exposed.'

'Was the whole of her body on the passage side of the door?' – 'Partly between the two. It [the door] was pushed back away from her.'

'Did she also show you how the light was? – the kitchen gas?' – 'Yes.'

'The jet is in the centre of the room, over the kitchen table?' – 'Approximately, yes.'

'How did she put the light?' – 'Rather low, just a small jet.'

'Did she say whether or not the man came downstairs then?' – 'Yes, when she was preparing to go out.'

'During these several interviews you had with Mrs Haskell, was every consideration shown to her throughout?' – 'Oh, yes, certainly.'

'What was her demeanour while she was making these statements?' – 'Quiet, cool and collected, but she became agitated when she was shown the knife.'

'After these statements had been made by Mrs Haskell, did you on November eleventh go to Plymouth and meet Mold?' – 'I did, on the night of the eleventh.'

'Was the *Adriatic* in port at that time?' – 'Oh dear, no, she only comes inside the Sound; she lands her passengers and mails on a tender. She was just inside the breakwater, which is two or three miles out.'

'Did you go out to her?' – 'Yes, I went out on a tender with Mr Richardson.'

'Did you find Mold on board?' – 'Yes, after some difficulty. It is a twenty-five thousand-ton boat, like a small town. He was in bed, and before Mr Mold could be got out of bed the *Adriatic* had sailed away and we sailed with her.'

'You *sailed with her?*' – 'We had no alternative.'

'You were quite satisfied that Mold had come over from New York on her?' – 'Yes.'

That was all Parr had to ask; now came Trethowan's opportunity. He began by asking drily 'I hope you had a nice trip over to Cherbourg?' – 'Anything to do with tragic affairs . . .' Unimpressed by Dew's not inconsiderable reputation in his field, Trethowan snapped 'Please answer my question.' – 'I repeat that anything connected to tragic affairs cannot be pleasant to me.'

'You can say "yes" or "no", or refuse to answer.' – 'I *have* answered your question.'

'Please don't speak to me in that manner. I won't be spoken to like that. Don't speak to me like that again. If you won't answer, say so. Why did you go to Plymouth? – the letter was in the house.' – 'I don't know that I had seen it in the house.'

'Was it in consequence of reading that letter that you went down?' – 'Not altogether.'

'Was it in consequence of a letter handed to you?' – 'There was another letter which came after that one, while Mrs Haskell was in custody.'

'Where is that letter? I want it produced.'

The coroner produced the letter, and Trethowan barked 'I want it read.'

Smith read 'Pier forty-eight, New York. Dear Flo, I shall try to get back home for the evening of November thirteenth. I hope you are well and Mother improved. Thanks very much, dear, for looking after

her. I am very well. Looking forward to see you again. I am sending by this – the *Lusitania* – so you ought to get this on Thursday. Much love, dear. Yours sincerely, Alf.'

Trethowan asked 'Was it in consequence of that letter?' – 'I don't know that it was altogether. We thought Mr Mold might be able to throw some light on this matter.'

'Did you have a statement in reference to Mold having some connection with this woman?' – 'No, I think not, I only heard she was keeping company with him.'

'When you saw Mold did you ask him whether he had heard anything of the serious affair which had happened in Salisbury?' – 'I probably did.'

'Did he say no?' – 'He did.'

'Did you then say to him "You must have seen it in the New York paper"?' – 'No, sir.'

'Nothing to that effect?' – 'No, sir.'

'Did you tell him he ought to come forward and try to save this poor woman?' – 'No, certainly I did not.'

'Or anything to that effect?' – 'No, I certainly did not.'

'"Yes" or "No" will be sufficient. Did he ask you what you wanted?' – 'I'll tell you if you like.'

'Yes, please tell me.' – 'I apologised because it was late at night when I saw Mr Mold. As I had to remain on the boat until it arrived at Southampton I said I should probably see him before I went off. I did see him the next day, before I left the boat at Southampton, and he asked me if I thought he would have to attend the inquest because, if so, it would put him in a very awkward position and he might lose his berth. I told him that as far as I was concerned "Certainly not". He said "Can I sign on?" and I told him that as far as I was concerned "Certainly he could." He told me he should be in Salisbury on the Saturday, and he would call at the police station. In addition to this I saw the purser and explained as much as I thought necessary in connection with my visit, and I said I hoped it would not in any way prejudice Mr Mold.'

'You did take a statement?' – 'Oh, yes.'

'Was it necessary to take a statement under the circumstances?' – 'I think so, yes. It is always necessary to have some sort of statement, but it is not always necessary to make use of it.'

'I formally call for that statement.'

Smith, the coroner, said 'I don't think the statement is evidence. If the jury would like to hear it they can have it.' The jury deferred to the coroner, who told them 'It isn't evidence', and the foreman replied 'Why read it?' So the statement was not read, but Trethowan maintained he had done his duty in calling for it, and would call Mold at the trial. He then turned to the events of October 31, starting with the state of the knife, to which Dew replied 'The knife was in a piece of brown paper when I saw it.'

'Would you not think that the opening of the kitchen door and the appearance of the man coming downstairs were instantaneous [*sic, i.e.* simultaneous]? – 'She led me to believe that he was on the second or third stair from the bottom.'

'You heard Percy Noble give evidence. Did you hear him say she moved back one of the chairs?' – 'I heard him say the chair was moved.'

Trethowan then read out, from Percy's statement, the part recalling the moment when, at his aunt's back door, he heard what sounded like a jump from the stairs. He pressed Dew on whether he thought the opening of the door and the emergence of the strange man would not be simultaneous, and whether the jump from the stairs that Percy recalled was the jump Flora heard. Dew replied 'I am sure I don't know what jump she heard.' The court laughed when they heard Dew's response, and the mood of comedy was maintained over the next few exchanges, with Trethowan remarking 'Oh, you are not so dull as all that.' – 'I am not dull at all.'

'Perhaps you are too smart.' Amid laughter, Dew replied 'Oh, no I am not!'

'If, on hearing the thump on the stairs, Mrs Haskell went there instead of to Percy Noble, the appearance of the man and the opening of the door would happen almost simultaneously?' – 'I should think it was done very quickly.'

'If that were so the man would not see her until he was at the bottom of the stairs?' – 'I take it so.'

'You say that when making her statements Mrs Haskell's demeanour was calm, collected and cool. A rather extraordinary thing if she were?' – 'That is what struck me.'

'Did you hear what Dr Wilks said about her?' – 'Oh yes.'

'Did you hear the evidence of the other witnesses, who spoke of her agitated condition?' – 'Yes, sir.'

'Did you hear that she fainted almost immediately after making her statement to you?' – 'Yes, I was told so.'

'Have you any reason to doubt it?' – 'No, I have seen her faint, many times.'

'Have you spoken to Mrs Haskell at all at any other times than when she was making her statements?' – 'I think I spoke to her the night she was arrested, and told her not to be agitated.'

'No towels have been taken away from the house?' – 'I have never suggested it.'

'I don't say you have.'

Parr interjected 'After the question about the towels on Saturday and further enquiries had been made, were you satisfied?' – 'I never was dissatisfied. The point about it was that they were described as towels, but were found to be cloths.'

'You have been asked as to the condition of Mrs Haskell when seen by Dr Wilks and others, but you can only speak to her condition when you got there?' – 'Yes, and I did not take any statement from her till late on Sunday.'

And with that, the examination of the police witnesses, sometimes gruelling, sometimes knockabout, but always searching, was concluded.

8

'I saw a man come from a house', The Inquest, Thursday 26 – Friday 27 November: closing stages

THE NEXT WITNESS on the Thursday was Thomas Alfred Rawlins, the dairyman who lived at 26 Meadow Road, and who had gone into No. 40 with Walter Steer on the night of the murder. He had been at the hearing and had heard the Chief Constable's testimony the previous Saturday, 21 November, and had reported the blood marks he saw on the kitchen tablecloth. That cloth was now produced and he identified it. Parr asked 'About what time did you see it on the table that night?' – 'At about eleven thirty. I was in the house some time.'

'When you saw the blood marks, were they the same in colour as they are now?' – 'No, sir, they were very bright.' The jury then asked whether Rawlins reported the blood spots to the police as soon as he had seen them, and he replied that he did not, adding that there were several people in the room at the time, and he called someone's attention to the marks then.

Trethowan's cross-examination began, as with other neighbours with the relationship between mother and son, and Rawlins testified to their good relations, and that he had nothing to say against Flora as a mother.

'When', asked Trethowan 'did you first make a statement to the police?' – 'On Sunday November first.'

'You said nothing about these blood marks then?' – 'Not [those] on the table cloth.'

'I take it that you simply recognise the tablecloth because you see blood on it?' – 'Yes.'

'You don't recognise the *tablecloth*, you recognise the blood on it?' – 'Yes, because the spots are similar to what I saw three weeks ago.'

'So if there were two tablecloths with similar bloodstains on them, you could not tell one from another?' – 'Not if they were precisely the same.'

'For three weeks you said nothing about it, and you now say you can tell exactly the spots on the tablecloth, how they were formed, whether they were little ones or big ones?' – 'I could show the position of the spots, if I could not swear to the cloth.'

'You can't say that that is the same cloth you saw at 40 Meadow Road, three weeks ago?' – 'No.'

'After making your statement to the police, have you made a statement to my clerk?' – 'Yes, a very good statement. I think I gave you more than the police.' The court laughed as Trethowan conceded 'I have nothing to complain about.' He added 'Did you say anything about the blood marks on the table cloth?' – 'No, sir.'

Parr asked 'When you were there last Saturday afternoon, was Superintendent Stephens there, and after you had placed the table in position as you saw it that night, did he take measurements?' – 'Yes, sir.'

At that point Stephens was recalled to explain the measurements. Under cross-examination he had to admit that unless the table were replaced in its exact position, his measurements would be useless.

Emily Sweetman was recalled to give evidence about the tablecloth. She said to the coroner 'When I went into the kitchen on the night of the murder, I saw the tablecloth on the table, and noticed the blood marks on the side nearest the staircase – on the same side as the door that leads from the kitchen to the passage. It was after Dr Wilks had been.'

'Did you tell anybody about these marks?' – 'I pointed them out to Superintendent Stephens.' Trethowan asked 'Except for the blood marks could you identify the tablecloth?' – '[No], except that it is a large white one.'

'When was it you pointed it out to Superintendent Stephens?' – 'Saturday the thirty-first.'

'Saturday thirty-first. Any other police officers with him?' – 'I don't remember. There were several other people there.'

'Were you in court when Superintendent Stephens gave his evidence?' – 'Yes.'

'Was anything said by him about it?' – 'I think he knew of it.'

Trethowan then pointed out to Mrs Sweetman that Stephens had said that neither on that night nor on the days immediately following did anyone point out to him any blood marks on the tablecloth. Mrs Sweetman stood her ground: notwithstanding Stephens' statement she did tell him about the blood marks.

'When did you first make your statement to the police?' – 'On November third.'

'Did you say anything about these blood marks then?' – 'No, I did not.'

'Did you afterwards make a statement to my clerk?' – 'Yes, I did.'

'Can you tell us the date?' – 'A fortnight last Tuesday [10 November]'

'Did you say anything about blood marks on the table cloth then?' – 'No, I did not.'

The final question came from the jury, as to the colour of the stains, and Mrs Sweetman testified that when she first saw them they were bright red.

Next to speak was Rosa Manning, Flora's next door neighbour to the south at No. 42. In response to the coroner she recalled 'On October thirty-first, I went to bed between nine thirty and ten p.m. I was expecting a parcel that night from the Co-operative Stores, and after I had been in bed a short time I heard someone knock at my door; I thought it was about ten p.m. I did not answer, and heard another knock which sounded [as if it was] next door. I went to sleep, and some screams woke me up. I rushed downstairs having put on my coat and boots, and went to the front door. There were several people outside, and Mrs Cooper said "They say someone has murdered little Teddy."' Smith was about to ask Mrs Manning about a conversation between her and Flora a couple of months previously, but Trethowan objected.

Parr interjected 'I will put the question, and the coroner can decide whether it may be answered. In view of the letters which have been put in, I consider it important that the jury should be in possession of all the facts.' Trethowan countered 'This question will open up all sorts of things, and as it goes back to two months I do not see that it has anything to do with this enquiry.' Smith said he would leave it up to the jury. Parr observed that Trethowan had raised the point when he asked about 'the man on the *Adriatic*'. He continued 'I do suggest, with all respect, that it is a matter on which we should have further information', at which Trethowan reminded the coroner that Mold's statement had remained unread, and argued that there was no need to take up the matter now. But Parr persisted: 'The point is whether she had any matrimonial intentions.' Smith wearily replied 'I really don't think my enquiry goes back further than the date of death of the boy. If the jury want the question answered it can be.' A member of the jury enquired whether the point would lead to the suggestion of any motive, and Parr replied 'That is for the jury to decide.' Trethowan, clearly exasperated, said 'We cannot go back two months, and I shall ask the coroner not to allow such a question to be put. We shall be here for months!' Smith, playing by the rules, said the jury wanted an answer to the question, and Parr asked Mrs Manning 'Did you at any time recently have a conversation with Mrs Haskell about her re-marriage?' – 'Yes, about three or four months ago she told me that Mr Mold had asked her to marry him, but it took a lot of thinking about.' The court chuckled at this little insight into Flora's sense of caution and even decorum. 'Did she say anything more?' – 'She said if ever she did, she would always work and keep little Teddy.'

'Did she say anything as to who Mr Mold was?' – 'No, sir.'

Trethowan's cross-examination began with Wyatt's errand before eliciting Mrs Manning's view on her neighbours. 'Have you ascertained that the boy who came with your boots was called John Stanley Wyatt?' – 'I read it in the papers.'

'Could you tell how long he stayed out side your door knocking?' – 'About a minute.'

Mrs Manning added 'I have known Mrs Haskell about two years, and saw her and Teddy every day. Mrs Haskell was kind to Teddy and she was a nice, kind neighbour. I always liked her. I never heard her say an unkind word to Teddy, who always looked bright, cheerful and happy. I last saw Mrs Haskell before that evening, on Sunday [*i.e.* 25 October], but I heard her call Teddy the same evening [*i.e.* 31]. She said "I shall not be going long, Teddy." I did not see Teddy after that.'

The next witness was Alfred Walter Noble, Flora's nephew and next-door neighbour to the north. The elder son of the family, he was, like his two neighbours, Walter Steer and Walter Cossor, a compositor by trade. He recalled first hearing about the murder. 'On the night of October 31 I was in Fisherton Street with two or three friends when someone told me of the affair, and I then went to 40 Meadow Road, going in the back way. The back door was locked. I knocked, and someone inside said "That's Bob", and they opened the door.' Noble also had interesting evidence from earlier that day. 'In the early part of the evening I had a conversation with Mrs Haskell. It was at about quarter-past seven. She said she could not help thinking about a man who came the night before for lodgings. It worried her so, that she woke up two or three times during the night. She said she had thought of it several times during the day, and could not make out who had recommended the man to her.' He also commented on the Mold connection. 'I heard Mrs Haskell say, in a joking manner, that she was going to get married: she said it to my father. I cannot remember when, but it was this year, [and] she told him it was to Mr Alfred Mold.'

From the jury came a question on Flora's emotional state, and Noble replied 'Mrs Haskell appeared quite rational when she had the conversation with me in the evening.'

Trethowan's line of questioning moved gradually from the possibility of marriage to the events of the early evening, and to his enquiries Noble responded 'This conversation about her re-marriage was treated as a joke by everyone there. She was laughing when she said it, [and] I heard nothing about the marriage from Mrs Haskell since. Mrs Haskell had a brother called Richard Carter, and Mr Carter and Mr Mold were boys together and had been exceedingly friendly ever since. I knew there was great affection between Mr Mold and Teddy, and that when he came home Mold always gave him a penny or twopence. Mrs Haskell and Mr Mold had been great friends since childhood, and I was always friendly with Mold too, but Mold never told me he was going to marry Mrs Haskell. Two or three days before the murder I was with Teddy playing cards. Teddy's ear bled, and he took out his handkerchief and applied it to his ear. On one occasion when I slept with Teddy there was a discharge of blood from the stump of his leg, and he said it often bled. I and my brother Percy came back from Dean about six thirty on the evening of October thirty-first. On the way home we went into Mrs Haskell's house, and at about a quarter-past seven I went into the town with Mrs Haskell and Miss Lawrence. Mrs Haskell went shopping, and at the Poultry Cross bought some sweets for Teddy. I left her at Fisherton Bridge with Mrs Hawkins, and the two went up [towards] Fisherton together.'

Trethowan asked 'She was in her usual spirits, nothing wrong with her, and bright and cheerful?' – 'Yes.'

'You got to Meadow Road, somewhere about eleven thirty, didn't you?' – 'Yes.'

'Where was she then?' – 'Sitting down in the kitchen, crying. I said 'Good God, Flo, what's happened?' She did not reply, she was crying so much. I put my arm round her neck, and she laid her head on my breast and cried bitterly.'

The penultimate witness that day was Noble's father, Alfred John, for whom on account of his deafness his son had to act as intermediary. He said,

'I saw Teddy at nine o'clock on the night of the murder, and I last saw Mrs Haskell at about twenty-five minutes to ten. At that time she brought the washing with her. She said, "You are up late for a Saturday night, aren't you?" and I replied that I had been into the town, and hadn't had time to read the paper. She asked me if I knew of an empty house with a larger back [yard] in which she could dry her clothes. She shortly after wished me goodnight and went home, after being in the house about five minutes.'

Trethowan's cross-examination again focused on her demeanour and her relationship with her son. Noble said that Flora was in her usual spirits when she left. He continued, 'I have known her a long time, and she always treated Teddy kindly', and 'When Teddy left the house he said 'Mam is calling me, I must go into supper.'

And so to Thursday's last witness, Edwin Daniels, an employee of the building firm of Billett and Musselwhite, who lived in Meadow Road, but over York Road, at No. 54. His testimony was that 'At ten o'clock on October 31, I was in a barber's shop in Fisherton Street. I was kept about ten minutes, and then walked up Fisherton [Street], down St Paul's Road [and] into Meadow Road. I stood at my door several seconds, and then saw something shuffle round the corner in the direction of York Road, coming from the direction of Mrs Haskell's. After that, I went in, and stayed three or four minutes. I then went round to the *Duke of York*, and on my way saw people running about. I asked what was up, and, of course, went and told my missus about it. I heard no screams. I did not take any particular notice of the person I saw shuffling round the corner.'

Parr asked, 'When did you first tell the police about this?' – 'Last night, sir.'

'Are you able to say whether that 'something' you saw was a man or woman?' – 'I could not say sir, it was something in light clothes.'

'Were you able to see clearly?' – 'No, sir.'

Trethowan then asked, 'Is it right to say that the person you saw "scrambled at a half-trot round the corner"?' – 'Yes, sir.'

'And that corner would be the corner of Mrs Cooper's house?' – 'Yes.'

'Was that person holding his or her head down?'

SIDNEY BUCHANAN SMITH, SALISBURY CITY CORONER, DEPICTED IN THE MORNING LEADER, 1908.

– 'Yes, sir.'

'You made your statement to my clerk on November twenty-fourth, before you made it to the police?' – 'Yes.'

The jury then asked whereabouts was the barber's shop Daniels had visited: 'It was Mr Sparks', opposite Fisherton Church.'

The coroner asked the final question: 'Can you tell me what time it was that someone was shuffling round the corner?' – 'Between a quarter and twenty past ten, I should think, sir, or three or four minutes before that.' Trethowan added that the time was fixed by the fact that when Daniels came out of his house, people were running in the direction of No. 40.

And with that, at twenty past seven on Thursday, 26 November, the inquest was adjourned until 10.30 the next morning, for what was to be its eighth and final day. Again before a crowded court, the final witness, and not someone from the area, was Francis Samuel Leate, a saddler, of 29 St Mark's Road. He stated that between ten o'clock and ten thirty on the night of October thirty-first, he was in the neighbourhood of Meadow Road. The coroner continued, 'Did you see anything?' Leate's testimony was electrifying . . . but uncorroborated by any other witness. 'I entered Meadow Road from Cold Harbour Lane. I was walking on the left-hand side of the road, and saw a man come from a house on the right-hand side of the road, followed almost immediately by a woman, who went in the same direction. The woman then stopped, turned and walked back, apparently to the house from which she came. Whilst returning to the house she stopped once or twice. She was sobbing. By this time I was opposite the house, and she was standing in the doorway. I glanced back, but the man was out of sight. I did not pay any particular attention to this, but walked on until I was half way between York Road and St Paul's Road. Then, hearing the woman sobbing louder, and the sound of hurried footsteps behind me, I turned and saw a crowd collecting round the house where the woman was standing at the door. I went back to where the crowd was collecting, and heard the woman, who was still sobbing at the door, saying something about a man who had killed or murdered her Teddy. I am not quite clear now as to what the words were. I stayed outside the house about ten minutes I should think, and then walked away. I saw the woman go into her house, but who it was I could not say.'

'Could you give a description of the man you saw?' – 'As far as I can remember – I did not pay any particular attention to him – he was rather under average height, five foot five inches, or five foot six inches, rather slightly built, dressed in clothes or dark material, and did not appear to be wearing a collar. I think he was wearing a cap.'

'Did you see his face at all?' – 'No.'

'Do you think you would know him again if you saw him?' – 'Oh, no, sir.'

Parr then asked, 'Is your recollection about this as clear now as it was on Monday, November second?' – 'No, sir, certainly not.'

'On Monday, November second, did you make a statement at the City Police Station?' – 'Yes, I suppose it was that date; I can't quite remember.'

'Is that your signature?' asked Parr, holding out Leate's statement. 'It is, sir.'

'Was the statement taken down in writing by Mr Richardson, and read over before you signed it?' – 'Yes.'

'When you first saw a man or woman leaving the house where were you?' – 'Just by Davidson's, the cabinet-maker. I don't know which house it was.'

'You told us you saw a woman following a man in the same direction up towards James Street -?' – 'Yes.'

'Was the man walking fast or slow?' – 'Rapidly.'

'You were walking on down Meadow Road?' – 'Yes.'

'What point had you reached when the man passed you on the opposite side?' – 'I can't clearly remember. I think I must have got to about No. 23.'

'If 28 is opposite 23, the man would be at about 28?' – 'Yes.'

'At that time how far was the woman behind the man?' – 'I can't clearly say. I think the woman had stopped.'

'Where did she stop?' – 'I can't clearly say.'

'Then is it correct to say "I passed them both on the opposite side of the road, and the man was about eight or a dozen yards in front of the woman" – 'Probably not, if my statement doesn't agree with it.'

'After you passed, did you hear a woman say "Stop that man, he has murdered my boy"?' – 'I tried to make that as clear to the police as I could. It was after I had turned round and come back that I heard her say what she did say.'

'Did you tell Mr Richardson 'After I had passed them I heard her say "Stop him, he has killed my boy."?' – 'Yes, if it is in my statement.'

'Is this a correct account of what took place: 'She was following a man in the direction of Cold Harbour Lane. After they had passed me, I heard a woman say 'Stop him, he has murdered my boy'?' – 'I can't remember the exact words.'

So Parr repeated the question, and Leate said he would like to explain. Parr retorted 'I would rather you answered the question first and explained afterwards.' – 'Yes.'

'Was the woman screaming at all until you had got back to the house after having gone down towards St Paul's Road?' – 'Not what I would describe as screaming.'

'How far do you now say the woman walked after the man until she turned back?'

Leate looked at the plan of the locality and said, 'I had just passed the passage of 36 Meadow Road. I point out the spot opposite No. 34, near the passage. It was thereabout.'

'How long did you stay outside No. 40, when you went back again after going to St Paul's Road?' – 'I should think about ten minutes, but I am not clear.'

'How long did Mrs Haskell stay at the door?' – 'I can't stay how long, but she went in while I was standing there.'

'Did you tell the police on Monday, November second, that you stayed there about a quarter of an hour and she was there the whole time?' – 'If you have it in the statement I must have said so.'

'You think the woman following the man must have seen him?' – 'Yes, sir.'

'Was the light clear in the road near Mrs Haskell's house on the James Street side?' – 'Yes, I could clearly see the houses.'

'Did you see whether or not the woman leaned up against any of the houses?' – 'I saw her stop once or twice and lean against houses as she passed.'

'Was that before she got back to her own house?' – 'Oh, yes.'

'Has your attention been called to the statement made by Mrs Haskell with regard to what you say?' – 'I heard Mr Richardson read a statement in which Mrs Haskell contradicted my evidence.'

Trethowan's cross-examination – and the unpicking of Leate's testimony – began. 'In your first statement you told the police you were outside Mrs Haskell's house for about a quarter of an hour -?' – 'Apparently.'

'You have said today about ten minutes?' – 'Yes.'

'Did you tell my clerk some time this week that it was no more than five minutes?' – 'If I said so, it is so.'

'You said "I think the woman following the man must have seen him." Are you prepared to say that the woman would see the man?' – 'I am not prepared to say she *must* have seen him, but she could have seen him.'

'If he hadn't in the meantime disappeared?' – 'Yes.'

'You passed the man first?' – 'Yes.'

'And when the woman appeared he might have been out of sight?' – 'Oh, no. I saw the man and woman in the street at the same time. They were *both* in the street at the same time as I was.'

'Are you prepared to swear that the woman you saw passed beyond No. 36?' – 'I am not prepared to swear to it.'

Trethowan pressed the point, and Leate replied 'I am not prepared to say Mrs Haskell was making an untrue statement when she said she did not pass Mr Steer's.' Then he was tackled about the distance between the couple. 'I am not prepared to say how far the man was in front of the woman when I first saw them: I am no judge of distance.'

'Was the sobbing you heard pretty much the same as when you got half-way down York Road?' – It was louder as I walked away, but of the same sort.'

'You say you heard Mrs Haskell say 'Someone has killed – or murdered – my boy'. Was that after you came back?' – 'I didn't hear anything said until I came back to the house.'

'You had not seen Mrs Haskell before?' – 'Not to my knowledge.'

'And therefore the story you have told us about this man and this woman might, as far as you know, apply to somebody totally different from Mrs Haskell?' – 'Oh, yes, quite possible.' Leate added that when he got back the woman outside the house, whom he had identified as Mrs Haskell, was crying hysterically and begging someone to go upstairs.

Smith then asked, 'The jury want to know whether you are positive that the man you saw did not return and go along York Road.' – 'He may have done after my back was turned. My back was to the house.'

'You cannot say?' – 'I can't say; I didn't see him as far as I am aware.'

Trethowan asked, 'Didn't you look back and see he was gone?' – 'Oh, yes.'

Mary Carter had been the first witness at the inquest; now, on its final day, she was recalled to explain how she had cleared up the hallway at No. 40. In response to Trethowan she said, 'About six o'clock in the morning on the day after the murder I was in the kitchen of 40, Meadow Road, and told Police Sergeant Golding and Miss Lawrence that I would clean up the passage.'

'Tell us what you did.' – 'I took a soft brush first, and swept. I then got a pail of water and flannel, and began at the front doorstep.'

'When you came to the kitchen door you saw a patch of blood?' – 'Yes, I did.'

'What was about the length of that patch of

blood?' – 'To the best of my knowledge it was about six inches.'

'And when you got to the patch of blood, what did you do?' – 'Washed it up as best I could.'

'And how?' – 'With a flannel and cold water, in the ordinary way that you would wash anything.'

'Did you remove any of the blood?' – 'Yes, nearly all. I don't think I got out every mark, because I only had cold water and no soap or brush.'

'Did you get up as much as you could?' – 'Yes.'

The last witness was Dr Pepper, down from London to comment on the bloodstains. The kitchen table from No. 40 was brought into the court, and Emily Sweetman carefully placed the tablecloth as she had seen it on the night of the murder. The coroner asked how he had first come to see the tablecloth, and Pepper replied, 'The tablecloth was brought to me by Chief Inspector Dew and the Chief Constable of Salisbury on Sunday.'

'Were there any stains on it?' – 'Yes.'

'Have you tested those marks?' – 'Yes.'

'Can you tell me what they were?' – 'Blood.'

'Will you describe the marks?' – 'On the right of the central ridge are a few marks. Some object with blood on it has caught the central ridge nine and a half inches from the hem border. From that ridge, for ten inches to the left, is a series of smears, mostly linear. The first set are oblique, the rest are horizontal. Between the smears on the border of the cloth below there are six roundish spots, the largest half an inch in diameter. I removed half of this by cutting the cloth. Close to the left border is one round spot and one linear smear. Close to the right border, there is a small smear. The spots and many of the smears show on the other side of the cloth, the blood having soaked through. The spots were formed by drops of blood falling on the cloth or being sprinkled or splashed on it. The linear smears were not, in my opinion, caused by a hand. There are too many and they are too linear for that. They were caused by some soft material, such as a towel-cloth, or handkerchief, or dress, or something of that sort. I think', said Pepper, pointing to the cloth, 'this object moved in a sweeping direction, first obliquely and then horizontally, from right to left.'

'Am I to take it you cannot say they are human

bloodstains?' – 'No, but they are mammalian.'

'About the age?' – 'They are comparatively recent, but I could not say within weeks or even months. It depends how the thing has been preserved.'

Parr then asked, 'Doctor, can you say whether they are of the same age as the stains on the blouse and skirt?' – 'Yes, approximately. One could tell from their appearance and by the way in which they react to the tests.'

Smith said, 'The jury want to know whether any of the smudges, or smears, on the upper part of the skirt could be made to correspond with those on the tablecloth.' – 'No, I believe not. Firstly, on account of the direction of the smears. They could not have been caused by anyone taking a step. Secondly, there are no smears on the skirt corresponding in direction with these stains. Those on the skirt are vertical: these are horizontal, or mainly horizontal. Thirdly, there are a number of spots on the tablecloth which are not merely impressions made by blood coming from any object. They have fallen on, or have been sprinkled on and they, obviously, could not have come from the blood on the skirt.' Smith said, 'That is all the evidence I have to offer.'

Trethowan declared, 'I reserve my cross-examination', and then asked, 'Am I to take it that you do not consent to my addressing the jury?' – 'No, I think not. I think it is better that neither of you should. I think that the jury have gone into the matter very carefully, and I think it would be best not to.' – 'Very well. I have made the application. My client was anxious that I should. If I have not your permission, of course, I cannot.'

And so, after eight days and the summoning of thirty-five witnesses, the inquest was drawing to a close. Smith delivered his summing up. 'That is all the evidence I propose to call. I don't intend to take you all through the evidence again. You have taken very careful notes, and I think it will be sufficient. There are a few things, however, I should like to say to you before you consider your verdict. It is quite clear in the present instance that you are inquiring into the death of a boy who has been murdered. I need scarcely remind you that a murder is when a person of sound mind, memory and discretion unlawfully kills any reasonable creature in being and under the

King's peace by any means with malice aforethought, either express or implied. I am glad to tell you that in this city this crime has been very rare. My clerk has been very carefully through the records since 1875, and there have only been three cases of murder in that time, and in all those cases the verdicts have always been against persons unknown.

In the present case it has been given in evidence that on the night of the thirty-first October this boy, known as Teddy Haskell, was alive at nine o'clock, and at half-past ten the same night was found in his bed, dead, in his mother's house, with his throat cut. It has been shown that at a quarter to ten on the night in question, Miss Steer called there to fit Mrs Haskell with a jacket, and she was then quite happy and in her usual state. Again, at twenty minutes past ten the lad Wyatt called and delivered a parcel for Mrs Manning. He says Mrs Haskell was in a quiet state of mind. The next thing we hear is that Percy Noble says he was there at ten thirty. He knocked twice at the back door and heard Mrs Haskell moving a chair. He also heard what he said was a thump, and when asked where he heard the sound came from, he said 'Near the stairs.' Mrs Haskell then comes to the door screaming. She says, 'Go and see if you can see that man, he has murdered my poor Teddy. After that she seems to have gone to the front door, and Steer hearing her screams came in. He seems to have been the first person who was at the house after the murder. He tells you what he found, and that he touched the little boy's face and it was warm.

They sent for the doctor. The doctor arrived at about ten thirty-five. You have got the time from a quarter to ten till ten thirty five. The doctor's evidence is that he arrived within a quarter of an hour of the death, and he says the cause of death is haemorrhage. Then we have the finding of the bloodstains in the bedroom, on the landing, and on Mrs Haskell's blouse, and the finding of the knife afterwards, lying at the kitchen door. You have also heard what Mrs Haskell said as to a man running down the stairs. You heard the evidence of Dr Pepper as to the bloodstains on the articles he examined being a few days old, and he says it might have been weeks or months, as after a week changes take place very slowly. He says they were all of comparatively recent

date and all about the same age. I don't propose to go into the question of the money, as I don't think there is anything I need call your attention to on that point, after the very careful attention you have given through this enquiry. The points which will be in your minds, and [which] I shall ask you to consider are these:

1. When and how Teddy Haskell died?
2. What was the cause of his death and by what means it was caused?
3. Was he murdered?
4. And if so, can you say who committed the crime?

I am sure the answers you will give me will be in accordance with the terms of your oath, and that you will give a verdict to the best of your skill and knowledge.'

With that, at twenty-five to one, the jury asked to retire for deliberation, and were escorted by Inspector Stroud of the City Police Force to the Grand Jury Room.

At eight minutes to three the jury trooped back into the court. Smith asked, 'Have you agreed upon your verdict?' Miles, their foreman replied, 'As

INSPECTOR HERBERT STROUD WHO ATTENDED THE INQUEST
© J.B. MOODY COLLECTION

regards some of the questions we have'

'With regard to no. 1, can you say when and where Edwin Haskell died?' – 'On the night of October thirty-first in the middle bedroom of No. 40 Meadow Road.'

'What was the cause of death?' – 'Haemorrhage, by having his throat cut with a knife.'

'Was he murdered?' – 'Yes.'

'Can you say who committed the crime?' – 'We are not agreed as to who committed the murder.'

'I shall take that as an open verdict against some person unknown.'

Parr interjected, 'They must, of course, agree as to that.'

Miles responded, 'There is no agreement as to that.'

Smith advised him, 'Then you must retire again. I must have twelve men agree upon it.'

Miles, wanting clarification, asked, 'We must agree as to its being an open verdict, must we?' – 'Yes, an open verdict, or by somebody.'

As the jury left for the Grand Jury Room just after three o'clock, Miles turned to Smith and said, 'I don't think, Mr Coroner, there is much possibility of agreement.' – 'Then you will have to go to the Assizes. That's what it means.'

Parr added, 'They must adjourn to the Assizes.'

Trethowan countered, perhaps more in hope than expectation, 'Or he can discharge them.' – 'No, he cannot', snapped Parr.

Smith said, 'I will adjourn from time to time, and if they cannot agree then I must adjourn to the Assizes.' – 'Then', replied Miles, 'We must retire again.'

At four o'clock the Jury returned, and Smith asked, 'Have you agreed upon your verdict?' Miles replied, 'In answer to your fourth question, we find Mrs Haskell committed the murder, but from the evidence given as to the nature of the woman, we are convinced the crime must have been committed during a moment of temporary insanity.' Smith

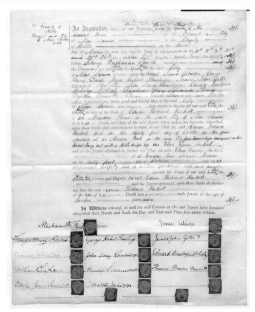

INQUEST DOCUMENT SIGNED BY THE INQUEST JURY, 1908. © *PRO*

replied 'I have no right to enquire into that'; Miles protested, 'We wish to state that.' The coroner, Miles' scruples notwithstanding, repeated the formula of the verdict of wilful murder and asked, 'That is your verdict, gentlemen?' – 'Yes, that is the verdict of twelve of the jurors.' – 'Only those who agree with the verdict must sign it', replied Smith. At this, some of the jurymen baulked at having publicly to sign the verdict, and the court was then cleared. The document recording the verdict bears the names and seals of the coroner and Asbridge, Bennett, Bingham, Cripps, Davies, Gater, Rambridge, Rawlings, Simmonds, Sly, Summers and Whaley; the doubters were James Miles, the jury's foreman, Howard Lapham and Elisha Sims. Smith then formally committed Flora for trial at the County Assizes in January, on the charge of murder. Flora was not present to hear her fate. With an exchange of compliments between coroner and counsel, the inquest was over.

9
'Not a syllable can be uttered unless the prisoner be present': the speech for the prosecution at the Magisterial hearing, Monday 30 November.

NO SOONER had the inquest been concluded than Flora's trial before the Magistrates commenced. The fact that on a majority verdict the inquest had found that Teddy had been murdered, and by her hand, did not make of the magisterial hearing a mere formality. If anything the trial would be a sterner test of her mettle, if only because, as the *Salisbury Times* explained, it had, in its entirety, to take place in her presence. The case began relatively late at 11.15 a.m. on Monday 30 November, perhaps because Flora had had to come all the way from Devizes by car, and even so she had a careworn and weary air about her as Constable John Tucker and a female attendant escorted her into the court. There she was allowed to take her place not in the dock but in a chair below it, beside her solicitor William Trethowan, with whom she would confer frequently. The concern for Flora's emotional and physical frailty was not misplaced, as, during Prosecuting Counsel's opening address she again collapsed.

The Bench before whom the case was heard comprised the new mayor, Tom Perkins in the chair, his predecessor Robert Hall, Samuel Atkins and John Folliott. As in the later stages of the inquest T.H. Parr was the prosecuting counsel and, in the words of the *Salisbury Times*, he 'conducted the case . . . with conspicuous ability and fairness, while the prisoner's

interests were zealously watched' by Trethowan. Also there were the three senior police officers Richardson, Stephens and Dew. As with the inquest there was no shortage of spectators, 'particularly of women, who occupied the large balcony.' And so the stage was set for a compelling drama, of which the opening act was Parr's speech, a disquisition as lucid as it was persuasive, which took practically the two hours before the lunchtime recess, and which was listened to with the silence of concentrated attention.

'May it please the bench, I appear on behalf of the Director of Public Prosecutions to prosecute in this case, and I am very glad to know that the prisoner is defended by Mr Trethowan. Her interests throughout this inquiry are in safe hands, and one feels that they will be ably looked after. The charge against this woman is that on the night of October thirty-first she wilfully murdered Edwin Richard Haskell, her only son, a boy twelve years old. And before I come to the facts of this case, may I say this? We are here entering upon an entirely independent inquiry. We are bound to put out of our minds anything we may have heard that has happened elsewhere, either at the Inquest, or anywhere else — anything we have seen in the newspapers, or any comments we may have heard passed upon this case in the ordinary private conversation of the man in the street. I know this intimation of mine is not necessary, but at the same time one feels bound, when approaching a serious charge of this sort, to take care that these proceedings are properly guarded and are absolutely independent of anything that has taken place. We are entering upon an inquiry which must of necessity last some time. It will no doubt be a severe tax upon the time of the Court, but one is sure with an important case of this kind that the time and trouble which must be expended upon it will be freely given by the tribunal which I am now addressing.

'The murder is alleged to have taken place at a home known as No. 40, Meadow Road. There, there lived alone at the time of the murder, the accused woman and her only son. She was a widow. Her husband had died five or six years before. The boy was a cripple owing to some tubercular disease, and his leg had been amputated some five or six years ago. He was known generally to his friends and the neighbours as 'Teddy Haskell', and he seems to have been a popular little fellow with all his playmates and in spite of the infirmity from which he suffered he seems to have taken part in games and so on, and always seemed a cheerful, happy child. The woman earned her livelihood by taking in laundry work, and I may say at once that at any rate up to the time of the murder there can, I think, be little doubt that she had always treated this child as far as the neighbours and acquaintances knew with the greatest of care and the greatest of affection. There is one other circum-stance I must mention because it is important in a case of this kind that all the environment and surroundings pointing to the position of the woman at the time should be fully known. I don't think, when you have heard the evidence there will be much doubt that she was at the time contemplating marriage with a man of the name of Mold, a steward on the *Adriatic*, and upon that point very little evidence, but some evidence, will be placed in due course before you.

'Now I come to the description of the house in which I have said the woman and her boy lived alone. It is a six-roomed house. It is approached downstairs by the front door in Meadow Road. You then go along a narrow passage, and on your right, soon after entering the front door, is the front room.

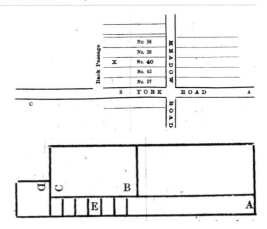

DIAGRAMS OF THE STREETS SURROUNDING 40 MEADOW ROAD AND THE GROUND FLOOR PLAN OF THE HOUSE, PUBLISHED IN THE DEVIZES GAZETTE, 1909.
© DEVIZES & WILTSHIRE GAZETTE

You then go on a little further, and you come to a door leading to a passage into the kitchen. You enter from the kitchen into the scullery by a door which communi-cated between these two rooms. From the scullery there is a door leading into the back of the house. The staircase leads up with no turn at all in it till you get onto a landing at the top. You then turn sharply to the right, and there is a door leading to into a bedroom which is generally called the middle room, where the murder was undoubtedly committed by someone. Leaving the house by the back door you go through a little garden and come to a wicket-gate which leads into a passage running into York Road. There was communication to next door, by means of that passage, so that people going into No. 38 could easily get round that way to the back of no. 40.

'I ought to say here that a light is thrown upon the front of No.40 from a street lamp, the position of which will be proved to you to be almost exactly opposite No. 40. I think I shall be able to prove it has fifty candle power of incandescent gas.' Parr then sketched the geography of the neighbourhood, adding 'I feel no need to go into the matter at great length, because I am addressing a bench of magistrates who probably know the locality. I call [your] attention to the position of St Paul's Church, because some evidence will turn on it. Some of the witnesses passed near it along St Paul's Road, and another point is that the church clock was heard to strike by some of the witnesses in this case.' Counsel also explained that he would place before the bench nine or ten photographs of the street, the house and the position of the furniture and things in the bedroom as they were when the killing took place. 'Now', Parr continued, 'I come to the facts of the case itself. The boy was undoubtedly murdered on that Saturday night between about ten seventeen or ten twenty, and ten thirty. He was murdered in that middle bedroom.

'At nine o'clock Alfred John Noble, who lives at No. 38 next door, saw the little boy. I think he was the last person who ever saw that little boy alive. The boy left him to go home to supper. About half an hour afterwards, at five and twenty to ten, the accused woman went by the back door and round the back way to Alfred Noble's to take home the week's washing. She saw Alfred Noble, and for a few minutes had a conversation with him about going to look at a house. It appears to have been an ordinary conversation and, certainly, at that time, as far as Alfred Noble was concerned there appears to have been nothing to attract his attention – nothing the matter with the woman, which leads me to suppose that she was not to her usual spirits. At a quarter to ten a girl called Gertrude Steer, who lives at No. 36 with her parents, two doors off and on the same side of the street, called with a jacket she had been making for Mrs Haskell. She came in from the back way, from that passage in York Road. She does not remember whether the back door was then locked or not. She came into the kitchen and noticed some things on the table. The accused woman tried the jacket on, and she was then dressed, as the girl will tell you, in a light cotton blouse and a dark skirt which were undoubtedly the same things she was wearing immediately after the murder had been committed. Gertrude Steer did not see or hear anything of the boy Teddy. Probably at that time he was in bed, and possibly he was asleep. There was, of course, ample time since nine o'clock for the boy and the woman to have had supper and for the boy to have been put to bed by her. Gertrude Steer stayed there about ten minutes and she then left to meet someone at the Great Western Railway Station from Warminster somewhere about ten. She got there just about ten.

From that time, for about seventeen or twenty minutes there was an interval.

'About ten seventeen or ten twenty a boy called Wyatt, who is employed at the Co-operative Stores arrived at the house. He had left the Stores after they had closed at ten o'clock. He left about five minutes past ten on a bicycle, with a parcel for a Mrs Manning, who lives at No. 42 – next door to No. 40. He did not know where Mrs Manning lived, and he seems to have made one or two enquiries. He saw a woman – the only person he did see anywhere near Meadow Road – of whom he asked where Mrs Manning lived. Having found the house he knocked at No. 42. He knocked several times, but could get no answer. Mrs Manning was in bed, and then, not knowing what to do with the parcel he went next door – No. 40 – and knocked for the purpose of asking anyone who lived there to look after the parcel, and to give it to Mrs Manning. He knocked several times – certainly more than once – and the door was opened by a woman. He does not know the woman. He was unable to recognise her. He did not study her face, but there can be no doubt that the woman who opened the door was Mrs Haskell. He remembers distinctly that she unlocked the front door. In delivering the parcel he had a very short conversation with her, and he does not remember whether the door was re-locked, when he left, by the woman who had opened it. He was only there for a matter of a minute or so – possibly less. Since the Saturday evening when he cycled from the Stores, he has, I think, taken the same route on a similar evening, with similar conditions of traffic, so as to test the time it took him, and he will be able to tell you it took him just under twelve minutes, so that that would bring him to the house at somewhere about ten seventeen. There is then an interval of something like ten or twelve minutes, an interval – if the case for the prosecution is true – of the very utmost importance, because that was the time at which, according to the doctor's evidence, death undoubtedly took place. The doctor got there at about ten thirty-five, and he will tell you that death had taken place within about a quarter of an hour of that time.

'At ten thirty, the woman's little nephew, Percy Noble, who lives with his parents next door at No.

38 came to the back door up the passage from York Road. He came there for the purpose of paying back a shilling to Mrs Haskell which he had borrowed earlier in the day. That back door at that time of night appears sometimes to have been locked and sometimes to have been open. He tried to open the door, but found it locked, and he knocked twice at the door. He heard Mrs Haskell answer, apparently from the kitchen. He heard a certain noise, which he will describe, and he saw Mrs Haskell's shadow through the scullery window. The kitchen is lit by a gas jet, approximately in the centre of the kitchen, and there is a window just to the right of the scullery door. He saw the shadow caused by a figure between the gas jet and the scullery gradually lengthen as it came towards the back door. The shadow was undoubtedly that of Mrs Haskell, because she immediately opened the back door. She had been screaming just before, and she told the boy to run off for the doctor, saying something about a man having killed Teddy. He ran off down the passage into York Road. He did not see anyone moving hurriedly or running down York Road. He went off for the doctor, and he must have gone very quickly, because Dr Wilks, who lives on the Wilton Road, got there within five minutes.

'Now I come to what I may call the critical points in this case. From the evidence of very many witnesses who will be called before you, it is abundantly clear that within a few seconds after the moment at which the boy Noble had knocked at the back door Mrs

Haskell was on her front doorstep, and she only moved from it a yard or two towards Mr Steer's house. She was on her doorstep screaming 'Somebody has killed . . .' or 'Somebody has murdered my little Teddy.' It is impossible, if that statement were true – apart from the statement subsequently made by Mrs Haskell – that she could have gone upstairs after the boy knocked at the back door and before her appearance at the front door. The time is fixed in more than one way. It would probably take Mrs Haskell about the same time to appear at the front door as it would the boy Noble to appear in York Road after he had run from the back door and down the passage. The door from the scullery to the kitchen would be open and the kitchen door was probably open at that time, and therefore there was nothing to impede Mrs Haskell's progress as she passed, probably hurrriedly, from the back door to the front door. The boy, we know, was running. This is not only a question of the clock. There are several witnesses who were, at that moment, placed at various points near that house. The time is fixed by some of these witnesses by the fact not only of the clock, but by the fact that they saw the boy Noble run across the road. Those witnesses are very important witnesses for two reasons – first from the point of view of the prosecution, they prove that within a few seconds or so of the boy leaving the back door Mrs Haskell was at the front door immediately screaming 'My poor boy has been murdered' or 'Someone has murdered my Teddy', and also for another reason.

'From a statement subsequently made the same evening to people who were in the house – neighbours and so on – Mrs Haskell appears to have stated that she heard a man coming down the stairs, and as she went to the kitchen door he threw a knife at her. From a statement made later, but before her arrest, she described rather more minutely what happened at the kitchen door; that just as the boy had knocked, a man passed the door and threw something at her, a man she could not recognise, that she came back from the back door, after answering it, into the passage, and found the front door open, and that she was screaming very loudly at the front door all the time. A girl called Lily Stretch, who was coming from George Street with a young man named Primmer, with whom she was walking out that night, came from George Street into your Road, and she saw the boy run across York Road from the direction of the passage.'

And then, as she had done on three occasions during the inquest,[1] Flora fainted dead away, and had to be carried from the court. She was attended by John Armitage, MRCS, LRCP, who was in practice at 26 Endless Street, and she was away from the court for about 35 minutes. On her return Flora looked dreadful, and at Parr's kindly suggestion an armchair and some cushions were found from somewhere and 'the frail little woman was placed in it.'[2] Parr continued:

'The Bench will see the witnesses who were near the house, and who will be able to say whether Mrs Haskell was at the door immediately, and whether it is possible that anyone could have left the front door without being seen. It is only a matter of seconds, and the questions will have to be looked at very carefully as to whether or not somebody might possibly just have time to get away from the front door of No. 40. A witness who came out at once is a man called Steer who lives at No. 36. He met Mrs Haskell just between her house and his own – somewhere near Noble's front door, and she said 'Man round the corner!' He ran round the corner close by York Road, but he saw no-one running away or moving hurriedly. He only saw two men by the *Duke of York* gate. He knew one by sight and the other man he did not know, but it will be perfectly and clearly proved that these two men were Butt and Eccott. Steer, having seen these two men came back, and he was the first to go upstairs. He saw no light. When he got upstairs he was unable to see anything. He called for a lamp and one was immediately brought, and then with a man named Rawlings [*sic, i.e.* Rawlins] and Mrs Butt he went upstairs into the middle bedroom. He will describe to you in detail what he there saw – how he saw the boy lying peacefully in bed, nothing disturbed and nothing moved, but everything in order.

'He waited till the doctors came, at about twenty-five minutes to eleven – Dr Wilks and Dr Row who was staying with him. They will describe the position of the boy, the wound and so on. From their evidence I do not think there is any doubt that death was instantaneous, that the boy did not realise that he was being killed, and that, whoever committed this deed, he felt no pain. They will also explain to you how a small wound that was found on the fourth finger of one of the boy's hands, a small incised wound, was caused; they will explain to you that that was caused by an involuntary movement of the hand, that the boy felt something going up to the throat, and that this wound was caused by one movement of the instrument which caused death, that the finger would be taken away by the same involuntary movement, and that the left hand was found outside the bed, while the right hand was found inside. Just outside the landing, Mrs Butt found a small brass lamp, which was out, and which you will hear of further on. There were no marks of blood on the lamp, and if it had been used at the time the murder was committed, it must have been moved by the hand other than that which committed the deed, to account for no blood marks being on it.

'Immediately after the doctors had come, Sergeant Golding arrived, and he was the first police officer to arrive on the scene. He met the witness Steer, who had been upstairs, and Steer gave him a description of the man he had seen outside the *Duke of York*. That was a description of Eccott, as to whose identity Steer was not then clear. Golding went to the *Duke of York*, and then down to Slade's, which is a shop towards St Paul's Road, to telephone to the police station. He then came back. The prisoner appears to have been on her doorstep for a minute or so, she was only in the passage for a moment and she then went into the front room where she was sitting with several women neighbours who had come in. Some of these people had already noticed a knife lying on the threshold of the kitchen doorway close to the jamb, but they did not take it up. Golding, after telephoning, came back to the house, saw the knife, picked it up and wrapped it up in paper. He will tell you how it was lying, that there was a stain of blood under the knife, corresponding more or less with the length of the blade, and I do not think he noticed any splashes of blood anywhere near. He handed the knife to the Chief Constable. Golding and a police constable called Cutler were on duty at the bottom of the staircase, and the Chief Constable was the next important witness to arrive on the scene. He seems to have got there at five minutes to eleven. [The] prisoner was still in the front room. I do not think there is any doubt whatever that she did not then, and that she did not till a considerably later stage go upstairs.

'Chief Constable Richardson had obtained the assistance of Superintendent Stephens of the County Police, who went with him into the front room and there they saw Mrs Haskell, and she mentioned something about some money in a drawer upstairs. Richardson and Stephens went upstairs, and after some searching they found in the top left-hand drawer of a chest of drawers, in the folds of a double cloth, three pounds ten shillings in gold. There were no marks of blood whatever on that particular drawer, either on the china knob or inside the drawer, but there was observable something very important with regard to the lock. At the time Richardson and Stephens first saw it, the lock, which had only been fixed by tin tacks, was hanging at a slight angle, so that the lock, which was then thrown and would have been locked if it had been in position, was free. It was hanging, as I have said, by only one tin-tack, the head of which was off. One tin-tack was still in position, with its head on, and it appears, from attempts which have been made since, that the eye will not go over that tin tack. It may be that it has some projections which prevent it going on, especially if any pressure has been applied. It is rather a curious thing that one is not able to see the explanation of. Inside the drawer were two tin-tacks, and also the head of the tin-tack by which the lock was then hanging. I think it quite right to say at once that the very least possible force applied to the handle of the drawer would have opened it, and I don't think it would have made any great noise.

'Having found this money in the drawer, the police officers did not at once go down to Mrs Haskell, because it was the first time they had been in the room, and they had to make a careful examination of it, and of the house and premises, and you will hear the details of that examination, and where they found marks of blood. I do not want to go into it in detail, but I must for the purposes of the Bench understanding the case deal with the position of these marks. Just by the side of the bed were some spots of blood, and at the foot of the bed were several spots, and outside on the landing, where Mrs Butt found the brass lamp, were one or two more spots of blood. There were blood marks on the right-hand wall as you go down the stairs on the paper, and there was the stain I have already referred to at the threshold of the kitchen door where the knife was found. There were no marks of blood from the end of the passage to the front door, and there were no marks of blood on the front door. There were no blood marks at all found at a subsequent examination of the scullery, or on the door leading into the scullery, or the sink, or anywhere there. That is the general result of the very careful examination made by Richardson and Stephens that night.

'After they had made that examination they came back again to Mrs Haskell, who gave to the Chief Constable a description of a man who called for lodgings the night before, and to whom I shall refer later on. No description was given to him of the man who she afterwards said passed her, because she did not recognise him. She gave a description of a man who had called the night before. That description was circulated, and that was followed up by every possible investigation. Enquiries were made at the railway station, trains were watched and search parties were organised in the neighbourhood in which many people seem to have taken part, and some of the witnesses who will be called took part in it, but nobody was found. I desire to say that if any appreciable time elapsed I think there would be very little difficulty in a neighbourhood of that sort of a man being able to conceal himself. At the same time no-one was seen that night either entering or leaving the house. The doctors who had been in the house some time left to get a draught for Mrs Haskell who was in a hysterical condition and required some medicine.

'They did not come back until about eleven thirty and I do not think it was until that time that Mrs Haskell expressed any wish at all to go upstairs. She certainly had not gone upstairs when the doctors came back a second time. Here again will be a matter of consideration as to why that was. I want to put it quite fairly both ways. If she really believed that the boy had been murdered by someone it may be that there was a natural reluctance on her part to go up. That may be, but at the same time, as I have already pointed out, you find her drawing a conclusion at once from this little incident which took place at the kitchen door, that the boy had been murdered. You find she never went upstairs to see whether the little boy had been killed or not, but you see her outside saying somebody had murdered him. There are two ways of looking at the position taken up by Mrs Haskell. She did go upstairs after the doctors came a second time. Dr Wilks, naturally and very kindly, thought the sight would not be a pleasant one for the mother, and steps were taken to clear the room up, to make the room presentable by removing the blood and so on. When she went upstairs, her mother, Mrs Carter, who had come into the house, also went upstairs. Dr Wilks was with her and she touched nothing in the room. She came into contact with no blood. She merely kissed the little boy once and came straight downstairs.'

Flora, as on several occasions during the inquest, burst into tears, shaking uncontrollably with sobs for some time. Conscious of the distress his address was causing her, Parr lowered his voice as he continued. 'At about half-past three, the matter of the drawer cropped up again. Richardson and Stephens had found the money directly they went up, but it was necessary for them to make an examination of the house, and having seen what they saw in the room it was quite natural that they should go off to give directions to the police, and not trouble themselves any further with what had been found in the drawer. We find Mrs Haskell, not having had her question answered as to whether any money had been taken from the drawers, asking Sergeant Golding, who was on duty in the house, about the drawer. He went up and brought the drawer down, and satisfied her that there was only three pounds ten shillings in it. So the night went on. I am not going into all the details of the conversation of these women, a great many of whom were in the house. I propose merely to deal with the material incidents of the night, taking them one by one.

'I have already referred to the knife picked up by Golding. That knife was subsequently examined by Mr Pepper. It had been recently sharpened, and there

were several marks of blood on the handle, evidently caused by a hand with blood on it. The blade was generally smeared, and there were some round spots on it, and some marks running vertically near the back of the blade. The sharpening was distinctly seen through the film of blood on it. I do not think there can be any doubt whatever in this case that death had been caused by the use of that knife. And here I desire to say that the question arose as to who that knife belonged to. There was no concealment as to that whatever by Mrs Haskell. Immediately the question was asked as to whether she had missed a knife, she and her mother looked about and found that a knife was missing from one of the drawers, and subsequently, when making a statement to the police officers, before her arrest, this knife was shown to her, and she said it was the one that was missing, the one which the boy had been sharpening on the Thursday before, and she had not seen it since. I think it fair to point out that that was so, and at any rate there doesn't seem to have been any attempt on Mrs Haskell's part to conceal the fact that a knife was missing from the house. The whetstone on which the knife might have been sharpened was subsequently found at the back of the premises.

'Another matter I have to call attention to, which may be of considerable importance on this night was the matter of the tablecloth. The girl Steer, at a quarter to ten, had noticed the supper things on the table. Golding, when he came back, noticed the tablecloth with some crockery on it. When he came in the third time, the table had been cleared, and Mrs Carter, the prisoner's mother, very naturally put away the cups and saucers which had been used by some people, or possibly used earlier for supper. At about eleven thirty a man called Rawlings, who was in the house, noticed marks of blood on the tablecloth on the edge of the top of the kitchen table on the side nearest the staircase door. You will see the cloth and hear all that is to be said about it. They were noticed also by Mrs Sweetman in the same position, and her evidence is very much the same as that of Rawlings. They were not noticed by any of the police who were there. Chief Constable Richardson and Super-intendent Stephens did not, as far as I can understand, examine any further than the doorway going out into the kitchen. They did not then examine the kitchen and scullery, but merely the passage and outside. Rawlings and Mrs Sweetman do not appear to have remembered about this, or to have said anything about it, at any rate to the police, till the end of the last week, but when that information did reach the police, the police who had been in possession of the house since Mrs Haskell's arrest (and indeed before her arrest, a police officer was, with Mrs Haskell's approval, left at the house) made a search in the house, and they found in a drawer in the kitchen a tablecloth with blood upon it.

'That tablecloth will be shown to Rawlings and Mrs Sweetman, and you will hear what they say about it. How were these marks made on the tablecloth? Were they made after Mrs Haskell had appeared at her front door and after she had been seen that evening, or were they made by anyone carrying something which might have had blood on it, and quite legitimately carrying it from the bedroom to the wash-house? Were they made either by the doctors, who might have had some blood on their hands and might have gone into the scullery to wash them? On that I shall be able to place evidence before you. You will hear from the doctors that the marks on the tablecloth could not possibly have been made by them because they washed their hands upstairs. You will hear also that they were seen before the doctors came in their second visit, and before any washing took place in the bedroom, before the witness who attended to this matter had taken up the cloths and water to the bedroom and had brought them back through the kitchen. It is a matter for your very careful consideration as to how those marks on the tablecloth could possibly have been caused.

'The blouse which Mrs Haskell was wearing that evening was noticed by several witnesses that evening – there was no concealment about it – to have a certain number of blood spots on it, not only by witnesses other than the police, but by the police themselves, and by Dr Wilks. It was subsequently taken off and handed to the police. That was a light cotton blouse, on which marks were easily noticed. She had on also a skirt of dark material, which will be produced. On that dark skirt it would be very

difficult to notice bloodstains without a close examination. No-one certainly appears to have noticed any bloodstains on the skirt that evening, and one of the questions that arises is whether the woman herself knew that evening that there were any bloodstains on the skirt she was wearing. There was no blood on her hands when she was first seen by neighbours.

'A handkerchief with blood on it was seen when she was in the front room. While she was in the front room Mrs Cooper, Mrs Butt and Mrs Sweetman noticed a handkerchief in her hand. It was a handkerchief which had a considerable amount of blood on it, and no doubt that handkerchief was in that room soon after the murder had been committed. There was, on Mrs Haskell's nose, a small scratch. It was not then bleeding, but was a recent scratch and it was seen by several people, and the same explanation was given by Mrs Haskell to Superintendent Stephens and Mrs Sweetman, in which she said that she cut it with her ring on the previous Thursday. It was also clear that the boy had a small abrasion on the left ear, caused by knocking it against a clothes peg at school a day or two before. Evidence as to the nature of the scar will be given by Dr Kempe. Two other handkerchiefs were subsequently found with bloodstains on them in a copper at the back by Chief Inspector Dew who had been sent down from Scotland Yard to assist the Chief Constable and Superintendent Stephens in this case. There were three handkerchiefs on the premises with a considerable amount of blood on them. It may be that the handkerchiefs in the copper had been used by the boy, and that accounts for the blood on them. A certain amount of blood had come from the ear, and if he had scratched it, it would bleed again, and if he had used the handkerchiefs, that no doubt might account for the blood on them. It appears to be a little more difficult to account for the blood which was on the handkerchief in the front room, where Mrs Haskell was seen after the murder. You will hear evidence as to that handkerchief.

'Mrs Haskell was not wearing any apron that night. She could not have been wearing an apron if these blood marks on the skirt were caused by anything that happened that night because the apron, which later she said she was wearing, was found to have no blood on it. It could not possibly have been in position on her at the time the blood marks were produced on the dark skirt. Another matter of importance which took place in the house on that night was that several statements were made by Mrs Haskell to several witnesses as to a man coming for lodgings on the Friday night. I think she said something about it to Mrs Cooper, Mrs Steer and Dr Wilks, and it was in consequence of that that the description was circulated by the police. It is important to remember that that was said by Mrs Haskell almost directly after this terrible affair had happened upstairs. The night drew on, and it was getting towards morning when it was suggested to Mrs Haskell and her mother should leave the house and go to some friends. She appears to have wished to stay, and some bedding was arranged for her in the front room downstairs. As I have already said, the Chief Constable left an officer in charge of the rooms with the full approval of Mrs Haskell.

'We then get to the early morning of the next day, Sunday, November first. Sergeant Golding, who was in charge of the premises, was still there, till at six o'clock in the morning. At that time the floor of the passage leading to the front door, the kitchen door and the kitchen were washed over by Mrs Carter, the prisoner's mother. They seem to have been washed over in the ordinary way, with a wet rag, dipped into a bucket of cold water, and rubbed over the floor, and then wiped after the rag had been squeezed out. I have referred to this because it may be that some importance may hereafter be attached to it. It could not have been anything in the nature of a scrubbing, because the linoleum on which the knife was, was afterwards very carefully examined by Mr Pepper, the consulting expert to the Home Office, and he, I think, is clear on this point, that the blood marks on the linoleum in the kitchen doorway show no signs whatever of having been interfered with by any washing or scrubbing. And he will tell you there were no marks of any smears away from the knife mark, which must have been shown if that spot had been vigorously rubbed by anybody with a view to removing the blood. It may be a little unfortunate that this washing took place at all, but there it is,

and that is how the matter stands. And in that connection it is important to remember that, after all, long before six o'clock that Sunday morning, at the earliest opportunity the night before, a very careful examination had been made by the Chief Constable and Superintendent Stephens, so that they will be able to give you, to the best of their recollection, the actual result of the examination of the house before the washing on the Sunday.

'The Chief Constable had sent up for Chief Inspector Dew, and he arrived on the Sunday. I desire here to say how grateful the city ought to be for the untiring labours which have been expended on this case ever since the night of the murder, not only by the Chief Constable, but by Superintendent Stephens and also Chief Inspector Dew. I do not wish to prevent the defence from making any legitimate criticisms on the conduct of the police, but I do say this, that they have devoted an enormous amount of time and sacrificed an enormous amount of sleep in their efforts to clear up the case. All three made a careful examination of the premises on the Sunday, and subsequent examinations by Mr Pepper, who came down from London to examine the premises on the eighth.

'One thing that is quite clear is that the boy was lying rather on the side of the bed close to the chest of drawers. At the time when the knife was passed across the throat there was an arterial spurting of blood to the left. There was no arterial spurting of blood to the right, but there was a spray of blood projecting to the right, not from an artery, but projected by the air from the windpipe which was severed. That is manifest, because on the wall between the bed and the chest of drawers there were some spots of blood. On the cushion on the chair there was some blood and on the right-hand side of the chair were some spots of blood. The medical evidence is conclusive that they were caused by the spray of blood from the windpipe. The spots at the foot of the bed, on the landing outside and the marks going down the stairs were caused by blood dropping from the hand when the assailant left the house. The marks on the wall going downstairs were probably caused by a person, possibly stumbling and jerking the knife. It is important to observe that there were no marks of blood found on the floor at the threshold of the kitchen doorway except where the knife lay. There were no marks of blood on the door itself or on the adjacent woodwork or the adjacent wall. In the kitchen there were no marks. There was a sink in the scullery with a tap in working order. In the bedroom there were no marks of a knife being laid down unless it were laid down where there was a mass of blood on the pillow close to the boy's head. It certainly had not been laid down anywhere else.

'On the Sunday when Dew came down, and the following days, the police made all possible enquiries for the purpose of tracing anyone who might have left the home, and they also took statements from witnesses who could throw light on the matter. These enquiries were made to assist Mrs Haskell, and from the time of the murder down to her arrest I do not think there can be any doubt that she was treated by Mr Richardson, Mr Stephens and Mr Dew with every possible consideration.' After reading to the court some extracts from Flora's statements, Parr continued. 'The skirt and blouse she had been wearing were carefully examined by Dr Kempe, the divisional surgeon, on the following Tuesday, and he found, in addition to the marks on the blouse, a quantity of blood on the skirt, and following the report which came from the doctor, Mrs Haskell was arrested on a charge of murder, but to that charge she only at the time said 'No, no!' There was no reason, if she still wished to put forward the same account of what had happened, that she should say anything else. She had given the fullest statement to the police, and I attach no importance to the fact that she just said 'No, no.'

'After she was arrested the skirt and blouse were very carefully examined by Mr Pepper, and the result of his examination is a matter of the very gravest importance in this case. On the light blouse twenty-eight spots were found on the right front, and on the sleeve about fifty, reaching on the sleeve from within about an inch of the yoke to about an inch and a half of the free part of the wrist. They were small, rounded spots, very widely scattered. On the skirt were about nineteen blood marks, and some of these were rounded. Those were the ones on the upper part of the skirt. The other spots on the skirt, lower down,

were mostly of an elongated character, elongated in a vertical direction straight down – one of them, one and a half inches down. On the front of the skirt was an irregular smear about five inches long, and among the spots on the sleeve is one very characteristic spot with two little lines on it, showing, in Mr Pepper's opinion, that the blood went in an upward direction. The marks on the blouse and the upper part of the skirt must obviously have been sprayed or sprinkled on by some means. Those on the lower part of the skirt were caused by blood dropping down the front of the skirt. Was the prisoner's explanation of how this blood got on her a true one? Could these marks have been caused by something thrown at her at the kitchen door, or anything thrown down at the kitchen door? Was anything thrown down except the knife? Was the object thrown a knife, and a knife only?

'The knife – if it was the knife with which the murder was committed – must have been brought down from the bedroom. There would, no doubt, be a certain amount of blood on the knife. The knife would be closely gripped and you would not get very much blood inside the hand. You would get some on some parts. We know these spots of blood had been dropped from some object and there were some of them from the room right down the stairs and on the wall. By the time the knife got to the kitchen door a considerable amount of blood must have dropped off and to some extent the amount of liquid blood must have been exhausted. We have found, as I have pointed out, no marks on the floor, but on that point you must bear in mind this subsequent washing by Mrs Carter. It is very important that we found no marks of blood on the door itself, on the kitchen door or on the adjacent woodwork. Putting all these facts together, the deliberate opinion of Mr Pepper, the medical expert in this case, as to the possible throwing of the knife accounting for the seventy-eight marks of blood on the blouse and the marks on the skirt is one which must meet with the very greatest consideration.

'That she was wearing an apron, as she said she was at the time, must be impossible. It might be possible that not knowing of the marks of blood on the skirt she might have thought she was wearing an apron at the time. That might be so: one has to look at all the possibilities, but at the same time one must remember that it is quite possible that she did not at that moment realise the amount of blood which might be found on the skirt. That the knife hit her body when it was thrown is almost impossible, because there were no aggregate marks. If the marks on the blouse and skirt were not caused by the throwing of a knife at her, what is the explanation? She never went upstairs except under the circumstances I have already referred to when she only touched the boy and nothing else. How did the blood get on to the blouse and skirt? That is a question of the utmost importance and on the answer to this question depends the ultimate issue of this case. We know where the assailant must have been standing, between the bed and the chest of drawers. He or she must have been in a direct line of spray projected from the windpipe of the boy as he lay in bed. Is it consistent or is it not that the marks on the blouse and on the upper part of the skirt could have been caused by the spray so projected? On that point you will hear the medical opinion of Mr Pepper and the other doctors in this case.

'As to the lower part of the skirt, is it possible that all that blood was caused by a knife being thrown at her? If it was not so caused was it caused by a knife held in the hand parallel with the skirt and dropping blood on the skirt as the wearer of it passed the table? If Mrs Haskell's explanation is true, the assailant never went into the kitchen at all. If the tablecloth was on the table, if these marks were caused at the time of the commission of the crime, how did they get there? Another question which the tribunal – which I suppose must ultimately decide this case – will have to answer is this: did they [the marks on the tablecloth] get there from someone with some soft material in their hands covered with blood passing along the kitchen doorway between [it and] the scullery, and in so passing along, smeared the tablecloth with blood, and one or two drops of blood dropped onto the table. Passing for what purpose? Was it for the purpose of washing the hands in the scullery, where there was a sink and a tap and cold water available and a towel? There was a jack towel hanging there, but there are no marks of blood on it, and the hands might have been wiped on it after they

had been thoroughly washed if they were not wiped on something else which has not been found. These are grave questions arising out of the explanation which has been given by Mrs Haskell. If that explanation is not true as regards the possibility of the blood marks on the clothes having been caused that way, does it bear investigation from other points of view?

'How came the mother to jump at the conclusion that her boy upstairs had been killed when she only sees a man run away and throwing something at her which she doesn't know the nature of, and why does she send the little nephew for the doctor? What are the probabilities? Would a mother in these circum-stances go to the back door where someone was knocking, to answer perhaps a casual messenger, before she either pursued the man out into the street or went upstairs to see what had happened or, if you like, call upstairs loudly to the boy to know if he was all right? Why allow the little boy to run off down the passage when the man – if a man was there at all – was obviously running away from the front?

'Take the case, if you like, for a moment on the hypothesis that someone who nobody saw go into the house, and someone who nobody saw leaving the house, but who somehow had got in for the purpose of robbery – of robbing a woman earning a precarious living from laundry work, robbing her of money of which she said no-one knew the existence except herself, her mother and the boy Teddy. How did he know of the existence of money in the house? How did he become possessed of the knife which was sometimes kept in the kitchen and sometimes in the backyard? If for robbery, did the robbery take place before the murder? On the left-hand drawer there isn't a trace of blood – not a trace! There are no drops of blood between the bed up towards the right of the drawer, which would have been caused after leaving the bed if the assailant had gone to the chest of drawers for the purpose of examining it. I have already said that a very slight pull might open the drawer. There was nothing disarranged in the room. There were no signs of disturbance, everything was tidy, no disorder. The drawer was closed when it was found by the police, and, still stranger, the sum of three pounds ten shillings in gold was still lying in the drawer with no signs of disturbance. Is it possible that the three pounds ten shillings escaped the notice of the robber? Is it likely?

'If a robbery was committed it must have been committed, one would think, before the murder, otherwise one has to suppose that the knife which certainly caused no blood marks must have been laid down on the bed, and means must have been taken in order to prevent any blood dropping off the right hand onto the drawer, or the whole of the opening must have been done with the left hand. Take the hypothesis, the only possible one, that the robbery took place before the murder. Then how and why was the boy murdered? What occasion was there for anyone to murder the boy in his sleep? – because that boy had made no conscious movement before he was murdered. If the robber had already attained his object he could easily have got away from that room. Whoever was in that room was certainly not hurried or disturbed. The lamp had been carefully placed outside. The whole thing shows signs of deliberation which one would hardly have found in a case of a robber entering a house for the purpose of robbery. With regard to the question of whether there was ever more than three pounds, ten shillings in gold in that drawer on that night before the murder, it may be that in the course of this case some evidence will be forthcoming which I shall be able to place before you.

'It may be that a man did come for lodgings on the Friday night. There is nothing unusual about that if he did. It was known that someone had stayed there. This man Mold, who was on the most affectionate terms with the family, had stayed there, and as far as I know had slept there by himself in the front room. It might have been imagined by a stranger that the room was to let. One doesn't know. There is nothing unusual or wonderful in a man having come there for lodgings the previous night. And with regard to a man asking the boy for his name and address there is nothing extraordinary in that. He

may have wanted, out of kindness to this poor cripple, to give him some money, or some little present. But that isn't the important thing. The important thing is whether, if this incident happened, it was used by Mrs Haskell for the foundation of the story which was subsequently told. I have dealt with the question as to whether the explanation Mrs Haskell gave can, under the circumstances, be accepted, or whether it has been absolutely destroyed. All these questions I have asked must, I submit, be answered by the tribunal which has to draw the proper inference from these facts.

'As to the motive there may have been in this case, if the deed was done by Mrs Haskell and the prosecution were a true one, that again is a question for a jury, knowing all the circumstances, knowing all her environment, to draw such proper inferences with regard to motive as they may think fit. It is not necessary in a case of wilful murder for the prosecution to prove any motive at all. The commission of the deed is the establishment of a case of wilful murder as far as the prosecution is concerned. It has been said that there is no adequate motive, no really logical motive, that can possibly exist. I felt it my duty in opening this case to deal with the facts, summarising them as far as I was able, having regard to the enormous amount of evidence which will be given in this case. I felt it my duty, particularly as the prisoner is defended, to point out the kind of questions which will have to be answered before the truth in this case can be arrived at. That duty has not been a pleasant one, and in the discharge of it I have had to make comments of weight with regard to the inference which must be drawn from all these facts. I submit, before I sit down, that the prosecution, on the facts which will be given in evidence before you, will have established a *prima facie* case, on which it will be your duty, and on which the only course open to you, will be to commit this woman for trial on a charge of wilful murder.'

10

'Easier for a man to inflict the wound than a woman': evidence at the Magisterial hearing, Monday 30 November-Saturday 5 December 1908

WITH PARR'S ELOQUENT ADDRESS ringing in their ears the court adjourned for lunch, and for the afternoon session Flora resumed her place in the armchair at the foot of the dock. Again the public gallery was full, peopled, as the *Salisbury Times* primly commented, with 'the class that, somehow, always finds leisure for proceedings of this sort' – two long rows of women with a scattering of men, a police constable by the entrance. By agreement between Parr and Trethowan, witnesses, with the exception of the police and medical experts, were kept out of the court unless actually giving evidence. But as at the inquest, their depositions were recorded in longhand, surviving to this day in over a hundred pages in the National Archives.

And so the witnesses appeared, in rather a different order from that of the inquest, beginning with Notley, the Assistant City Surveyor. His plan of the house and yard had measurements, furniture and bloodstains on it, and he laid before the court a mass of data which, as the *Salisbury Times* reported, 'uninterpreted, puzzled the listeners, but which, undoubtedly, when taken together, will provide a circumstantial account of the movements of somebody, whoever it may be, whose trail is marked in blood'. Notley also produced a plan which showed that there was a street light of fifty candle-power directly opposite Flora's house, which shone through

the fanlight over the door, lighting the hallway for seven feet, but not reaching the stairs at all. Notley's testimony lasted over an hour, and not much less time was given to Horace Charles Messer.

One of Salisbury's seven professional photographers, and active from the late nineteenth century until just after the Great War, Messer operated from 29 Castle Street, opposite the recently built Post Office and today the home of Purple Life, selling mobile telephone accessories. He advertised 'Wedding, family, cricket, football and all kinds of groups photographed – distance no object.' Among his more widely known collective portraits is one taken of the 127 members of the Salisbury Philharmonic Society in 1896 and another of the City Police Force in 1905, from which individual portraits have been taken for this book. Apart from his studio and peripatetic photography and technical work, Messer was one of Salisbury's five photographic dealers: his advertisement in Brown's Directory of 1912 claimed "We carry the largest stock of Kodak cameras, films, plates and everything necessary for photography in the district – developing, printing, etc. for amateurs." Today Messer is remembered for a little illustrated history of the city called *The graphic guide to Salisbury*, published in the Edwardian era, and for a souvenir guide to the 1902 Coronation celebrations in the city, as well as numerous picture postcards of Salisbury and environs. In the

FLORA HASKELL'S BEDROOM TAKEN BY HORACE
MESSER SHORTLY AFTER THE MURDER, 1908
© *Timothy W. Frank Walker and Ann Richardson Whittle,*
grandchildren of Frank Richardson, Chief Constable.

magistrates' and assize trials of Flora Haskell his contribution was to present and speak to thirteen large prints of photographs inside the house and in its immediate environs. The *Salisbury Times* observed somewhat tartly that they were of 'places decidedly uninteresting but for their connection with this extraordinary case having turned the camera upon them.'

Just after four o'clock the court adjourned for tea, and Walter Steer was called to give evidence on his part in the events of October 31st. His testimony took the whole of the evening session. The following morning, Tuesday 1 December, Steer was cross-examined by Trethowan. He described how, after the doctors had washed their hands in Teddy's bedroom, he had brought down the pail of bloody water and the bloodstained cloths, taking them through the kitchen in the gap between the table and the wall next to the stairs, to empty the pail into the sink and to rinse the cloths in several changes of water. Trethowan asked, 'What for?' — 'To wash the blood out.'

Counsel's questioning now followed a new tack, one not thoroughly pursued hitherto. 'Do you know that Teddy's leg was constantly discharging blood?' — 'I have heard that the wound was an obstinate one, and would not heal properly.' Trethowan resumed his inquiry into the night of the murder, and asked about Flora. Steer answered that he saw her three times that night, but did not notice any blood on her hands. Asked by her whether Teddy was all right, Steer did not say what he had found, and, out of

kindness, dissuaded her from going upstairs. Steer also spoke of Golding picking up the knife, adding that he thought he saw the constable put the knife into his pocket.

Edward Butt and William Eccott, the men at the *Duke of York* were next to testify, describing how Steer had appeared in York Road, and immediately afterwards they had heard screaming coming from the direction of Meadow Road. Steer had stated in his evidence to the coroner's inquest that he had come across two men outside the *Duke of York*. But Eccott now said that he came out of the public house and straight into the yard to the side, and therefore could *not* have been one of the pair whom Steer claimed to have seen, even though Steer had identified him in court! The consequence was that when Eccott joined in the search for the presumed killer he was the object of that exercise. As Trethowan now said to him, 'You didn't realise that you were looking for a man of the same description as yourself? — 'No.'

'You didn't *know* you were looking for yourself, did you?' — 'No.'

'What description was given to you of the man?' — 'No description at all. We were only looking for a strange man.'

Alfred Noble senior again testified to his sister-in-law bringing the week's consignment of washing round at twenty-five to ten in the evening of October 31st, and discussing the possibility of her taking another house. The questioning turned to Teddy's health: Noble knew, he said, that the wound at the boy's hip was constantly discharging blood.

Gertrude Steer told of Flora's light-hearted remark, "I *shall* be a toff tomorrow!", barely half an hour before the murder was estimated to have taken place. Under cross-examination she said that she did not notice any bloodstains on Flora's blouse, and also confirmed that there were no bloodstains on the tablecloth at that time, adding that she thought she would have noticed them had there been any.

Wyatt, the draper's apprentice, was called, and his evidence as to timing was crucial in light of the doctors' best estimate of the moment of death at around 10.20. He repeated that he left the stores at 10.05 to take a parcel of boots to Mrs Manning of Meadow Road. He took, by reference to subsequent timed journeys, twelve minutes to arrive at Meadow Road, but, not finding anyone at home at No. 42, he left the parcel next door at No. 40, where it was taken in by a woman whom, as at the inquest, he did not recognise. Nevertheless, when asked by Trethowan whether he noticed any blood on Flora's hands, Wyatt replied that he did not; by way of confirmation, Parr handed to Trethowan the parcel's brown paper wrapping, perfectly clean.

Rosa Manning, on whose behalf Flora had taken in the boots, gave evidence of their conversation some four months previously about an offer of marriage from a young steward on the *Adriatic*, whom Flora did not name. The offer was one which according to Flora "took a lot of thinking about, and if I ever remarry I will always work and keep little Teddy." 'Did you take the conversation seriously?' asked counsel. 'I did – I thought it was meant.' Rosa also took the opportunity to add that she had received her new pair of boots only last Sunday – four weeks after they had been delivered to her neighbour. Parr apologised for the inconvenience, unavoidable as it was, to which she had been put.

Then came a new witness, Mrs Emma Louisa Lodge, of 20 Meadow Road. The last of the witnesses at the previous Thursday's session of the inquest, Edwin Daniels, had testified to seeing, between 10.00 and 10.30, a figure shuffling along Meadow Road and into York Road, dressed in light clothing and moving briskly with their head held low. It transpired that it could have been she whom Daniels had seen, as she, in her white pinafore, covering her from top to toe, had walked briskly from Meadow Road to the *Duke of York* with a jug in her hand. She now testified that on October 31 she 'went marketing', and came back at about 10 p.m. After a few minutes, she went out again, to Alfred Uphill's shop, 36 Sidney Street, and then on to the *Duke of York*. She testified that she walked straight down Meadow Road, and round by Mrs Cooper's house, no. 27, which is on the corner of Meadow Road and York Road,[1] *en route* for the public house – implying that she had walked back along Sidney Street from Uphill's and past her own front door. Just before she reached the *Duke of York* she heard the church clock strike the quarter-hour. Trethowan, cross-examining, asked,

'Did you shuffle along?' – 'No: I am in the habit of walking quickly, but I don't shuffle along'

'And you don't scramble along at a half-trot?' – 'No.'

'Nor with your head down?' – 'No.' She added that she was carrying a jug at the time and did not see Daniels. Trethowan asked, 'Who suggested to you that you might have had an apron on that night?' – 'I did myself.'

'You weren't trying to hide your head, as you went by, so that people should not know who you were?' – 'No, sir.' Mrs Lodge added that she did not see anyone in Meadow Road between York Road and St Paul's Road.

Alfred Noble junior told of Flora's story of the man calling for lodgings and her wondering who sent the man. His testimony included the little vignette of family life, in which Flora touched his father on the arm and said, lightheartedly, 'Alfie, I am thinking about marrying again.' She had laughed as she said it, and the family treated it as a bit of a joke at the time . . . and yet it was said. Noble again testified to Flora's grave concern about the man calling for lodgings and her consequent lack of sleep for worrying. Trethowan was keen, also, for the court to hear of Teddy's health. Noble gave evidence that the pair of them had shared a bed one night recently, and he had noticed in the morning a patch of blood in the bed. He said to his cousin, "Teddy, your leg has been bleeding", and Teddy replied "Yes, Bob, I know; it often does."

And so to the final witness of the Tuesday, young Percy Noble, who repeated his testimony of his aunt's initial, calm response of "All right" to his knock, the scraping of the kitchen chair, the thump, the scream that someone had murdered her Teddy . . . Under cross-examination he repeated his view that there would be no difficulty in anyone leaving his aunt's house without having to go into the road.

The hearing resumed on Wednesday, 2 December at 11.00, with Flora again exhausted, and throughout the day on the point of collapse, kept conscious only with plenty of water to drink and the use of smelling salts to revive her.

The first witness was Lily Stretch, the nursemaid who had been taking the air with her young man

Herbert Primmer. As she did on Thursday 19th, Lily recounted the sequence of events, fixing the hour between 10.20 and 10.30, and measuring the time elapsed between Percy dashing across York Road, and the emergence of Flora, screaming, at her front door, as being the time for her to walk a few paces. Her key points of evidence were of Flora standing on her doorstep, sobbing, crying, "Someone has killed my Teddy", and without, Lily thought, while not being certain, moving from her doorstep. And although she could not swear to looking up Meadow Road, Lily was sure that she would have noticed a fugitive. Primmer had much the same to say, and Gertrude Skutt's account of her brief appearance before dashing back indoors to check on her own child was corroborative.

The last witness before the court adjourned for lunch was Ernest House who had been out with his brother-in-law Walter Haynes. Again, his evidence was crucial for establishing timing, for he heard the church clock strike the half-hour and at once heard Flora's first scream from the other end of the street, but saw no-one running away. Later he joined in the manhunt, and Trethowan asked 'If you had found a man, what would you have done to him?', and House growled 'He would have found that out.' As the court rose, Flora was met by her brother Richard, who had been attending the proceedings from the beginning. She kissed him and collapsed.

Walter Haynes's testimony, the first after lunch, again established that at the time of Flora's screaming, there was no-one walking or running away from the scene. As at the inquest, he confirmed that the fences between the back gardens were but three feet high, and no barrier to anyone bent on escape.

Alice Steer gave evidence of her and her husband hearing Flora's screams at about 10.25 p.m., and with the rest of her testimony the story of that evening went forward to the time when neighbours were crowding into the front room at No., 40, and she confirmed that after she had fetched Mrs Carter she heard Flora say 'something about a man having called the previous evening for lodgings.' Trethowan's cross-examination returned to Teddy. 'You know that the wound in Teddy's leg had never properly healed

and was constantly bleeding?' – 'Yes.'

'And that Mrs Haskell herself sometimes had to lance it?' – 'Yes.' There followed an insight into Flora's personal circumstances. 'Do you know what kind of skirt Mrs Haskell had been wearing for the last twelve months?' – 'No, I don't.'

'Not even the colour?' – 'It was a dark one.'

'Did she appear to you to have had the same skirt on for the last twelve months?' – 'Yes.' Trethowan's last question was about the man seeking accommodation. 'When you heard her say something about a man coming for lodgings, that might have been said in answer to a question addressed to her?' – 'Yes.'

Next to speak was Alice's mother, Emma Chivers. As at the inquest she testified that when Flora told her that someone had murdered Teddy, she replied "Oh, don't say that!", and Flora said "Something must be wrong with him, or he would not stay there so quiet". She again referred to Flora's claim of hearing footsteps upstairs and of her crying out "Look! There is the knife", and pointing to it at the bottom of the stairs. She added that when Sergeant Golding arrived he went upstairs with Steer, and the pair came back down almost at once. She pointed out the knife to Golding, and he picked it up, but Mrs Chivers did not, she said, know what he did with it. And while she could testify to Flora remarking on the blood spots on her blouse, Mrs Chivers did not notice any blood on Flora's hands.

Mrs Langmead spoke of staying with her mother, Mrs Cooper, in York Road, then of hearing Flora's screams and, while at No. 40, noticing the knife lying in the kitchen doorway.

Mrs Butt, like Mrs Langmead, provided further corroboration of the screams, fixing the time as 10.25. She spoke of running to the house, and of Flora asking someone to go upstairs, and of going upstairs behind Walter Steer to come upon the dead child. She told of finding the small brass lamp outside the bedroom, with its globe quite cold. Trethowan asked her why Flora did not go upstairs herself, and Mrs Butt replied that she thought that she was prevented from so doing.

The last witness of the day was Emily Sweetman, who recalled hearing about the murder and joining the people in the front room at No. 40 Meadow

THE MURDERED BOYS BEDROOM. PHOTOGRAPH TAKEN BY MESSER SHORTLY AFTER THE CRIME.
© *Timothy W. Frank Walker and Ann Richardson Whittle, grandchildren of Frank Richardson, Chief Constable*

Road. She gave evidence of Flora's worries about the man who had called for lodgings, and repeated her account of bathing Flora's face with some eau-de-Cologne, and the proffered handkerchief being bloodstained and damp. She testified, as she had done when recalled at the inquest, to the bloodstains on the kitchen tablecloth on the side nearest the staircase wall – the side by which anyone going to the scullery would pass on their way there. She confirmed that when she noticed these marks, Superintendent Stephens and others were present, and she pointed out the marks to Stephens, and admitted, as before, that were it not for the blood marks on the cloth, she would not be able to identify it as the one she saw on the night of the thirty-first. Trethowan asked her, 'How did you remember about these blood spots?' – 'Mr Dew asked me, a week ago.'

'What did he ask?' – 'He asked me if I saw anything in the kitchen, and I said "Yes, I saw bloodstains on the tablecloth."'

Thursday's first witness was Thomas Rawlins, who had heard Flora's screams, and with Walter Steer and Sarah Butt had gone up to the bedroom. He said that on his arriving at the house Flora had taken hold of his arm and said "My Teddy is dead: do go up.", and on his return she had asked him what had happened. Rawlins added that he saw the bloodstains on the tablecloth at about 11.30. Trethowan then cross-examined, and Rawlins had to concede that he could not be certain that Flora had actually said "Teddy is dead." When asked when it was that he saw the bloodstains on the tablecloth Rawlins said it was after he had been to the scullery to fetch some water.

The second new witness at the Magistrates' hearing was James Asbridge, the watchmaker and jeweller of Fisherton Street who had served on the inquest jury. He maintained the clock in the tower of St Paul's church, and he testified that on the morning of October 31 he had examined it and put it right.

Next to testify was another new witness, the accused's sister-in-law Emily Thirza Haskell, who stated that she was currently an inmate of the Hampstead Workhouse Infirmary. She continued, 'I have known Mrs Haskell for many years, and have stayed with her in the summer on and off during the last seven years. I came to visit her at 40 Meadow Road on the Tuesday after Bank Holiday, and remained there until the tenth of October. I slept in the middle room, over the kitchen, and Mrs Haskell and the boy slept in the front room. While I was staying there Mrs Haskell was kind to the boy and showed him affection.'

Parr then asked, 'While you were there did she say anything about marrying anyone?' – 'She told me someone wanted to marry her, but it took some thinking about.'

'Did she say who it was?' – 'Mr Mold.'

'Did she say what Mold did, or who he was?' – 'She said he was [a] steward on board ship.'

'Did she say anything further about what she would do if she married him?' – 'She said she would still do some work to keep her little boy "Teddy".'

'Did you ever see Mr Mold there yourself?' – 'I saw him once.'

'About when?' – 'Somewhere towards the end of August or at the beginning of September.'

Miss Haskell was then asked whether Mold had stayed over and what were the sleeping arrangements. She replied, 'Mr Mold slept at 40 Meadow Road on two nights while I was there. Mrs Haskell and I slept together on these occasions, and Mr Mold occupied Teddy's room. I think Teddy then slept at his uncle's.'

'Did Mr Mold, himself, in Mrs Haskell's presence, say anything about her marriage?' – 'He told me he wanted to marry.'

'Was Mrs Haskell present?' – 'Yes.'

'Did Mrs Haskell say anything to that?' – 'She did not give any reply.' Miss Haskell added that after the second night when Mold stayed at No. 40, she did not see him again during her visit. Parr continued, 'Did Mrs Haskell say anything more to you while you were there about Mold?' – 'She said nothing more than what I have said.'

'When you were staying there how was Mrs Haskell getting her living?' – 'By laundry work.'

'Did she talk to you about the rent of the house?' – 'I know it was five shillings and sixpence a week.'

'Did you know from her at all how much she was

making at the laundry work?' – 'No, I could not tell you.'

'Before you left, did you have any conversation with her about money matters?' – 'No.'

'You knew about Teddy's leg -?' – 'Yes.'

'Did you have any conversation with Mrs Haskell about that?' – 'She said he was going to have a cork leg as soon as he was old enough and had done growing.'

'Did she say anything about the getting of the cork leg?' – 'She told me her mother had given money to her for Teddy.'

'Did she say how much it was?' – 'No.'

'Did Mrs Haskell say anything about it?' – 'She told me that she had it, but had had to take something away from it.'

'Did she say why?' – 'Because she said she had not sufficient to go on with.'

'When you left on the 16 October, did you leave any money there?' – 'Yes, I left ten shillings behind.'

Trethowan now cross-examined and wanted to know the background to Mold's stay at No. 40. Miss Haskell explained that Mrs Mold, who took lodgers, came and asked Flora if Alfred could stay with her, as she, Mrs Mold, was full up.

'May I take it,' Trethowan continued, 'your impression was that Mr Mold wanted to marry Mrs Haskell?' – 'Yes.'

'But that Mrs Haskell had never agreed to it?' – 'Yes.'

The magistrates now heard from the first of the medical witnesses, the Haskells' family doctor, Herbert Wilks. He testified as he had done at the inquest, the substantive addition to his testimony about the state of the room when he arrived on the night of the murder being that when he took her upstairs, Flora had stayed with Teddy's body for about a minute. As he had done others, earlier, Trethowan asked the doctor about Teddy's amputation. Wilks replied that the site did discharge from time to time, but he could not say whether it had done so in the week ending 31 October.

At the end of Wilks's testimony, Trethowan had something to say. 'I think it is only right to inform the Bench – so that there shall be no misconstruction of my position – that I have seen the persons instructing me today, and have partly gone through with them the theoretical evidence the doctors have already given. I have told them that in my opinion if I now raise all the points which I think I ought to raise it will, at all events, take up another day. I am bound to say – and I don't think they [my clients] will object to this – that funds are not as I hoped they would have been, and I want to limit this inquiry as much as possible. If I only cross-examine as to some of the issues raised by the doctors, and do not go into all the theoretical evidence, I do not want my action misunderstood. I simply want – out of kindness more than anything else – to limit this inquiry, so that when we go to another place – and I am afraid we must go there – the examination can be gone into much more fully. I want to say this, so that people will not misconstrue the position I take up.'

Parr generously responded, 'I think I can help Mr Trethowan. I will say at once that I accept that [i.e. the defence's] position in this sense. It will not be suggested by the prosecution that the defence accepts the theories put forward by the doctors. The position taken up by the defence is that they reserve any cross-examination until hereafter, and they reserve the right to fully test the theories of the doctors.' Perkins replied, 'I think the bench clearly understand the situation, and I am sure the public will do so. I don't think, therefore, that there will be anything lost by your [i.e. Trethowan's] action.

Everard Row, Wilks's house guest, was next to testify, and he corroborated what his host had had to say, adding, tellingly, 'If the knife was thrown as it is suggested it was, I should have expected to find a splash of blood on the oilcloth, not such a mark as was found.'

Augustus Pepper spoke next, again repeating his testimony to the inquest, and, echoing Rowe's comment, added, 'If the knife had been thrown at a person, I should have expected to find a general shaking off of blood round the blood mark on the linoleum at the foot of the stairs. I do not think the blood marks on the blouse and skirt could have been caused by a knife being thrown at Mrs Haskell.' The hearing was adjourned part-way through Pepper's evidence, and at its resumption on Friday, 4 December, he again put forward his view that Teddy's dying breaths, through the cut windpipe, would have

carried forth a spray of blood droplets which may have extended to two or three yards. An assailant standing at the head of the bed, he added, would be in the direct line of the spray.

Flora, meanwhile, had started the day looking ever more deathly pale. Sobbing as she was brought into the court and for some time afterwards, rather than relax in the armchair with the cushions, she buried her face in her hands, generally oblivious to the proceedings, except when Pepper's evidence prompted more bitter tears from time to time. Then, at 12.15, just as she had done during the inquest, Flora collapsed and had to be carried out. Another half-hour passed before she was fit enough to return to hear the rest of the consultant's testimony. Once that was read back to Pepper and signed, the magistrates ordered a long adjournment, and the court did not reconvene until three o'clock that afternoon.

Herbert Wilks was then cross-examined by Trethowan, who questioned him about the injury: 'Considerable force must have been used to cause the wound in the boy's throat?' – 'Yes.'

'And easier for a man to inflict the wound than a woman' – 'I think so.'

'Knowing Mrs Haskell as you do, do you think she would be likely to be joking with Miss Steer just before ten o'clock and murdering her son at ten twenty?' – 'From my impression of Mrs Haskell that was not probable. When I first went into Mrs Haskell's house and asked her what was the matter, she said, "I want to find out: go upstairs."'

Wilks added that he went up, and subsequently took Mrs Haskell up to see the boy, and she kissed him.

'Do you think she would have done that if she had murdered the boy?' – 'Not as an ordinary individual.'

Trethowan questioned him about the amputation, and Wilks testified that when he examined Teddy he saw no signs of lancing there.

The next witness was John Moxham Cooper, who had a potentially dramatic revelation to make. He testified to visiting 40 Meadow Road at about 10.30 p.m. on the night of the murder, and of hearing Flora say that the man who had thrown a knife at her had offered or given Teddy twopence a day or two before. Trethowan had given Cooper pretty short shrift at the inquest, and he now pointed out that he was saying for the first time that Flora said the man who offered or gave Teddy twopence was the same man who threw the knife at her. Cooper had to admit that he did not mean what he had just said.

The last layman to be called was another new witness, Gertrude Skutt's husband Jesse, whose testimony was limited to that fact that he took part in the manhunt.

Now came the turn of the police witnesses, beginning with Constable William Cutler, a new witness. He stated that in consequence of information he had received he went to 40, Meadow Road on October 31st, arriving just before eleven o'clock. Mrs Haskell, he said, was saying "My boy has been killed"; Cutler also testified to the Chief Constable asking for a description of the man who had called for lodgings on the Friday.

Next to testify was the hapless Sergeant Golding. He related how he had come to the house, and was left in charge over night, when, at about six o'clock on the Sunday morning Mrs Carter washed the hallway with a flannel and a bucket of water. Trethowan asked, 'Why didn't you stop her?' – 'My instructions were not to allow anyone upstairs.'

'And you stuck to them?' – 'Yes.'

Questioning then turned to the knife, when Cutler revealed that not merely had he picked the knife up, but had also put it in his pocket. Trethowan asked him, 'How long was the knife in your pocket?' – 'Until I handed it over to the Chief Constable.'

'How long was that?' – 'About two hours. The Chief Constable arrived at the house about eleven o'clock, and I told him I had the knife.'

'You say you had it in your pocket?' – 'Yes.'

'And you say he told you to keep it there?' – 'Yes.' Enough, perhaps, said.

The last witness of the day was Frank Richardson, Salisbury's Chief Constable. His evidence was limited to establishing a context for his activities on the night of the thirty-first – his arrival at No. 40, and his examination of the house.

The following day, Saturday 5 December, would be the final day of the hearing. Overnight, Flora had recovered her composure, and was able to smile at her two brothers who were sitting next to Trethowan.

Richardson resumed his testimony, again recounting Flora's questions about the money, the state of the drawer and the presence of only the three sovereigns and a half-sovereign, his request for her help in tracing the murder and her response – the description of the man calling for lodgings – on which basis the Chief Constable had instituted a search. He recalled taking possession of the knife and ascertaining that it was one which belonged to the family, and the account of the man paying Teddy twopence for providing family information and his name and address, and noticing the bloodstains on Flora's blouse and taking possession of it on learning that she had worn it when the knife was thrown at her. He continued, 'I suggested that Mrs Haskell and her mother should go and sleep with some friends, but she said she preferred to stay in the house.' His testimony then turned to the interview on Sunday, 1 November in the company of Superintendent Stephens, Chief Inspector Dew and Chief Constable Llewellyn, which had resulted in Flora's first statement. He read extracts from the statement – Mrs Haskell washing the boy and putting him to bed, sitting for a while in the kitchen, hearing someone coming downstairs and having something thrown at her which splashed her sleeve. He continued: 'Her nephew, Percy Noble, knocked at the back door, and she went to the back door screaming, and asked Percy to go for a doctor. She could not tell why she said that, only because she saw splashes of blood on her sleeve.' Richardson concluded with reference to the money in the drawer and the fact that it was savings for an artificial leg, and that only Mrs Haskell and her mother and son knew of it.

Parr then asked about the arrest on the evening of Tuesday 3 November, and Richardson recalled the charge of wilful murder, and Flora's shocked response, "No, no!" before she was taken to the police station. At that point Flora became hysterical, crying so violently that members of the bench stepped down to try to console her, to no avail, and she had to be taken out of the court. After about ten minutes, she had calmed down, and returned, and Richardson continued, with an account of Mold's letter. 'At the prisoner's second remand, I showed her a letter from Alfred Mold, a steward on the *Adriatic*. The letter was posted from New York on November third, and was received in Salisbury on November eleventh. In this letter Mold expressed his thanks to Mrs Haskell for looking after his mother, and said he was looking forward to seeing her again.'

Trethowan now cross-examined Richardson, and he replied 'I told Sergeant Golding to take care of the knife. I did not examine it when I first saw it. It was carried about in Golding's pocket wrapped up in brown paper. I afterwards examined it for finger-marks but could find none.'

'Didn't you realise that if the knife had been examined at the time a great amount of this inquiry might have been unnecessary?' Richardson had no answer, and Trethowan continued. 'Did Chief Inspector Dew ask her about this man Mold?' – 'He asked her whether she had got a young man.'

'Will you say he did not ask her anything about Mold, and did not mention Mold's name?' – 'Nothing was said about Mold.'

'What was it that induced you and Chief Inspector Dew to go down to Plymouth on the eleventh?' – 'In the course of enquiries.'

Trethowan now called for Mold's signature to be produced, and Parr replied 'If Mr Trethowan wants the signature he is entitled to it. He cannot have anything else.' Trethowan continued his questioning: 'Did you get a signed statement from Mold?' – 'Yes.' – 'Then', said Trethowan', 'I am entitled to have it put in.'

At this the mayor demurred, saying that the Bench was of the opinion that Trethowan was not entitled to have the document put in, but, if the prosecution were prepared to grant the concession, the document could be put in, sealed, so that only the signature was exposed. Parr agreed, adding , 'I am quite willing that that course should be taken.' Trethowan's huffy response was to say that he should like a note made of the fact that he had asked for the production of the document and that it was refused. As to whether he was entitled to have the document put in – that could be argued elsewhere.

Following Richardson, Stephens testified, and then Dew. During Dew's evidence, Flora again

fainted, and Wilks was summoned to attend. On arrival he administered restoratives, and Flora recovered enough to take a place in the easy chair

The last witness, appearing for the first time, was Matilda Sheppard, the wardress who had had charge of Flora during her custody in Salisbury. She testified that 'When Mrs Haskell was searched after the arrest I found a black purse containing seven sovereigns and two half-sovereigns in the pocket of her skirt. Mrs Haskell told me that the purse belonged to her mother, who gave it to her on the previous day [*i.e.* 3 November], while she went to the inquest. It was handed to the Chief Constable with a request from the accused that it should be returned to her mother.'

Richardson was recalled to give evidence about the money, and said 'I got the message from Mrs Sheppard as to the purse and eight pounds in it. I made the necessary enquiries and satisfied myself that both were the property of Mrs Carter, and afterwards handed the purse and money in it to Mr Richard Carter, the eldest son.'

And with Richardson's testimony, the inquiry was at an end. Parr said, 'So far as I am concerned, I have now reached the end of this investigation, and that is the case for the prosecution.' The last word was with Trethowan; 'I think everybody will be glad that this painful inquiry is nearly at an end. My instructions at first were to bring my witnesses before you, and to state my client's defence at once. Only with some difficulty have I been able to convince them that owing to the extraordinary verdict arrived at by the Coroner's jury, whatever were done here, even if we brought our witnesses and defence before you, and could prove there was no *prima facie* case to enable you to send the prisoner to Devizes, yet the verdict of the Coroner's jury is still in existence, and the case would still have to go to Devizes. Therefore my client has left herself in my hands, and she has taken my advice. We don't propose to call any evidence before you today. I feel the case must go to Devizes, and it is better the inquiry should not be protracted any longer, for the poor woman has hardly been able to stand the investigation so far. For that and other reasons we propose to call no evidence. But I want to say this, because reports are going all over the country, and I don't want it to be thought that we have no defence. I want the public to know we have a defence, and the people who are advising Mrs Haskell consider they have a good defence.'

The time by now was seven o'clock, and the charge was merely a formality. Flora remained seated, her face buried in her hands as Arthur Jonas softly read over the charge. Even without the playing out of the whole ghastly affair at the inquest, the verdict implicit in the charge was a foregone conclusion, and it was perhaps as well that it was not incumbent upon Flora to give answer herself to the charge, serious as it was. Trethowan spoke for her, 'I plead not guilty and reserve my defence.' The deposition was written out, and Henry Vincent, Trethowan's clerk, took it across for Flora, who falteringly signed it. Then the magistrates quietly signed the committal to the Assizes, and John Folliott, "with characteristic kindliness", stepped down from the bench to open the door out of the court to allow Flora to be led away with the help of both of her attendants. Then, and only then, were the witnesses bound over to appear at the Assizes.

Flora's circumstances were by now parlous in the extreme. The inquest – an inquiry, not a trial – had determined that she had killed her son, and had already committed her for trial at the Winter Assizes.

Now, following Parr's detailed narrative and cogent analysis, the city bench had confirmed that judgement. The ineluctable implication of the inquest was that she was already guilty, despite Trethowan's robust defence and assertion of her innocence. The appeals for donations to pay for her defence seem to have been channeled through more than one route, into "Mrs Haskell's Defence Fund", organised by *Lloyd's Weekly News*. It will be recalled that within three days of Flora's arrest, the call went abroad for a fund supported by public appeal for her defence,[2] responded to by a letter from Frank Baker, sometime Mayor of Salisbury, published in the *Salisbury Journal* published exactly a week after the murder, declaring he would receive funds for that purpose.[3] The next day, *Lloyd's Weekly News*, publishing letters on its front page from the Mayor and Canon Thwaites, Rector of St Paul's, calling for a defence fund, started one with a gift of ten guineas.[4] During succeeding weeks, the paper published details of sums large and small paid into the fund – two guineas from Sir Edward Tennant, four individuals identifying themselves simply as "Friend", one shilling each. As well as Mr Baker, who set up an account for donations at the National and Provincial Bank at 48, Blue Boar Row, George Hawkins and his wife, who ran the *Malmesbury Arms* on the Wilton Road[5]

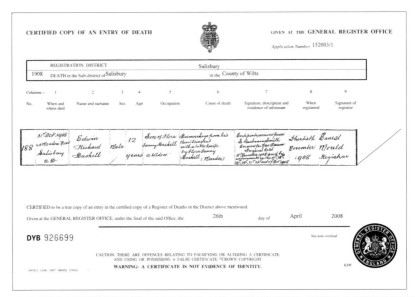

THE DEATH CERTIFICATE OF EDWIN RICHARD HASKELL, 1908. NOTE THAT HIS MOTHER IS ACCUSED OF THE CRIME
© CROWN COPYRIGHT

amassed £5 1s. 6d. from local well-wishers, while the associates of one F.E. Lyne gave 6s. 1d. The total recorded for one week in Lloyd's News was £9 3s. 6d., for another, £10 3s. od.,[6] and for another, £5 11s. 7d.[7] However, finances were precarious. At the end of the magistrates' hearing Frank Baker wrote to the Editor of the *Journal*, under the heading 'Mrs Haskell's defence fund',

SIR, – Now that this poor woman has been committed to take her trial at Devizes in the early part of January, it is important that all subscriptions should be paid to me or to the account which I have opened at the National Provincial Bank, Salisbury, as early as possible, to enable her solicitors to prepare for trial and brief counsel.

The lengthened inquiries before the Coroner and the Magistrates have more than exhausted the funds already subscribed.

Yours faithfully,

FRANK BAKER.

'Sturminster', Victoria Road, Salisbury, December 10 1908.[8]

Flora's straits were not merely financial. During the inquest, as we know, Dew had been hard at work, travelling far and wide – even overseas – to gather evidence relating to the case. After her committal at the magistrates' hearing, he travelled to Goole, in Yorkshire, and to Gosport, Hampshire, following the discovery of a pocket-book containing the names and addresses of, among others, three men whose identities Dew thought would bear further investigation. Mr Bryant of Alverstoke, near Gosport, turned out to be an uncle by marriage of Flora's, while Mr Edwards of Goole, who by 1908 had moved to London, was in fact one of Flora's brothers. In the report to his superintendent on Boxing Day 1908 Dew commented that this might 'be regarded as somewhat singular inasmuch as prisoner[']s maiden name was Carter, but, the explanation may be, that the mother was married twice'; or, he added darkly, 'a more probable explanation may be easily surmised.' The last address was of a Mr Mills of Gosport, endorsed with a military service number and an address in the Forton Barracks there. The service number related to another brother of Flora's, and Mr Mills was a

Salisburian, and Dew inferred that Mills appeared in the pocket book simply as a putative acquaintance of her brother the Royal Marine.

Far more serious was the information gleaned from reports of conversations between Flora and the Rector of St Paul's, Canon Thwaites, and of one between her and the Police Matron, Matilda Sheppard, reported by Dew to his superintendent on New Year's Eve 1908 and on 7 January 1909. In the latter report, Dew records taking a statement from Constable John Tucker, in which he reported an exchange between Flora and the Rector on 30 November, in which Thwaites warned her that the charge against her was a matter of life or death, and 'whatever there is between you and God you must tell God, and he will put everything right.' Tucker then repeated what Thwaites reported Flora saying, when he visited her on 5 December: 'She is so grateful to you all for your kindness, and she says herself the evidence was strong against her, and points straight to her; and [she said] "If I did do it I don[']t know anything about it"'. Thwaites, said Tucker, added 'do you think a woman in her right senses would do such a thing [?]', and Tucker replied, 'I, as a Police officer dare not say'.

In the same report Dew records taking a statement from Inspector Herbert Stroud, recording a conversation between himself and Canon Thwaites which again smacks of Flora being fitted up: Stroud overheard Thwaites say to her, 'If you are guilty you had better say so, as you will have to appear before the great Judge which will know all hearts and [from whom] no secrets are hid'. The Rector had added the pious but self-absolving rider as Stroud let him out of the Guildhall, 'Something has passed between me and Mrs Haskell which would not be right for me to tell you.' This turn of phrase, with some embellishment, had also been used by Thwaites to Tucker in a conversation relayed to Stroud on 5 December: as the Rector left he said to the constable 'that something had passed between him and Mrs Haskell which would not be right for him to tell him, but that it looked very black against her.'[9]

The next day, Stroud, Mrs Sheppard and Flora had driven back to Devizes, and on the return journey the Police Matron passed on Flora's damning words

RAYNER GODDARD, DEFENDING COUNSEL FOR FLORA HASKELL

to the Inspector, in consequence of which Dew had taken a statement from Mrs Sheppard. She said 'Yes, I did tell Mr Stroud something on our way back from Devizes, I said to him, I think if Mr Thwaites could have seen her again, she would have told him, if anyone, because she said to me after his leaving on Saturday evening, the last day, "Oh, Mrs Sheppard if I did it, I don't remember it"; and she did say this.' The matron added that she was alone with Flora when this conversation occurred, but that it was immediately after Thwaites had left.

Nevertheless, help was at hand. Flora's saviour was a young barrister, Rayner Goddard. Born in 1877, Goddard was the second son and third of five children of Charles and Janet Goddard, and was named after his paternal grandmother. His antecedents were solidly professional, his grandfather being a doctor, and his father a solicitor and the co-founder of the partnership of Peacock and Goddard in Gray's Inn.[10] At Marlborough College, Goddard gained prizes for athletics and for English and history and was Captain of the Rifle Corps and a Victor Ludorum when he left for Trinity College,

Oxford, in 1895. There he gained a full Blue in athletics, while perhaps gaining no greater knowledge of the law than he learned from his solicitor father. While he impressed his undergraduate contemporaries with his knowledge of arcane legal topics such as demurrer, replevin and estoppel, some at least of his tutors were not altogether won over. A parting shot from Sir William Anson, then Warden of All Souls' was 'I hope you get on well. You will make an income at the Bar, but you will never make a lawyer!' Having graduated in 1898, Goddard completed his Bar examinations in January 1899. From there he joined the Western Circuit chambers of A. Clavell Salter. He learned his craft as an advocate by attaching himself to the Wiltshire Quarter Sessions, claiming later never to have missed a session before the Great War.

The Winter Assizes for the county of Wiltshire opened at Devizes in February 1909, with the circuit judge, Sir Edward Ridley, arriving from Waterloo to a fanfare of trumpeters just before 5 p.m. on Thursday 11th. He was greeted by the High Sheriff and the Sheriff's Chaplain before proceeding with a police escort to the Judge's Lodgings opposite the Court. Goddard and the other counsel, meanwhile, were driven to The Bear Hotel, a quarter of a mile away in the Market Place, and reserved for the Bar for the Assizes. After a service in St John's Church, the proceedings began at 11 a.m., and a variety of cases, beginning with an attempted suicide and including bigamy, attempted murder, concealment of the birth of a child and malicious wounding, were all dealt with in fairly short order.

The prelude to Flora's case was that of an elderly gentleman indicted for indecently assaulting a child, the case being heard on the morning of Saturday, 13 February. As with Flora, Goddard, instructed by Messrs Nodder and Trethowan, acted for the defendant, a Salisbury man, who was a member of the Town Council and had served on the Education Committee. The case took just two and a half hours and the defendant was acquitted. Fresh from this success, Goddard would, after the weekend, face his sternest test to date in the role of defending counsel; indeed, as it turned out, his sternest case ever in such a role.

11

'Send an experienced officer at once by motor': Chief Inspector Dew

WHEN FRANK RICHARDSON, Chief Constable of Salisbury received Golding's telephone call at 10.40 on October 31st, he must have suspected not only that the case would be a severe test of his experience and abilities, but that he would need to summon outside assistance: his arrival at 40 Meadow Road would only have confirmed his worst suspicions. His first act on returning to the station in Endless Street was to send off a telegram Scotland Yard. The man on the 8.30 from Waterloo next morning who met the Chief Constable three hours later was Walter Dew, who had discovered the last of Jack the Ripper's victims.

Walter Dew was born at Hardingstone, just outside Northampton, on 7 April 1863. Having no academic bent he left school at thirteen, and began work as a solicitor's clerk near Chancery Lane, a post which afforded him the opportunity of regularly attending the Law Courts at Westminster. That was

TELEGRAM SENT BY FRANK RICHARDSON TO SCOTLAND YARD ASKING FOR THEIR ASSISTANCE.
© PRO

the chief consolation of an otherwise boring job which Dew kept at for a year before securing another clerical post in Holborn which was even more short-lived. His father and brother were railwaymen, and, passionate about railways, Dew joined their company, the London and North Western Railway, a move he never regretted, and which he expected would be his career. However, at the age of nineteen, he applied to join the Metropolitan Police. He did so on someone else's suggestion, and without any expectation of success, as he had harboured an instinctive fear of the Police in the big city. However, his application was successful, and Dew was issued with the warrant number 66711, and sent for training on 15s. a week at the Wellington Barracks. His first substantive post was at Paddington Green, on 24s. a week, in June 1882. There he remained for five years during which time he married and settled down in Bethnal Green.

As a uniformed officer Dew was not slow to demonstrate considerable prowess, being commended for his work by members of the judiciary, and gaining, after five years' service in the uniformed branch, a transfer to the Criminal Investigation Department. After policing the suburbs of Paddington and Bayswater, his new posting tempered the elation of his promotion with a sense of foreboding, for it was H Division – Whitechapel. Dew later recalled, 'Whitechapel, Spitalfields and Shoreditch were now my hunting-ground, with hundreds of criminals of the worst type as my quarry. Whitechapel in those days was full of slums in which vice of all kinds was rampant. Sordid narrow streets, still narrower courts, filthy and practically unlighted. Woe betide any innocent wayfarer venturing alone down any of those dark and sinister passages.' Dew's colleagues at Whitechapel included Detective Inspector Edmund Reid, a man who, at this period, known as the heroic period in the history of criminal investigation, was the inspiration for Dier, the hero of Charles Gibbon's series of ten detective novels of the 1880s. There were other characters, including William 'Johnny Upright' Thick, Eli 'Tommy Roundhead' Caunter, 'The Russian' and 'The Shah'. Scarcely had Dew arrived than the notorious, and to this day unsolved, series of murders by 'Jack the Ripper' began.

The problem for Dew was that there was neither motive, nor circumstantial evidence. As he wrote, 'The hope and ambition of every East-End policeman – myself included – was to catch the Ripper red-handed. This seemed the only way. There was small chance of the killer being caught and convicted through circumstantial evidence. Of such evidence there was virtually none.' And as the murders continued, with ever-mounting yet silent ferocity, and the public panicked and the press fulminated, the police continued to be frustrated in their efforts. Even the presence of Henry Moore, Walter Andrews and Frederick Abberline from Scotland Yard failed to progress matters. With Emma Smith, Martha Tabram and Mary Ann Nichols killed within the space of five months, and the last two within the month of August 1888, Dew wrote 'These were wretched days for me. The hunt became an obsession. I spent long, long hours on duty, only to return home worn out but sleepless. Night after night I tossed about on my bed seeing again and again the terrible sights I had witnessed. In this I was not alone. There were dozens of other police officers whose lives Jack the Ripper had made scarcely worth living. My food sickened me. The sight of a butcher's shop nauseated me.' Nine days after Mary Ann Nichols's death, Annie Chapman was found, eviscerated, on 8 September, in the yard of 29 Hanbury Street, from whence the killer had slipped away through streets swarming with police on patrol throughout the night. The killer had even paused to arrange Chapman's belongings by her feet. Four suspects were apprehen-

ded – George 'Squibby' Cullen, John 'Leather Apron' Pizer, William Pigott and Joseph Isenschmidt – and, in due course, eliminated from enquiries.

Had 'Jack the Ripper' been all that Dew and his colleagues had to worry about, life would have been quite hard enough; but the search for the killer was being conducted in addition to all the other work thrown up by the most lawless corner of the Metropolis. A further burden, from 27 September was the first of a shoal of letters purporting to be from the killer, signed 'Jack the Ripper' – whence the soubriquet associated with the series of murders – and sent to the Central News Agency. The next two of the Ripper's murders were discovered in the early hours of 30 September: that of Elizabeth 'Long Liz' Stride in Duffield's Yard, off Berner Street, and that of Catherine Eddowes in Mitre Square. In the search for Stride's murderer, 80,000 leaflets were distributed, 2,000 denizens of common lodging houses were searched; 300 had their movements traced, 80 people were brought in for questioning, and out of all this there were just three descriptions of a man or men who had been seen with Long Liz on the night she died.

There then followed a month and more of relative peace while the Ripper stayed his hand. Increasing pressure, meanwhile, on the Commissioner, Sir Charles Warren, from the Home Secretary on the one hand and the British press on the other, forced his resignation on 8 November. However, almost as if for a leaving present for the Commissioner, the Ripper struck that night. A rent-collector, calling at 13 Miller's Court, Dorset Street received no answer from Mary Jane Kelly, and looked through a window, to come upon the seventh murder. Inspector Beck and Dew were summoned from Commercial Street police station, taking uniformed officers on their way to the crime scene. There, despite Beck's warning to Dew not to look, the Detective Constable confronted what he later described as the most gruesome memory of his police career, the eviscerated, dismembered and partially flayed body of Mary Jane Kelly, an Irish prostitute whom Dew knew well by sight. The frenzy with which the attack convinced Dew both that the Ripper was quite deranged and also, given the likely state of his clothes after the attack, that he was being sheltered. There were three

CHIEF INSPECTOR DEW (LEFT) OF SCOTLAND YARD
WHO TOOK CHARGE OF THE INVESTIGATION.
© *STEWART P. EVANS*

possible sightings, but nothing came of them. At that point, the pinnacle of ferocity, the storm abated. Dew was promoted to Detective Sergeant, and transferred to F Division, Paddington. There were three further murders of prostitutes in the East End, in December 1888, July 1889 and February 1891, but none of them bore the hallmarks of the Ripper, and Dew was no longer directly involved.

Dew's career progressed, with promotion to Inspector and transfer to Scotland Yard in October 1898. Almost at once he was presented with the theft of jewellery worth £30,000 from an unattended railway carriage at the Gare du Nord, Paris, on 17 October. The owner of the collection, the Duchess of Sutherland, noticed that the jewellery box was gone only as the train was drawing from the station, and did not notify the authorities until the train stopped at Amiens. At that point telegrams were sent to the police in London, Paris and Amsterdam, with the Duchess and her husband, Sir Albert Rollit returning to Paris to report the loss before proceeding to

London to provide a full description of the missing jewellery. In London, Dew was assigned to the case with Inspectors Walter Dinnie and Frank Froest. Dew reasoned that the theft had to be the work of an international villain, and his enquiries began with the premise that the culprit was on the continent at the time of the theft. He had a hunch that the thief was English, and connected with the London underworld, and learned pretty quickly that a likely suspect, William 'Harry the Valet' Johnson had come into money and had been out of the country until 22 October. On 23 October, back in London, Johnson visited a jeweller in Houndsditch to have some gems set, and subsequently was seen drinking at the *Brown Bear* in Worship Street and laundering some money there. And then he disappeared.

But then Johnson made the mistake that would lead to his arrest. Six months earlier he had taken up with an actress, Maude Richardson and, in essence, had sponged off her during their time together, with him pursuing her to the continent. They had fallen out by the time of the robbery, but Johnson lured Maude back with the news of the haul, which he implied was in his possession only as a result of handling stolen goods. Overwhelmed by the sight of the jewellery, Maude wore it when the couple were out, and refused to hand it back to Johnson the following morning. A row ensued and Maude returned to England to give a statement about the jewellery, pursued by Johnson. Despite an attempt to cover his tracks – he had told Mrs Richardson that he was going abroad and that she would never see him again – Johnson took rooms in South Kensington. Acting on a tip-off early on 28 November, Dew, Dinnie and Froest visited the premise, 5 Cathcart Road and smashed the door down to arrest Johnson, who had on him £320 in cash and £800 worth of jewellery. Although he as good as admitted the theft of the Duchess's jewellery, and pleaded guilty to the charge, Johnson was remarkably uncooperative as to the whereabouts of the rest of the haul. His stubbornness earned him a sentence of seven years, but only some £5,000 worth of the Duchess's jewellery was ever recovered and returned to her.

Dew served two years at Scotland Yard, and was

HOME OFFICE,
WHITEHALL,

3rd November, 1908.

Sir,

I am directed by the Secretary of State to
acknowledge the receipt of your letter of the 1st
instant, and to say that he approves of your action in
sending Chief Inspector Dew to assist in the investigation
of the Salisbury Murder.

I am,

Sir,

Your obedient Servant,

E. Blackwell

The Assistant Commissioner of Police,

Criminal Investigation Department.

LETTER INSTRUCTING CHIEF INSPECTOR DEW TO
INVESTIGATE THE HASKELL CRIME.
© PRO

then transferred to T Division, Hammersmith. In 1903, he was promoted to Inspector, First Class, and transferred again to E Division, Bow Street. After a further three years, the opportunity for advancement arose when Frank Froest was promoted to Superintendent at Scotland Yard. Dew was his replacement as Chief Inspector, and it was during this stage of his career that he was summoned to Salisbury to oversee the Haskell case.

From conversations between the local police and Scotland Yard the day after the murder, as reported by Inspector Arthur Hailstone, it seems that there was an inkling of Flora's guilt as early as that Sunday, even before Dew's arrival on the scene by midday. Indeed, Trethowan's second brief to counsel refers to a conversation between Richardson and a local magistrate as early as 8.30 on Sunday 1 November, indicating that Flora was under suspicion and already believed to be the perpetrator. Dew examined the crime scene and took a statement from Flora in the presence of Richardson and Captain Llewellyn, 'who', in Dew's words, 'happened to be in the house'.

Dew was working flat-out to gather information and marshall it in such a way as to be able to construct a hypothesis, a narrative about how the murder happened and hence who might be under suspicion. In his first report to the DPP, dated 4 November 1908, he wrote: 'Since my arrival on Sunday I have been engaged with the Chief Constable and Superintendent Stephens making inquiries etc with but a few hours rest, and there is still an immense amount of work to do and I therefore do not propose to make a detailed report or fully summarise the statements I have taken at this moment; the statements speak for themselves.'

Indicative of his working methods, he stated elsewhere in the report, 'I obtained signed statements at the earliest possible moment from as many persons that I thought could throw light on the matter and from these it will be seen that Mr Steer contradicts prisoner in many particulars.' Although he acknowledged in the above remarks that, less than four days after the event, enquiries were necessarily at an early stage, Dew was already convinced of Flora's guilt, or at the very least, that she was the prime suspect. So sure was he that only hours before the report was filed, he brought against Flora a charge of murder: he reported, 'Having regard to all the circumstances and enquiries made by me, and. in the absence of any real corroboration of Mrs Haskell's statement, I was of the opinion that we should be justified in arresting her. At about 10.30. p.m. [on the] 3rd [November] we arrested her at her house, and when told the charge she simply said "No, No", and when charge was read over she said "No".' When this report was filed, the issue of motive had not been addressed; perhaps it had not even been considered.

How had Dew come so promptly and so firmly to the conclusion he did; a conclusion which he was never to alter? There were five points in Flora's statements which aroused Dew's suspicion – apart, that is, from the lack of corroboration by those of other witnesses, specifically Walter Steer's, with whose account Flora's was at variance.

When the alleged assailant came flying down the stairs and throwing the object at her which turned out to be a knife, she could not see him well enough to be able to describe him; yet the light was good enough for her to see the blood splashes on her sleeve which led her to believe that Teddy had been murdered. However, we know that one of the splashes penetrated the blouse deeply enough that Flora could feel the blood on her arm.

The kitchen was directly below the scene of the crime; yet Flora said she heard nothing. However, against this there is Emma Chivers' testimony both at the inquest and the magisterial hearing that Flora heard movement upstairs which at the time she assumed came from next door.

No-one knew about the money except for Flora, Teddy and Mrs Carter – hence it could not have been a motive for a burglary attempt ending in the taking of Teddy's life. However, Emily Thirza Haskell testified to knowing of the money, and Trethowan's case notes refer to a neighbour, Mrs Hawkins at 29 Meadow Road, and a friend of Flora's, Miss Lawrence, knowing of the money. It could have been common knowledge, therefore, that there was money about the house.

Flora was certain that she wore an apron on the night of 31 October 31, which claim was belied by the presence of blood on her clothing and the discovery and identification of a clean apron. But this is to ignore the possibility that Flora was wearing an apron in the earlier part of the evening – perhaps when she was bathing Teddy – and took it off before she was exposed to the blood.

Flora wanted to amend that part of her statement relating to Walter Steer, and made a supplementary statement on 3 November; yet Dew dismissed this, adding, 'I beg special attention to the greater part of this statement, as it seems an afterthought', adding, in the next sentence, 'Mr Steer contradicts prisoner in many particulars.'

Dew had other grounds, he felt, for suspicion. The testimony of Lily Stretch, corroborated by Herbert Primmer, that she saw Flora screaming but noticed no-one disappearing up Meadow Road, was reckoned to contradict Flora's story. She was crying out that her child had been killed, without, apparently, having looked to see whether this was indeed so; 'and yet', remarked Dew, 'she herself practically contradicted this.'

Finally, the clincher was the bloodstained blouse. Dew remarked 'To my mind the position of the bloodstains on the blouse are consistent with her having cut the boy's throat, and not consistent as being caused in the manner described by her, because I found several blood spots on the oilcloth floor of the bedroom, one on landing at top of stairs, one or two spots and smears on right side of [the] wall … [and] I suggest that that the running blood on [the] knife was practically exhausted before being taken from [the] bedroom.' One wonders how come Dew was so confident that such a horrific injury as Teddy had suffered resulted in such a minuscule amount of staining on Flora's blouse. Doubtless, by the time he compiled the report, Dew had discussed the matter with the local police surgeon, Gilbert Kempe, who examined the crime scene, the body and Flora's clothing. At the time of the magistrates' hearing Kempe stated that he considered that the blood on Flora's blouse was the result of spray exhaled from the severed windpipe. But he was never called upon to account for the exact point in the process of cutting the boy's throat at which that amount of blood, and only that amount of blood, would end up on someone's clothing. And although Kempe was a police surgeon, he was not an expert in forensics. That person was Pepper, and given that he did not arrive at the scene of the crime until 8 November, Dew's judgment on the blouse four days earlier would seem not to rest on the strongest of foundations.

Pepper's role was considered in some depth in Trethowan's brief to counsel for the second trial. Of the medical witnesses, Wilks, the Haskells' family doctor, was reckoned to be most favourable to Flora's cause, having stated in court his belief that the assailant was most likely a man, and a maniac at that. And yet Wilks seems to have been overawed by the gravity of the occasion and in particular the reputation of Pepper. He frequently qualified his testimony by prefacing his remarks, 'as an ordinary man.' In Trethowan's words, 'He [Wilks] never is a strong witness. Dr. Kempe however is, and is somewhat of a partisan always.' Most tellingly, Pepper took two steps to engineer the medical evidence. Firstly, he convened a case conference with the three doctors before they appeared at the inquest.

Next, he directed the prosecution's questioning of them, until, as Trethowan recorded, 'although no objection could be raised to the form of the question asked, yet if the answers given were not exactly in the form which Professor Pepper required, the questions were put again differently until Profr. Pepper appeared to be satisfied.'

Thus, Trethowan cautioned Goddard, the medical evidence was not truly independent, and if a way could be found of intimating that to the jury, it should be.

What would have added to Dew's difficulties was the treatment of the crime scene: the fact that, despite Hailstone's plea that care be taken in handling evidence at the crime scene – so as not to disturb, for instance, any finger or hand-prints – the damage was already done. Golding had wrapped up the knife and put it into his coat pocket, and had allowed Mrs Carter to wash the passage and, as Trethowan's case-notes reveal, Miss Lawrence to wash the kitchen floor. Much evidence of bloodstaining had gone: Wilks testified under cross-examination before the magistrates that there had been a great deal more blood on the kitchen floor where the knife was found than remained on the specimens of linoleum exhibited in court. None of this is alluded to in Dew's first report, by way of a *caveat* to his conclusions, and the police and prosecution subsequently closed ranks to aver that the evidence thus lost was not crucial to their case.

The alternative theory, that a man had gained entrance to 40 Meadow Road and killed Teddy Haskell, leaving his mother in a state of shock and horror as she claimed, was dismissed within hours, possibly because the investigation predicated on that theory was handled so poorly. The response of the local police, following Richardson's interview of Flora at her home, was to send out search parties, either of their own personnel or using local volunteers from among the neighbours. So, on the one hand, P.C. William Cutler was dispatched to the railway stations to ask after left luggage and to watch for people boarding trains, despite the fact that it was then over 24 hours since Flora's mysterious visitor had called. And on the other hand, William Eccott ended up searching for a man based on a third party's

description of him, so he was actually looking for himself. Trethowan's brief to counsel described the search operation as 'a perfect farce'.

As a result, Leate's story of a woman weeping and following for a few yards a man walking briskly away from 40 Meadow Road in the direction of Coldharbour Lane came to be discounted. Even though Trethowan noted that 'He [Leate] has always been understood to be a truthful witness, and that he saw somebody in Meadow Road about the time mentioned by him may be taken for granted', it was discounted by Dew, partly because Leate, in a faintly lackadaisical manner, left it until the Monday morning, 2 November, to make a statement; by which time Dew's mind was made up. He would say, in his final report to the DPP in April 1909, 'I satisfied myself that he was an absolute liar.' One reason why Dew was able to come to this conclusion was that he had elicited from Flora a series of assertions, in her third statement, which flatly contradict Leate's testimony. Trethowan was highly critical of the way that statement – indeed all of Flora's – had been gathered, remarking, 'The cross examination of the Chief Constable before the Coroner & Magistrates will shew the extraordinary way in which the Police acted in this matter in obtaining the three statements from the Prisoner.' It is quite clear, despite Dew's remark on 4 November, that 'she [Flora] absolutely, (without of course knowing what he [Leate] had said) contradicted it in every detail', that his questions were leading. Thus, in Flora's statement, she said, 'It would not be true if anyone says that I followed a man down Meadow Road . . .', 'It would not be true if anyone says that I walked back to my house after following the man . . .' and 'It would be quite untrue for anyone to say that I was weeping and wailing quietly . . .' With that, a whole line of inquiry was dispensed with.

That someone left 40 Meadow Road in the manner Flora described seemed at least possible. Among the witnesses interviewed by Richardson and Dew was the wife of Henry Hawkins, a railway fireman, at 29 Meadow Road, diagonally opposite No. 40 and about 40 feet distant. The couple had a dog, said to be 'quiet with neighbours' but possessed of a keen sense of smell and a marked antipathy to strangers. The dog, evidently not a large one, was frenziedly trying to clear their fence at about 10.25 p.m. on October 31 in pursuit of such a stranger, and its fury was heard by their neighbour John Philpott. Dew and Richardson's reaction to the story was to cut it short. The possibility of a local suspect, identified in Trethowan's brief to counsel, who promptly 'went to ground' was never followed up. As Trethowan noted, 'Nothing of this of course was stated by the Prosecution either before the Coroner or before the Magistrates, and great stress was put on the fact that a search was made for some man, & no man could be found, or was known to be missing.' Indeed, instead of pursuing that line of inquiry, Dew, perhaps subconsciously pursuing the idea of the man fleeing No. 40, in the direction of James Street, where Flora's friend Mrs Mold lived, latched onto the notion that the man might be her son Alfred, whose name was romantically linked with Flora's. It was, of course, quickly realised that Mold was nowhere near the scene of the crime, but in Dew's eyes he provided the missing piece of the jigsaw – *a motive*. That, to one of Dew's mindset, was sufficient excuse to intercept the *Adriatic*, on board which Mold was a steward; but it led to him being out of the country for some short time while the liner crossed the channel to Cherbourg.

Despite this and other motives being discounted by both prosecution and defence, Dew continued to believe in Flora's ill intent. His premise of her guilt was reinforced time and time again, and can be charted through his reports to the Director of Public Prosecutions. Thus, in that dated 26 December 1908 he refers to addresses in a pocket-book, resulting in trips to Gosport and to Goole, in pursuit of people with whom Flora might have been liaising. In that dated 7 January he reports a fourth-hand conversation in which Flora acknowledged to Thwaites over a month earlier that the case looked black against her, and that, as she would also say to Matilda Sheppard, that if she had killed Teddy she did not know it. In that dated 1 March 1909, Dew goes so far as to relate a story about Flora threatening to have Teddy put away for some misdeed, as illustrative of her intentions with regard to the boy. In his final report to the DPP, he described Flora as 'a cool, calculating woman', who 'found that this poor cripple boy, was either a hindrance to her getting married to Mold, or to her carrying on intrigues with men, and so she determined to get rid of him.'

Walter Dew was a man captivated by a sense of the dramatic in his vocation, from the thrill of pursuit to the shock of mutual recognition. Reference has already been made to his dream of catching Jack the Ripper red-handed, and in his memoirs he compares meeting Crippen face-to-face with the encounter between Stanley and Livingstone. Whether that view – typical of what has been described as the heroic age of police detective-work, and in a tradition indebted to the work of Jack Whicher in fact and Sherlock Holmes in fiction – was appropriate to the case of Teddy Haskell would now be tested in the scales of justice.

12

'Who could have done it?': The First Trial, Day One: 15 February 1909

O N THE EAST SIDE of Northgate Street in Devizes, between an outstation of Wadworth's brewery – the former White Lion Inn – and a row of cottages named Cyprus Terrace, stands the Assize Court. A handsome classical building of Bath stone of 1835, designed by T.H. Wyatt, its centrepiece is an ionic portico of four columns with the arms of Salisbury on the tympanum. Disused for a quarter of a century, its windows boarded up, the Court stands today a forlorn reminder of its career as the crucible of the County's justice a century ago. The case to be heard was the most sensational murder trial in the county for a generation at least, and perhaps since the notorious Road Hill case of 1860.

Monday 15 February 1909, the date fixed at the Winter Assizes for Flora Haskell's trial, dawned dull and blustery.[1] Even so, crowds gathered round the Court House soon after 9 a.m. As the doors opened the crowd surged forward for the public gallery, women at the forefront, pushing for a place and climbing over the benches to gain places at the front of the gallery. In a scene reminiscent of a London stage show, as the barrier to the gallery was cleared, an excited shout of 'Hurrah! I'm first' was heard, amidst giggles of satisfaction. In the words of the *Devizes and Wiltshire Gazette*, 'The officer in charge has his work cut out to regulate the admissions to the [lower gallery], and before he could look round he found the two front [rows of] seats, kept for the jurymen, quite full. Much to the chagrin of those who had obtained seats, upon which they were

congratulating each other, they had to turn out. Most of the other seats were full, and they had to retire.' Once there, some who had secured seats stayed put for the day: others less lucky, many of whom had travelled from afar, hung around for the whole day on the off-chance of gaining admission. There was considerable press interest, with reporters from the four Wiltshire newspapers which are the main source of the foregoing account, and from five or six London newspapers. At 10.30, the judge, Mr Justice Ridley, left his lodgings across the road from the court in the High Sheriff's carriage. His arrival was heralded by a fanfare of trumpets, and he took his seat in the plain, cheerless courtroom at 10.34, accompanied by the High Sheriff of the County, Mr F.H. Goldney, resplendent in court dress, the Sheriff's chaplain, the Revd W.H. Weeks, in hood and gown, and the Chief Constable of the Wiltshire Constabulary, Captain Hoël Llewellyn, and his immediate predecessor, Captain Robert Sterne, R.N.

The twelve good men and true who made up the jury comprised Frank Billington, Herbert Blake, Frederick George Butler, George Frederick Church, Herbert Beesley Coles, George Douglas Crook, Robert Hooper, Robert Henry Jefferies, George Long, James Henry Vernon Lucas, William Edward Morse and Lewis Snelgrove Newman. Three of them were business neighbours in the Market Place: Billington a grocer at No. 36, Lucas a draper at Nos 43-44, and Coles a hairdresser and tobacconist at No. 45. They filed into the box, and then the Clerk of

LORD JUSTICE RIDLEY, WHO CONDUCTED THE FIRST
TRIAL. *from Vanity Fair*

Assize issued his command to the Governor of the Gaol, to 'Put up Haskell!' Flora, accompanied by three prison staff, was led up the stone steps from the cells below the court, and up the steep wooden steps into the dock, a decanter of water and a tumbler to hand. There she took her place 'with more ease and less concern than might have been expected', a slight, hollow-cheeked figure dressed in black, accompanied by a kind-faced prison chaplain and one of the wardresses. Flora now had some colour in her cheeks, and looked much better than she did at her committal in November.

The indictment, that she did 'feloniously, wilfully and of your malice aforethought kill and murder Edwin Richard Haskell at 40 Meadow Road, Salisbury, on October 31st' was read out. Asked by the Clerk of the Court, James Read, 'What say you, Flora Fanny Haskell, are you guilty or not guilty?',

Flora readily replied, in a voice described variously as "low" but "firm [and] clear", 'I plead not guilty, my Lord'. The Clerk advised Flora of her right to object to any juryman being sworn, but she offered no such objection, and the jury was sworn in, with Billington being appointed foreman. Counsel for the Crown comprised Mr J. Alderson Foote and Mr T.H. Parr, who had represented the Director of Public Prosecutions from the third day of the inquest, 19 October. Foote, then 60, had had, like the judge, a distinguished academic career. A Carthusian, he had gained a first in classics at St John's, Cambridge, and, following a Whewell Scholarship in international law, had written *A treatise on private international jurisprudence*, 1878, with a second edition in 1892. But, while respected and liked within the Bar, and always courteous in court, his obituarist noted that he was prone to "a certain polite intolerance, which was more amusing than successful." Defending Flora was Rayner Goddard, described by the *Salisbury Times* as "a brilliant young barrister", instructed by W.J. Trethowan (who had defended Flora at the inquest), and assisted by Alfred Felix Schuster, a relative of Goddard's by marriage, and, in fact, his senior in the profession.

Opening the prosecution's case at twenty to eleven, Foote began with the charge: that 'Flora Fanny Haskell is charged with the wilful murder of her son, Edwin Richard Haskell, aged twelve years. I need hardly remind you that you have a most painful and difficult duty to perform. It will be necessary to go with considerable detail into the case, and it will occupy a good deal of your time. You will have to enquire into a great many things that appear small, and which actually are small, but it will be necessary that you attend to them all, and follow as closely as you can in order to appreciate the strength or weakness – as you may regard it – of the case presented to you.

'The prisoner is a widow, aged 34, and she lived with her little boy, twelve years old, who was a cripple, having lost a leg which had been amputated.' Foote then showed the jury the large-scale plan of the neighbourhood, and Notley's diagram of the house. 'You will observe that Meadow Road and York Road cross each other. The prisoner lives at No. 40,

Meadow Road. The houses on that road are small houses, such as working people would have, with, on the ground floor, a front room, a back room or kitchen, and a scullery, and on the upper floor, two rooms, back and front. You will see that from York Road, a back passage runs up behind Meadow Road, giving access to the back doors. The back door of the house opens into the scullery, close to the door of which is the sink. The scullery opens into the kitchen. Above the kitchen is the bedroom, where the boy was found murdered, lying in his bed. There is no doubt that after he had gone to sleep someone did go up and murder the child, and that he died probably very quickly – certainly without being able to call out and, we hope, without a great deal of suffering.

40 MEADOW RD 1908, X MARKS THE SPOT

Living in this house the mother gains her living by taking in washing, earning a small but steady livelihood. There is no evidence that she is in want any more than all people who earn a small wage are to a certain extent in want, nor in worse circumstances than her neighbours. I don't suppose she was never pressed from day to day, [but nor] was [she] pressed more than usual, and I do not suggest that she is anything but an honest and industrious woman, living with her child and supporting him. Although the little boy had suffered the terrible calamity of losing his leg by amputation, he was an active, bright and cheerful little fellow, who went to school and got on well with his school mates, and generally enjoyed his poor little life more than one would expect possible under such circumstances.

'The day when this dreadful event took place was October the thirty-first, and roughly about ten-thirty at night, perhaps a few minutes before. The lad was murdered as near as we can put it, at twenty-five minutes past ten; it was a Saturday night. Mrs Haskell was seen by several people about the city within an hour of the time when the tragedy occurred, and she appeared to be in her normal state of health. According to her own statement she had been doing the usual things a woman in her position does on a Saturday night – going shopping and things of that kind. About nine thirty-five she was seen by a man next door, No. 38, a Mr Noble. He was her brother-in-law, and she was in his house about nine thirty-five. Except that she made some remark about intending to take another house there was nothing worthy of comment in what she then said; she was, so far as can be judged, an ordinary, rational woman at nine thirty-five. At nine o'clock the little boy himself was in the Nobles' house, also in his ordinary condition, cheerful and well. That was the last time anybody saw the little boy alive.

'The prisoner appeared to have gone back into her house, and in ten minutes or less she was seen there by a Miss Steer, a dressmaker. Miss Steer lives next door but one, No. 36, and had been making an article of dress for Mrs Haskell – a little coat – and brought it in [for her] to try on at ten minutes to ten. As far as Miss Steer could judge Mrs Haskell was then in her ordinary, usual state of mind. According to her statement she had before this point put the little boy to bed – [at] about nine o'clock or very near it.

'The next person going to the house was a boy named Wyatt, and as nearly as we can calculate – [and] it is important to try and ascertain the time – that was at ten-seventeen. He was an errand-boy who had a pair of boots to take to Mrs Manning, who lived at No. 42, but Mrs Manning was in bed, and he went to Mrs Haskell's house and knocked at the front door to ask her to take them in for Mrs Manning. The front door was locked – I ask you to notice that at, as nearly as we can tell, ten-seventeen, the front door was locked. He gave the parcel to her, but saw nothing in Mrs Haskell to draw attention to her condition. You have therefore got to within a few minutes before the deed was actually committed, and I do not think it conceivable that there was anybody inside the house beside Mrs Haskell and her son, whom she put to bed. The fact that the front door was locked conclusively shows that there was nobody else was in the house at this time except the prisoner and the little boy. . . . Or, I will not say *that*: it is conceivable, of course, that a man had concealed himself in the house at an earlier period of the day, and I do not want to prejudice the case; but short of some such supposition as that, Mrs Haskell was alone in the house with the boy, upstairs and asleep at ten-seventeen or ten-twenty. Between that time and ten-thirty exactly the child was killed by having his throat cut.

'The next thing, so far as it was seen by anybody, was [seen] by one of the Nobles, a boy named Percy, whose age is about sixteen years. He is a nephew of the prisoner and lives next door. That boy had borrowed a shilling earlier in the day from the prisoner, and as he was passing the back of the house, No. 40, to go to his own house, going by way of the back passage, and seeing a light in Mrs Haskell's kitchen he thought he would call and pay the shilling. So he went to the back door of No. 40 – leading into the scullery – and there being no knocker he knocked at the back door with his knee.

What Percy Noble then heard and saw is of the greatest importance, and you must pay attention to what the boy himself will say rather than to what I say about it. He thinks Mrs Haskell did not answer instantaneously, but certainly there was no delay such as to arouse the boy's suspicions. He saw the light burning in the kitchen – a good light – and he heard the sound of a chair being moved. That may have been that the woman was sitting in the chair and that as she got up she pushed the chair, or that she knocked against a chair as she passed it. In fact it may have been caused in a variety of ways. The lad also says he heard another noise which he described variously as a fall or a thump. That was the only other noise he heard; he certainly did not hear the noise as of a door being opened, or shut. Almost immediately after, he saw the shadow of the woman on the blind, coming between the gas and the window to where the kitchen opened by a door into the scullery.

'Before or after that, exactly which he could not say, he heard Mrs Haskell scream; there was no doubt she screamed within a few seconds of opening

40 MEADOW ROAD. THE BACK DOOR KNOCKED BY PERCY NOBLE ON THE NIGHT OF THE MURDER.
© *Timothy W. Frank Walker and Ann Richardson Whittle, grandchildren of Frank Richardson, Chief Constable*

the outer scullery door. As she opened it she said to him, "Run for the doctor. There's a man killed my poor Teddy." The boy ran off quickly to get help from a doctor, so that his evidence as to the woman's condition at this time is probably not very minute, and probably not very accurate. He ran quickly out the same way that he came in – down the back way into York Road. As he emerged from the passage into York Road he was at once seen by a young man and young woman, respectable, credible witnesses, who were walking along York Road to where it is crossed by Meadow Road.' At this point Foote pointed out where, on the block plan, the young couple were. 'They walked on, and had passed Meadow Road, and had got half way between the corner and the back way, a distance of about twenty-five yards when the boy emerged, when they heard screams coming from Meadow Road. These two witnesses heard the scream, and they went back some fifteen yards to the corner to see what it was, and saw Mrs Haskell at her front door, screaming.

The importance of that lies in this. You will see that if Mrs Haskell, after telling the boy Noble to go for help, had rushed straight to the front door to scream, she would have got there in a short time, as quickly as the boy could emerge from the back passage into York Road, because it was a shorter distance for her to go. But as a matter of fact she was slower than the boy by the time it took these two people to walk some twenty-five yards, therefore she did not rush directly from the back door to the front door, and did not reach it until some little time after Noble got to York Road. That is, if you can rely on the evidence of the two people I have just mentioned, the young man and young woman, as I think you can, you will see that there is an interval. It was not very long, but you will notice from the plan that near the back door was a sink, and a tap, and it is quite plain that she would have had time under the circumstances, if there were blood upon her hands, to rinse her hands. She certainly could have run from the back door to the front door, as the sequence of events would prove. She would have had time to wash her hands, but nothing else.

'I must now tell you what Mrs Haskell's own story was. She says that she was sitting in the kitchen, and, intending to go out to see a neighbour or buy something, she lowered the gas and went to the door leading from the kitchen into the passage. The door opened into the passage at the foot of the staircase, and the passage went straight to the front door. As she got to the door a man came down the stairs, threw something at her which did not hit her; he then ran down the passage, and got away. At the moment of the knife being thrown at her she heard a knock at the back door and immediately ran to answer it. Then it was that she saw the boy Noble, and told him to run for the doctor. Roughly, that is her account of what took place. I must point out that the passage leads straight to the front door, and that going to open the front door from inside, the handle is on the right and the hinge on the left, so that the obvious, ordinary way of opening the front door is with the right hand. It is important to observe that, because although you will hear a lot about traces and spots of blood in the house, there was no blood on the front door, nor on the door handle, nor anywhere nearer the door than some marks in the passage where the kitchen door opened.

To go on with the story: it is not disputed that when the woman came screaming to the door to answer Percy Noble she had not gone upstairs to see what was the matter, nor had she followed the man she alleged she saw in the house. Although, of course, it is very difficult, almost impossible to imagine what a woman would do under such circumstances, whether she were guilty or innocent, yet I am bound

to suggest to you that when the mother saw a man running down from upstairs with a knife and some signs of blood – because, apparently, she saw signs of blood – her instinct would be either to run upstairs to see what had happened to the child, or to follow the man. Or, if hearing a knock at the back door, she would naturally go there first, to see if there was anybody who could help her. I could conceive that, but surely, having done that and sent Percy Noble for the doctor, or for help, she would then go upstairs to see whether her child was safe.

'She did not – she did nothing of the sort. She ran – after that short interval of time which I have described – to the front door instead, and screamed, and then she made no attempt to follow the man. Her screams at the front door attracted the attention of the Steers who live at No. 38. At the time all the family of Steers were in their kitchen, and hearing the first scream, which seemed to come from the back – it must have been the scream which the woman gave just as she opened the door to Percy Noble – Mr Steer ran out to he back [of the] premises and looked that way. No sooner had he got out to the back than he heard screams that seemed to come from the front. Without going through his own premises he ran to the front by way of the narrow passage leading direct into Meadow Road, followed rather more deliberately by his wife and mother-in-law. In Meadow Road he was the first person actually on the scene: the young man and woman who were walking down York Road were not actually on the scene, [and] their evidence was confined to fixing when Mrs Haskell got to the front door. When Steer came out of the passage way into Meadow Road, Mrs Haskell was either at her front door, or a few feet or a yard away from it nearer to Mr Steer, and she called out to him, "Man round the corner", and repeated to him that someone had killed her Teddy. One must try to understand what she meant by "Man round the corner". Naturally, having regard to the fact that her house is on the corner, one takes it that she meant Mr Steer to understand that the man had turned from her house to the right, and gone either up or down York Road. Mr Steer ran to that corner, and, looking up, saw no-one; looking down, he saw two men outside the *Duke of York* public house, one man standing and the other going in. These men were afterwards found to be respectable inhabitants of the neighbourhood; both they and the police were occupied some time in enquiring as to the two men whom Mr Steer saw, but it has been satisfactorily cleared up. Mr Steer went as far as the *Duke of York*, and then made his way back to 40 Meadow Road, and he was practically the first person in the house. He went upstairs, followed by Mrs Butt, a witness who arrived early on the scene, and [he] had no possible means of knowing what had happened.

'He is quite clear that up to that time Mrs Haskell had not gone upstairs, and although she had called out that her child was killed she certainly had no means of knowing it from anything she had seen. The only possible means she could have had of knowing it was that she says she saw a man coming downstairs, that he threw a knife at her and that there was blood about. It may be that that is enough – I am not expressing any opinion – and it may be that it is not enough, but I submit that you are bound to consider very carefully the fact that Mrs Haskell did not go upstairs to see what had happened. Later on she attempted to go upstairs, but you will find that that was not until after her mother, Mrs Carter,

had come to the house that she made any offer to go upstairs, and that it was not earlier than eleven-fifteen, three-quarters of an hour after the tragedy took place. Somewhere about that time, she and Mrs Carter did offer to go upstairs, but Mr Steer advised her not to go yet. Later on still, Mrs Haskell asked Steer to tell her what had happened to her boy, but that does not detract from the gravity of the fact that immediately after the thing happened she made no attempt to go upstairs, or to enquire what had occurred.'

'Mr Steer went upstairs and saw the child lying on the bed.' Referring to Notley's plan of the first floor of No. 40, he continued, 'The bedstead was in the corner, the head and one side being against the wall. Against the other wall, opposite to the head of the bed, was a chest of drawers, [and] between the two was a chair. The door opened against the foot of the bed. These are the material points. There was a great deal of blood on both pillows. From the medical evidence there could be no doubt that the person who killed the child, whoever it was, stood at the head of the bed near the chair, and leant over, probably putting the left hand out to hold or to steady the boy's head, and then with the right hand drew a sharp knife across the throat, severing the jugular vein and the

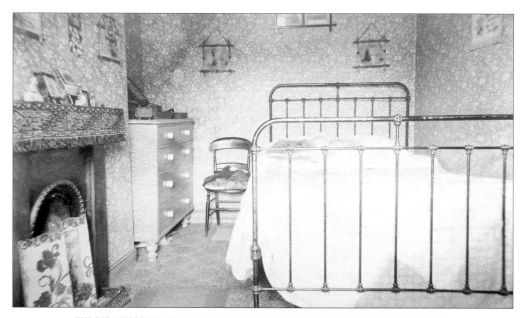

THE BED WHERE THE CRIME WAS COMMITTED SHOWING THE BLOOD STAINED PILLOW.
© *Timothy W.Frank Walker and Ann Richardson Whittle, grandchildren of Frank Richardson, Chief Constable*

windpipe with one deep slash. It required considerable force in one sense, but it depended upon the keenness of the knife and the steadiness of the hand. The spurting of blood caused by the severance of the vein was away from where the person would be standing. But there would be a certain amount of blood blown also from the windpipe – the breathing would go on until the air in the lungs was exhausted, and as it was expelled it would blow some of the blood – and the child's head being turned somewhat that blood would be blown in the direction towards the chest of drawers. There was some blood on the pillow that side, some on the chest of drawers, a little on the chair, a little on the floor, a little on the wall – a little, that is, compared with the amount there was on the pillows.' At this graphic description, Flora burst into tears.

Foote continued: '[There were] also found traces of blood on the bars at the bottom of the bedstead, and dripping or splashing of blood on the wall of the staircase – the right-hand wall coming down. With indications of blood all the way it needs no argument to show that the person who killed the child fled across the landing, down the staircase, to the bottom of the stairs. From that spot the blood did not go on to the front door. This is important,' he continued, 'it is a factor in the case that the knife with which unquestionably the murderer committed the deed was found lying just there, at the entrance to the door of the kitchen, at the bottom of the staircase. As it lay, the handle was in a diagonal direction, not towards the kitchen but towards the passage.' At this point, Mr Justice Ridley queried this detail of Foote's exposition, and the counsel agreed to ask the jury to reserve opinion on the point until they had heard the evidence. He continued, 'The knife was lying for at least an hour before it was picked up, though many people were in and out, and conclusive evidence as to the direction in which it was lying would be found in the mark made by the bloody blade as it lay on the floor – not the whole length of the blade, however, because the handle of the table knife elevated the blade from the floor. You should observe that the only blood down the stairs appeared to be that shaken from the knife, and that [the murderer] having got rid of the knife there was no reason why more blood should be

shaken. That is for you to consider in relation to the fact that no blood appeared on the passage or at the front door.

'Steer came down from the bedroom to the kitchen and almost immediately afterwards two doctors arrived – Dr Wilks and Dr Row. One doctor happened to be visiting the other, who lived a short distance off, and their bicycles were in the hall, so that they could come instantaneously. Mrs Haskell appeared to have been then in the kitchen and made a statement concerning a man coming down the stairs, and Steer went out and made further enquiries with the police as to the two men he saw standing by the *Duke of York*. It took him an appreciable time, and going back once more to 40, Meadow Road, he found that Mrs Carter, Mrs Haskell's mother, was there. He went again to the bedroom and found a watch. He went downstairs and asked Mrs Haskell if the watch belonged to the little boy, and Mrs Haskell then said, "Is my Teddy all right?" He went upstairs again, and here the case may vary a little from the way in which it has previously been presented. Steer went downstairs again, and I suggest that it was not until then, at eleven-fifteen, that Mrs Haskell and her mother made the offer to go upstairs; she did not offer to go upstairs earlier than that, not when he came downstairs asking her about the watch. The doctors went away a short time, and [on their] coming back about eleven-thirty Mrs Haskell asked what was the matter with the boy. Other statements were made by her, all of which I will presently read out to the jury.

'I now come to another point. Mrs Haskell was that night wearing a light blouse and dark skirt, and there were a great many spots of blood upon both – fifty upon the skirt and twenty-eight upon the blouse, the bulk of the spots being mainly on the right half, extending downwards from the shoulder, the biggest spot being just at the wrist of the sleeve. The spots on the skirt were mainly on the right-hand side.

'The doctors and Professor Pepper have made minute and scientific examination of the spots, and will tell you that in their opinion it is impossible for the spots to have come from a knife being thrown at the woman, whether the knife was covered with blood or not. Some were spots that may have spurted on,

FLORA HASKELL'S KITCHEN WHERE SHE WAS SITTING WHEN PERCY NOBLE KNOCKED THE BACK DOOR.
© *Timothy W. Frank Walker and Ann Richardson Whittle, grandchildren of Frank Richardson, Chief Constable*

some had fallen and trickled down a little, being bigger at one end than at the other. You are as well able to judge as the doctors are, or as I am — fortunately it is your duty, not mine to judge, how far spots of that kind could be thrown upon the woman from a knife thrown at her; [and] she never said it hit her. It is obvious that the amount of blood which can be carried on a knife is comparatively small, and if it had been dripping [blood] in the bedroom and as it was carried to the passage down the staircase, by the time the bearer of it had got to the bottom of the stairs there would be much less than when the man started from the bedside. These are matters to which you will have to direct your most careful attention, because these are the facts which bear most strongly against the prisoner.

'That is not all. In the kitchen were three chairs standing against the wall separating the room from the staircase; also in the room was a table with a white tablecloth upon it. There was very little room — only one foot seven inches — to allow a person who wished to get to the scullery to pass between the stairs and the table, and it is not easy to pass without coming into contact with the chairs or the table. Upon the part of the tablecloth which hung down on that side of the table there were smudges and spots of blood. It cannot be suggested that anybody but Mrs Haskell passed between the chairs and the table to [reach] the scullery, and a careful examination has been made by the doctors to see if upon her skirt or clothing there appeared to be any corresponding smears or smudges. No such traces could be found after [a] very careful and anxious search. The expert evidence was that the smears were more consistent with something carried in the hand than with anything else. One of the women in the place came in shortly after the discovery of the murder, before Mrs Haskell had been upstairs, and offered the prisoner some *eau de Cologne*. Finding that the prisoner had a handkerchief in her hand which was bloodstained she took it from her and placed it on the mantelpiece, and then gave her the *eau de Cologne*. There were one or two handkerchiefs which will be spoken of as having marks of blood. This handkerchief has an amount of blood which cannot be accounted for in the way that is suggested by the defence – that the boy hit his ear at school a few days before, knocked a scab off and dabbed it with the handkerchief. I don't know of any suggestion which sufficiently accounts for the blood found upon this handkerchief. At this time, certainly, the prisoner had not been upstairs, and the only way in which she can have got blood on her clothing or the handkerchief she carried would be from the passing of the man who threw the knife at her without hitting her. It has been suggested that she had a scratch upon the nose caused by a ring she wore a few days before. But in the first place the evidence shows that that was dry and healed and in any case that would be quite inadequate to account for the amount of blood on the handkerchief. I have not seen the handkerchief, and I do not suggest it was soaked in blood, but the blood was in larger quantities than could be accounted for by either of the ways suggested. If it is true if Mrs Haskell passed along between chairs and the table – and it is true – and if it is true that no-one else passed between the chairs and the table, then the blood upon the table cloth would be caused by her clothing, or her hand, or something she carried. Someone did presently pass between the chairs and the table, but there was no evidence they had blood upon them, while the smeared tablecloth could be accounted for by Mrs Haskell carrying the bloodstained handkerchief.

'You must consider this evidence of the blood together – the blood upstairs, the blood upon the knife, the blood upon the woman – but at this stage of the case you must not endeavour to make up your minds. You must hear the expert evidence, which I will not undertake to repeat, [for] I prefer that you hear the medical men themselves.'

Next, Foote discussed the money missing from that which Teddy was saving for a new artificial leg, kept in a chest of drawers in the lad's bedroom. 'There is one other thing it is difficult to understand. In the chest of drawers in the bedroom where the murder was committed, the prisoner said [there] was a sum of money. After the murder, the prisoner enquired several times during the night whether the boy's

money was safe, and said there should be eight pounds two shillings in one of the drawers in the bedroom. But when the police examined the drawer they found only three pounds ten shillings, underneath a cloth which was inside the drawer. It would appear that the money was collected, or given to the boy, for the purpose of enabling him, later on, to buy a cork leg, which would not, however, be bought until he finished growing. It was money given him largely by his grandmother, who, though a poor woman, was in possession of the King's Bounty at Christmas time. Perhaps the most difficult thing to understand in relation to this drawer, was not so much the fact that three pounds ten shillings was there – although that was a little difficult to account for. If the murder was committed for robbery one would have expected all the money to be taken, and not three pounds ten shillings left, but the most difficult thing to understand was the condition and position of the lock of the drawer. When the police saw the drawer it was apparently shut and fastened, but, on drawing it out, it was found that the lock was hanging, so to speak, by a thread – on the point of one tin tack, from which the head was gone. The lock should have been secured by four or more tacks or nails or screws, one in each corner, but they were of a light and fragile character, and evidently at some time or another – when, no-one knows – the drawer had been burst open – no, I will not say "burst", because there was no appearance of any bursting nor of any instrument being used to open it. But it had been pulled so strongly that the lock had come off, and, suspended as it was by one tin tack without a head, it must have fallen into the drawer if the drawer was roughly opened and shut. This is the difficulty. It is not for me to [do] more than indicate the fact and tell you the view I take of it for the Crown.

'Assuming for a moment that there was a man in the room, you have also to assume that he knew there was money kept upstairs in the child's room, and that he went there to steal it. We must also assume that he opened the drawer before he murdered the boy, because though there was a little spurt of blood from the boy's windpipe upon the drawers there were no blood-marks on the handle of the drawer, nor on the lock, nor on the cloth in which the money was wrapped. The robbery must, therefore, have been committed first, and the murder afterwards, and it is difficult to understand why the murder took place at all, and why three pounds ten shillings was left.

'On the other hand we have nothing but the statement of the woman herself to show what amount of money was originally in the drawer. It would appear from the evidence that Mrs Haskell had taken part of the money and put it to another use, but do not let it be thought that I am attributing that to her as a crime. It might have been better if she had left the money for the purpose for which it was intended, but I would never dream of suggesting in this Court that it was an act committed by Mrs Haskell which should be treated as a crime. But we do not know: practically all we know is that there was three pounds ten shillings found in the drawer and Mrs Haskell said there ought to have been eight pounds two shillings. We do not know when the drawer was last opened – there was a key to it in the little basket standing on the chest of drawers, but we do not know when it was last used. I am telling you these things, but I do not present the facts on behalf of the Crown as having any bearing on the case, although they are facts you ought to have your attention drawn to. I will tell you also that the sum of eight pounds was found on Mrs Haskell when the arrest was made, but the Chief Constable of Salisbury has satisfied himself that it belonged to Mrs Carter. If I were to make a suggestion at all, it would be that the condition of this drawer has nothing to do with the case, that it was something which happened before the murder, and not for the purposes of robbery. Though it makes an additional difficulty in the case, it has no material bearing upon the charge you have to try'

Foote then read out the three statements which Flora had made on various occasions to the police. 'The material points have already been made in my opening, but I draw your attention to two circumstances which Mrs Haskell put forward as being suspicious in character. One is, that on the night before the murder, a strange man, whom she has described, called at her house and was very anxious to get a lodging there, saying that he had been told that she let lodgings, and seemed upset because she

refused to take him in. She has never let lodgings', Foote continued. 'Only her brother and a man named Alfred Mold, steward on the *Adriatic*, slept there once or twice. This man Mold is the one to whom, it is said, the prisoner is to be married – but his movements have been satisfactorily explained. There is not the slightest suggestion that there has been any impropriety, or any calling for censure, nor is there any evidence on which the Crown could make the suggestion that there is any motive arising out of the proposed marriage which would account for the murder. The other is that somebody – a man in the street – offered Teddy money to write down his address, and that he was seen writing it at home a few days before the murder. But enquiries have been made at Fisherton School, and there is no doubt that someone *in the school* did ask him to write down his name for the purpose of sending him some postage stamps – or some such boyish thing.'

'A very important piece of evidence will be placed before you which I do not propose to repeat. When she was in the cells the prisoner made a statement to Mrs Shepherd, the wardress at Salisbury, which will probably have a material bearing on the question of the prisoner's innocence or guilt. I will not tell you what it is, but will let it come from the mouth of the witness when she is called.'

And so, Foote came to the conclusion of his speech for the prosecution, and with it an astonishing admission which was to hobble the Crown's case from the outset – that there was no motive – let alone one involving Mold – for Flora to have committed the murder.

'Substantially, I have said all that I have to say on the evidence,' he continued, 'but I have said nothing yet upon a question which I have no doubt will be impressed upon you. What motive could the prisoner have in doing this? That is one of the problems it is impossible for me to answer. You must remember that I who address you know no more of the case than you know now, except that I know more of the details; I know no more than his lordship knows, nor than those instructing the defence know.

'Gentlemen of the Jury, we are simply here to ascertain the truth. If I knew why this little boy was murdered, or who murdered him, I should be here in a different capacity from that wherein I stand; and I tell you frankly, on the part of the Crown, that I am not able to place before you any reason why the prisoner should have murdered this child, nor am I able to suggest to you any reason why anyone else should have murdered him. But we know he is dead, and we know that his throat was cut, and that whoever cut that child's throat must have done so without any adequate – indeed without *any* motive.' (At this, Flora broke down, again). 'I do not understand the workings of the human mind. I cannot tell you what state of mind that woman was in when she cut the boy's throat, if she did it. In the history of the world there have been many cases in which murders are committed, either in an abnormal state of mind – for the moment, a state of frenzy, or a state of obliviousness, or a state of passion – quite consistent with sanity, so far as medical men are able to judge of sanity afterwards.

'The prisoner has been under the observation of the prison surgeon, who has experience in these matters, and I shall place him in the box, and he will tell you that he regards her as perfectly sane. It is you, gentlemen, who have to speculate as to the cause, and decide as to the possibility, of this woman, or anybody else, committing the crime. It is as much your duty as it is mine. I see no sufficient evidence which would justify me, on behalf of the Crown, in putting any theory before you. I could suggest possible theories, but I do not put them forward. You might say that the woman was going to be married, and it may be that the boy was an impediment, but, gentlemen, as far as I can test that, and as far as the evidence goes, there is no ground for it. I do not put it forward, and I do not ask you to accept it. You might say the woman had stolen the boy's money, and wanted to hide it. But I see no evidence on which I should be justified in making that submission to you, even if it offered any explanation why she should take that course. Nor should I offer any reason why the deed was done, because, if the mother wanted the money, nothing would have been easier than for her to take it. But if she had taken it, or any part of it, I cannot see, and I don't think you can see, any reason why she should cut the child's throat. The two things do not appear to me to bear on each other, and therefore

I do not put that theory before you. It would be wrong of me to put it before you unless I could bear it out.

'When you consider this evidence, I ask you to remember that the theory, as far as the Crown is able to present a theory at all, is that the woman committed the act in one of those extraordinary abnormal conditions of mind, which do overtake human beings sometimes, and of which it is impossible for medical men or legal experts to give any adequate explanation. Unquestionably, the absence of motive does add greatly to the difficulty of your task and mine. It adds to it in every way, because if you accept the theory of the man you still have to construct a theory of why he murdered the child. Take the sort of thing shadowed out in Mrs Haskell's statement, that some man came to the house to ask for lodgings, some man asked the boy to write his address on paper, does it seem a reasonable theory that there should be anybody in the world who would cut this little cripple's throat with no motive, but simply that he was a cripple and a little boy. There is still no motive: you are just as far from any rational explanation. That is the initial difficulty. Then you are met with the physical difficulties of the case. How did the man know the money was there? How did he get into the room? How did he get the knife, which was generally kept in the kitchen? You are met with all these physical difficulties directly.

'But apart from the physical difficulties, the difficulty would be as great in suggesting a motive if a maniac in the form of a madman had got there. No-one cuts the throat of a twelve year-old child without adequate or reasonable motive. It must be that at the moment when the act is committed the will of the person who commits it is not to be judged in the same way as we judge the will of an ordinary person performing the ordinary duties of life. Therefore you must address yourselves to this dreadful problem, and decide whether the evidence I shall call is sufficient to satisfy you of the prisoner's guilt, remembering what I have said as to the question of motive, and bearing in mind that whoever committed this deed committed an act for which no adequate motive can be suggested by any advocate who addresses you.'

Having held the court's ear for two hours, Foote handed over to Parr to examine the first two witnesses, Charles Notley, Assistant City Surveyor, and Horace Charles Messer, the local photographer. Their duty was to set the topographical scene for the events of October 31st.

Notley explained how he had examined the house at 40, Meadow Road, and the neighbouring streets, and took measurements for a block plan of the house which was shown in court. He continued, 'I have heard Mr Foote's description of the plan. The front door does open inward, with the handle on the left hand side going out. The width of the bottom of the stairs is 2ft 6in, and it is the same all the way up. On the 23 of November I took the distance of the kitchen table from the wall parting the kitchen from the staircase. Chief Inspector Dew was then present. I found [that the distance] from the corner of the table nearest the door to the wall was 3ft 2¼ inches. From the other corner of the table to the same wall it was not quite the same: it was 3ft 1inch. On 28 of November I took further evidence of the table, and besides the Chief Constable there was a Mr. Rawlins there who placed a chair near the door leading to the passage and it was close against the wall. Mr Rawlins also, at the same time, placed the table in the same position as it was when I took the measurement. From the front edge of the chair to the line of the kitchen table was 1ft 7½ inches. I have seen the house at night. If the front door is shut, and there is no light in the kitchen, there will be no light in the passage, and the staircase is not lighted. There is a glass fanlight over the front door, and very nearly opposite is a street lamp, but that does not show any light on the stairs.'

Notley had also prepared a block plan of the bedroom, having taken the measurements on Thursday 11 February. 'The bed is 4ft 4½ inches wide, and the height from the floor to the top of the mattress on the bed was 2ft. I took some paper off the wall of the bedroom, where a chair was, about 3ft from the floor. I gave the paper to Dr Kempe, the police surgeon. I also took off from the right hand wall of the staircase, going down, another piece of paper, which was a strip right down the staircase, parallel with the stairs. The bottom of the paper was

about 3ft from the bottom of the treads underneath.' Notley also surveyed the neighbourhood for a plan of the streets around Meadow Road on display in the court. Asked about the gas street lighting he explained that the contract with the Gas Company stipulated a minimum output of 50 candle-power, and that would show [some light] on the front door of the prisoner's house. Cross-examined by Goddard, Notley stated that 'The model correctly shows the staircase, and the bottom step of the stairs comes level with the jamb of the door', and that 'In Meadow Road there is no lamp on Mrs Haskell's side of the road, nearer than the corner of James Street, and the distance is 147 feet.'

Next came the photographer Horace Charles Messer. He said: 'I took photos under the instruction of the Chief Constable [of the City Police Force, Frank Richardson]. The first is a photograph of Meadow Road, showing the front doors, and the end of the passage at Steer's house. The second is a photo of the staircase. By this photo you can just see into the kitchen. The third is a photo of the back of the

MESSER'S PHOTOGRAPH OF THE STAIRCASE
© *Timothy W. Frank Walker and Ann Richardson Whittle, grandchildren of Frank Richardson, Chief Constable*

house, and the door at which Percy Noble knocked. The fourth is a view looking down from the corner of Meadow Road and York Road, in the direction of the *Duke of York*, to show the passage which goes along at the back of the prisoner's house. The fifth shows the point where a young woman, Miss Stretch, and a man with her saw Percy Noble running across when they were there, and shows the passage out of which he ran. The sixth is a photograph of the bedroom and its contents immediately after the crime. The bedroom was arranged for the photograph under the direction of the Chief Constable, just as it would be when the crime was committed, and undoubtedly was so, within an inch or two. It shows where the paper was removed by the Surveyor to be sent to the analyst to analyse certain spots on it.' Also on display was a model of the house, showing the layout of the ground and first floors.

The first of those directly involved with the events of October 31 was Flora's neighbour, Alfred Walter Noble, the eldest son in the household at 38 Meadow Road. He explained how he came to see Flora on the Saturday, around dinnertime, and that there was nothing unusual about her demeanour.

Foote asked, 'Did you see her again?' – 'I walked down the street with her at about a quarter to seven.'

'What did she talk about?' – 'Things in general, but she said to me "I cannot help thinking of the man who called for lodgings. I was so worried that I could not get it off my mind, and I woke up several times during the night. I could not sleep for it"'

Foote interjected 'Did she say why she was so worried?' – 'She could not understand a man coming to her, as she never took any lodgers. She could not think who recommended the man to go there.'

'Have you known anyone stopping there?' – 'Only her friends'

'You mean Mold?' – 'Yes.'

'Have you ever heard her say anything in particular in your presence?' – 'She said once before in my presence, and my father's presence, "Alf," – that is, my father – "I think about getting married again." She never named any particular man to me; I took the whole matter as a joke.'

'Did you see her again that night in her kitchen?'

– 'Yes. I got to the house an hour after the murder had happened'

'Was she crying?' – 'Yes, Mrs Haskell was crying bitterly. There were a lot more people there. At the time Mold was staying at the house, Mrs Haskell's sister-in-law was there as well. I knew Teddy Haskell all his life, and [he] was a very cheerful lad. He kept goal for his football club.'

Under cross-examination by Goddard, Noble continued: 'On the evening of the murder, when I saw Mrs Haskell she was in her usual spirits. She mentioned the man coming for lodgings as we were going down town, [and she] bought a penny-worth of sweets for Teddy while she was out.'

'Did you help her collect her money as a laundress?' – 'Yes, I made up her books for her sometimes.'

'What would her earnings be?' – 'About twenty-two shillings per week in the winter, and in the summer they would be more, because of the blouses.' Every week it would be over a pound.'

'What was her rent?' – 'Five shillings and sixpence a week.'

'She also has a little money in the Co-operative Stores?' – 'Yes, sir. Mrs Haskell only has a one-pound share in the Co-operative Society, and she gets cheques for amounts of goods bought by her, for which she receives a dividend.'

'Have you known her many years?' – 'Yes, and I know her three brothers in London, who are respectable people in decent positions.'

The examination turned to the subject of Teddy's injured leg.

'Did Teddy Haskell sleep with you sometimes?' – 'Yes.'

'Did you notice anything on one occasion?' – 'When I woke up I noticed some blood on the bedclothes, and I said, "Teddy, your leg had been bleeding", and he replied, "Yes, Bob, I know, it very often does."'

Next to speak was Alfred's father, Alfred John Noble, and his testimony was rather shorter. 'I married Mrs Haskell's sister. The boy Teddy was her only child, and his full name was Edwin Richard.'

'When did you first see Teddy Haskell on this day [31 October]? – 'About nine o'clock at night, in my house.'

'Did he leave your house by the back door?' – 'Yes, sir, at nine o'clock.

'Did you see Mrs Haskell later that evening?' – 'Yes, at about nine thirty-five.'

'She came to your house?' – 'Yes, sir, with my washing. She asked if I knew of an empty house, because she wanted a house with a larger back to dry her clothes. I told her there was one in Ashley Road. She told me that Mrs Mold had asked for that one, and if she did not have it, she, Mrs Haskell, should. That was all she said.'

'She returned after that?' – 'Yes, by the back way. She was not with me for [more than] about five minutes. I did not notice anything about her [that was] unusual. She was quite as usual.' Cross-examined by Goddard, Noble added: 'Mrs Haskell was always a good and affectionate mother to Teddy'.

Following an adjournment for lunch of just thirty minutes Gertrude Steer was called, and her evidence started to set the scene. 'I live at no. 36 Meadow Road, [and] I am a dressmaker.'

'Did you go up to Mrs Haskell's house on the thirty-first of October, and, if so, [at] what time?' – 'Yes, at about a quarter to ten. I fixed the time by going to meet someone at the station at ten.'

'Did you go to the door, and Mrs Haskell opened it?' – 'Yes, sir, I went the back way.'

'What did you go for?' – 'To fit a little jacket I made for Mrs Haskell.'

'You went inside the kitchen?' – 'Yes, sir.'

'How long did you stay?' – 'About five minutes.'

'Did you fit the jacket on her?' – 'Yes, sir.'

'Did she say anything?' – 'She said she was very pleased with it.'

'Did you see the little boy?' – 'No, sir.'

'How was Mrs Haskell dressed?' – 'In a light blouse and a dark skirt, as near as I can remember.'

'You fitted the coat over the blouse?' – 'Yes, sir.'

'And you did not notice anything on the blouse then?' – 'No, sir, I saw nothing at all on it.'

'Did you notice whether she had an apron on?' – 'No, sir, I did not, and don't know if I should have noticed it even if she had on a long one.'

'As to the kitchen table, had that a cloth on it?' – 'Yes, there was a long white tablecloth on the table.'

'Was it laid for a meal?' – 'Yes, there were cups

and saucers on it.'

Gertrude's testimony continued, 'I was standing by the fireplace, between the fireplace and the table, but I did not notice whether there were any chairs on the other side of the table. When I went out, I went the same way as I went in, and went on to the G.W.R. station. It was there that I met my father and my grandmother. There was plenty of time for the ten o'clock train from Warminster, which we had to wait for. My sister came by that train.' Cross-examined by Goddard, she added 'I have known Mrs Haskell all my life, and also Teddy, and I have not heard an angry word at all. Mrs Haskell and her son were on the best of terms.'

Next to be called was John Stanley Wyatt, whose evidence was key in establishing the chronology of events on the 31st. 'I live at Salisbury, and work for the Co-operative Stores at Salisbury, at Winchester Street. That street is near the Council Chamber, but I cannot say whether it is near the centre of the city or not. On Saturday the 31 October I was at the Stores in the evening. They closed at ten o'clock, but I was there later, and was sent a message by Mr Slade, the Manager. I was to go to Mrs Manning of Meadow Road, with a parcel, which I had to deliver. The address on the parcel gave no number, but simply "Mrs Manning, Meadow Road". I went on a bicycle, and did not know the proper number. On my way I made enquiries. I spoke to a lady first, at the corner of Meadow Road. I then went to Slade's shop, and enquired there also. That was half way up, between York Road and St Paul's Road.'

'Did you go to 42 Meadow Road?' – 'Yes'

'What did you do there?' – 'Knocked at the door.'

'Did you get an answer?' – 'No.'

'What did you do afterwards?' – 'Knocked next door, at No. 40.'

'Did someone come?' – 'Yes.'

'At once?' – 'I cannot remember if at once.'

'When they came, was the door opened to you? Did you hear if it was unlocked?' – 'I heard it being unlocked.'

'Was it a man or a woman who came?' – 'A woman.'

'Can you recognise her again?' – 'No.'

'Did you say something to her, in consequence of

which she took the parcel in?' – 'Yes'

'And you left?' – 'Yes.'

'As you left did you hear if the door was locked again?' – 'No.'

'Had you seen anyone else in Meadow Road as you were going up St Paul's Road, except the woman you met at the bottom? – 'No.'

'You left the stores at ten five?' – 'Yes.'

'What time did you get to No. 40?' – 'About ten twenty.'

'Did you look at the Stores clock before you left?' – 'Yes.'

'Since that evening have you gone the same route on your bicycle on a Saturday the same time at night? – 'Yes.'

'Twice?' – 'Yes. I did that once in the evening and once in the dinner hour. The first time I went to test the time there was someone with me, although I cannot remember who.'

'The second time, did you go with the Chief Constable and Superintendent Stephens?' – 'Yes'

'That time, did you stop on the way?' – 'Yes, exactly as I did on the night of the murder'

'The time that that took was taken by the Chief Constable?' – 'Yes'

Goddard then asked Wyatt to rehearse his exchange with Flora: 'I stood for a moment or two at Mrs Manning's door knocking, and I was not kept long at Mrs Haskell's house. When the woman came I asked her if she would take the parcel, and we [*i.e.* I] had a little conversation with her about the parcel.

The next witness was Rosa Manning, Flora's neighbour at 42 Meadow Road at the time of the murder. She said 'On the evening of the 31 October I was expecting a parcel. I had gone to bed before it arrived. Whilst in bed I heard someone knocking at the front door: I did not answer this, [and] I heard the knocking at the next door. I knew Mrs Haskell and used to talk to her.'

'Did Mrs Haskell ever say anything to you about marrying?' – 'She told me that a steward on board a ship had asked her to marry him, but it took a lot of thinking about. She said if she did, she would always work and keep little Teddy.'

'Did she say who the steward was?' – 'She did not mention a name at that time, but [on] one

occasion she said he was Mrs Mold's son.' Judge Ridley asked when the conversation about the proposal took place. 'I think it was in August' replied Rosa. Goddard had no questions.

Percy Noble, next to give evidence, recounted the first seconds after the discovery of the attack on Teddy. As such, he was a key witness. Aged 16 the previous June, and the younger brother of Alfred Walter, he was the youngest to take the witness stand. Foote began by asking him 'Were you coming home late on this night [*i.e.* that of October 31]' – 'Yes: I was going home by the passage from York Road. I had to pass Mrs Haskell's to get to my home.'

'Did you intend to stop at Mrs Haskell's?' – 'Yes, sir.'

'And then go home?' – 'Yes.'

'What time was it when you were at Mrs Haskell's?' – 'Ten thirty, by my watch'

'When did you last look at it?' – 'At York Road corner.'

Judge Ridley interjected, 'Was it a good watch?' – 'I could not rely on it, [but] my watch was right when St Thomas's [church] clock struck ten. I was going to pay Mrs Haskell a shilling.'

He continued 'Did Mrs Haskell know you were coming?' – 'I don't know, sir. I told Teddy that I was coming. The light in the kitchen was not at all bright. There was gas in the room, and I should think it was the gas that was alight. That door was sometimes kept locked and sometimes it was not. On this occasion it was locked, and I knocked with my knee.' The judge asked 'When you knocked, had you to wait?' – ' No, sir; I did not have to wait long.'

Foote then asked 'What was the first thing you saw or heard after?' – ' Mrs Haskell said "All right".'

'Where did the voice come from?' – 'I can't say; it came from the room somewhere, inside.'

'Had you knocked more than once?' – 'Twice – a double knock'

'What did you hear next?' – 'I then heard a chair pushed back, or moved … I think that a chair would make the same noise whether it was pushed back or forward.'

'What was the next thing?' – 'I heard a thumping noise.'

'Where did it come from?' – 'From the bottom

of the stairs.'

Foote asked 'What sort of a noise?' Percy then stamped his foot, and said 'It was similar to that.'

'How soon afterwards did you hear Mrs Haskell?' – 'Immediately'

'What was it?' – 'A scream, although I don't think she [Mrs Haskell] said anything. I did not hear any words.'

'When you heard the scream did you see a shadow in the kitchen?' – 'Yes: I was looking into the window, and after I heard the scream I saw the shadow coming towards me. I did not notice whether the woman ran. The shadow seemed to come pretty fast.'

'Did she open the door?' – Yes.'

'Was it locked?' – 'Yes.'

'What did she say?' – '"Go and see if you can see that man. He has killed my poor Teddy. Go for the doctor, quick!"'

'When she said "that man" did she point in any direction?' – 'No, sir, she said the words directly one after another. She did not point to any way, or do anything to indicate who she was talking about. I ran off without asking her anything.'

'You heard no door being opened or shut?' – 'No. When I got into York Road I turned to the left. I looked up and down, and there was nobody to be seen. I looked up and down Meadow Road, and ran down York Road. I was fairly quick getting to York Road. If I had not been frightened I could have gone quicker. I did not see anyone in York Road until I got up to the Co-operative Stores which were some distance. There was a man and a woman and a few children there. Dr Wilks lives in Wilton Road, nearby. It would take about five minutes to run from Meadow Road to Dr Wilks's. On the way back I saw P.C. [sic., i.e. Police Sergeant] Golding. After that I went home. I had been with a boy named Walker near the *County Hotel* at Salisbury. I walked home with Walker, and it would take about ten minutes or a quarter of an hour to get to Walker's house.'

Goddard asked the boy to go over some of the details of his story again. Percy replied, 'When I got to Mrs Haskell's house I gave a double knock. I was often in and out of Mrs Haskell's house, and I know that Mrs Haskell generally sat close against the

fireplace, and the sound of the moving chair came back from that direction. The next thing I heard was the sound of a thump, which I thought came from the bottom of the stairs. I cannot remember whether it was a loud thump, or if it was in or out of the kitchen. Mrs Haskell screamed as soon as I heard the thump. When she said "All right" the voice seemed as usual. At ten o'clock I was by the *County Hotel*, and I was with Walker. We stopped at Sidney Street for about a quarter of an hour.'

The young woman whom Percy had seen as he sprinted along York Road was Lily Stretch, the nursemaid who lived at 32 George Street. In her evidence she described the unfolding scene from when she saw Percy run across the road. 'On the 31 October, in the evening I was coming away from George Street with a young man named Primmer. It was nearly half-past ten. We were going up York Road. We were on the right-hand side of the road, and were going on an errand to the *Duke of York*. We were going along at an ordinary pace. While walking along I noticed no-one except the lad named Noble, who ran across the road. I think he came from the back of the houses of Meadow Road, and ran in the same direction as we were [headed]. We were opposite the South Wilts Dairy gates, near the lamp, in York Road. We continued to walk along York Road, and crossed into Meadow Road. As we crossed Meadow Road, after seeing the boy, there was no-one up Meadow Road, walking or running away, and no-one was near No. 40, Mrs Haskell's house. We had got to No. 27, when our attention was arrested by a scream, which seemed to come from Meadow Road. I turned round at once and went to the corner of Meadow Road. When I got to the corner, I saw Mrs Haskell at her door step, and she was saying, "Someone has killed my little Teddy." She said that more than once. I know Mr Steer, and saw him shortly after. Before that I had not seen anyone up Meadow Road, besides Mrs Haskell, although we had a good view up the road. No-one came by us. As Mrs Haskell screamed, Mr Steer came running down and passed us at the corner, on the way to the *Duke of York*. Several other people came afterwards, and we went home. The neighbourhood was very quiet that evening, although it was not usually so quiet. It would have been easy to hear anyone if they had run away. I think it was about half-past ten when I left George Street.'

Lily's escort that evening was Herbert Primmer, the gardener from Quidhampton. His testimony was as follows. 'I left 32 George Street with the last witness, at between [a] quarter and twenty past ten. I am speaking generally, and I did not look at my watch [at the time]. I did not notice anything before we came to Meadow Road. I did not notice anyone run across the road. I heard a scream after we had got half-a-dozen yards beyond Meadow Road, which appeared to come from Meadow Road. When I heard it, I turned and went to see where it came from. I saw Mrs Haskell, and it looked as if she was on her door-step. I heard her say "Someone has killed my poor Teddy." She screamed that out more than once. While she was there I saw Mr Steer come, but [I] did not see him stop by Mrs Haskell. All I saw was that he went to the *Duke of York*. When he went away he went towards York Road. We stayed at the bottom of Meadow Road for about ten minutes or a quarter of an hour. I did not hear anyone run away. When we crossed Meadow Road, we did not look either up or down Meadow Road.'

The next witness to be called was Gertrude Skutt, who lived on the other side of Meadow Road from the Haskells, at No 23. 'On the evening of Saturday 31 October I was at my mother's house at 13 York Street. I stayed there until about twenty past ten. When I left I went towards Meadow Road. As I was going along I saw Percy Noble come from the passage of Mrs Haskell's house, and he ran straight up York Road, in [the] direction of Devizes Road. As he ran out I heard some screams which seemed to come from the front of Mrs Haskell's house. I looked down the passage, and then heard one more scream. I then went to the corner of Meadow Road, where I saw Miss Stretch and her young man. I saw Mrs Haskell standing on the doorstep, and heard her say "Someone has murdered my Teddy." I only heard that once, although it was rather long. I stayed at the corner of Meadow Road a minute or two, and then went home. Besides the young man and girl, and Mrs Haskell, I did not see anyone else near Meadow Road, nor did I hear anyone. I did not even see Mr

Steer. When I heard the first scream, I was just about opposite Mrs Haskell's back passage. Percy Noble heard the scream at about the same time.'

Walter Steer, the neighbour two doors along from the Haskells at 36 Meadow Road, was the next key witness. He recalled, 'I was at the station at ten o'clock meeting my daughter, and it was [a] quarter past ten when I got home. In going home I passed Mrs Haskell's door, but did not see anything. Soon after I got home – about five minutes – I heard a scream. I was in the back part of the house. When I heard the scream I ran into the garden, and the screams seemed to come from the front. When I got into the garden I did not see Percy Noble. The wall is four or five feet high. I could not have seen Percy Noble if he had run down the garden. If a boy ran down Mrs Haskell's yard I don't think I should hear him. I ran down the passage into Meadow Road, and I got there before anyone [else].

'I first saw Mrs Haskell between her own house and mine. I passed her at Mr Noble's window. She said, "Man, round the corner!" When she said that, I continued running. She did not point or give any indication which corner she meant. I ran several yards up York Road, and looked in front of me. I looked up York Road, towards the *Duke of York*. I did not look the other way at all, down towards the meadows, and did not hear anyone run away. I did not notice whether any of the previous witnesses were near the corner. I saw two men at the *Duke of York* gate. One man went inside the gate and the other was standing outside. I recognised the man who stood outside as a Salisbury man, but did not know his name. On [the] Monday I saw a man named Eccott, and he was the man who went into the yard. I pushed the gate back and pushed up against the other man who said "What's up?" I waited for him to come out, and asked the other man if he knew him and he said "No." I followed the man to the corner of Meadow Road, and I then heard Mrs Haskell scream again, so I went back. She was only crying out and not screaming any words.

'When I got to the house I ran up the stairs into the front bedroom, and there was no-one there. I went to the back room, and it was so dark that I called for a light. My son brought a lamp from our

WALTER STEER © *THE WEEKLY DISPATCH*

own house. Mrs Butt was close behind me.'

'Did you see the boy dead?' – 'Yes, sir, I saw the boy lying on the bed with his throat cut, and the bed was saturated with blood.'

'Which way was the boy turned?' – 'His head was turned slightly to his left.'

'He was dead?' – 'Yes.'

'Was he nearest to the wall or the chair?' – 'Nearest the chair.'

Steer's testimony continued, 'When I saw that I left the room, and sent for a doctor. I remained on the landing until the doctor arrived. There was nothing knocked about in the room. Everything was in the best of order, and the drawers had not been moved. Dr Row and Dr Wilks came after the discovery had been made, within five minutes. I went into the bedroom with them, and then, hearing the confusion downstairs, I went down. I gave expression to my thoughts by saying "Who could have done it?" Mrs Haskell was still down there. She said she was sitting in the kitchen, and heard someone come downstairs, and a man threw a knife at her.

'I went upstairs again, and P.C. Golding was there. I gave him a description of the man I saw in Meadow Road, going into the *Duke of York*. I was

there about five minutes with the constable, who went back before me. I saw Mrs Carter there and she came to the foot of the stairs where she said "Is Teddy dead? Oh, let me see him!" I said "Don't." She went into the front room and from there into the kitchen. Mrs Haskell was in the front room at the time. After that I went upstairs again, and the Chief Constable and Superintendent Stephens were there also. A watch was found under the pillow. After that I went down and asked Mrs Haskell if it belonged to Teddy. Mrs Haskell asked "Is my Teddy all right?" I asked her again, and she answered, "Yes, it is Teddy's, and there is some money in the drawer." That was the first I heard of the drawers.

'I then went upstairs again, and stayed there some time, and while I was there the second time the police were examining the drawers. The doctors had gone away by that time. While I was at the foot of the stairs and Dr Wilks was in the room, Mrs Carter and Mrs Haskell wanted to see the boy, but I said "Don't." Dr Wilks said he would make him presentable and then they could see him. That was the first I saw of Dr Wilks after I came back. Dr Wilks told me to get a bucket of water and a towel, which I did. I had not been into the kitchen before then. The doctor washed the child's face after the water was taken up. The doctor also asked for a handkerchief, and then Mrs Carter went upstairs. I took the water and towel into the back kitchen, where I washed the towel out and threw the water away. Mrs Haskell was downstairs at this time. The towels were in the bucket when I carried them down. The bucket was about half-full, and I am sure I did not spill any of its contents when I brought it down.'

'Did you notice anything on Mrs Haskell's blouse, and if so, at what time? – 'I noticed a splash of blood on her wrist,' Steer replied, showing his right forearm, 'when I asked about the watch. It was a splash on the wrist of the bodice.'

Goddard then said, 'Describe what Mrs Haskell was as a mother.' – 'I have known Mrs Haskell for twenty years, and I am no relation to her. Mrs Haskell is everything that a mother ought to be.'

'Was she a quiet, respectable and well-conducted woman?' – 'Yes, she has always been, and the boy was always a bright, merry little fellow'.

There were further questions, about the moments when the alarm was raised. 'It would be right that it was only a matter of seconds between the scream in the back and the ones in the front. Mrs Haskell was in the front when I got there.'

'And were you able to form an opinion as to the time between the first scream and the arrival of Sergeant Golding?' – 'From the time when I heard the screams until Sergeant Golding arrived, I think about ten minutes or a quarter of an hour elapsed.' When Mrs Haskell told me of the statement about the man, she was in the kitchen. The excitement was very great at the time.'

The judge asked, 'Did she want to go upstairs?' – 'Not that I know of – not until she asked the doctor, but that was some time after the thing took place.'

Foote asked, 'When was your attention first directed to the knife?' – 'Sergeant Golding came and said he must get on the telephone, and then the knife was pointed out to him. The sergeant picked it up with a piece of brown paper, and put it in his pocket at the back of his coat. Mrs Carter drew our attention to it, the doctors being in the bedroom at the time.'

The next witnesses were the two men at the *Duke of York* inn. First was Edward Butt, of 27 George Street. 'On Saturday 31 October I was outside the *Duke of York* [at] about half-past ten. I was on the pavement near the side gates. Mr Steer came from Meadow Road. I saw another man come from behind the gates. I know the man well by sight, and he is the man Eccott.'

William Eccott was another of the Haskells' neighbours at 48 Meadow Road. He testified that 'I was at the *Duke of York* inn, and I left about ten twenty-four' and added that it was half-past ten by the time he arrived home, as his wife called his attention to the time. 'When I came from the public house I went into the yard. On coming out of the yard I saw Mr Steer, who did not say anything to me. When I passed Meadow Road I heard some screaming in No. 40, but did not see Mrs Haskell. I waited outside the house, and then went to my own house. There were not many people about. After I went indoors, I came out, and helped to search the neighbourhood. I was identified by Steer at the Police Station as the man he saw in the yard at the inn.'

Also a neighbour of the Haskells, Ernest James House, of 27 Meadow Road, testified that 'On the Saturday night – 31 October – I was at Fisherton Street with my brother. I left a shop in Fisherton [at] about quarter past ten. I fixed the time by hearing the clock of St Paul's church strike. I and Haynes then walked up to Meadow Road and went home. I passed close by the front door of No. 40, and got home at about twenty minutes past ten. I did not notice anyone near the front door of No. 40. After staying in for two or three minutes I went out again, and went to Slade's shop. When I walked down the road I did not notice anyone, and that was about twenty-five minutes past ten. I went inside the shop and stopped five or six minutes, and then came out of the shop, and Mr Slade stood by the shop door. When I got by the door, I heard a woman scream. The clock struck half-past as the woman screamed. I made a remark to Mr Slade about it. When I heard the scream, which came from Meadow Road, I went straight along, and saw only a young man and girl at the corner of the road. The street lamps were burning brightly. When I got by No. 40 I saw Mrs Haskell, who was standing in her doorway then. She said "My poor boy", or "My poor Teddy", I forget which. The streets in Meadow Road were lit as usual. I did not see anyone run up the road, or walk hurriedly. I was able to see from No. 40, right up to Coldharbour Lane. Later I helped in searching the back[s of the] houses.'

House's travelling companion, Walter Ernest Haynes, was another neighbour, at 31 Meadow Road. 'On the 31 October I came with the last witness to Meadow Street [*sic*] from Fisherton Road [*sic*]. We left Fisherton Street at quarter past ten, and it was about twenty past ten when I got home. I did not notice anyone in Meadow Road. After I had been in home for ten minutes I heard a scream from Mrs Haskell's house. When I got into the road I heard some words, "Someone has killed my Teddy." I saw Mr Steer, who was by Mrs Haskell's door. He seemed as if he was waiting for a light, because someone brought him one.'

Corroborating the testimony of Walter Steer was that of his wife, Alice, and her mother, Emma Chivers, who lived with the Steers. Alice testified: 'I had been to the G.W.R. station, and on coming back passed from [sic] the door of No. 40. I did not notice anyone about there. We got into the house at about quarter past ten. After we had been indoors for a few minutes we heard a scream. My husband was by the kitchen door when I heard the scream. He went down the passage, and I went after him. When we got into the road, I heard Mrs Haskell at the front door, screaming. My husband was in front, and I followed after about a minute. Mrs Haskell said "Someone has murdered my Teddy", and asked me to go for my mother and a policeman. Having gone for my mother and the policeman, Mrs Haskell was in the front room when I returned. It may have taken me a quarter of an hour to go for my mother and the policeman. The only thing I heard Mrs Haskell say was that someone had come for lodgings the night before. I only heard her say it once, neither did I hear anyone answer, because the Superintendent came and ordered everyone out of the room.'

Cross-examined by Goddard, she added, 'Mrs Haskell was wearing a light blouse, and I saw some blood on the right wrist. She was wearing a dark skirt, which she has had a good long time.' She agreed with earlier witnesses that Mrs Haskell had always treated Teddy kindly and well.

Mrs Chivers added 'On the 31 October I went to [the] station with [my daughter and son-in-law], and passed the front door of No. 40 on the way back. I went into the kitchen, and my daughter and [her] husband had gone into the back kitchen when we got back. I heard two screams – one from the back and the other from the front. There were about two seconds between the two screams. I followed my daughter [and her husband] to the front road, although I did not see them there. Mrs Haskell was coming towards the house, and said "Oh, do come, do come, someone has killed my Teddy." We both turned round and went into the house. I said "Oh, no, don't say that" when Mrs Haskell said someone had murdered her boy, and Mrs Haskell said "Oh, yes, I am sure something has happened to him – look at the knife –", or else he would not be so quiet", and she pointed to the knife lying cross-ways. She also said [that] when she was coming from the back that she heard footsteps on the stairs, and someone threw

something at her. At that time I did not notice anything on Mrs Haskell's sleeve. When we spoke about someone throwing the knife, Mrs Haskell said "Look at my wrist." There were also spots of blood on her blouse. Mrs Haskell asked me if I could go upstairs, and I replied that I could not. Mrs Haskell did not go upstairs while I was there. I was in the house about ten minutes. My son [-in-law] came down and asked for a light, and I sent my son-in-law for one in our house, because I did not know where to get one in the house. Mrs Haskell was in a dreadful state at this time. I had seen Mrs Haskell in the city [earlier] in the evening, and she was in her usual spirits then.'

Next to give evidence were Matilda Cooper of 27 York Road, and Edith Langmead, her daughter staying with her at the time. Mrs Cooper recalled 'I was at home on the night of 31 October. After ten o'clock I heard a scream, and went to the front door. My daughter came out with me. Two people were at the corner when I came to the door. I looked up Meadow Road, and saw Mrs Haskell at her door, on her doorstep, but [I] did not see anyone else. Mrs Haskell went into the sitting room, and I went with her. There was no-one else there then, but Mrs Sweetman came in soon after, and then Mrs Chivers and some others came in. I asked who could have done such a thing, and she [Mrs Haskell] kept saying, "A man who came for lodgings yesterday". She kept talking about the man, but I could not understand all that she said. She was very much distressed, and sobbing very much. That was all I can remember Mrs Haskell saying, although she kept on saying other things. While I was comforting her I saw her take out of her pocket a handkerchief which was bloodstained. Before I saw it someone suggested giving Mrs Haskell some eau-de-Cologne, and Mrs Sweetman showed me a handkerchief. I noticed blood on it, but did not notice whether it was much or little, or whether it was wet or dry. I noticed the blouse, and there were some small spots of blood on the blouse, as I was comforting her.'

To this her daughter added 'I went to the door with my mother and there was a young man and woman at the corner, and I asked them what was the matter. There was only [a] little light in the house [*i.e.* No. 40] and so I went back to my house and got a candle. I put the candle on Mrs Haskell's front room on the table. Mrs Sweetman went into the house with me. I saw a knife lying in the doorway which I showed to Mrs Sweetman. I asked if anyone knew who the woman's mother [*i.e.* Mrs Carter] was as she was a stranger. The knife was lying in the centre of the doorway, and the blade was towards the kitchen and the handle towards the doorway, but it was laid diagonally and not straight.'

By now the day's proceedings were drawing to a close, and Foote took the opportunity to ask the Judge to release all the witnesses who had already testified, unless they were directly concerned. With this Goddard concurred, subject to being allowed to recall Alfred Walter Noble, the elder of Teddy's two neighbouring cousins, to give evidence about Alfred Mold. He testified, 'I have known the man Alfred Mold all my life, and I and Mrs Haskell's family and the Molds have been friends for years. Mold was a steward on [a] White Star liner, and he would leave his ship at times and come home. He used to call in Mrs Haskell's very often. I have also seen Mold with the little boy, and they were very good friends. He was very fond of Teddy, and frequently gave him coppers and played with him.'

The final witness called on Monday 15 February was Sarah Butt, of 40 York Road, who had followed Walter Steer into the bedroom, and who later held the light for the doctors. Her evidence, like that of Wyatt, Percy Noble and Steer was crucial in establishing the sequence of events. She said 'On the evening of 31 October I was called by hearing some screams at about twenty-five past ten. I went to the door and saw several people at the corner of Meadow Road, and I then went to Mrs Haskell's house. She was just outside of her door when I got there and heard her say "Someone has killed my Teddy." I followed Mrs Haskell in. There was no light on the staircase when I went in. Mrs Haskell screamed "Someone go and see my Teddy." Mr Steer came in with a lamp, and I followed him. Rawlins came up into the bedroom where I and Mr Steer were. The condition of the bedroom was in good order. Mr Steer and I both waited in the house until the doctors arrived five or ten minutes after. I held the lamp for the doctors and stayed there while the doctors examined the room. I did not touch the boy, but saw everything that happened. The doctors examined the boy for about twenty minutes, and while they were there Rawlins came up with some water to wash their hands. He [Rawlins] then went down again, but I don't know whether he took anything down. It was a basin that the water was in. When the doctors went, I stayed on the landing, and Mr Steer took the lamp down. I saw a small brass lamp, just outside the door of the bedroom, on the landing, which was out and quite cold. On the second visit to the house I saw Mr Steer bring up the water. I was in the house about three quarters of an hour. After staying until Dr Wilks had nearly finished washing the little boy, I came down, because I was not wanted. The doctors paid two visits to the house, one twenty-five minutes after the other, and Mrs Haskell wanted to go upstairs between the two visits of the doctors, but they did not think she ought to, so they did not let her. Mrs Carter was with Mrs Haskell when she wanted to come up. It was Mrs Carter who first asked to go up. When she came downstairs she went into the front sitting room, and sat in an armchair. Mrs Sweetman and others were also there. I saw someone give Mrs Haskell a handkerchief, and heard someone say "Don't give her that, it is dirty: give her a clean one." It was Mrs Sweetman who gave Mrs Haskell the handkerchief. Afterwards, in the kitchen Mrs Carter said she was sure the handkerchiefs were Teddy's, because she gave them to him. Mrs Haskell was present. I am sure Mrs Haskell said "Someone go and see my Teddy."

With that, and at the end of a long and distressing day, the trial was adjourned for the night. After a drive, no doubt to clear their minds, the jury was taken to the *Castle Hotel* in New Park Street, where they were kept under lock and key, in the charge of the Sheriff's officer. Counsel, meanwhile, returned to another of Devizes' famous old coaching inns, the *Bear*, which had been reserved for the Bar for the duration of the Assizes.

13

'Have you ever seen a throat cut?': The First Trial, Days Two and Three: 16–17 February 1909

THE NEXT MORNING, Tuesday 16 February, was fine, bright and clear and another large gathering had built up outside the Assize Court by half-past nine. The crowd – mainly women, many of whom had come for the day, as they came with packed lunches – rushed excitedly for seats in the public gallery when the doors opened at ten o'clock. Within a quarter of an hour the gallery was packed, and as on Monday many were disappointed. Some of those strolled towards the prison to catch sight of Flora. Two carriages left the prison, one enclosed, bringing the governor, and the second, a brougham drawn by white horses, in which sat Flora with a warder and two wardresses. In court, she looked well, as she had done the day before, and maintained a close interest in the proceedings. Whilst at times the strain of concentration showed in her face, Flora held a whispered conversation with the prison doctor after lunch, and smiled quite brightly.

At half-past ten sharp Mr Justice Ridley took his seat, and Thomas Alfred Rawlins, of 26 Meadow Road, was called to give evidence which would corroborate and add to the accounts of Walter Steer and Sarah Butt. 'I went home on 31 October, and heard a scream. I went out and saw Mrs Haskell first. She was on the pavement, by the side of her door. I went and spoke to her, asking what was the matter. I am not sure what she said, but it made me think something terrible had happened to Teddy. She said "Oh, do go up," and caught hold of me. I went in and when I got to the foot of the stairs I saw Mr Steer with a lamp, and Mrs Butt was stood behind

him. I then went upstairs and into the bedroom, and saw what had happened. When I went down Mrs Haskell said "Do tell me, Mr Rawlins, what is the matter?" I said "I can't, Mrs Haskell, but I am afraid it is very bad."

'I then went out and sent for the doctor and the police and fetched Mrs Mold, whom Mrs Haskell had asked for. Later on I went upstairs again, and afterwards fetched a basin for the doctor from the kitchen. That was before the doctors had gone away the first time. I saw the doctors wash their hands. I gave the basin and water to Mrs Butt. Superintendent Stephens came soon after the doctors went. I had been to the foot of the bed, and stood near it, but did not touch the boy. I had, at that time, taken special notice of the bloodstains on the landing. After we had examined the blood marks I went down with Mr Stephens and Mr Richardson, and went into the kitchen. Mrs Carter was in the kitchen then, sitting in a chair, close to where the knife had been lying, but it was not there then. The back of the chair was towards the partition that parted the staircase off. There were two or three other chairs in the same position with their backs to the partition. There was a white tablecloth on the table, and there was some blood on the sides of the cloth. The side nearest to the staircase, on the edge, and the part that was hanging down was also stained. Along the edge it was like a smudge, but on the part that hung down it was spots. The marks were about two inches long.'

The oblong tablecloth was brought into the Court, and Rawlins placed the cloth onto a table as it was when he saw it. The tablecloth had been examined by the Home Office pathologist Dr Augustus Pepper, who had taken a sample from it, and placed a yellow mark upon it. Rawlins continued: 'The light was very bright on that night, and as I walked round the table I could not help noticing the bloodstains.' The bloodstains still visible on the cloth, were, Rawlins confirmed, 'the ones I saw on the 31 October. When I saw the blood on the table first, it was before the doctors had been, and I first told the police about it, about three weeks after – but I had said it before in the kitchen, so everyone who was in there could have heard it. Mrs Carter answered me. Mrs Haskell was not there. I said 'There is blood on the table cloth.' I have known Mrs Haskell a long time, and Teddy as well, and they were on the best of terms, and [she] was all that a mother could be. I do not remember where there was an armchair by the fireplace. I noticed the bloodstains on the tablecloth about half past eleven. I had been into the kitchen before that, and it was on the 21 November I made the statement to the police.'

In response to Goddard's query, Rawlins agreed, 'Mrs Haskell undoubtedly treated her boy very kindly'

The last lay witness to the night of the murder was Emily Sweetman of 42 York Road. 'I was at home on Saturday the 31 of October, and a man named Eccott brought a message about half-past ten or soon after. In consequence of this I went to Mrs Haskell's house. Mr Rawlins was at the front door, and Mrs Haskell was in the passage. I then went with Mrs Haskell to the front room, and stayed there some time. While I was there Mrs Haskell said 'Someone has killed my little Teddy.' She also spoke about a man coming the previous night for lodgings, and that he worried her, and that he seemed very much upset because she would not have him, as she never took any lodger in. There was a small scratch on Mrs Haskell's nose, but it was not bleeding at the time.'

At that point, Mrs Sweetman was asked about the bloodstained handkerchief. 'I was going to bathe Mrs Haskell's face with some eau de Cologne, and went to take her handkerchief, but noticed that it was bloodstained. I took that from her and put it on the mantel-shelf. It was a little damp at the time. There

was one big stain, and other stains as well. On the 15 of November I was shown three handkerchiefs by the police at the police station and picked one out and marked it with the letter E.' The handkerchief was shown to the court. 'The blood on the handkerchief was brighter than it is now. That was before the doctor had been to the house at all. I could have seen the doctors if they had come. While we were in the front room, Mrs Haskell was going out and said to all in the room "I was in my kitchen, and I was just going out when I heard footsteps, and then a man came down the stairs, he threw something at me, and then went out of the front door." I was in the front room for about half an hour. My attention was called to a knife that was lying on the threshold of the kitchen door, the blade pointing to the kitchen. It was about a quarter of an hour after I was in the room before I saw the knife, and then after seeing it I went into the front room again. When I went it was on the arrival of the Chief Constable, and all the women were asked to go.

'I and other women – Mrs Carter and others – went into the kitchen just after the Chief Constable came. When I went into the kitchen I saw bloodstains on the tablecloth. The cloth was a white one, and it was on the side nearest the staircase that the blood was on. We were nearest the end of the table towards the scullery door. The spots were about the size of a threepenny piece. That spot was about the middle of the cloth. There was nothing on the top of the table, but a smudge right along the edge. The large spot was about at the bottom of the tablecloth. I called the attention of Superintendent Stephens to the blood, but he did not make any answer or come round. On the following Monday [2 November] I saw Mrs Haskell to fit on a mourning dress and I asked her if the mark on her nose was where the man hit her with the knife, and she replied "No, I cut it with my rings on Thursday." I first made a statement to the police about three weeks after, but I had spoken to other people about it.'

Cross-examined by Goddard, Mrs Sweetman added, 'Mrs Haskell held the handkerchief quite openly. It felt damp, but I cannot say whether it [the dampness] came from the blood [from the cut on her nose] or not. The scar on Mrs Haskell's nose looked as if a little rub would make it bleed, and it looked fresh. I understood from the blood on Mrs Haskell and on the handkerchief that the knife hit her.'

Next there was the brief and touching testimony of Harold Webb, Teddy's 13 year-old school pal, of 22 Devizes Road. 'In October I was living on the Devizes Road with my parents. I knew the little boy Teddy Haskell, and went to the same school. I was in the same standard as little Teddy, and we were good friends.'

He was then asked, 'Do you remember anything being said by you to little Teddy about his address?' – 'Yes.'

'What was it?' – 'I asked him if he would like some foreign stamps, and he said 'Yes,' and I asked him if he would give me his address.'

'Did he give it you?' – 'Yes. He wrote his address on a bit of paper, and gave it to me the same day, although it was after he had been home. It was at playtime, after he had been home. It was about a week before he died.'

Dr Taylor of Hampstead was then called, to give evidence on behalf of Flora's sister-in-law, Miss Emily Thirza Haskell, at that time in an infirmary in Hampstead, and too ill to attend. Her deposition was read out to the court. She stated that Flora had confided to her the previous summer that Mold wanted to marry her, but that it took a lot of thinking about; also that she would always work to keep little Teddy. Flora had added that Teddy had saved up money for a cork leg, but she had had to take some of it, because she 'hadn't sufficient to go on with'.

The first police witness was Sergeant William Golding of the Salisbury City force. He recalled 'I was sent for to go to 40 Meadow Road on 31 October, and got there about ten thirty-five. I saw Mr Steer first, and from what Steer told me he went into York Road looking for someone. We then went into Mr Slade's shop, which was in Meadow Road. There was a telephone there and I telephoned to the Chief Constable, and after doing so I returned to the house with Steer. When I got back and got into the house, Steer first showed me a knife, which was lying slanting-wise at the bottom of the stairs, on the threshold of the kitchen door.' He produced the knife, and said it was the one. 'There was a mark on the

floor. I took it [the knife] up and examined it, and found a lot of blood on it, which was almost dry.'

Foote asked, 'Was it so dry that you could wrap it up in brown paper without altering it?' – 'Yes. I picked it up so that the blood should not be rubbed off.'

'Was it so dry that it did not mark the paper?' – 'I did not see it afterwards.'

The judge interjected, 'You did not keep it?' – 'No, I gave it to my Chief Constable.'

Foot resumed his questioning: 'When did you give it to the Chief Constable?' – 'About three o'clock in the morning, [some] hours after I found it.

'The next thing was [that] I went upstairs and saw the doctors there, and came down when they did. I only went into the kitchen to get the paper. When I got down there I looked in the kitchen and there was no-one there, so I went into the front room. When I looked into the kitchen I saw there was a white tablecloth on the table, and some cups and saucers; there was blood on the tablecloth. Mrs Haskell was in the front room, and was dressed in a light blouse and a dark skirt, with no apron. I noticed some blood marks on the right arm of Mrs Haskell's blouse, although I did not make any examination of them. I did not stand in the kitchen all the time: I sat down – in a chair near the stairs. I stayed there all night until about three thirty.

'It was then Mrs Carter and Mrs Haskell asked if the money was all right: Mrs Carter and Mrs Haskell also stopped in the house all night, and did not lay down but sat in chairs. Mrs Haskell may have laid down in the front room, but she did not stay there only a few minutes. Mrs Carter and Mrs Haskell asked me if the money was all right, and I replied that I did not know. They asked me to go up and see. Mrs Carter asked first. I was told by Mrs Haskell that the money was in a draw[er] upstairs.'

Judge Ridley asked, 'Did she say how much there was' – 'Yes: she said there should be eight pounds. "The drawer," she said, "would be locked," and I would find the key near there. When I got up to the bedroom the drawer was opened partly, and there was three pounds ten shillings in it. I took it down, and showed it to Mrs Haskell. She said there should be eight pounds two shillings, and she did not know where the other money was gone to. I then took the drawer back again and put it in the [chest of] drawers.

'About six o'clock in the morning, Mrs Carter, the mother of the prisoner, was in the house, and she brushed the floor of the passage, the doorway, and the kitchen. After that she washed the passage and the kitchen, and nothing was said about her doing it.' This admission was a bombshell; so much so that Goddard repeated the sergeant's testimony for confirmation: 'About six o'clock, Mrs Carter got a bucket, some water, and a cloth, and swabbed the passage?' – 'Yes.'

'You stood by and watched her.' – 'Yes: I did not stop her.'

'Did she swab down the front door?' – 'Mrs Carter started washing at the front door, and went towards the kitchen.

'You saw the linoleum, and on it a mark of the knife?' – 'Yes.'

'Did the mark, when you saw it at the police court appear different from when you saw it on the night?' – There was more of a mark of blood on the linoleum at the police court, when I saw it, and it seemed larger than it did when I was at the house.'

'Do you mean that? As if more blood had got on it?' – 'No. The streaks seemed longer.'

'It was not quite the same?' – 'No.'

Judge Ridley interjected, 'Did she wash where the knife had been?' – 'Yes.'

He continued: 'Why did you allow that? What were your instructions?' – 'My instructions were to allow no-one to go upstairs.'

'Go upstairs?! Why did you allow her to wash the marks on the floor?' – 'I was told to let them do as they liked downstairs.'

'Dear! Dear!! I cannot imagine such a piece of folly. It was the one piece of evidence in the case, and now it has been washed over. It is all your fault that the marks are different.'

Goddard interjected, 'And on the passage?'

Ridley retorted, 'Never mind the passage. I have not heard it stated that there were any marks there . . . it is open to you to say there were.'

Foote interceded, 'I don't think that very much harm was done, my lord, but it is incredible that a policeman should sit up in the house all night, and

then in the morning allow the very thing he had been sitting up to prevent.' – 'I only had to stop anyone going upstairs,' Cutler protested.

Ridley repeated, 'I am not aware that there were any marks on the passage', to which Foote responded 'It had been examined as far as it could be. It is not as bad as it sounds.'

Ridley repeated to Golding, 'You should not have allowed such a thing as washing the floor.'

Goddard continued, 'You were the only police officer on the spot?' – 'Yes.'

'You did not send out anybody, but you went out yourself.' – 'I went out at once. I did not know then that the boy had been murdered.'

'You did not leave any orders not to let anyone go upstairs before you went to telephone the Chief Constable. When you got back did anyone go up?' – 'No, no-one tried to go up at all. I did not give any orders until I telephoned to the Chief Constable.'

Golding added that there was an armchair in the kitchen, and that it was by the fireplace.

Next to speak was Police Constable William Cutler of the Salisbury force, who went to the scene of the crime with Chief Constable Richardson, and

WILLIAN CUTLER WHO WAS SENT TO PATROL SALISBURY TRAIN STATION. © *J.B. MOODY COLLECTION*

recounted the description given to him by Flora of the man who had called to inquire about lodgings. He continued 'I went to the railway stations in Salisbury and made inquiries for such a man or for luggage which Mrs Haskell said the man stated he had left there. I found no such a man [*sic*] or any luggage incounted [*sic*] for.

The last of the local officers to be called was Frank Richardson, Chief Constable of the Salisbury force. He said 'On the thirty-first of October I got to 40 Meadow Street [*sic*] at five or ten minutes to eleven; Superintendent Stephens was with me. We went in consequence of a telephone message. P.C. Cutler and Sergeant Golding were at the house, as also was Mrs Haskell and several other witnesses as well. I sent the women out into the kitchen soon after I got there in order to speak to Mrs Haskell. I asked her if she could throw any light on the matter. She told me there was some money upstairs in the drawer. She was very depressed. There was eight pounds, two shillings: seven sovereigns, two half-sovereigns and a two-shilling piece. She said it was in the chest of drawers upstairs, in the middle bedroom, and asked if it was all right. I then went upstairs with Stephens. That was all she said before I went upstairs. I found, when I went upstairs, that the chest of drawers was shut. Mr Butt was up there on the landing. The doctor had gone then.'

At this point the drawer was produced, and was identified by the Chief Constable, and examined closely by the jury 'It was I who opened the drawer, which came out easily when I pulled.' He then placed the lock as he had found it on first opening the drawer, hanging on a headless tack with the others in the bottom of the drawer.' Richardson continued: 'In the drawer under a cloth there was some money: three pounds ten shillings: three pounds and a ten-shilling piece. That was the money about which Mrs Haskell spoke, only it was four pounds twelve shillings less than it ought to have been. There was no indication that the lock had been forced by a chisel or anything of the sort.

'I found two spots of blood at the head of the bed on the floor by the chair, several spots at the foot of the bed, and one by the dressing table which was on the way to the door. I did not at that time make any examination of the wall. There was another spot on the landing by the bedroom door, but [I] did not notice any on the stairs. I only looked on the floor. When I got to the bottom of the stairs I examined the passage right up to the door, but did not see any blood. I examined the door, the lock, and [the] handle, but there was no blood there. The next spot of blood I found was near the jamb of the door of the kitchen inside the threshold of the door – more inside than out. The blood was of a bright red colour, and dry. I did not go inside the kitchen, and that was all the blood I noticed at that time. There were no marks on the drawer, though the following day some blood was found on the chest of drawers.

'After that I went to the front room where Mrs Cooper and Mrs Haskell were. I asked Mrs Haskell if she could help in the matter, and she said that the only thing she could do was to describe the man who came for the lodgings. I gave instructions to the officers and had the neighbourhood searched, and they searched as much as was possible. I acted in conjunction with Superintendent Stephens, who is of the County Police, and policemen were sent out on bicycles. Superintendent Stephens and I went back to the house at about one o'clock, and Mrs Haskell was in the kitchen. Golding had not given me the knife. I asked Mrs Haskell if a knife was missing, and Mrs Carter opened a drawer in the kitchen, and Mrs Haskell helped search to see if the [*sic*, *i.e.* a] knife was missing. It was Mrs Carter who said there was a knife gone, and that it was a brown-handled one, and that it was the one that Teddy used.

'I was also told about the man asking Teddy for his name and address – Mrs Haskell said this. [She said that] the man also asked if he had any brothers or sisters, and that he had asked Teddy to write his name and address on a piece of paper, but [she] did not say that he [Teddy] did it and that she had seen him doing it. There were a lot of other knives in the drawer, but they were not of the same appearance as the knife produced. It was then [that] I noticed blood marks on Mrs Haskell's blouse.' At that point the blouse, of thin silk, was produced, and the bloodstains were easily visible. 'Mrs Haskell took the blouse off then, and sent it to Dr Pepper. The marks at the time I first saw them were brighter than

THE FRONT ROOM OF 40 MEADOW ROAD PHOTOGRAPHED BY MESSER IN 1908.
© *Timothy W. Frank Walker and Ann Richardson Whittle, grandchildren of Frank Richardson, Chief Constable.*

they are now. When I received the knife from Golding there were no marks left on the paper in which the knife was wrapped.

[Chief] Inspector Dew of Scotland Yard arrived, and we examined the house. There were some smears of blood on the left of the stairs, on the paper, at about the height of one's arm. After we got up the stairs, on the cushion cover on a little chair by the head of the bed I found seven spots of blood, and several spots on the paper on the wall behind the chair, and several spots on the chest of drawers, which I pointed out. There was a toilet cover on top of the [chest of] drawers, and there were several spots on that. This was on Sunday [1 November], and I knew Mrs Haskell had stayed there all night. A bed was made in the front room for Mrs Haskell.

At that point Flora's four statements, made on the Sunday, Monday and Tuesday, 1-3 November, were read out by Foote, with Richardson explaining that Dew had questioned her, while he, Richardson, had written down her answers.

'The first statement was made on the Sunday, which was the long statement that was read at the opening of the Jury [*i.e.* the inquest]. The next day, Mrs Haskell made another statement, which was only a short one, about the boy from the Co-op. who

brought a parcel to her house, and [to say] that some time ago her sister stayed with her for ten weeks. She also saw her little boy writing his name and address on a piece of paper, which he wanted for someone. On the afternoon of the Monday, when the Chief Inspector and I went to the house, Mrs Haskell made a third statement, which was read when Inspector Dew gave his evidence. A point in the fourth statement made by Mrs Haskell was that a day or so before the murder, Teddy had a scar on his ear, and told her that he had knocked it against a clothes peg at school. That, she said, accounted for the bloodstains on the handkerchiefs.' Two handkerchiefs were produced, and Richardson confirmed that these were the ones shown to Mrs Haskell.

He continued: 'The skirt was taken off on the Sunday afternoon, and it was given to me by Mrs Shepherd. I was with Inspector Stephens, and arrested Mrs Haskell, and charged her with murdering her son, and she said "No, no." The skirt was a black one, and the spots were not visible to an unskilled person. I gave Mr [*sic*] Pepper a knife sharpening stone, two handkerchiefs, [a] pair of drawers chemise, blouse, skirt, and black apron, and the things were the clothing, etcetera, belonging to the prisoner. On Sunday the 8 November, I was there when Professor Pepper took certain things away, and I was also present when Mr Messer took a photograph of the bedroom. I also made an experiment with the boy Wyatt, to see how long it would take him to do what he did, to see what time it would take to get to Meadow Road. It took eleven minutes fifty-five seconds to get from the Co-operative Stores to the house.'

At that point, two letters, written by Alfred Mold while on the liner *Adriatic*, and delivered while Flora was in custody, were read out in court. The first, from New York, was as follows: 'Dear Flo. – I shall try to come home on Friday evening, Nov. 13th, and I hope you are well, and mother improved. Thanks for looking after her. I am looking forward to seeing you again. I am sending this letter by the 'Lusitania'. Much love. – Yours sincerely, ALF.' The second, written when the *Adriatic* had docked in Southampton, was as follows: 'Dear Flo. – Thanks for letter. Sorry mother is poorly, and hope she will soon be better. I think the doctor should see her right away. Thanks for looking after her. I am scribbling these lines before going into the town. – Yours Sincerely, ALF.'

Richardson's testimony continued: 'About the money in the drawer, when I examined the drawer, I found the money was in folds of cloths. I found some spots of blood, and some of the spots were not far from the bed, and the spot of blood on the landing would have been on the left-hand side of a person going downstairs. The interview I had with the other two police officers took two or three hours. On the day after the murder I received a communication from a man called Leate, and he called in the morning. He was the son of a tradesman of the town, and was a respectable man. I saw Leate, and that made me put further questions to Mrs Haskell.'

At that point Foote read another statement made by Flora. In it she said that when she heard someone come downstairs, she went to the back door and told Percy Noble what she had told the police. She then went to the front of her house and shouted, and went a few paces towards Coldharbour Lane. Had she seen a man in Meadow Road when she reached the front of her house she would have followed him.

Concluding his testimony, Richardson said 'I went to Plymouth Docks, and saw Alfred John Mold there aboard the *Adriatic*, and was in his company for about half an hour. I saw him writing, and it was in the same style as the letters were. I did not get the table cloth, exhibit no. 18, from the table but from a drawer, where it had been put to. With regard to the money, it was handed to me by Mrs Sheppard, and the money that was on Mrs Haskell was not in the black dress pocket.'

At that point, the trial was adjourned for lunch

After lunch Chief Constable Richardson returned to the witness box, to be cross-examined by Goddard: 'This is the first murder case you have had cognizance of in this Division?' – 'Yes, it is the first murder case I have conducted.'

'And when you returned on the Sunday you did find blood marks in the house that had escaped attention on the Saturday?' – 'That had escaped my attention early on Sunday morning.'

'I think your memory is not very clear, is it, with regard to the statement Mrs Haskell made to you on the night of the murder about a man asking Teddy for his name and so on?' – 'I think it is. Mrs Haskell told me that someone had asked Teddy for his name and address.'

'She didn't tell you that Teddy said the name was for a man?' – 'No, she simply said she saw him writing his name and address down.'

'On the Saturday night, when she made a statement to you, you did not make a note of what she told you?' – 'No.'

'On November second, when she made a statement, it was taken down in writing, and what she said was this: "On Wednesday evening my little boy was writing his name and address on a piece of paper. I asked him what he was doing. He said: Someone wants it, mam, at school; he is going to bring me something tomorrow if I take my name and address – I did not ask him any question about it, neither can I say he took it on Thursday. I was quite alone when he told me this." Now, Mr Richardson, enquiry has been made about that and we have heard the little boy Harold Webb who was to have given him some foreign stamps?' – 'That is so.'

Judge Ridley interjected, 'Did she say a man wanted the name and address?' – 'No, my lord.'

'I thought you said so before.' – 'No, I have not said that'.

'It sounded like that.'

Foote chipped in, 'I was watching the difference between 'a man' and 'someone'.

Goddard continued, 'When you got her statement you made such enquiry as you could to ascertain the truth or falsity of it? – 'I did.'

'And did you ascertain that the statement that Mrs Haskell made as to her movements on that night was correct?' – 'Yes.'

'Did you ascertain that the statement she made about the insurance policy was also correct?' – 'Yes, sir'

'And that she would get no immediate benefit from it for some twelve months?' – 'That is so.'

'Was it from her statement made, I think, on November second, that you first learned about the boy Wyatt coming to the house with the parcel?' – 'Yes.'

'There were no bloodstains on the parcel at all?' – 'No.'

'The knife described by her in her statement had not been shown to her when she made her statement?' – 'No.'

'And she accurately described the knife?' – 'Yes.'

'Now, one question about this money in the drawer. When you examined the drawer did you find the coins concealed in the folds of a cloth?' – 'They were in the folds of a cloth. You could not see them when you opened the drawer.'

'You told us you found some spots of blood at the foot of the bed.' – 'Yes.'

'Were some of the spots close to the bed?' – 'Not very far away.'

'And was the spot of blood that you noticed on the landing on the left-hand side of the person who left to go downstairs?' – 'Yes.'

'I think the interview you had with this woman on the Sunday lasted some hours?' – 'Yes.'

'There was no other woman present, and she was alone with you and the other three officers?' – 'She was.'

'On the Monday after the murder did you receive a communication from a man of the name of Leate?' – 'Yes.'

'What time of the day did he make a com-munication to you?' – 'He called at the police station.'

'What time?' – 'I did not see him personally.'

'Can you tell us?' – 'I think it was in the morning.'

'Leate is a tradesman in Salisbury?' – 'The son of a tradesman.'

'He works, himself, and as far as you know he is a respectable man?' – 'Yes, he assists his father in the business.'

'You saw Leate, and you took a statement from him?' – 'Yes.'

'And that resulted in you seeing Mrs Haskell again, and putting certain matters to her?' – 'Yes.'

With the end of Goddard's cross-examination, Foote sought clarification about the blood marks from the Chief Constable. He replied that 'No fresh marks of blood were discovered on the floor after the first examination. The fresh marks discovered after the first examination were the marks on the chair, on the chest of drawers, and on the wall of the staircase.'

The next police witness was Superintendent Thomas Stephens of the Wiltshire Constabulary, Salisbury Division. He testified that 'I went with the Chief Constable to 40 Meadow Road, on the 31 October, and I was desirous to give assistance. I arrived at the house with Richardson. I was in court when he gave evidence, and I agree with what was said about the money. We did not see the money at first. Mrs Haskell said that it was "in the top drawer [of the chest] nearest the fireplace. It is locked and it is in the box." Stephens corroborated Richardson's testimony on the drawer. He added that he sent cyclist messengers into the country district, and had a cordon of men drawn round the district for a radius of ten miles. He continued 'I heard Mrs Haskell say that she was wearing an apron on the night of the murder, and I went out to Mrs Carter and brought one in to her, and the accused said that that was the one she was wearing. I did not go into the kitchen till one o'clock, and Mrs Sweetman is mistaken when she said she saw me there.'

Next, the question of the armchair was raised. The judge asked 'Is there any importance attached to that chair?', and Parr replied 'I was only asked that question because my friend Mr Goddard seemed to attach such importance to it.' A handkerchief, almost covered with blood, which Mrs Haskell had handed to Stephens was exhibited, and his comments was that 'Mrs Haskell said that was one of the handkerchiefs Teddy had used when he made his ear bleed.' A second handkerchief, recovered from Teddy's jacket, was exhibited: this too was bloodstained. Stephens's final contribution was that he had found the whetstone used to sharpen the fatal knife.

Chief Inspector Dew's testimony was relatively brief; probably because most of the forensic investigation which could be carried out had been by the time he arrived. 'I was sent to assist in this inquiry. What Chief Constable Richardson and Superintendent Stephens said with regard to what I did is correct. I went into the kitchen and found two handkerchiefs in the copper.' Heavily bloodstained, these were then produced in court.'

Foote then asked how the police statements were obtained. Dew replied, 'I told Mrs Haskell who I was, and that I was very anxious to detect the person who had committed the murder. Mrs Haskell said she would tell me all she knew, and she then made her statement[s] [with me] asking a few questions. [It is these statements] which have been read in court. With regard to the fourth statement, about an injury to the boy's ear, I made enquiries at the school, and am perfectly satisfied that the boy knocked his ear at school, that blood came from the ear, and that he had been seen mopping it with his handkerchief. This explains one or two of the handkerchiefs produced. I was present when Mrs Haskell made her statements. She was cool, calm and collected until I showed her the knife, when she became very much agitated.'

Goddard had no questions to ask.

With the next group of witnesses, the hearing moved into its final and sternest phase: consideration of the medical evidence, testimony being given by the family doctor, the police surgeon and the Home Office pathologist.

H.L.E. Wilks, whose surgery was on the Wilton Road, was the Haskells' family doctor. 'I went at once with Dr Row on being called by the lad Noble. I went upstairs.' After setting the scene in the

bedroom Wilks continued, 'The main artery of the neck was severed and death must have been instantaneous, and the expression on the face was quite peaceful. Air was bubbling through the wound, which led me to believe that death had taken place about a quarter of an hour.' There ensued a detailed description of the wound, which, Wilks added 'was of such a nature as could be caused by the knife produced.' He explained how blood would spurt through such a wound, 'which must have take considerable force' to inflict. There was [also] a slight wound on one of the fingers, which was quite consistent with the suggestion that he might have put his hand up involuntarily when the wound in the throat was inflicted.'

Judge Ridley asked, 'Did you think the boy had seen the person who had struck him with the knife?' – 'I should say not.'

Wilks continued, 'Mrs Haskell was in the kitchen in a very hysterical condition. I went to get her a soothing draught. I took Mrs Haskell upstairs because she asked to be taken up. The room had been made presentable. We had to wash the boy and remove the blood. I made the bed presentable by putting the blood-stained clothes at the foot of the bed. I first brought up Mrs Carter and then Mrs Haskell. She – Mrs Haskell – only went up and kissed the boy, and then went out again. The prisoner made a statement to me that she thought the man who came downstairs was the same as came for lodgings. The knife produced [in court] was what I saw. I saw blood on the blade, which was partially dry. The edge was bright, as if it had recently been roughly sharpened. My attention was called to a mark on the threshold of the door, about three or four inches long. It was on the linoleum, which was on the floor, and was such a mark which might have been made by the knife resting on the floor. It was of course a mark of blood, and appeared to have been done within half an hour. That was the only distinct mark I saw anywhere near the door. I formed the opinion from the character of the mark that if a knife had been thrown from any height it would not have made a mark like that. It looked as if it had been placed there.

Goddard's cross-examination, like those with others who knew Flora, began with an enquiry about her relations with her son. Wilks replied, 'I attended the boy all his life, and to my knowledge, no discharge had taken place from the boy's leg. I attended Teddy Haskell, who lost his leg two years ago, and when the operation took place the mother did all she could, and was always a good nurse to him.'

And then, Goddard requested that a reminder be produced of the night's events even more grisly than the murder weapon – the blood-drenched pillows. He turned his questioning to the evidence on the pillows of swift and dramatic blood-loss, and Wilks responded as follows:

'The spots of blood on the pillow in my opinion was [the result of] a spurt on either side, and the drainage was by the head after the head had been moved. Some of the spots were clear arterial spurting. The big mark would be caused by the artery. I knew from what I saw at the time that the artery was obstructed by some tissues. The artery had spurted at the beginning. I cannot say whether the spots were caused by the spurting or the flow. What blood came from the lungs would be lighter than that which came from the artery. The bed was up against the wall, and the boy was lying on the left pillow. There was blood on the handle of the knife, which would indicate to me that the hand that held the knife must have had blood upon it.'

Goddard continued his cross-examination: 'Your view was that whoever killed that boy put their left hand on the boy's head?' – 'Yes. [I have already said so].'

'Can you tell me whether there were any spots of blood on the right cheek or [on] the hair of the child?' – 'I don't think there were.'

'The person who cut the boy's throat must have stood by the side of the bed?' – 'Yes.'

'This wound was, as I understand [it], one clean cut?' – 'Yes; there was one little jag in it, in the middle.'

'That might have been caused by the roughness of the knife, or a notch?' – 'Yes.'

'Surgically speaking, this knife was a blunt thing?' – 'Yes.'

'The windpipe is a cartilage of some toughness?' – 'In between the rings there is loose tissue.'

'The wound you have spoken of was deeper at the end than at the beginning?' – 'Yes.'

'Which would show that the assailant kept the force up to the end, that there was no slackening of the force of the blow?' – 'No.'

'And that would convey to your mind that rather an exceptional amount of force was used?' – 'A considerable amount.'

'It would be more considerable with a man than [with] a woman?' – 'A man is stronger than a woman.'

'Did it indicate to you that more than ordinary determination was used?' – 'I should say, decided determination.'

'The wound was at about the most fatal spot that could have been selected in the throat?' – 'Yes.'

'Just where the main artery is nearest to the surface?' – 'It went through the main artery, and that means instantaneous death.'

'Blood would issue from this wound directly the incision was made?' – 'Yes.'

'And as the knife was drawn across would blood spurt out simultaneously?' – 'Yes.'

'And there would be a certain movement of the head, whether voluntary or involuntary?' – 'I should think so.'

'And, of course, the movement of the head would tend to cause the blood to fly?' – 'I think in this particular case it had an opposite effect, because of the tissues I have spoken of.'

Goddard then clarified with Wilks the exact sequence of events on his arrival on the scene, and he replied, 'When I came to the house I went straight up to the bedroom, and was there about ten minutes, and I got there within a quarter of an hour [of the attack]. When I went downstairs first Mrs Haskell wanted to know if he was bad, and it was on the second time that she wanted to see him, after I had told her that the boy was dead.'

'When you saw Mrs Haskell the first time she was in a state bordering on panic?' – 'She was hysterical.'

'The wound itself would prevent the boy making any articulate sound which could be heard downstairs?' – 'Yes, because the wound itself is below the vocal chords. He may have made a gasp, but he could not have made more.'

'When you had the bed made presentable you took Mrs Haskell up?' – 'Yes.'

'Was she able to control herself?' — 'She kissed the boy and then burst out crying.'

'Would you suggest that the left hand was put on the head to steady it?' — 'It was not necessarily so.'

'The neck must have been stretched [for the assailant] to have been able to inflict such a wound?' — 'If the neck had not been stiff it would only have caused an ugly cut.'

Dr Row, Wilks' house guest at the time of the murder, confirmed his host's evidence.

Next to testify was Gilbert Kempe, the local police surgeon. 'On the Tuesday after the murder, the third November I examined the body as police surgeon. I noticed a small scab on the left ear. I removed the scab and examined the flesh underneath, and it was healing. It had not bled for some hours before. The scab was only a small one. On the same day I was shown the skirt and blouse which have been produced. The skirt is black and I saw some bloodstains on them [*i.e.* it], although it wanted close attention to see them. I would describe the ones on the upper part as irregularly rounded, but they cannot be seen now. I have no doubt that the bloodstains are there, a group on the top side, and on the lower part as if blood had been on there and had dropped a little — about the shape of a long pear drop. It does not look as if there has been any arterial spurting on it. They [the blood marks] are all on the right-hand side. There is no mark where a bloody knife could have struck her. I have seen the knife in this case, and assuming it had some blood on it and was thrown at the person who was wearing the blouse, the blood marks could not have been caused in that manner, neither could they have been caused by a knife striking the floor and the blood sprinkling upwards.

In my opinion all the marks on the blouse were caused by blood being blown from the windpipe. With regard to the blood on the skirt, the long pear-shape ones could have been done by that. If the blood had been blown it would have took [*sic*] a sort of curve, and then have dropped onto the skirt. That is how I think they were caused. In my opinion all the marks were caused by blood being blown out from the windpipe. There are distinct indication[s] of the way the blood was smeared on the [table] cloth. There is a raised crease, and there is a lot of blood on one

side, and on the other side of the crease there is a gap where there is no blood, and then the marks begin again. The marks show that the thing which smeared the cloth travelled along the direction which was pointed out — namely, towards the wash-house.

The third medical — and expert — witness was Professor Pepper, consultative adviser to the Government. As at the inquest, he expounded his inspection of the linoleum, the wallpaper, the tablecloth and other bloodstained specimens. 'I found no marks of blood on the front door, or on the button and latch of the back door. There were no blood marks on the small brass lamp which has been spoken of. On the piece of floorcloth which was taken from the staircase there is a circular mark about three and a half inches long and four small spots of blood. A knife fallen from any distance would not have left a mark like that: there would have been many more splashes around; probably the knife would have rebounded.

'I agree with the previous witness as to the position of the bloodstains in the bedroom. I examined the paper from behind the chair and found bloodstains thereon. They were such spots as might have been caused by the spray of blood from the wound in the windpipe. There were several other spots of blood on the linoleum in the bedroom, one lot by the bed and another near the door. There was also a large spot on the landing and another smaller one. This would have been caused, in my opinion, by dripping from something. There was no trace of smearing. On the wallpaper from the staircase there was a blood mark such as might have been caused by a person carrying something downstairs. It was not smeared, it was projected. The whole of the blood marks were distinctly recent, probably a week old. It was all approximately of the same age. It was mammalian blood, but I cannot go further than that.

'On the blouse, the spots of blood are of the same character. There are twenty-eight spots on the front and nearly fifty on the right sleeve, extending to a little below the yoke. They go to the wrist. One mark seems to indicate that the blood struck the sleeve upwards: I arrive at this from the shape of the spots. It would be quite impossible for the marks to have been caused by a bloody knife being thrown. There was no sign of a knife having struck the blouse. If a knife had been thrown at a person there would be a large aggregated mark showing the point of contact, and I would have expected to find more splashes.'

At that point, Pepper was shown the skirt, and invited to comment on the bloodstains on the skirt. With some difficulty he found the stains and continued his testimony: 'There are nineteen to twenty spots on the skirt. The marks were very evident when I first saw the skirt, but they have been rubbed since and are rather difficult to find.' Pepper then showed the exhibits to the jury and to the judge: all examined them with interest. He pointed out one particularly large spot. 'On the upper part of the skirt,' Pepper continued, ' they are of the same character as those on the blouse – rounded. The majority of the marks are elongated. This would be caused by dropping down from some object held near to the skirt. The marks on the skirt could not have been caused by a knife being thrown. If that had been the case there would be one large mark, and the marks would not be scattered around as is the case. The shower of spots is too uniform for that. I am quite confident the spots could not have been caused in that way. If the blood had come from the knife as it was passing her the stains would not all have been in one direction, and if the knife had struck the floor there would be more spots on the bottom of the skirt than at the top.'

Par interjected, 'Would you have expected to find more marks on or about the kitchen door?' – 'I should.'

Ridley added, 'A knife can only carry a certain amount of blood.' – 'Not only the knife, my lord, but there would be blood on the hand.'

Parr continued, 'In giving your opinion, have you allowed for the blood that might have been in the hand?' – 'Yes. I am quite convinced that the marks were not caused by anything thrown at her.' He added that the bloodstain caused by the knife contradicted any notion that it had been thrown.

At that point – it was by then five o'clock – the court rose, and the case was adjourned until the morrow.

The third day of the trial, Wednesday 17th, again witnessed large crowds outside the court, and a packed public gallery within. Mr Justice Ridley again took his seat at 10.30, and Parr proceeded with his cross-examination of Professor Pepper. Continuing his exposition of the bloodstaining, he said 'I have already told you of the blood from the windpipe on the wall and the chest of drawers. Marks on the blouse are consistent with having been blown from the windpipe, [as were] those on the lower part of the skirt. There are indications of the spray going to the right of the blouse. My opinion is that the assassin would stand with her back to the wall. In that case the blood would be on the right side because that was the direction the spots would go. I cannot say whether the cause of the spots on the blouse was that they came from the artery or from the windpipe; but I should think they came from the windpipe. Such a spray would continue for some little time after the assailant had left the room, presuming she left the room at once.

'With regard to the handkerchiefs that were got from the copper, the blood [on one] might have been produced by it being dabbed on the scar. I should think it was all from the nose. [On] the handkerchief, [exhibit] no. 33, there was more blood on it than I should have expected. The worst part is the aggregated mark on the handkerchief. If it had been dabbed on the ear or the nose it [the blood] would have been more scattered.

'With regard to the tablecloth, I have heard Dr Kempe's evidence about the direction of the smear, and I agree with it. There are two sorts of mark on the tablecloth. One took a slanting direction, and the other was a horizontal one. There is no mark on the skirt which could have caused the marks on the tablecloth. There is a mark on the skirt which seems as if it has rubbed against it [the tablecloth], but that was lower down than the level of the tablecloth. Therefore the blood marks on the tablecloth cannot possibly have been caused by the skirt. The marks would have been straight if caused by the skirt.

Parr interjected, 'Are there any indications of these smears on the table cloth being caused by blood from a person's hand passing by?' – 'They may possibly have been caused by a hand being rubbed against the cloth; but I would rather think that it was being done by something held in the hand. If this had been done [by a hand] there would only have been the one mark, but instead of that there are a number of marks. If the marks had been made at the same time they could not have been made by the skirt. That is quite impossible. The spots indicate that they were dropped from some article onto the cloth. The largest spot on the tablecloth measures about half an inch across. I examined the knife on the eighth of November, and there was a considerable amount of blood on it, and it was on the handle as well as on the blade.'

In response to cross-examination by Goddard, Pepper replied, 'I should think the person who committed the murder must have stood with her back towards the wall, behind the head and rather behind the pillow. The spots of blood that have been found in the house are mammalian blood, but that does not imply that it is human blood. There are tests which would enable an approximate opinion to be formed whether the blood is animal or human, but it would be no certain opinion. Spots of blood, like any fluid, have a tendency to show from which direction they come, and the tendency of the marks on the sleeve of the blouse would depend on whether the arm were held up or down.'

Goddard interjected, 'If a knife having any quantity of blood upon it were thrown, and in its flight struck against some hard inanimate object, might there not be a tendency of the blood to spray?' – 'Spray of a certain kind, but it would not spread far and widely.'

Ridley asked, 'I suppose you mean the side of the door-post?'

Goddard replied, 'Something of that sort, my lord. Am I right in saying that the tendency of the direction of the spots is from somewhere about the left front, down towards the right?' – 'Yes.'

Goddard then asked 'Have you ever seen a throat cut?' The judge interjected 'I hope not.' The professor continued, 'As a surgeon I have seen throats cut. Small arteries would spurt.' Mr Foote asked, 'The spray would be intermittent?' – 'Yes' replied Pepper.

'And would last while the child was dying?' – 'Yes'.

While this exchange was taking place, Flora wept bitterly.

The judge then asked, 'Is there any indication to your mind that there were two people in the room at the time of the murder?' – 'No, my lord, there is nothing to suggest that. Of course, there might have been, but from my investigation there is nothing to suggest it.'

Foote interjected with an assurance that the matter had been considered by the Crown, but Ridley pressed the point: 'Is there anything to indicate that there were two people [standing] apart from each other "doing the job" in the room or the house at the time?' – 'Not the slightest indication'.

The final witness was Mrs Sheppard, police matron at Salisbury who had charge of Flora whilst she was in custody in Salisbury. She testified that after Flora was committed for trial on 5 December, she made a statement. Parr asked, 'At Salisbury, in a room adjoining the cells?' – 'Yes.'

'Did she say anything to you?' – 'Yes. After the Reverend Mr Thwaites had left she had a conversation with me, and she said, 'Oh! Mrs Sheppard, if I did it I don't remember it'. Under cross-examination Mrs Sheppard acknowledged that 'It is true that the accused was before the magistrates from Monday morning till Saturday night. The magistrates sat long days, and Mrs Haskell had frequent collapses. The remark was made late at night, and during the day Mrs Haskell had been attended by a doctor.'

The two witnesses who were not called were Edwin Daniels and Francis Samuel Leate, the one person who may have witnessed the mysterious man whom Flora claimed to have been the killer. Foote said he did not propose to place them in the witness box, unless his learned friend wished to put any question to them. Goddard replied that he had no desire to do so. Both prosecution and defence had their reasons.

14

'A horrid task': the closing speeches at the first trial, 17 February 1909.

WITH ALL THE EVIDENCE in a most harrowing case reviewed, the trial reached its *dénouement* with the closing speeches. For the Crown, Foote spent half an hour, during which he scrutinised the evidence in great detail, starting with the points which, he said, were beyond dispute, leading to the conclusion that some of the prisoner's statements were improbable, indeed impossible.

Thus, 'according to Mrs Haskell's own statement, she passed from the door between the kitchen and the passage to the wash-house door, and you know that when she passed along there, there was blood upon her blouse and upon her skirt. Nobody is going to suggest that the blood came upon her garments after that. You know that the tablecloth on the side on which she passed was discovered to be smeared and spotted with fresh blood. You know that the accused was seen by Mrs Sweetman within five minutes after the alarm with a blood-stained handkerchief in her hand. After hearing the evidence of Mrs Sweetman, as trustworthy a witness as anybody who has been called before you, will you resist the inference that when Mrs Haskell passed the tablecloth she had that bloodstained handkerchief in her hand? You have also the fact that the boy Noble heard a noise as of a chair being pushed or moved. How was that chair pushed back or moved, and why? If her statement is true it could not have been Mrs Haskell who pushed it back.

'Listen to what she said: "Then I sat down in the kitchen for about a quarter of an hour. Then I got up and locked the back door, and lowered the gas [light] in the kitchen." I do not want to be hypercritical, but you will remember that the boy's evidence was that there was an ordinary light in the kitchen, sufficient to throw a shadow of the accused into the scullery. She may have lowered the gas, as she said, but she cannot have lowered it much, because had she done so there would not have been sufficient light to cast her shadow. But that is not my point. Mrs Haskell went on to say "I had locked the back door and lowered the gas in the kitchen, and as I was going to open the kitchen door leading to the passage my little nephew came and knocked at the back door. As I was going towards the back door I heard someone coming downstairs, and they threw something at me and splashed me."

'According to the statement, Mrs Haskell was not sitting at the time, but if the little boy was right, someone was sitting. I think I am justified in submitting that if Mrs Haskell was sitting at all, she could only have been sitting in the chair immediately adjoining the passage door, and is it not a conceivable theory that if this unhappy woman had just done this dreadful thing she may have come down the stairs with the knife in her hand and sank into the first chair? And then hearing a knock, she knew it must be answered, and it would be natural and easy for her then, still holding the knife in her hand, to put it down. It could then have been put down exactly where it was found, and that theory would explain the fact that there was the distinct mark of a knife resting on the floor, and not a mark such as would be caused by a knife thrown violently from the stairs. One would have thought that a knife thrown from a height would have moved, would have rebounded, jumped, and would have made more than one mark.

'As to the "thump" which Percy Noble said he heard after he knocked at the door, I suggest that what the boy heard was made by the woman starting, and not being in a calm state she would get up hastily and make a staggering noise with her foot. You know, according to Mrs Haskell's statement, that she was greatly alarmed and agitated. I do not wish to put it in a theatrical way; I do not want to appeal to your sentiment, but it is almost inconceivable, if Mrs Haskell's statement about a man coming down the stairs and throwing a bloodstained knife at her is true, that she did not go immediately upstairs. I would have thought she would have gone upstairs before she went to the little boy, but at any rate after she had sent for help one would have thought she would have gone up to see if any serious injury had been done to her Teddy. One cannot understand the conduct of this woman, who, I don't doubt, was at ordinary times, an affectionate and good mother. She did not go up, nor did she attempt to go up for some considerable time after the doctors had left the first time. The first time she attempted to go up was after Mrs Carter, her mother, came, and I am bound to point that out to you, and I am also bound to remind you that without going upstairs Mrs Haskell appeared quite certain that the child was dead.'

Discussing the handkerchiefs, Foote continued, 'I remind you that Mrs Sweetman put the bloodstained article on the mantelpiece, and the next that was heard of it was Mrs Carter offering it to the police as little Teddy's handkerchief. I suggest that that handkerchief was in Mrs Haskell's hand when she passed through the kitchen to unlock the back door, and it was that that smeared the tablecloth.'

Foote's next point concerned the spots on the blouse and the skirt: 'I direct your attention to the emphatic statement made by Dr Pepper that it was impossible that they could have been caused by a thrown knife.' On the question of the knife, Foote continued, 'It was ordinarily kept in the drawer, and that was where it was looked for and missed. Can it

be thought probable that the knife was lying on Teddy's bed, or on the chest of drawers, ready to the hand of a hypothetical murderer who came without a knife on the chance of finding one? You cannot ignore the problem: "How did the murderer get the knife?" If in fact the knife was left in the room in such a prominent position that it was ready to the hand of the man who rushed into the house in this way, mustn't Mrs Haskell have seen it, and wouldn't she have told the Chief Constable afterwards that it was there? It appears to me that the question of the knife is a very difficult and a very significant one.'

The final point addressed the question of the would-be lodger. '[I would refer you to] Mrs Haskell's statement to the young man Alfred [Walter] Noble, some hours before the murder, that she was worried about a man who called for lodgings the previous night. The inference you can draw from that is that if she really felt nervous about a thing of that kind she was in a very nervous and excited state. What is there to terrify a woman in the fact that a man, a well-spoken man of medium height and build and well-dressed, called for lodgings and that she declined to take him in? Of course, I know that women are more nervous about these things than men are, and it is quite natural that a woman living alone should be nervous, but it is for you to judge whether excessive nervousness isn't shown by this woman, which rather indicates a neurotic state of mind. You must take the facts and all the circumstances into consideration, and give your verdict on the evidence before you. If I have selected those facts which are against this prisoner, it is not because I desire to do so, but because it is the duty I am sent here to discharge.'

The silence was electric as Goddard rose to his feet. Unlike the prosecution, he would speak for an hour and a half, in a measured, deliberate tone of voice.[1] Turning to the jury, he said

'If your lordship pleases, gentlemen of the jury, Edwin Richard Haskell was murdered on the night of October 31st. The prisoner, his mother, was arrested and charged with the crime on November 3rd, and this is the first occasion in all these months that have elapsed — time that must have seemed like as many centuries to this unhappy woman — that any opportunity has [been] offered for the evidence to be criticised and for a defence to be put forward on her behalf. This is the first opportunity, and I know full well that I am addressing a jury who has paid most careful attention to the case, and that you will not have made up your mind on it one way or the other until you have heard the criticisms I, on behalf of the prisoner, have to make upon the evidence, and the points I desire to put before you in order that you may come to a just decision. I should like, at the very outset of my remarks, to pay a tribute of thanks for the exemplary fairness in which this case has been conducted from start to finish.

'This is no ordinary case of murder which you have to try. It is not a case in which the nature or the quality of the crime comes into consideration; that is to say, you are not here to consider whether this is a case of murder or manslaughter, nor are you concerned with the state of the prisoner's mind, whether she is sane or insane. It is simply and solely a question of *murder*, and at the outset of my remarks, I would ask you most earnestly to bear this question in mind, that the question you have to try is not who committed this murder – the question you are sworn to try is a much narrower one than that. It is this: *has the prosecution proved that this woman committed the murder?* One cannot help feeling in a case of this kind, in which, so far as any witness has been produced, the prisoner is the only person who is known to have been in the house at, or about, the time of the murder, that there must inevitably be a temptation to put the question to oneself, "If the prisoner did not do it who did?"

'Gentlemen, I venture to think that that is a most dangerous speculation, but whether it is a dangerous speculation or not, it is not a question we are here to try. The question we are here to try is as I have already said, aye or no, beyond a shadow of doubt, beyond the possibility of mistake, is it true that this woman slew her only child that night? That is the question the prosecution has undertaken to prove, and it is for them to prove it. I hope I shall be able to show you before I conclude the remarks I have to make, that the only real evidence against this woman is the fact that there were bloodstains on her clothing and the other evidence is the various conjectures which

medical men of eminence and of fairness have drawn from it. And I think that before you have come to the end of this case you will find that the matter comes down to this: Are you content to condemn a fellow-creature to death on the evidence, on theories of doctors, however eminent? Gentlemen, I hope I shall be able to show that this is so.

'Let us take the general conduct of this woman, because it is agreed on all hands that she was a most loving and devoted mother – a mother who had not only devoted herself to her child in health, but also in sickness. Dr Wilks told us that from the time this little boy was maimed by illness the mother nursed him, and proved herself a loving nurse. Teddy himself, this happy little cripple, showed by his own brightness and happiness what a happy home he had. The little fellow was handicapped in the race of life – handicapped among his fellows by the loss of a leg, yet he was so brave and fine a little character that he managed to take part in football, and kept goal for his school team. The best evidence of a happy home life is the little cripple himself, who showed such cheerfulness in the face of his great misfortune. [By now Flora was weeping bitterly] You will not forget that remark of Mr Steer's, when I asked him what sort of a mother she was to Teddy, and he said that she was "all that a mother should be". I wonder how many women there are in this world of whom this could be said, and I wonder how many women there are who would give anything to feel that that could be said of them.

'Not only was the accused a good mother, she also showed herself to be a brave, hard-working woman. Deprived several years ago of a husband's help and care – a man in a decent position – she did not sit down under her misfortune, but she worked, and worked hard, to keep herself and her boy, and she worked successfully, because we find that here she was, with herself and her boy to keep, making a little income of something over a pound a week as a laundress – a very nice income for a woman in that position – having to pay five shillings and sixpence a week for rent, and some small amount for the materials she had to use in her trade , but an ample sum for a woman in that position. We have heard that her brothers are in good positions, so that if she had been in financial trouble or straits she had friends to turn to. No sort of suggestion can be made that this woman was not comfortably off in life. You start with the fact that we have a woman in a decent position, in want of nothing, a loving, devoted and tender mother, and yet it is suggested that almost in a moment of time she turned into a monster.

'This prosecution has been put forward from first to last as against a sane woman. I have met the prosecution on that ground, and no theory or suggestion of insanity has been raised by the defence. Had it been suggested that she was insane, different considerations altogether would arise. It is suggested that this woman, whose movements can be traced up to within a minute or two of the murder as a sane woman, a woman who has been able to tell a connected story, that this woman turned from a loving and devoted mother into such a monster that words almost fail one in attempting to give a true description of her. Now, gentlemen, I cannot help feeling that the Crown have put forward their case as one of a premeditated crime. I had some doubt at first as to whether that was the thing put forward by the Crown. But all doubt must have been cleared away by the remarks of my friend Mr Foote, towards the close of his speech, because when he was referring to the knife he suggested that it was not likely to have been in the hands of the murderer before he came to the house; that it must have been taken out of the drawer, and that Mrs Haskell must have made her story up. Gentlemen, it was not a story that a woman of her education, a woman in her position, could have made up on the spur of the moment. With regard to that knife you will remember she said it was the knife that Teddy used to cut a tip-cat, and it is easily conceivable that it may have been in the child's room, and that some murderer might have laid his hand on it. But if this was a premeditated murder, there must have been some overwhelming motive that induced this woman to commit it.

'The Crown have been unable, so they say, to suggest a motive, but at the same time they have not eliminated from the case a certain portion of the evidence which could have been put forward for no other reason than to suggest a motive. We have heard letters read about this woman's association with Mold. We have heard that somewhere back in August she had been mentioning to someone the question of marriage, and we have had letters read which passed between her and Mold. But, gentlemen, the prosecution have expressly disclaimed the view that the suggested motive was marriage, and I think you will probably feel that they did well to drop that suggestion. A more hideously inadequate suggestion could not possibly be put forward, especially when you remember that it is in evidence that Mold used to make this little lad his companion, that he gave him money, and went about with him. If Mold had been some fiend, some man who it could be proved, or suggested, had said to this woman, "Get rid of the cripple and I'll marry you," would he have been a man who would have made this lad his companion when he was at home in Salisbury?

'Of course, if a maniac committed the crime, one does not look for motive. And if there was no motive a maniac may have committed it. Is there anything in the evidence which will justify you in saying that this woman is a maniac? It has often been said, and it is true, that there can be no adequate motive for murder. But if a sane person does commit a murder, if a murder is committed in cold blood, there must be some motive. I want you to observe this point closely. If this case is proved at all, it is proved by evidence which I suppose would be called circumstantial, though I confess it seems to me to be more theoretical. But circumstantial evidence, at its best, is dangerous ground, because at its highest it establishes a case on probablility only. And if you are to convict a person on circumstantial evidence, surely the question of motive must be of overwhelming importance, because if it is true – and I think you will agree that it is – that circumstantial evidence establishes a case on probability, and probability only, you will want to carry that probability further, and to see if the probability exists in the evidence. Gentlemen, there is no motive in this case against this woman, and no motive is put forward by the Crown.

'Now I am going to come at once to the most difficult part of the case, to that part of the case which I am well aware conveys the most suspicion against this woman. That is the evidence that deals with the stains on the clothing, and the medical evidence drawn therefrom. It is almost a platitude to say that the theories you draw from the facts must in their nature be the most dangerous ground to act upon, because, I don't care how eminent a gentleman may be in his profession, or how fairly he gives his evidence, human judgement is always fallible, and it is not at all certain that a man has not made a mistake because he is eminent in his profession. There is no more reason why Dr Pepper should not have made a mistake than anybody else, and I can't help feeling that you will require something very much stronger than has been adduced in this case before you can possibly accept theories, however plausible they may be, as sufficient to find a verdict in a case of life and death.

'Let us briefly recall the circumstances of this night. You will remember there is the circumstance of Miss Steer's call with the little coat. She fitted the coat on this woman, and some little conversation took place about payment. The woman was in her ordinary spirits, in her usual health, and nothing unnatural was noticed about her demeanour. From that time to the time of Wyatt's call, we do not know what happened, but it is quite clear, from the way in which she went out and took in that parcel for a neighbour that she talked in the ordinary way, and in a way which did not excite any suspicion in Wyatt's mind. The next thing we know is Noble's visit. Now, gentlemen, the prosecution are inviting you to find that the circumstances prove that Mrs Haskell is a murderess. I am going to invite you to say that her story is by no means impossible, and I believe I am not overstating my case when I say that unless you find that these circumstances could not have come about by any other conceivable means, you will not be entitled to return a verdict of murder against her. I have no dispute with the doctors as the facts. I have no dispute with anybody as to any single fact that has been proved.

'Where I do join issue is in the theories drawn from the facts. The first matter I wish to mention is the tablecloth. A great deal has been made of the tablecloth, and nothing has been said which is not fair. The suggestion is that Mrs Haskell put those stains on that cloth when she had some bloody thing

in her hand which could have made the stains. Did you notice that with the exception of the stains on the tablecloth, no single stain, or mark of blood, is found in the kitchen, and not a single stain or mark of blood is found in the scullery, nor on the back door which she opened to Percy Noble. It has been suggested and put forward by the Crown that those marks got onto the tablecloth from a handkerchief reeking with blood which was held in her hand as she went to answer the door to Percy Noble.

'Why then is there no mark of blood on the scullery door which she opened? Why is there no mark of blood anywhere in the kitchen? Why is there no mark of blood between the kitchen and the scullery? Remember that with regard to the tablecloth there was some doubt at the very outset, and we don't know with certainty that it is human blood upon it. Some of that blood may have got there in anyway. The woman was living at home, cutting up her own meat and occasionally having little accidents to her own nose and the boy's ear, and anything may have happened. It may have got on in exactly the same way as the Crown suggest. It may have got on from some bloodstained handkerchief. But we know that the boy had been mopping his ear, and we know the woman had a scar on the nose which needed some staunching.

'Where is the proof that those stains got onto the tablecloth from a handkerchief which she held, wet with the blood of the child she had just murdered? It seems to me inconceivable that if she put those smears on that tablecloth that some other traces have not been found in the kitchen or on the scullery door. It is said that the blood on the tablecloth was bright red. It is a fair remark to make, but it is a most extraordinary thing that these bloodstains were only seen that night by Mrs Sweetman and the man Rawlins, neither of whom are trained observers, and that the police did not notice them at all. Undoubtedly there were stains on the cloth, but when did they get there?

'Many people went into that bloodstained bedroom that night and passed through the kitchen, and though they said they had no blood upon them, who is to tell exactly what they did in the agitation which must have come over them all when they saw what a horrid deed had been committed?

Undoubtedly the handkerchief which Mrs Haskell held in her hand had bloodstains upon it. This woman who has committed this premeditated murder has this handkerchief in her hand for all to see. Is it wonderful that she had this blood-stained handkerchief? We know that someone's nose has been bleeding, because Dr Pepper says there was mucus on it. You know well enough that a woman would not be able to get all the blood off her hands with a handkerchief, and have left no trace of it, and it has never been suggested that there was a mark or trace of blood on her hands that night. I suggest that in artificial light the two witnesses who saw the stains on the handkerchief could not tell whether the colour was that of fresh blood or not.

'And as for the spots of blood on the blouse,' Goddard continued, 'The suggestion is, gentlemen, that the blood got onto the blouse as the result of a spray from the larynx. You have seen the pillows. It was a horrid task, but I had to bring them out. You have heard a description of the room. Can you believe that if this woman cut the boy's throat she could have got so little blood on her as is on this blouse? You have seen the blouse, and the amount of blood on it is infinitesimal. Can you believe that if that blood got on the blouse by the accused cutting the boy's throat there would not be infinitely more? Dr Pepper has said in his evidence that the whole thing depends upon the position – as to whether she was in the line of the spray, whether she moved or whether she did not. What is it more than the purest conjecture? On that conjecture you are asked to find a verdict of guilty. You know the doctors don't agree on the most important matter, namely, *where* this woman stood or *how* she stood. You will remember I asked Dr Wilks, and he said she stood facing the pillow. Dr Kempe thought she stood facing the corner of the bed, and Dr Pepper says she stood with her back to the wall. There you get three absolutely divergent views as to the position, which is admitted by Dr Pepper to be an important thing. Does that not bring doubt into a man's mind?

'But there is another matter. How is it, accepting the theories of the doctors, that there is no blood on the left side of the blouse? If it all depends on position and the woman came into the line of spray, I can conceive that you might be able to frame a theory. But does that fit in with the facts of the case? You must pardon me if I uncover this pillow once more. We know, because there is undoubted evidence of it, that the boy's head was lying *there*, and as I stand here I should be looking straight in the boy's face. We know there is blood on the wall and we know there is blood on the chair. We know there is blood on the chest of drawers which would be on my left as I stand here. Does it not occur to you as a most astonishing thing, that whichever way the woman stood she had not got any blood on her left side? Gentlemen, there is not a trace or mark of blood anywhere other than on the right front of this blouse, and I venture to think you will pause before you draw an unfavourable inference against this woman on that account.

'Let us see whether the explanation which this woman has given fits in. She has said that as a man came downstairs she looked out, that he threw a knife at her and it splashed her. Dr Pepper has agreed with me that with a knife thrown and hitting some firm inanimate object, blood might spray from it, although he does not think the spray found on this woman's blouse looks like that. Dr Pepper has not told us of any experiments he has made to find out what pattern of spray would come, and I suggest to a most distinguished medical man that it is exceedingly difficult to say what spray might come off a knife. Supposing a butcher gets blood on his hand and throws it off, how can anybody say what pattern it will make, and what direction it will take?

'One point in Dr Pepper's evidence that is of the utmost importance is that coming downstairs there was a mark on the right-hand side as if blood had been projected. Is it not a strong point to bear in mind when we are deciding whether this woman's story is impossible, as they would have you believe? I want you to remember that this staircase comes down flush with the jamb of the door, and the kitchen door opens in. I want you to picture yourself for a moment the position a person would be in who suddenly hears footsteps and looks out up that staircase. I think a person coming hurriedly in that way would look up the stairs and in so doing would expose her right side and her left side would be covered to some extent by

DEPICTION OF THE MURDERER AND THE DISCOVERY OF THE MURDER IN THE ILLUSTRATED POLICE NEWS

the right. I suggest that if blood were thrown by a man coming downstairs at that moment there is nothing surprising in finding it on the right side; it is exactly where you would expect to find it.

'On the other hand, how could the blood have got on her in that room where we know the blood spurted to the left and no blood got to the right at all. As to the skirt, remember that this is an old skirt, which she must have been wearing for some time, and you ought not to take it as proved that every mark of blood got on that skirt on that day. You will, no doubt, be of [the] opinion that some of the blood got on the skirt on that day, but when you have to deal with facts which, if proved, are of such frightful importance to a fellow-creature, I submit that you ought not to start with the presumption that every one of these bloodstains – which Professor Pepper said might be days or weeks old – got on the skirt that day. Here is a little lad with a bad leg. We have heard that a short time before the murder, when he had been sleeping with young Noble, that [sic] there was some blood in the bed.

'Anything might have happened to account for the blood on the skirt. I do not suggest that some blood did not get on that night. Although Dr Pepper disagrees that the whole of the stains could have been caused by the fall of a knife he does not deny that taking the stains individually they could not have been caused by a knife falling against the skirt. The doctors say that this knife could not have fallen or been dropped from a high position because there is only one mark of blood where it fell with the exception of four minute marks around it; they say they would have expected more splashes around. Dr Wilks has said that in his opinion the knife was placed there. Does it seem to you likely that a woman coming down with the weapon in her hand with which she had murdered her only child, would have stooped down to place it at her own door? Would she not have wished, at all costs, to get rid of the horrid thing?

'See if an explanation is forthcoming from her story. Suppose a woman to be coming out and seeing a man coming downstairs, what would she naturally do? Would she not draw back, and might not the knife in falling have struck her skirt? I know she says it did not strike her, but she does not know. Might it not have struck her skirt low down, and, its fall being broken, would it not fall gently? Would not that account for the one mark and the four minute spots? I suggest that to you, and I suggest that it fits in with her story. I suggest to you, with some confidence, that it is incredible that this woman could have come downstairs and placed the knife on the floor as suggested. It is only one degree less intelligible than the theory adduced by the prosecution from the spots at the foot of the bed. They are said to show that whoever had that knife in their hand stayed there, and the blood dripped from the knife onto the floor. I agree that that is what they do show; but can you imagine that if a mother had just killed her only child, she could have stood at the foot of the bed, stood in the room where she had done this ghastly thing, and let blood drip from her knife? I suggest to you that it is incredible that a mother could have done it.

'We have had four doctors, distinguished in their profession, who have given their evidence with a fairness that is most noticeable, but I cannot help thinking that you are every bit as good judges as the doctors. To bring down famous experts to tell you what sort of a mark a bloody knife is likely to make when striking a black skirt, seems a little out of proportion, seems like bringing down a steam hammer to crack a walnut. You are just as well able to form an opinion as any eminent surgeon. I suggest that taking the two things together, the marks on the skirt more towards the right at the bottom than they are at the top, and the fact of the absence of splash marks around the knife, they do go to show that it is not beyond the point of possibility or probability that this woman's story is true, and that these marks on the skirt are caused by a knife falling on it. When you are dealing with evidence of bloodstains, you are dealing with things which must at best be very unreliable.

'So many things may happen that it is impossible to tell. I have already pointed out to you that these doctors do not agree in the most material point of the case: the position in which the assailant stood. I put it to Dr Pepper as to whether he had ever seen a

throat cut in this way, and it caused some amusement. But my point is this, that no-one has seen such a thing and one has to speculate about it, and there is no certainty. No doctor has said that these stains on the woman's clothes *must* have been caused by a spray from that boy's throat. The most they have said is that they *could* have been caused or *might* have been caused. I suggest that nothing short of certainty, beyond any doubt, *must* and not *may* will entitle you to find a verdict of guilty.

'I want now to pass to the other circumstances surrounding this crime. It is of the utmost importance that you should come to a conclusion in your own minds as to what time this murder was committed. It is clear by the evidence that the murder was committed some time before half-past ten. You only have the evidence of Dr Wilks and the time that Mrs Haskell was at her door. You have to consider what time Mrs Haskell was found giving the alarm, and I think that somewhere about ten-twenty-five is probably right, although I suggest to you that the evidence points if anything to Mrs Haskell being found rather before that time than afterwards. One cannot be certain to a minute or two. I want you to remember the evidence of the boy Wyatt – and to my mind Wyatt's is the most important in this case – who came to this house at about ten-seventeen, or it might have been as late as ten-twenty.

'If this woman was the murderess she must at that moment have been almost starting to go upstairs to kill the boy. She comes to the door, and I think I am justified in saying she comes without hesitation, because he cannot even say he knocked more than once. She comes to the door without hesitation and took the parcel, and on the parcel we know that there was no trace of blood. The murder had not been committed then. She came to the door, and she could hold a conversation with him, discuss taking the parcel for a neighbour when she must almost have been ascending the stairs to commit the awful act, if she did it. Does it not occur to you that if she had been contemplating it, interrupting her almost in the act would have shaken the strongest nerves? Do you think that feeble woman, if she had been contemplating immediate murder and was disturbed, could have held a quiet conversation with this boy?

JOHN WYATT DEPICTED IN THE MORNING LEADER

'I venture to think it is impossible, and I venture to think that if she had been contemplating such a deed the visit of Wyatt would have been sufficient to put her off her purpose. Think what she must have done if she committed the murder. Between the time of Wyatt's visit and the time when she gave the alarm she had not got much, if any, more than five minutes. She had to take the parcel in and put it in the front room where it was found the next day, to get the knife, to go upstairs and murder that boy, to come down and place the knife where it was found, to remove the traces of blood, and sufficiently compose herself so that when Percy Noble came she could answer "all right" in her usual quiet voice.

It has been suggested that between the time when she gave the alarm to Percy Noble and the time when she was found at the front door, there was time for her to rinse her hands. We know that that cannot be accepted, because the evidence of Mr and Mrs Steer, who I am perfectly certain you will accept as careful and accurate witnesses, shows that it was a question of seconds only. Where, then, did this woman cleanse her hands? You will not consider it possible that she could have committed the murder and not have got a considerable amount of blood on her right hand. Is it conceivable that she could have got it out of her nails in the time? It does not come off at all easily, and yet we know we know it has never been suggested from first to last that she had any blood on her hands. If she had not any blood on her hands she must have washed it off somewhere. There is no trace of blood on the sink, on the tap, or on the door which she opened to Percy Noble. There was only blood downstairs in the kitchen on the table, and the mark where the knife was found.

'Something was said about all traces of blood ceasing at the kitchen door, but of course the murderer dropped the knife there, which was the most bloody thing about him. Not only that, but we know the passage was washed over, and we know also that many women with skirts that trailed on the ground had come into the house, that people had walked over it, and might not that, combined with the washing over, have obliterated any marks there were. Gentlemen, I do not really think that much can be gathered from the fact that there were no marks after the bottom of the stairs. Remember that this woman's movements were traced from about seven o'clock that evening, when she was out shopping with her friends, with her usual bright demeanour; that she mentioned the fact about a man who had called at her house for lodgings, then going home later in the evening she sees her brother-in-law, the elder Noble, next she sees Miss Steer, and then Wyatt, and the next witness who sees her is the Noble boy at the back of the door.

'Just remember for one moment the story told by Percy Noble. Just remember that thump. It is all very well for my friend to say that that thump was no more than a footfall. The boy said he heard it, and that she answered 'all right', and that the sound of the movement of the chair came from the place where Mrs Haskell usually sat. Can you believe that that thump was not caused by somebody stepping off or jumping off those stairs? It was either the prisoner or someone else. If it was the prisoner, can you believe that she would have thought of such a detail as to go to the stairs and jump off to give the idea that somebody was coming down? To my mind it is inconceivable that that could have taken place.

'Take the woman's demeanour on the night. A great deal has been made of the fact that she did not go upstairs at once, but how can anyone say what inference can be drawn from what anyone does in a moment of panic? She might have had time to recover, but she knew that some man had come down from the place where the only person who was there was her only child, that he had come downstairs and threw something at her which splashed her. What inference can anybody draw from the ghastly tragedy enacted there? She is seized with panic. She feels the shrinking which people always have from a terrible thing, from a thing she feared to come to grips with – as people are – fearing the worst. In considering this point, remember that this is not a man but a woman; the person you have to deal with is a woman, a mother, a loving mother, a weak woman. You see the poor woman in the dock. You can judge for yourself whether you think she has the bravery, the resolution, which is needed to come to grips with the worst. Is any inference unfavourable to her to be drawn from what she did then, when she knew that some disaster had happened to her only child? From first to last this woman never tried to conceal a single thing against herself. Why did she give the alarm?

'If she was a woman who could calmly and deliberately murder the boy and make up a story and answer Percy Noble in her usual quiet voice, is she not a woman who could have told Noble to go away, that she was going to bed, when she would have had all night to discover this, when she might have destroyed her clothing? But she volunteered to give her clothing to the police. There was no attempt to get rid of the skirt. She describes the knife that is missing, she openly holds the handkerchief in her hand, and now that is made the chiefest evidence of her guilt. The story she told, she told from the earliest possible moment, and I am going to ask your attention to that story for a moment, because you will see that in many respects it is most strangely corroborated.

You have to remember that witnesses have been called to show that no man was seen running, but not one of the witnesses who has been called could have seen a man running away if there had been one, because he would have gone away before Mrs Haskell got to the door. Not a single witness has been called to tell you that they saw Mrs Haskell come to the door. The people who went there, went there because they heard screaming, and the Crown has not been able to produce a single witness who saw Mrs Haskell come to her door. You have been left in the dark by

the Crown as to one of the most important points. Mrs Haskell says that the door was open and that she went into the street. No witness has been produced to say that they saw her open the door. If such a witness could have been called the evidence would have been proof positive that the prisoner's story was not true, [and] my case would have been gone if that had been shown.

'People were standing quite close to the corner, and they have not even said that they heard the door open. So that if a man had run away there was not a single person who could have seen him. It was a dark night, and the road is lit with only two lamps, so that a man could easily have skulked away underneath the houses. If there had been a murderer there, it was his business to get away unseen. It would have been the simplest thing for a murderer to skulk along the road for about forty yards, to James Street, and get away. The doctors say it was possible for Mrs Haskell to have committed this crime, and to have got such an infinitesimal amount of blood upon her. If, therefore a man had committed the crime, it is possible that he had so little blood upon him that he would have no difficulty in concealing it, especially if he was wearing dark clothes. It was not as if the man had to go out into the street reeking of blood, he could have got away with a few spots, according to the doctor. He may have [had] black clothes on, and the bit of blood he would have got on him would not have shown up very much. I venture to think that it is by no means impossible or improbable that a person could have got away and not be seen by anyone, because there was no-one there at the critical moment.

'The most remarkable fact about Mrs Haskell's story is that the story is corroborated at every turn. If she had made it up to cover her crime, you may be perfectly certain that it would soon have broken down on immaterial points. It is, no doubt, incorrect in some details, but just remember the circumstances in which it was taken. This first statement fills several pages of closely-typed characters, and it was taken just after that poor creature, whether innocent or guilty, had suffered the most tremendous shock that any human being could suffer. She was alone, without any single woman, with four police officers, and it is not to be wondered at that you find some discrepancies in her story in one place and another. Thus, she said she was wearing an apron, and it is quite conceivable that she thought she was, but it is most probable, I should think, that she was not. Then her story differed a little bit from the story given by Percy Noble as to whether she was sitting in the chair when she saw the man coming down, before Percy knocked at the door. But surely, that is a small detail; it is a detail that the woman might easily get confused ideas about. But these little points go to show the honesty of her story. Take the main features and see if there is corroboration. It is a remarkable fact, and I am going to mention it to show you that not only is corroboration forthcoming at every turn, but she has never tried to twist things into her favour, or overstate facts which are true in order to give a favourable impression.

'You will remember that on November 2nd, she told the police that on the previous Wednesday evening her little boy was writing his name and address on a piece of paper, that she asked him what he was doing, and that he said, "Someone wants it, mam, at school." Obviously that was a point she should tell the police, and it turned out to be a point of no importance at all from the point of view of detecting the murderer, but it does turn out to be a point of the utmost importance as showing she was a truthful woman, because the police have ascertained that her statement was true. I am much obliged to the prosecution who have proved that this is right because they have brought the boy to prove it.

'Let us see about this man who came for lodgings. If a person is in a tight corner, and tells a story about some person who is not forthcoming, the usual thing which any person of common sense does is to ask, "Have you told that story before to a living soul?" If someone has been told, it is corroboration to some extent. We know that Mrs Haskell did tell Alfred Noble that night, however, before the murder about this man coming for lodgings. I do not think that you will believe that when Mrs Haskell was in the town shopping, talking and joking with her friends, and buying sweets for that little boy, that she was plotting this murder then. Do not think that I am saying that the man who called for lodgings that Friday night was necessarily the man who was concealed in the

house. It is not a part of my business to say it was even likely that that was the man. I do not know, and no-one knows. What is important is that you find Mrs Haskell, when she was in her usual health and spirits, telling her friends the same story.

'There are other small points. Take, for instance, the story of the boy hurting his ear. When she is asked to account for the spots on her handkerchief she says at once that the boy has hurt his ear, and Chief Inspector Dew tells you that he has enquired at the school and has satisfied himself that that is true. In all these little points where she has made a statement to account for unlikely things and so forth, you find they are true. There is the point of the insurance, and we know that the policy had been altered so that she would get no benefit. It was Mrs Haskell who told the police about Wyatt, and if she had not told them of it a most valuable piece of evidence might have gone undiscovered. There are some other matters I must call your attention to before I sit down, but it has just occurred to me that if that woman had been guilty she must have broken down at some time. She has never faltered.

'At the last moment the Crown brought up Mrs Sheppard, the police matron, in whose charge this poor thing was after she had been committed for trial. Think of the ordeal that woman had gone through – days and days before the Coroner, listening to these terrible details, repeated over and over again, and continuously before the magistrates for a whole week. We know she broke down frequently during the trial, hysterical sobs, weeping fits and so forth. Is it to be wondered at, when she heard all the evidence that has been piled up against her, when in her weak and broken condition she was sent back to prison to lie for three months before the trial came on that she said "If I did it I don't remember it"? The wonder is that she did not say anything much worse. Gentlemen, there is nothing in it. If that is a guilty woman, she made up this story. Do you think she would have made up the story of the spraying? Would it have occurred to a woman of that degree of intelligence to make up that theory that the knife did not hit her, but that the blood sprayed off?

'There is one more matter. Do you remember that Dr Wilks told us how when she did go up she controlled herself, how she went into the room and kissed the boy?' At this point, Flora, who had been in tears practically throughout Goddard's speech, broke into bitter sobs. 'If that woman is the guilty woman, what would you say of that kiss? Gentlemen, it was the most infamous kiss ever recorded. It shows that she was not only one of the worst criminals, but one of the greatest actresses that ever lived. This woman is a humble woman of the people, and is not trained in the arts of society of restraining and repressing her feelings in this way. Do you think she could have turned into such a consummate actress as she must have been if this charge is true?

'Now, gentlemen, I do not think any useful purpose would be served by my labouring the points in this case. You will remember what I said to you about the absence of motive, that you are dealing with evidence which at best only establishes a probability. You will remember what I have said to you with regard to the extraordinary absence of stains on the left, and the extremely little amount of blood that woman had on her after she came out of that room which was no better than a shambles. You will remember how I have gone through the details of that night. Remember Percy Noble's story about the chair being pushed back from where she sat, and the thump at the bottom of the stairs. Remember her demeanour that night and remember how her story is corroborated at every turn where it can be corroborated. Take all these things together, gentlemen, and ask yourselves whether you think the Crown have established such a case against this woman, beyond any shadow of doubt, that will justify you in finding her guilty.

'Gentlemen, I shall not detain you longer. I have been over all the evidence, and I have said all I have got to say upon it. I am certain you will give such attention to it as you think proper. I assure you I speak in no spirit of idle affectation when I say that I feel, and bitterly feel, how inadequate the efforts have been on my part on behalf of this woman. The responsibility which rests upon me is indeed a heavy one, but I am comforted and sustained in the remembrance that my responsibility is after all as nothing compared with yours. Upon you is placed the heaviest and most solemn duty that citizenship can enforce. In a moment you will be receiving the charge from my lord, and you will then go to your room to decide that question which is of such awful import to this woman whose life is now hanging on a thread. I would ask you to remember, and I know that you will, that your word in this matter is final; that once the verdict of guilty is returned that word is gone beyond recall. I would ask you to remember that in these cases there is no half-way house, and that so surely as you return that verdict, as surely must my lord, as his office compels him, pass upon this woman the last sentence of the law.

'I would ask you to remember that it is not for me to draw aside the mantle of the night which hides this deed, but it is for the Crown to prove by evidence, cogent and conclusive, that the prisoner slew the boy, and that she was guilty of his death. If this evidence, with all its inconsistencies, all its probabilities, all its theories, causes the woman's guilt to stand out red before you, gentlemen, you will convict her as your duty and your oath compels you, but if there is in the mind of one of you a lingering doubt whether this awful deed was done by that poor creature, if you can find anything in the case which does not bring home that proof, that certainty which alone can justify you in finding a verdict fatal to a fellow-creature, then I believe you will return a verdict which I believe would be hailed by a sigh of thankfulness and relief by every person in this court and in this county, a sigh of relief that this poor creature's sufferings are at an end, and a sigh of thankfulness that the sweet name of motherhood is not stained by so foul a crime.'

Throughout Goddard's speech, amongst many in that court, Flora wept.

Sir Edward Ridley, sometime Fellow of All Souls', Oxford, and a translator of Lucan's *Pharsalia*, was, according to his obituarist, " humane and high-minded, with plenty of Northumbrian shrewdness, but it was tempered by a kind of whimsical ingenuousness". But he could also be indiscreet, and too ready to reveal his opinion on a case. And so it proved on 17 February 1909. His summing-up took three-quarters of an hour. He began by referring to the entire absence of any motive. 'The Crown has not put before you any tangible motive that inspired this crime. In most cases the motive is of great importance, and it certainly would be of great importance in this case. If it could be shown why, and for what purpose the prisoner wanted to get rid of this boy, then the evidence which had been laid before the jury would leave her without the very smallest shadow of possibility of escape. I say this without fear of contradiction.

'The fact remains that there is an absence of motive, and it is the best topic that can be urged on the prisoner's behalf. Not only is there an absence of motive, but the prosecution admits – and nobody suggests anything to the contrary – that the prisoner has been a good mother to this crippled boy, and that she behaved to him as a mother should. I suppose it is partly owing to the character which she possesses, that during the whole of that terrible night no-one seems to have suspected her at all, because, although it was not given in evidence, it appears to me that the behaviour of the women, the behaviour of the constables and the behaviour of the doctors all point to the fact that they did not suspect her then, and they did not suspect her for a considerable time afterwards. That must not be forgotten. No motive has been assigned. Perhaps you might have suspicions that the story about Mold has something to do with it. That is rejected by the prosecution, and you must reject it too. The absence of motive has been eloquently spoken of by counsel, and his remarks on that point will probably have greater weight with than those on the material facts.

'This case shows some unusual circumstances. You must remember that the prisoner was not aware that the lads Noble or Wyatt were coming to the house that night. It may be that the prisoner had formed a plan to kill the child, and speak of a man as being concerned in it, but that Noble arrived too soon for her scheme to be carried out in this respect. There is no evidence of any man having been seen. [But] the prisoner said to Noble and several other persons that Teddy was murdered before anyone had been upstairs. This is significant.

'As to the knife, it is certainly suspicious that the crime should have been committed with a knife which was usually kept on the premises. Murderers do not usually wait for weapons to be provided on the premises. The bloodstains are very material in this case, especially those in the bedroom. I should have thought that the evidence of the doctors was satisfactory, and according to the laws of nature. The marks on the staircase are important, taken in conjunction with the fact that there are no stains in the passage towards the front door by which the man is supposed to have escaped. It is impossible to see how he could have got away without leaving some marks. Although the passage was washed, Chief Constable Richardson saw it before this, and there were no marks there then. The stain on the tablecloth in the kitchen could not have been caused by a man going out of the front door, but was most probably caused by the prisoner, who may also have had a minute or two in which to wash her hands. There is a good deal in Mr Goddard's remarks as to the absence of blood on the prisoner's hands, and this must be remembered in her favour. As to the mark of the knife, you must consider whether the weapon is more likely to have been thrown as stated or whether it was placed there.

'The stains on the blouse and skirt are most important. Nearly all of them are such as would be thrown by spraying. How could these have got there? Could there have been enough blood carried on a knife to make fifty spots on the blouse, especially on the right side, also twenty spots on the skirt. Is it any explanation that a knife thrown from a height did this? The blouse and skirt are most important elements. Then there is the handkerchief taken by Mrs Sweetman from the prisoner almost immediately after the crime was committed.

'Mr Goddard has dealt with the evidence in an able manner, but I disagree with him when he says that it is theoretical. There is no theory about it that I can see, except that Professor Pepper has been called to give evidence for the prosecution, but that does not make it theoretical. Circumstantial evidence it is, because there is no direct evidence of any kind at all from anyone who saw the deed done. Yet circumstances properly judged cannot lie, and it is from these circumstances you must take the facts and say what is the conclusion to which they point. Do they show beyond any reasonable doubt that the prisoner is the person who committed the crime? It will not do for you to say it could have been anybody else: you have been shown that the evidence points to the prisoner. That depends on the knife, on the marks of blood in the house, on the furniture, and upon the floor, and upon her own clothes. I think you will never believe there was any man on the spot at all. [As for the knife], it is possible that it might have been found in the house, but would not a murderer have come provided with his own weapon? If you take all the facts into consideration, and are guided by them in coming to a conclusion as to whether the prisoner is guilty, you cannot do wrong.

'You are to take the facts and see what they prove; you must see whether it is conclusively proved that the prisoner did the deed or if there was reasonable doubt. Many of the prisoner's statements have been proved, but there is a blank for the ten minutes which was most essential. There is no other issue — no question of insanity. If there is any reasonable doubt you must give the prisoner the benefit of it. If you do not find that reasonable doubt you must find her guilty.'

Just as the jury was about to retire, the foreman asked of Judge Ridley, 'Your Lordship, you say there was no blood on her hand?' — 'No.'

'Was it looked for, seeing she was never suspected?' — 'Whether it was looked for or not you must take it that there was not.'

Foote interjected 'There is no evidence one way or the other. She was not arrested till Tuesday night.' Ridley replied 'It may have been seen that night', and Foote agreed 'It might'.

The jury retired at 1.55 p.m., and returned after three hours' and ten minutes' deliberation, at 5.05. The Clerk of Arraigns, James Read, put the customary question: 'Gentlemen, have you agreed upon a verdict?'. The foreman replied 'No.' The clerk pressed his question: 'Is there any chance of your agreeing?'; the foreman replied 'I am afraid not.' Ridley asked 'Have you done your best to arrive at a conclusion in the case?' — 'Absolutely.'

'You have? If I sent you back again there would no chance of your coming to an agreement?' — Silence.

'What do you say in answer to that question?' — The silence continued.

'You must remember it is important you should

arrive at a verdict if possible, in many ways. That is why I put the question to you. If you tell me that you cannot arrive at a conclusion I should not send you back again after three hours of consideration. If you tell me there is any chance of your arriving at a conclusion, I should have to ask you to go back again. What is your answer to that? Tell me, and I will act accordingly.' — With a shrug of his shoulders the foreman replied 'I am afraid not, my lord.'

'Then I am loth to send you back again, after three hours, if there is no chance of your agreeing.' — 'There is no chance of our agreeing.'

'Upon that statement I don't think I can ask you to go back. I must say you are discharged. It is a great misfortune. This trial will have to take place again. You are discharged, gentlemen. As you have had a case of long duration I think you should be released for ten years from serving on juries.'

Parr interjected 'The trial is postponed till the next Assizes, and the witnesses' recognizances will be enlarged?'

The judge queried 'What is to be done with the prisoner?'

'The prisoner must remain in custody in the ordinary way. In a case of this kind it is impossible to take any other course.'

'The recognizances of the witnesses will be enlarged to the next Assizes. Unless there be some further advice on the part of counsel the trial will take place then. Of course, I cannot say anything about that. In the usual way the trial will take place at the next Assizes at Salisbury. It is impossible to try the case again this time, because I haven't got the time, and I don't think it would be advisable. I don't know what course can be recommended, but the prosecution might be advised . . .'

'The position will be carefully considered, my lord.'

'I am sorry the postponement has to take place. It [the trial] must be in June next, in Salisbury'

A stillness hung over the court as a crestfallen Flora was led from the dock, to be met by a huge gathering outside, watching silently as she left the court en route for the prison. And while Devizes' answer to the Lion Gate embraced Flora for a further four months, she was yet innocent, on the word of the one dissenter on the jury.[2]

15

'A strange delay, that is very difficult to understand': The Second Trial, 1-3 April 1909

FLORA'S PLIGHT, the subject of national interest, resulted in a question in the House of Commons on 25 February 1909, probably not unconnected with the fact that her defence costs were being borne by Sir Edward Tennant, the Liberal MP for Salisbury, and the concern that the case was by now so notorious that it would be difficult for Flora to receive a fair trial in her home town. Alexander Boulton, the Liberal MP for Ramsey, Hunts, asked whether the Attorney-General, Sir William Robson was 'aware that at a trial for murder at the Wiltshire Assizes the jury disagreed, and the presiding judge has ordered the accused to be tried again at the next Assizes; and, seeing that the accused woman has already been in prison three months, and that the next Assizes will not be held for another three months, if he will take steps either to secure that the trial shall take place at the Central Criminal Court or advise the appointment of a Special Commission for the trial of the accused woman at Assizes?' Robson replied, 'I do not think the delay apprehended by the honourable Member will take place. Arrangements are in progress according to which this prisoner's second trial will take place at the end of the business at the last place on the circuit. A judge will go down specially to try the case.'

Thus it was that on the conclusion of Mr Justice Ridley's circuit a special assize was convened at Devizes on 1 April. The case was heard before Charles Darling, not, like Sir Edward Ridley, a scholar, but a man of relatively humble origins whose career had begun in a Birmingham solicitor's office. A family bequest gave him the means to become a barrister in 1874 and to take silk in 1885. Following a less-than-happy Parliamentary career, he was appointed a judge of the Queen's Bench Division by Lord Halsbury in 1897, much to the surprise of his colleagues both in the House and at the Bar. But, in the words of his obituarist, 'so far from being a failure, as his critics expected, he made in some respects an admirable judge, and was not by any means the first to justify Lord Halsbury's shrewdness and knowledge of human nature.'[1]

So, just as in February, an enormous crowd gathered outside the Court House. Having motored down from Chippenham and now heralded by a trumpet fanfare, Judge Darling, in scarlet and ermine, opened the proceedings at 11 o'clock, accompanied by the new High Sheriff, Captain George Hounsam Fort, resplendent in black velvet, and his chaplain, Robert Stephenson Weallens 'in full canonicals, his long gown of solemn black being relieved by a fur hood of snowy whiteness.'[2] The jury comprised William Aldrick, Francis Bailey, A.W. Bryden, Isaac Butler, Mark Crook, Edwin Gilbert, H.J. Holly, J. Laughland, C.G. Matthews, W. Moore, George B. Nichol and A.W. Perren. This time the jury was possibly drawn from a wider social spectrum than at the first trial, certainly from a wider geographical spread. Aldrick and Butler were farmers in Rowde and Devizes and Gilbert was a farmer and carrier from Avebury, while Mark Crook was a farmhand from Urchfont.

Still in mourning, wearing a new black coat and skirt, finished with embellished crêpe, and a toque in

MR JUSTICE DARLING, WHO PRESIDED OVER THE
SECOND TRIAL, AS DEPICTED IN VANITY FAIR

matching trim, Flora was brought up from the cells to the bar, glancing nervously around. She gained confidence, however, as she was beckoned by her wardress to take her seat, responding with a smile, and likewise greeting her brother, who was among the small minority of the crowd to gain a place in the packed public gallery.[3] The *Salisbury Times* remarked that Flora looked 'remarkably well', and this bears out the Prison Medical Officer's opinion that she had 'eaten well, slept well, and gained in weight.'[4] Having pleaded not guilty in February, Flora was not called upon to plead now. As in February, Messrs Foote and Parr prosecuted, and Rayner Goddard defended.

Foote's speech lasted for an hour and a half. He began by admonishing the jury that they must clear their minds. 'I think in discharging my duty I first of all ought to tell you what of course you know already, that you should dismiss from your minds absolutely anything that you may have heard of this case before you came here. It is almost impossible that you have not heard of the case, but I earnestly warn you that you must come here as if you had heard nothing and know nothing of it, and give your verdict only on the evidence before you and on nothing you have heard of the evidence elsewhere, or of any rumour that may have reached your ears.' Turning to the case, Foote continued, 'It is a most difficult one, and most difficult to lay before a jury, and most difficult for a jury to appreciate, at any rate fully, before the close of it. What I have said about dismissing from your mind what you may have heard, I say more in the interests of the defence than in the interests of the Crown. You must endeavour to follow what I shall say to you now so as to understand the evidence as it comes, and do so with a mind absolutely fresh, as if you had never heard that such a crime – such a tragedy – had occurred.

He continued by reviewing and considering, as he had done in February, the salient points in the case. 'The prisoner is a widow, about thirty-four years of age, and the boy whom she is charged with murdering was about twelve years old. He was a cripple, and had had one leg amputated in consequence of some progenital disease, tuberculosis or something of that sort. Although a bright, cheerful and happy boy, as far as the witnesses can tell, yet, of course, one cannot help reflecting that he could not have had a very long nor a very happy and successful life before him. However, the child was happy and vigorous, and got on well with his playfellows. I do not think anyone would say, notwithstanding his misfortune, that he was an unhappy child. As far as the statements of the witnesses go, Mrs Haskell was a good mother to the boy, and lived with him on affectionate and proper terms, and took proper care of him. How far she might have brooded upon the fact of his misfortune, and the condition of health in which the child was, we do not know. Of course, one is bound to try and imagine what the woman's state of mind must have been with regard to that, but so far as the treatment of the child was concerned all the witnesses will agree in saying that the prisoner was a good mother, an affectionate mother and a kind mother.' At this, as on many previous occasions, Flora sobbed silently in the dock.

Foote turned to the events of the night of October 31. 'On the night of the murder, the woman was seen by the boy Noble, and she was then in her ordinary state of mind and body. There was nothing in her conduct to attract attention, and nothing to show she was either unhappy or ill. The murdered boy was in Noble's house as late as nine o'clock the same evening, and he was in his normal condition. The precise time at which the boy met his death was ten twenty-five p.m. A boy named Wyatt, who will be called, knocked at the door of Mrs Haskell's house at ten seventeen p.m. or ten twenty p.m., and he will say that the prisoner unlocked the door and took in a parcel which he had for Mrs Manning. Now, there can be no doubt that at that moment the boy was alive, lying upstairs in his bed, and it was equally certain that before half-past ten – as near as we can fix, ten twenty-five p.m. – that boy had his throat cut in bed and died instantly. At ten thirty p.m. Percy Noble, who is related to the prisoner, went to the back door of the prisoner's house and knocked at it with his knee. There is no doubt that Mrs Haskell was in the kitchen, and she was probably sitting down, because Percy Noble said that after he knocked twice at the door he heard a noise, which he describes as of a chair being either moved or pushed back, and he also heard a noise like a thump. Almost immediately afterwards Mrs Haskell screamed and went to open the door to Noble. She was then in an excited state and called out to him to go for the Police, saying that somebody had killed her Teddy.

'I think it is obvious that if Mrs Haskell had started running to her front door the moment she had sent young Noble from the back of her house for assistance, she would have got to the front door, screaming, at least as soon as the boy would have got to York Road. If you believe Miss Stretch, however, it will be plain that there was some slight delay before Mrs Haskell got to the front door. I don't want to make too much of it because it isn't a vital

part of the case, but if my times are right I think it will be apparent that she would have had time in the slight interval to at least have dipped her hands in water. There can be no doubt from the subsequent evidence that at the time Mrs Haskell opened the back door to the lad, she — one doesn't want to use stronger words — had a great deal of blood about her dress and clothes, but apparently no blood was ever seen upon her hands. It is quite conceivable, seeing that there was a delay, that she might have dipped her hands in water. The thought which naturally occurs to everybody is that if this unfortunate woman – of whom I desire to speak as considerately as I can — had reason to think that somebody had murdered her child, she would have gone immediately upstairs to see what had happened. As I shall tell you directly, the story, which she has told with great deliberation, is that she had just seen a man leave the house, that he hand thrown a knife at her, and had gone out. Is not almost inconceivable, if a mother had seen such a thing, and had reason to believe that a man had come from upstairs where her only child was sleeping, she did not go up to see what had happened? By her own account the man had gone and therefore there could be no danger in going up. On the other hand it might be said that she was paralysed with fear or alarm, and that that would not be a natural course for her to take. But I direct your attention to it because you will find there is a strange delay in Mrs Haskell asking to go upstairs or attempting to go upstairs. If the story she has told the Police is true, that delay is very difficult to understand.'

'It is very significant that there was no blood along the passage or on the front door, because if the murderer went out of the front door it seems impossible that he should not have dropped some blood to mark his trail.' As for the tablecloth, Foote continued, 'There was only a very narrow space between the kitchen table and the chairs which stood against the wall. The chairs in the kitchen were so arranged that no-one could get to the back door without touching the table. On the table was a white tablecloth, and that white tablecloth was smeared with blood: and I would suggest that the smears of blood on the cloth would leave no doubt in your minds that they were made by somebody passing along between the chairs and the table.

'Some blood was found on the woman's blouse and this, with her skirt was afterwards sent to an expert who will tell you that it is impossible for this number of spots to have got on the woman's dress in the way she suggested – by a knife being thrown at her. But it is all conjecture. Nobody [else] was there, and one can only put forward tentatively what one thinks is reasonable. The story she tells is that practically simultaneously with hearing a knock at the back door she heard the noise of a man coming downstairs. She opened the door which led to the passage, and as she stood there a man came downstairs and threw something at her, which she does not say hit her, but which she suggests was the knife, and that he then ran out of the front door and escaped somewhere. [On the other hand], it would appear to be a consistent and possible theory, that *if* the prisoner had come downstairs after committing this deed, she might possibly have sunk down in a chair close to the door to recover herself for a moment, holding the knife in her hand. At that moment there was a knock on the back door. The woman's hand would be then almost touching the floor, and she would only have to drop the knife down or place it where her hand was. That is exactly the place where it was found. If the knife had been thrown down violently, one would have expected to have found more blood on the passage floor. [But] the blood was a level, steady and uniform mark, such as would be made by a knife stained with blood being placed that way on the linoleum.'

Returning to the bloodstained tablecloth, Foote continued, 'One of the most serious things you have to consider in this case is that the blood marks on the tablecloth were made by *somebody*, either bloody or carrying something bloody, and it is not possible to suggest that any strange man ever passed through the kitchen. I think that after you have heard the evidence you will not think it possible to suggest that any of the people who came to the woman's assistance passed down there at any time, when it would have been possible for them to have got contaminated with blood, and so to have smeared the tablecloth in the way I have described to you. I suggest that it is impossible for anyone to pass between the chairs and the table except the prisoner.

'I have said that there was a strange delay in the prisoner's going up to see the child. There are a variety of statements made by the witnesses, and you will find that though she asked once or twice what had happened, and though she said more than once, and to more than one person, that someone had been up and killed her Teddy, she made no attempt to go upstairs and see the child until about eleven fifteen p.m. – three quarters of an hour afterwards, when many people had been upstairs. Somewhere about half-past eleven, after the doctors had put the boy's body in order, as far as they could, the prisoner went upstairs and saw the child. Until her mother, Mrs Carter, came upon the scene, I think it will be apparent that Mrs Haskell did not ask to go upstairs and did not attempt to go upstairs. When Mrs Carter arrived, she suggested to Steer, or Rawlins, or both, that she and the prisoner should go upstairs to see the boy, and one of the men said "Don't." It was Mrs Carter who made the suggestion, and not Mrs Haskell.'

The issue of the money was then rehearsed. 'According to the prisoner, one of the drawers in the chest contained eight pounds two shillings. It is beyond controversy that immediately after the murder the drawer contained three pounds ten shillings. I don't think that is a very important circumstance, except as indicating the idea of robbery having been the motive for the crime. It is difficult to conceive that a stranger, if he could have got into the house, would have only taken part of the money. That does not seem reasonable. According to the prisoner's statement the money was accumulated for the purpose of buying the boy an artificial leg, when he got older, and it was mainly, if not entirely, supplied to him by his grandmother, Mrs Carter, who lived close by, and received some money every Christmas. But perhaps, more perplexing is the state of the drawer. At some time or other the drawer had been so opened that, though there was no sign of violence outside, the lock, inside had given way and was hanging suspended by one tack without a head. I don't suggest to you that the condition of the drawer has anything to do with the murder.'

Then the Mold connection was examined. 'There is reasonable ground for saying that they were – I would not say *engaged* – but that marriage was contemplated by the prisoner with a man named Mold, a perfectly respectable man, who is a ship's steward, and who, at the time the murder was committed, was unquestionably on the high seas at the time. Mold was on board the *Adriatic*, and he was seen on his return by the Police, and they are satisfied, as far as anyone can be satisfied in these matters at all, that there is no ground for suggesting that the attentions Mold paid to this woman have anything to do with the crime. There is no ground for suggesting that the child was an obstacle in regard to the contemplated marriage. On the contrary, the evidence proves the opposite. It is only right and fair to Mold and the prisoner that I should say this; nor is there the slightest ground for any imputation against the woman's moral character or chastity.'

And so, finally to the question of motive. 'Gentlemen of the Jury', continued Foote, ' the most difficult point in this case arises from the fact that in laying this case before you, it impossible to suggest an intelligible motive for the crime. In one sense it is impossible to suggest an intelligible motive for any crime, but it is equally impossible to suggest why a strange man should come in and murder a little boy in bed, whom he does not know, for money, the existence of which he does not know, and which he does not take the whole of. Whoever committed this crime was actuated by some unnatural, abnormal motive, which a reasonable man cannot understand. Whether it is frenzy, whether it is a sort of temporary madness, produced perhaps by brooding over the child's state, we cannot say. Many people who are unhappy, appear to be happy, and no-one knows how far that poor woman may have been brooding upon this child's condition. I don't think doctors are able to say one way or the other, in any way that would satisfy [you as] the jury, what the causes of temporary frenzy are, how it happens, and how long it lasts. The doctors in this case can make no such suggestion, and you are left, as I am left, to deal with this case on the facts which I have laid before you at some length, facts which I suggest to you seem to

indicate that this woman must – whether or not in a moment of frenzy – have done this dreadful thing. I suggest that the physical objects and marks which remain and which [you], the jury can be guided by, are sufficient to lead you to the conclusion that this woman was the author of this crime, herself.'

As once more she heard this accusation of murder, Flora's eyes welled up with tears, and she buried her face in her handkerchief. Foote then read out Flora's Police statements, explaining that they had been obtained following questioning on those areas in which the Police wished to inquire. At this, Darling shot a glance to Goddard and asked him if he objected, but Goddard said he did not.

With that, the witnesses were called, as they had been six weeks earlier: Notley, with his plans, Messer with his crime-scene photographs. These were followed by those who set the scene on the night of the murder: Alfred Walter and Alfred John Noble, Gertrude Steer the dressmaker, John Wyatt the delivery-boy and Rosa Manning who had had to do without her boots for some weeks; and then the witnesses to Flora's screams and what ensued: Percy Noble, the courting couple Lily Stretch and Herbert Primmer, Gertrude Skutt, Walter Steer, Edward Butt and William Eccott, the men at the *Duke of York*, the brothers-in law Ernest House and Walter Haynes, Alice Steer and her mother Emma Chivers, Matilda Cooper and her daughter Edith Langmead, Sarah Butt and finally Teddy's school-mate Harold Webb who had come down from Gloucestershire to give evidence of their friendship.

Of all their testimonies, it was those of Percy Noble, Lily Stretch and Gertrude Skutt which were of key importance in establishing timings. Percy, having adjusted his watch by the chimes of the church clock less than half an hour earlier, noted that it was 10.28 p.m. as he went to the back door to repay the shilling he had borrowed. He recounted seeing that the kitchen light was not as bright as usual, and the blind being drawn; his trying the door before he knocked, and knocking the door and his aunt's response; and the scraping of her chair and the thump.

'What sort of a thump?' asked Darling. – 'As if someone jumped.'

'Did it sound as if it was a step?' asked Foote. – 'Yes.'

'More than one thump?' – 'Only one.'

'Was that after you heard the chair pushed back?' – 'Yes.'

'How long after that was the first scream?' – 'Immediately afterwards.'

'Did you then see Mrs Haskell coming towards you?' – 'I saw her shadow.' Percy went on to recount how Flora came to the door and stopped screaming, to tell him to "Go and see if you can see that man, he's killed my poor Teddy", and to "Go for a doctor – quick!", and of his dash to summon Dr Wilks, pausing only to tell a policeman to go to Meadow Road. Foote asked him, 'When at the back door did you hear any door open or shut?' – 'No, sir.' Goddard's cross-examination rehearsed Percy's adjusting his watch, the respective directions of the scraping of the chair – near the fireplace, and of the thump – near the foot of the foot of the stairs; the ordinary tone of voice in which his aunt acknowledged his knock, and that he did not notice her hands. Lily Stretch spoke of seeing Percy Noble as she and Primmer were walking along York Road, then of crossing Meadow Road, hearing the scream and turning back to the corner to seen Flora on her doorstep. On the other hand Mrs Skutt's evidence introduced another factor for the jury's deliberations on those supposedly first few moments after the murder, for she stated that there was *no* delay between Percy Noble sprinting into York Road and Flora screaming at her doorstep.

Walter Steer's testimony included his famous question in the kitchen at No. 40, "Who could have done it?", prompting Flora's response of the account of the man coming down the stairs and throwing a knife at her as he escaped. What he added, which he had not at the inquest or the first trial was that when he saw the murdered child, his lips were apart as if he had cried out. He referred also to the 'great deal of excitement in the district, at the time', and to the front passage of No. 40 being 'full of people'. At this Darling interjected, 'What? When the police came?' – 'Yes, my lord.'

'Was there a policeman at the front door?' – 'No, my lord.'

Emma Chivers' testimony confirmed Flora's man-with-knife story, and recalled Flora's chilling words that she 'knew her Teddy must be murdered, because it was so quiet up there.' The judge asked, 'Did either of you rush up and see what was the matter?' – 'No, I didn't.'

'Did she?' – 'No.'

The next day, proceedings opened at 10.30 a.m. The crowd outside the court, mainly women, were keen to catch sight of Flora as she was brought in a cab from the prison, looking quite cheerful, smiling and chatting to the wardress as she was driven along. In court, there was not the press of spectators there had been on earlier occasions. The first witness was Thomas Rawlins, the dairyman who, like Emily Sweetman, had spotted the bloodstains on the tablecloth. His account began with his hearing Flora's screams, and of her words to him about Teddy which led him to believe something awful had happened; his visit to Teddy's bedroom, and his returning downstairs to hear Flora's heartfelt plea to know what had happened, and his reply: "I can't [say], I am afraid it is very bad." He then sent someone to fetch the police and a doctor, and went himself to fetch Mrs Mold, as someone had told him Flora would like Mrs Mold there. Rawlins continued with an account of the doctors' examination of the crime scene, and of activity in the kitchen. With a new trial and a new judge, a great deal more attention was paid and given to exactly how the table was placed so as, according to the prosecution's hypothesis, for the cloth to have received the marks that it did. As Rawlins described the blood spots, Judge Darling ordered the cloth to be placed on it exactly as it had been the table in front of him and then for the witness – standing on the counsels' table – to point out with a quill pen where the blood spots were for the benefit of the jury, and to mark on a plan for the jury where the blood spots were and where the chairs were in relation to the table, with a gap of only 20 inches between chairs and table.

In cross-examination Rawlins had to admit that he never noticed the bloodstains when he first entered the kitchen, and did not see them until about 11.30 p.m. Goddard continued, 'It was not till three weeks after that you said anything about the blood on the tablecloth -?' – 'No.'

'You were present at the inquest and at the close of Chief Constable Richardson's evidence you sent up a note -?' – 'Yes.'

'You had not been asked about it before?' – 'No, I did not know that anyone else saw it.'

Darling then ordered the table to be placed into the gangway at the back of the court, so that the door there represented the kitchen door and the head of the jury box represented the scullery door, and had Rawlins place some chairs near to the table, to recreate the layout of the kitchen at No. 40. He then bade Rawlins leave the court, and return as if he were walking along the passage at No. 40 into the kitchen and past the chairs and table toward the scullery. Darling observed, 'So that the right arm of the person would pass very near the table?' Rawlins agreed. The re-enactment prompted much interest in court, not least from Flora going to look over the side of the dock, and commenting on Rawlins's placement of the chair.

Emily Sweetman gave evidence as she had at the first trial, referring again to the handkerchief she had taken from Flora – damp and bright red with fresh blood, also to Flora's story about the man with the knife and seeing the knife for herself. She again spoke of the bloodstains on the table cloth and of drawing the Superintendent's attention to them. She it was, too, who gave Flora the soothing draught prescribed by Wilks, adding, under cross-examination, that Flora was hysterical.

Emily Thirza Haskell appeared once more, straight off the train and, described by the *Devizes and Wiltshire Gazette* as "a great invalid", was accompanied by a hospital nurse. The sight of her in that state reduced Flora to tears. She spoke of Mold, and of how both Flora had said, and Mold had conceded, that at the time she had no wish to remarry. She referred, as she had done at the Magistrates'' trial, to the sleeping arrangements when Mold visited, to testify to the propriety of the relationship. Questioned by Goddard, Miss Haskell acknowledged that her sister-in-law was a kind and loving mother, and her testimony moved onto the plan to provide Teddy with an artificial limb, and the money put by for that purpose. As she was leaving the court, Darling called Miss Haskell back, and asked whether Flora had said whether all the money was there. She replied, 'She told me she had to take some of it.'

'Did she say what for?' – 'She said, to pay the rent, I believe.'

Goddard interjected, 'Did she say anything about putting it back again?' – 'She said she would replace it as she could – when she had the opportunity of doing so.'

As before, Herbert Wilks was the first to give medical evidence. He spoke of being Flora's family doctor for twelve years, and, remembering Teddy's amputation, he testified that there would be some discharge, on occasion, of pus from the stump.

Describing the scene he encountered with Row, Wilks mentioned the small abrasion on the fourth finger of Teddy's left hand, and added that blood from the main wound would spurt forth to the left and to the right once the artery had been cut. After some discussion of a bloodstain in the wallpaper which Darling had been the first to notice, Wilks added that the murderer was probably standing slightly above or below the boy's head, and would have been directly in the line of the blood spray, whereas he, Wilks, had got very little blood on his hands and had washed them in the bedroom, and, under examination by Parr, no blood on his clothes; by contrast, he did notice blood on the right sleeve of Flora's blouse. Wilks also recounted how Flora and her mother went upstairs, and how she kissed the dead boy and burst into tears, prompting fresh tears from Flora in the dock. At that point Wilks was handed the knife. He remarked that just inside the kitchen door he saw a mark of blood, as though an implement corresponding with the knife had been put there. Darling asked, 'If there was blood on the knife, would that account for the mark?' – 'Not', replied Wilks, 'if [it had been] dropped. If it was dropped it would have splashed. This was a linear mark.'

'Could the knife make the mark?' – 'Not, I think, if dropped, [but it would] if it had been put there.'

'Will you say why?' – 'Because it was a linear mark, and I could see no spots.'

At this point, at Goddard's, request just as at the first trial, the bloodstained pillows were brought in – by Foote – and Goddard had the chance to cross-examine. Wilks testified that Flora went upstairs of her own volition, and that she was a good mother. Goddard next asked Wilks how the assailant had stood to make the fatal cut, and at Darling's suggestion the doctor left the box in order to take the knife and re-enacted the killing for the jury's edification. As Goddard elicited how the blood had flowed from the wound, Flora became visibly distressed, the colour draining from her face, and her eyes closing. A glass of water from the wardress revived her somewhat, as Wilks's testimony drew to a close, with him stating that the murderer would have got blood on their hand, and that 'the cut was done with one severe swoop.' Finally, in answer to Foote, the doctor declared it was certain that the killer stood at the boy's head, and used his right hand to make the cut.

Wilks's guest Everard Row was next to speak, and with one exception agreed with what his host had had to say. The divergence of opinion was over Teddy's survival once the cut had been administered, with Row of the opinion that death was not instantaneous, but that Teddy had survived the cut to breathe for a few moments – perhaps two or three gasps. He also stated that he examined the body, and whilst blood could have got onto his clothes, he was sure that that did not happen. Row remained in the witness box to give evidence on behalf of Dr Kempe, who was indisposed through influenza, and whose deposition to the magistrates he read out. He, too, believed that the assailant stood near the head of the bed, rather behind where the wound was inflicted, and faced the foot of the bed. Like his colleagues, Kempe argued there was no possibility of the bloodstains on Flora's clothing being caused directly or indirectly by a thrown knife, nor indeed from the bloody hand of the person throwing the knife, but he was careful to preface his opinion by stating that the blood spots on the blouse 'did not fall into any regular pattern such as would be caused by an artery spurting.'

Dr Pepper next appeared, repeating his testimony that the wall bloodstains were projected, rather than smeared, as were those on the various articles of furniture in the bedroom, and there were blood spots on the linoleum from the bedroom, clearly produced by blood dropping onto the floor. Those on Flora's clothing were caused by a spray of blood, while the

mark on the linoleum by the kitchen door could not have been caused by anything falling from any height. He repeated his account of the upward direction of the bloodstain on the blouse, and the elongated marks on the skirt being brought about by blood dropping on it. After a detailed exposition of the blood marks which spanned the lunch break on the Friday, Pepper was examined by Parr. 'Could those marks [on the skirt] be caused by the person wearing it carrying something with blood dripping from it?' – 'Certainly.'

'If a knife was thrown at the person wearing the blouse or skirt standing near the foot of the stairs would it account for these spots?' – 'In my opinion it would account for neither, whether it struck the person or not.'

Pepper continued: 'The blood on the knife would have largely dripped off by the time it was carried to the foot of the stairs. There was too much blood on the oilcloth at the top of the stairs for much to remain. I think there was a good deal on the hands of the person who used the knife.' With a very detailed description of the marks on the tablecloth, Pepper added that the continuity was broken by a crease. He continued, 'The smear was evidently caused by someone carrying something in the hand. The blood on the blouse could not have caused it, because the spots on the blouse would be smeared, which they are not, and if it came from the skirt, you would not get an oblique direction [in the smear] but an horizontal one. [The mark] would have been parallel with the edge of the tablecloth. In my opinion, the marks were caused by a duster or handkerchief.' As for the handkerchiefs, 'There was enough on that which the prisoner had in her hand to cause the marks on the tablecloth.' The two handkerchiefs found in the copper had either no blood or far too little to account for the stains on the tablecloth: as Pepper said, 'The marks on one of the handkerchiefs found in the copper were nasal mucus, and on the other were spots of blood which might have come from the boy's ear.' There was on the other hand far too much blood on the handkerchief in the accused's possession to be accounted for by the injury at school to Teddy's ear.

Cross-examination was wide-ranging, from the age of the blood, which Pepper conceded could have been days or weeks old when it was examined, to the blood on the right side of the pillow, which Pepper explained must have spurted out in a shower and then fallen down onto the pillow. Finally, Goddard tackled the professor on the matter of the mark on the staircase, which he had said would be on the right hand of a person coming downstairs. Pepper replied that the mark was on the second stair from the bottom, three feet and five inches from the floor [of the passage]. How, Foote then asked, was such a mark to be accounted for? – 'The mark is such as would be caused by anyone hurrying down the stairs with a bloodstained knife. There is no doubt that is how the mark was made.'

'If a knife bearing a large quantity of blood was thrown at the woman, would there not be a big splatter of blood somewhere?' – 'Yes: more than I found.' Darling then explained to all parties that the professor 'is a very valuable official, and it would be very convenient if you could let him go back to London', to which both jury and counsel assented.

Sergeant Golding gave his account of his charge of the crime scene, wanting as it had been. He testified to picking up the murder weapon, even though the blood on it was 'not quite dry', wrapping it in brown paper and putting it into his overcoat pocket. He testified once more to seeing the bloodstains on Flora's sleeve, adding this time that he drew Richardson's attention to them when he came. On duty in the kitchen, Golding added, he noted that the table had on it a white cloth which he observed the prisoner's mother, Mrs Carter, take off, shake out and replace, but – although he did not so testify – took no action to stop Mrs Carter. He also recounted the story of the money missing from the drawer. Then, at 6 a.m. on Sunday 1 November, Mrs Carter swabbed down the passage and the kitchen floor with a bucketful of water and a cloth, again with Golding looking on. Darling asked, 'Didn't you stop her?' – 'No, my lord.'

'Why?' – 'I was carrying out my instructions, my lord. I was told to remain at the bottom of the stairs and to allow no-one to go upstairs or to interfere with anything downstairs.'

'I see,' replied Darling, flatly, stunned by Golding's reply.

Foote asked Golding, 'I suppose the passage and the kitchen were in a mess –?' – 'Yes.'

'Didn't it occur to you when you saw her doing it, that the washing ought to be stopped?' – 'It didn't, I am sorry to say.'

'Mrs Carter must have washed over the place where the knife was found -?' – 'She washed it all, sir; all over.'

Darling asked the policeman to confirm what he cannot have believed he just heard: 'All over the floor of the passage and the kitchen?' – 'Yes, my lord.'

Foote asked, 'Except the floor, did Mrs Carter wash the stairs or doorposts?' – 'No, I am quite sure of that.'

Goddard asked about the front room, and Golding replied that there were a lot of people there, and in the passage, and he did not turn them out, but no-one had been upstairs.

Next to testify was Golding's Chief Constable, Frank Richardson, who again recounted the story of the drawer and the missing money, and of his asking Flora whether she could shed any light on the matter or furnish him with any other clues. She replied, 'I can only give you a description of the man who called for lodgings' – medium height and build, 35 years of age, wearing dark clothes and a bowler hat. On the basis of Flora's description of the would-be lodger, a search party for the mysterious man, comprising 13 or 14 cyclists, was ordered, and Richardson sent P.C. Cutler, one of his officers already at the house, to go to the railway stations and check for comings and goings and find out whether any luggage had been left, in corroboration of Flora's story. His testimony included the discovery that a knife was missing and the man making inquiries of Teddy and requesting his name and address. Richardson referred to the account in her statement that Flora had just been about to go out to visit Mrs Mold, with the gas was turned down and no light in the passage when the man came down the stairs and fled under cover of darkness. Finally he described Flora's shocked reaction of denial to the charge of murder on 3 November 1908.

P.C. William Cutler was called, and testified to watching the GWR and L&SWR stations all night, having been deputed there by his Chief Constable from No. 40 Meadow Road, whither he had arrived with Golding earlier. He saw no-one leave by train, and confirmed that no luggage had been left for collection.

Stephens, the Divisional Superintendent of the County Force, spoke to corroborate the City Chief's evidence, and of receiving the mysterious caller's description. He sent out cyclist messengers with that description to each of the stations in his division, with orders to watch the roads. A cordon of ten miles' radius was thus drawn round the district; but no man was found. Stephens mentioned the scar on Flora's nose, but by the night of the murder it was quite healed over. He continued, 'When I was in the kitchen with Mrs Haskell and Mrs Carter, Mrs Carter said "Here is little Teddy's handkerchief which I found in the front room."' The handkerchief was produced in court, and it was that which Emily Sweetman had taken from Flora. It was steeped in blood, and Stephens took possession of it there and then. Under cross-examination he was compelled to retreat from his earlier assertion that the prisoner had said the man seeking lodgings and the man jumping down the stairs were at all similar. But Stephens refuted Mrs Sweetman's testimony regarding sight of the bloodstains on the tablecloth at 11.30 p.m., for he did not go into the kitchen until 1 a.m., and he denied her bringing the stains to his attention at all that night. He added that he examined the roller towel on the outer door of the scullery, but did not find any blood on it.

With Dew's testimony came a re-examination of one of the oddest aspects of the case, and one which was arguably central to the interpretation of events immediately after the murder. He referred to Flora's third statement, which was made on 2 November, and said that it had been obtained as a consequence of information received from Samuel Leate. At that point Darling interjected, 'Nobody places the least reliance on what Leate says!' and Foote backed him up, suavely remarking 'No, my lord, it is absolutely inconsistent with everything everybody else in the case says.'

The Judge turned to Goddard, 'You agree with that, Mr Goddard? You attach no importance to it?' – 'I have not cross-examined upon it.'

'I have a duty to perform,' Darling retorted, 'and whether you call him or not, if I thought Leate was a witness who ought to be called, *he would be called*, if I expressed that opinion to Mr Foote.' – 'If he is called I shall not ask him any questions.'

By way of explanation, Darling turned to the jury and said, 'The meaning of this is that the detectives were asking everybody they came across to give them information. A man named Leate said he had seen somebody, but now nobody attaches the slightest importance to anything he said.' To which the *Salisbury Times* added, 'It will be remembered that the witness Leate said that he saw a man come out of a house two doors from York Road, followed by a woman who was saying "Stop him! He has murdered my boy." She was crying and wailing, and was following the man in the direction of Cold Harbour Lane. After she turned round and came back towards her house she leant against the wall and sobbed.' He spoke of other aspects of Flora's statements, describing the position Flora had said she was in when, in her account of things, the man came down the stairs: she was just by the kitchen door. The gas was turned low, throwing a shadow which could be seen in the scullery. Foote asked, 'What was her demeanour whilst she was making the statements?' – 'She was quite cool, collected and intelligent until I showed her the knife, and then she was very much agitated.'

The last witness, the police matron Matilda Sheppard, recalled once more how after Canon Thwaites's visit on the day Flora was committed for trial, she had said, 'Oh, Mrs Sheppard, if I did it I don't remember it.' In cross-examination Mrs Sheppard conceded it was quite true that Flora had been before the Magistrates every day for a week before she had made her statement, and that on that day she had had an hysterical breakdown, the latest of many that week, leading to a half-hour adjournment of the hearing. With that anguished reminder the case for the Crown was concluded. The barristers and the judge then discussed whether there was any need for witnesses to be retained: they could see none but put the question to the jury. At this, George Nichol said, 'One question I should like to ask is whether the prisoner is left-handed or right-

FLORA AS SHE HAD APPEARED AT THE INQUEST WITH
FEMALE ATTENDANT, FROM THE MORNING LEADER

handed.' Richardson replied that Flora signed her name with her right hand; Goddard confirmed she was right-handed.

And so to Saturday 3 April 1909, the final day of Flora Haskell's ordeal. Perhaps because this was the last day there was a larger crowd outside the court than before. Inside the court were some who had attended the whole of the proceedings, including a couple of clergy, the *Devizes and Wiltshire Advertiser* reported, who had been present throughout the whole of the first trial; doubtless one of them was Canon Thwaites. The entire day was given over to the closing speeches – for the prosecution, for the defence, the judge's summing-up and the jury's deliberations. As if to bring the day's events full-circle back to those of that first Saturday, October 31st, the bloodstained pillows and bedding were brought in and laid on the table in front of the counsel for the defence. Flora arrived, looking flushed and nervous, but would listen to the proceedings with, in the *Salisbury Times'* words 'the keenest interest.' As soon as Judge Darling had taken his seat at 10.30 a.m., Foote opened for the prosecution. 'One of the first questions you have to decide,' he said to the jury, 'is whether the assailant went out of the house by the front door or through the kitchen. It cannot be said that it would be impossible for the

person to have gone out of the front door, having regard to the fact that the passage was washed; but I submit that it is very highly improbable that anybody could have gone downstairs and opened that door without leaving some marks of blood on the door, on the door handle, or on the jamb, or on the passage. That is one of the first grave difficulties you have to contend with. On the other hand, assuming that the assailant was the woman, what more natural than that, having escaped from the scene of the tragedy, she got downstairs and sank in the chair inside the kitchen with the knife held in her hand? I submit that upon the hypothesis that the woman committed the crime, and the knock coming unexpectedly at the back door, it was quite natural that she should grasp a pocket handkerchief and remove the superficial blood, which would account for the stains on the handkerchief which was subsequently found in her possession.

'The knife belonged to the house and was ordinarily kept in the house. [It] may be that the knife had been used by the boy in making a tip-cat, but that was the knife used by the murderer. Is it to be supposed that the knife was kept in the bedroom? If so, wouldn't Mrs Haskell have seen it when she put the boy to bed, and either have removed it or said to the police that she saw it when she put Teddy to bed?

'The theory of the defence is that the boy was murdered by a man who conceived an idea to murder the child simply from the fact of having seen him. One could not understand the extraordinary mania which impelled wicked murderers to do bloody deeds, but it was exceedingly difficult to understand why, after casually meeting the boy in the street, a man, a stranger, should be suddenly seized with the desire to cut his throat. If there was such a man, would he not have brought a knife with him? Is it to be conceived that a man would go into the house, and into the bedroom, with a dreadful intention of that kind, without a weapon, or that he went for the purpose of robbery, and did not take nearly all the money?'

Foote stressed the fact that 'from the beginning Mrs Haskell made up her mind that the boy was murdered', but then declared, 'I don't want to strain that point too much. It may be that if she did see a man rushing downstairs, that something was thrown at her, and that she saw blood on her sleeve, that she jumped hastily to the conclusion that that meant death, and that the boy had been killed. I suggest, however, that the more alarmed the mother was, the more certain she would have been to go up and see what had happened to her son.

'I submit that the facts are sufficient to bring the charge home to the prisoner in the dock. To the minds of all fair-minded men, desiring, as you all wish, to be merciful as well as just, the evidence is sufficient to bring home the fact that in some unaccountable frenzy, or in some morbid state of mind, possibly caused by brooding over the child's unhappy condition, this unfortunate woman did upon this night commit the act with which she is charged. It is your duty to return the verdict from which you all shrink, if you feel convinced of the truth of the charge.' With that conclusion to his closing speech, Foote fell back on the idea, first mooted at the inquest, that Flora may have been temporarily deranged: if he could plant that suggestion he knew the jury would find it easier to bring in a verdict of Guilty, knowing that it would be unlikely to bring Flora to the gallows.

Everything now depended on Goddard's response – his sole chance to convince the jury of the truth as well as the justice of the case for the defence. He began almost with an air of modesty, gradually, as he brought argument after argument to bear upon the prosecution case, increasing the emotional pitch to the point where the jury must be convinced of the rightness of Flora's case. 'It is now my duty to address you on behalf of the prisoner in the dock. I need not assure you that I am fully conscious of the responsible and difficult task which is laid before you: a task which I cannot approach without some sense of misgiving, because I know full well that I am quite incapable of doing full justice to the woman's cause. My task has been made lighter, if I may so put it, by the absolute fairness with which the case has been presented. I think I ought to say a word of thanks to my friends Mr Foote and Mr Parr, for the way they have helped me on every possible way whenever I have asked them anything. It is characteristic of the best traditions of English justice the way the case has been presented on behalf of the prosecution.

'I want you, at the outset of my remarks, to bear closely in mind the case you have to try. You are not here to consider who committed the murder. The issue you have to try is a narrower one than that. You are not here to consider the question, which I know there must be a temptation to do, 'If this woman did not commit the murder, who did?' That would be going into the realms of speculation – dangerous realms of speculation – and not the question you have to try. The question you have to prove is: Is it proved beyond the possibility of doubt, beyond the shadow of doubt or the possibility of mistake, that the woman in the dock killed her only child with this knife?' Goddard held up the knife for all to see. 'You will also remember that it is not for me to prove who did commit the murder. That is a task the prosecution has undertaken, and it is for you to say if they have proved beyond the possibility of doubt that the woman in the dock is the murderess. I do not deny – and it would be idle to do so – that a case of grave suspicion rests against the woman, but you are not here to send a fellow creature to her death upon mere suspicion. Nothing but proof – absolute, convincing proof – will justify a verdict of Guilty.

'It is agreed on all hands, by all the witnesses, and neighbours among whom she has lived the whole of her married life, that this woman is a tender and devoted mother – all that a mother should be; just the mother that every father would wish to have for his own children. You know, from the little boy himself, by his cheerful, happy demeanour, what a happy home life he had. Could you want any further evidence of the affection which the woman bore for her only child, than the fact that, cripple though he was, he had the pluck and cheerfulness to take part in games which one would have thought he would have been debarred from on account of his misfortune? He even kept goal for his school football team, and did whatever he could to bear up against his misfortune. Not only that, but you have heard not one word against Mrs Haskell's moral character. Mr Steer has told you that he looks upon her as a quiet, honest, respectable and hard-working woman. She is a woman who, some seven years ago, was deprived of a husband's love and protection, and instead of sinking down under her misfortune, applied herself to the task of keeping herself and her little boy. She worked, and it was at an arduous task. She is a laundress, earning, as you have heard from one of the witnesses, about a pound a week, and sometimes more – something like twenty-two or twenty-three shillings. It is an honest little income, quite sufficient to keep herself and her little child. You have heard yesterday from Mrs Haskell's sister-in-law that she frankly admitted that when a little short she borrowed from the boy's hoard upstairs. And why should she not do so? It might well be that people did not always pay their bills promptly, even to a poor laundress. Mrs Haskell was well enough off to entertain her sister-in-law and keep her for ten weeks in the summer. Here is a woman who, as shown by evidence that is not disputed, is making over a pound a week, paying five shillings and sixpence a week in rent, and having ample money to keep herself and her child in ordinary decent comfort, with three brothers, all of whom were in good positions, to whom she could always turn if she had needed their help.

'This is the woman who, you are asked to believe, in a moment of time, without any previous indication, was turned into such a monster that the mind almost refuses to picture. The prosecution has been put forward, against this woman, as against a sane person. I agree that the prisoner's demeanour the night previous to the murder was that of a sane woman. And that sane woman, you are asked to believe, turned in the twinkling of an eye, to be such a monster. A great deal has been said about the fact that the knife with which the murder was committed is one belonging to the woman, and one of the household ones, but it is an odd one. That is an important thing to remember. If the woman is a murderess, she has supplied the best evidence against herself. She could easily have denied all knowledge of the knife if she liked. You will have noticed, throughout the case, that the prosecution, with the fairness which has characterised it during the trial, has explicitly disclaimed to be able to suggest any motive for the crime. Of course, if an insane or maniacal person committed the crime, you would not look for motive. But this woman is not a maniac. If you are going to find she committed the crime you will also have to find a motive. Although you have heard evidence given that the prisoner was contemplating marriage, yet the prosecution has expressly disclaimed any idea that the marriage had anything to do with the crime. You know that the man Mold, whom Mrs Haskell was going to marry, was a friend and companion of the little boy, and the reluctance to marry came from the woman's side and not from Mold. The hideous inadequacy of such a motive is not for me to prove, because that has been laid aside by the prosecution.

'The evidence that there is against the woman is circumstantial – it is what is called circumstantial evidence, theoretical evidence, or what you like to call it. Circumstantial evidence can only establish a case of probability – that the prisoner was probably guilty. If you find evidence which points to the probability the prisoner is guilty, you should turn the probability into a certainty before you convict. You want to view the evidence to see if there is a circumstance or motive which would make the probability a certainty. But in this case you cannot find any such circumstance or motive. It is said, and said truly, that for murder there can be no adequate motive. But there is generally a motive of some sort. In this case there is nothing. If you have evidence before you which at its best would establish probability only, I venture to think that you, the jury, would pause long before you turned that probability into a certainty by returning a verdict of guilty.'

Goddard then recalled the circumstances of the night of the murder. Turning to the bloodstains and acknowledging that they were the most serious evidence against him, he said, 'They are dangerous things to deal with. So much may have happened. When you deduce facts from bloodstains, you must remember that human judgment – even of the very best – is fallible. Even in the judgment of an expert a mistake might crop up. The bloodstains cannot speak and tell you what happened. It may be that the witnesses who gave evidence concerning them made a mistake somewhere. A mistake might creep in anywhere which if detected would alter the whole significance. With regard to the tablecloth, that is a strong piece of evidence against the prisoner. There is not much doubt that the bloodstains were on the

FLORA HASKELL'S KITCHEN. PERCY NOBLE CLAIMS HE HEARD A THUMP AS MRS. HASKELL ANSWERED THE DOOR TO HIM. © *Timothy W. Frank Walker and Ann Richardson Whittle, grandchildren of Frank Richardson, Chief Constable*

cloth on the night of the murder. They either got there that night or were there before. As to when they were first seen, we are somewhat in the dark. It is a curious circumstance that of all the persons in the house that night – doctors and police, who were trained observers – and neighbours, no-one saw the stains, except Rawlins and Mrs Sweetman. Rawlins has fairly said that he did not know what time he saw them. Mrs Sweetman says she saw the stains about half-past eleven o'clock, and called the attention of Superintendent Stephens to them. We know she is mistaken because Superintendent Stephens has told us that he did not go into the kitchen until one o'clock, and no-one called his attention to the blood marks. The police, in fact, did not know anything about the blood on the tablecloth until three weeks afterwards.

'You cannot put from your minds [the fact] that several people, many, in fact, had been into the death chamber, which was reeking with blood, like a shambles, and had then gone into the kitchen in the course of the preceding hour. The blood may have got onto the cloth in many ways, but you do not know how. In fact you have no certain evidence that the blood on the cloth is human blood at all, much less the blood of the boy. It has been said the spots were bright red that night. But the witnesses who saw them are not trained observers, and they only saw them in artificial light. The prisoner had to cut up her meat or rabbits or whatever she may have for dinner, and the blood may possibly have got onto the tablecloth in this way. I do not deny that the bloodstains were there, but I cannot concede that they necessarily all got there that night. The theory of the prosecution is that the blood came from something carried in the hands of Mrs Haskell. I should think it is not impossible that the bloodstains got onto the table from some soft material such as a duster or handkerchief, but to my mind it is altogether improbable that all the stains could be communicated from one absorbent material to another in this way; and where is the proof that the blood is the blood of the little boy? You have heard that Mrs Haskell's nose had been bleeding, and she may possibly have gone by the table with a bloody handkerchief in her hand.

Is there any proof before you – this is the question – that the blood is the blood of the little boy? You, the jury, have seen the tablecloth, and you have seen the marks which have been pointed out by Dr Pepper. But you are able to judge them as well as he can. You will remember that besides the smears on the cloth there were also spots, and is it likely that spots would drop from a handkerchief? It might have caused the smear, but I fail to see how it could have caused the drops. But, of course, that is a matter for you.

'Another theory the prosecution has put before you is that the woman came downstairs with the bloody knife in her hand, and sank down into a chair by the door. Then, almost immediately, she heard Percy Noble at the door, and got up hurriedly to open the door, and brushed between the chair and the tablecloth. That would be a plausible story if it all fitted in with the evidence; but does it? It is entirely contrary to Percy Noble's evidence. He says that the chair he heard pushed back and the answering voice did not come from the direction of the door but from the fireplace, the chair where Mrs Haskell usually sat, the other side of the room. And then, if you note where the bloodstains were, is it not necessary to notice where they were not, for the remarkable facts about the case are not where blood was found, but where it was not. No trace of blood was found in the kitchen or scullery – except on the tablecloth. You will ask if the woman had come downstairs with her hands red with the blood of the little boy and the bloody knife in her hand, would there not have been blood by the chair where she sat? If she had got up immediately with her right hand holding this reeking handkerchief, to answer that back scullery door when Percy Noble knocked, how is it, gentlemen, that on that door you find no trace of blood? Comment has been made that there was no blood on the front door, but is it not much more remarkable, if this woman is the murderess, that there was no blood on the scullery door, nor upon the sink, nor upon the roller towel behind the back door, nor upon the woman's hand that night? She was seen by Dr Wilks, seen by the police, seen by Mrs Sweetman and by a policeman who was there all night, and there is no suggestion that there was any blood on her hand. Blood cannot be got rid of from the hands and nails

hurriedly, or merely by dipping them in water. Yet you know that never once by any living soul, by people who had every opportunity of seeing her, had it been suggested that one spot, or stain, or smear of blood was seen upon the prisoner's hand. If it had been upon her hand, seen as she was by many people, it must have been observed.

'It has been suggested that she got rid of the blood in the interval between opening the back door to Percy Noble and opening the front door and screaming. But bloodstains cannot be got rid of so easily, and had the woman rinsed her hand under the tap and wiped it, the roller towel would have had traces of blood. Mrs Haskell could not have had time to wash her hands between the time she answered Percy Noble at the back door and the time she was seen screaming in the front. Besides, If the blood on the handkerchief was the blood of the little boy that had been murdered, surely Mrs Haskell would not have held it for all the world to see? Does the woman in the dock appear to you as a cunning criminal who did not stop at killing her only child, but made up a story to shield herself? She brought out the damning evidence for all the world to see. She did not even put it in her pocket, for there was no trace of blood about the edges of the pocket.' Goddard then dealt with the bloodstains on Flora's blouse and skirt. 'Not a single spot of blood was found on the left side of the blouse. The suggested theory of the blood on the blouse was that it was blown from the child's windpipe. But all the blood in the bedroom would be to the left of the assassin. It was found on a chair at the head of the bed, on the upper part of the pillow, on a drawer, on the wallpaper, on the floor – all at the left side of the prisoner. And yet there was not a single spot on Mrs Haskell's left side! If this woman was there at the time the wound was inflicted, how is it that she got none of the blood that would be sprayed to her left side?

Yet the other theory accounts for the absence of blood on that side. As the woman came out of the kitchen door to the foot of the stairs her *right* side would be the side exposed to anyone coming down the stairs, and would receive the spots of blood from a thrown knife.' Goddard then took the model of the house, and showed how, if someone came down the stairs and threw down the knife and it were to strike the wall in its flight, any blood flying off it would land on Flora's right side, not on the left. Further, he argued that if the knife's fall were to be broken by glancing off the bottom of her skirt, that would account both for the mark on her skirt and the small amount of blood at the knife's final resting place. The mark where the knife had, according to Goddard's argument, struck the wall had been shown to the jury on the staircase wallpaper – a "projected" mark, as the medical witness had described it. To make the point Goddard gestured with the knife to show how blood would have been sprayed off it as it was projected forward. 'As for the blood on the skirt, would you assume that all that blood got on it that night? Dr Pepper admits that some of it might have been there three days, or even weeks before. It might easily have got there in the course of discharging ordinary domestic duty, and Dr Pepper agrees that some of it might have got there by the knife striking the skirt. And this leads me to a further point. It has been argued that the blood-mark made by the knife on the floor was not such as would be caused by a knife flung or falling from a height because the mark was too regular. But if the knife hit the fold of the woman's skirt before touching the ground the force of its fall would be so broken that it would fall gently and make the mark you have seen. The again, although the sprayed blood from the boy's throat went in an upward direction, there is only one stain – on the sleeve of the blouse – which shows that upward direction. And that might be [accounted for], that as the woman saw the man she threw up her arm in alarm, a natural action, and the apparently *upward* mark would be really a *downward* mark, the man being at a higher level than she.'

With that Goddard accounted for the blood on Flora's blouse, that on her skirt, and the bloodstain on the threshold corresponding only with the shape of the knife blade. He continued, 'I put it to you that not one witness has said that the spots on the woman *must* have been caused by the spray of blood from the lad's throat, only that it *may* have been. It is not a case of *may* that you ought to have, but *must*. And if she murdered the boy, is it conceivable that she left that room reeking with blood, that room little better than a shambles, with no more blood on her than these spots?'

As for when the murder was committed, he said, 'Mrs Haskell must just have been going upstairs to do the deed – if she did it – as the boy Wyatt called with the parcel at the front door. She must have been almost at the point of doing it. Her foot must have been upon the stair, the knife must almost have been in her hand, to go up and murder that child. And yet she was composed when she answered the door, and was quite in her ordinary mood. Could a person of the strongest nerves at such a moment converse quietly, in ordinary tones, with the lad at the door, take the parcel, put it in the front room, and then with hardly a minute interval go up and murder the boy? I contend that it would have shaken the strongest nerves if they were interrupted like that. This is a case of circumstantial evidence, and a circumstance such as that is every bit as important as that of the bloodstains or anything else in the case. No woman, not even the greatest brute of a man that ever lived, being interrupted on the way to murder the boy, could do all this calmly and then go on and do the murder. No-one suggests that she had committed the murder at the time that Wyatt called, and in the five or six minutes which elapsed between that and the knock at the back door by Percy Noble she must have committed the murder and so composed her nerves as to be able to answer Percy in her ordinary tone of voice. Then Percy heard the thump as of someone jumping from the stairs. As to that you have two alternatives. Either the thump was caused by Mrs Haskell or by someone else. Do you think the woman is capable of thinking out such a detail as that, to start the story which she afterwards told? That thump sounded like person jumping off the stairs, and if it was done by Mrs Haskell, it was a piece of consummate acting on her part, intended to give colour to her story of the man being on the stairs. Such an idea carries with it its own refutation: it is idle to think that a woman of this sort is capable of working out the story so artistically.'

Goddard then turned to the statements Flora had made, and the ring of truth which characterised them. 'You must not forget that this woman's movements were clearly traced from seven o'clock

– from the time that she was shopping in the city down to the last, and all her statements when tested were found to be true. Her main story was not made [up], either, when she found herself suspected and accused and had to make up a story. How easy it would have been not to tell Percy Noble, to tell him to come again tomorrow, and to give time to destroy all traces of the crime so far as they told against herself. Instead of which she gave every point that told against herself. She described the knife – a knife which she could have disowned without anyone being the wiser, for it was an odd one, not one of a set, which could be identified. She held the bloody handkerchief in her hand, and she put no difficulty in the way of the examination of her clothing. Her whole demeanour was consistent with innocence rather than guilt.'

Then Goddard dealt with the significance the crown had placed on Flora's failure to go upstairs to see her son until three-quarters of an hour after the murder. 'No-one knows what they would do if they were afraid. My learned friend has addressed you as man to men. But you have to remember that the prisoner is a weak woman, a loving mother, who knew some terrible thing had happened to her child. She rushed into the street, where she was quickly surrounded and comforted by loving neighbours, who wanted to keep the worst from her. Look at the poor, frail, weak thing in the dock! Are you surprised that she did not act bravely and at once come to grips with the worst that she thought or knew must have happened. Do not let yourselves draw an unfavourable inference from what might or might not be done at such a moment as that. We none of us know, thank God, what we may do when we are afraid.'

He again referred to Flora's statements to show that they were corroborated in every detail, except for some discrepancies between her account and Percy Noble's; nevertheless her statements included numerous odd little touches that showed their basic truthfulness. 'If she were guilty, when surrounded by her friends, by her mother, her story must have broken down and she must have given herself away. The most that can be said against this woman is that after eight weary days before the coroner, and six

weary days before the magistrates, after hearing the evidence piled up against her, after having hysterical fits, and having been committed for trial, and knowing that she had to lie in prison with this ghastly charge hanging over her for three months, when she had seen her clergyman, and had received spiritual consolation from him, she said to Mrs Sheppard, "If I did it I don't remember it". Do you remember that when Mrs Haskell went up with Dr Wilks, she bent across the bed and kissed the lad? If that woman is a guilty woman, could any words be found sufficient to describe the character of that kiss? Gentlemen, it would be a grim satisfaction to me, as it might be to you that if this woman did commit the crime, no words can be found adequate to describe its character. If this woman be guilty, she is not only one of the greatest criminals, but also one of the greatest actresses of the day, and not only that, but a great novelist to be able to make up such a story as she has done. This laundress, humble woman of the people, untrained by the arts of society and the conventions of a class higher than hers to restrain and repress her feelings – do you think that she could have gone up into the room and kissed that clay, that lifeless clay made lifeless by her own hand?

'In a moment you will be having the charge from the judge, and then you will debate amongst yourselves the question which is of such vital, awful importance to this woman, whose life since that Saturday, long ago in October has hung by a thread, and I would ask you to remember, when you debate the question, that your word alone now stands between this woman and her doom. So surely as she passes beyond that dock after the fatal verdict, she is dead in the sight of all who now behold her. Dark clouds of suspicion have gathered over her, but I ask you not to take a fellow creature's life unless there is *proof* – cogent, clear and compelling. It is the glory of our law, the great safeguard of our liberty, that no-one shall be convicted of even the meanest crime on suspicion, and doubly that must apply in this case. Is there any one of you to whom the evidence has brought home this woman's guilt with such certainty that there must be a verdict of Guilty? If there is even a lingering doubt in your minds as to whether those hands which have performed such acts of tenderness and loving kindness to that little boy are dyed with his blood, then I say to you, each one in this matter, individually, that the responsibility in this matter is an individual responsibility. If there is with any one of you a lingering doubt in your mind, uphold it, maintain it to the end, remembering that this woman's life is in your hands, no only collectively, but in [those of] each one of you. Now I commend her cause to your hands, and I ask you to judge her as we – you and I – would like to be judged if we ever stood in such sore need as stands this poor woman for whose life I plead.'

Goddard's speech took an hour and a quarter. His authorised biographer, Fenton Bresler, describes his speech as "almost a verbatim copy of his first, like an actor on the second night of a play". Nevertheless there were differences, and while Goddard in no sense eschewed the finer forensic points in his second speech, that address played more on the implausibility of Flora's guilt, when her character hitherto and her behaviour on the night were examined. The second speech is perhaps a more crafted piece of oratory, with successive phrases and clauses bringing to a climax each of his arguments. The *Salisbury Times* commented that the speech "created a profound impression in court, and Goddard's ability to work the jury's emotions doubtless bore on the outcome of the trial, for he was warmly commended by Darling.

Perhaps as important for the final outcome of the trial was the Judge's summing-up, in measured tones, over two hours. 'As you are aware, ' he said, 'and from what the learned counsel has said, it is for you to be satisfied that the prosecution had proved the charge which they made against the prisoner, but it must be a case of satisfaction to you, as it is to me, to know that the way the case has been laid before you has earned the entire approval and the thanks of the prisoner's counsel. Mr Goddard has said no point had been laid against the prisoner which should not have been. It must also be a matter of greater satisfaction that the prisoner has been defended with the very remarkable ability shown by Mr Goddard throughout the whole of the case.

'Mr Goddard has told you that if there is a lingering doubt in your minds you should find it in favour of the defendant, but it is *my* duty to tell you what sort of a doubt that must be. The doubt that lingers must be a reasonable one, and one which in your ordinary affairs you would act upon. You are not entitled – no-one is entitled – to have a doubt in a Court of Justice without a reason. If you have a doubt it must be a doubt for which you can give a reason. It does not mean a doubt which you can conjure up about the evidence. In this case the allegation against the prisoner that she murdered that little boy must be proved to them – proved beyond reasonable doubt – and proved, not by argument, but by the evidence to which you have listened. This is a charge of murder, there is no doubt about that, and no-one contends to the contrary. Mr Goddard asserted as plainly as Mr Foote that the little boy was murdered. *Someone* did the murder. The person who killed the child was a murderer, and deserved to be found guilty of murder and nothing else. The only question you have to consider is whether it is proved that the prisoner was the murderess or not. You know it is said she is not proved guilty of the murder, and it is obviously necessary to put before you some kind of thought as to who did it.

'When the people went into the house, after Mrs Haskell had been shouting, there was no-one else in the house besides the little child who was murdered. Who did it? The suggestion is that a man did it; that it was a man who ran downstairs just as the little boy Noble knocked at the back door. It is suggested that he did it. It might be, but is it? There is no suggestion who the man was, or why he committed the murder. Mr Goddard has told you that there is no motive for the woman committing the crime. It is true that no one gives a motive that a sane person committed the crime, and it would be also true to say that could not often be found in a murder committed by an insane person. Except in a case where a motive can be found, it is difficult to be sure that you know what the motive is. You all act differently. There are twelve jurymen here, and the same motive might not induce each of you to do the same thing. Some of you might do one thing, and some of you might do another from the same motive. It is a difficult thing to speculate on a motive. With regard to the man who is suggested to have done the deed, I ask, "Who is he?" You have heard no suggestion that there was anyone who bore any ill will against the child. When did he [the man] come to the house? How did he get there? Why did he go to the house? What motive had he for going? The name of no-one has been suggested. There was a man who slept in the house twice, and he was on excellent terms with the boy: I refer to the man Mold. I think it should be proclaimed that at the time Mold was on board the ship *Adriatic*. No suspicion whatever should be attached to him.

'Who knew the boy and would have done it? There is a suggestion in what the woman says about the man who called for lodgings the night before the murder, and she told him she did not take lodgers. The man replied that it was funny, because he had been recommended there. If the suggestion is that this man murdered the boy – and I suppose it is – why did he do it? What benefit was it to him to murder the little boy? If it was he who did it, it is a most extraordinary thing. Did he go with the intention of robbery? Mrs Haskell is a poor woman, who could just keep herself and her little boy. She was, in fact, so poor that on occasions she had to borrow some of the money that the little boy was saving to buy a cork leg. Did the man know of the money? No, certainly not. Did he take it? No, he did not. The money, eight pounds, was left in the drawer, as you are told, and when the drawer was opened the next time there was only three pounds ten shillings there. If it is suggested that the lock was broken open by the murderer, there would have been blood on the handle or on the drawer somewhere. But there was not a drop of blood on this drawer. Is the motive robbery? How can you say it is? If the man took the trouble to go there, and committed murder, would he go away and leave the drawer untouched? You have seen the drawer with the money under the piece of cloth, and would the man have gone away without lifting the stuff to see if there was any money there, or even have taken the stuff as well. The man did not take anything else, either. Then again, the murderer came without a knife, or if he brought one he did not use it. The knife with which the murder was committed belonged to the house, and it had been sharpened lately. Where did the man get it? If he

came to commit the murder why did he not bring a knife and use it? Is it suggested that the boy woke up while the robber was forcing the drawer? No. Then why should the man have killed him?' Darling considered other features of the case and said that after lunch he would deal with the evidence. The court then rose for a half-hour lunch break.

Darling continued his summing-up. 'I will now deal with the evidence which is said to prove the facts necessary to establish the case against the defendant. Really, although this is a remarkable case, and one which has attracted considerable attention, as you all know, yet it is a case in which the facts are very little in dispute until you come to the main fact as to who did really commit the murder. Really it is a case remarkable for that.' Darling then proceeded to review in detail the evidence of the witnesses and the statements made by Flora, going through them very carefully and contrasting them with the facts stated in evidence by the witnesses, particularly Percy Noble and Walter Steer. He showed significant discrepancies, particularly when Flora said to Percy and to Steer that Teddy had been murdered, whereas in her statement she said that she asked Steer to go and see what was the matter. The alleged throwing of the knife was another discrepancy. Percy's evidence, Darling continued, was 'undoubtedly correct, because there is one little touch in it about the shadow on the wall which a lad like that could not possibly have imagined.'

Having spent some time comparing Flora's statements with the evidence of the witnesses, Darling then tackled Goddard's theories. 'The defence are not obliged to give a theory at all. All they have to do is to prove that the prosecution has not established their case. But, [counsel for the defence] having put forward these theories, it is as well that they should be examined. With regard to the bloodstained handkerchief, for example, Mr Goddard has suggested that this was due to bleeding from the nose. That might be true, but it is mere conjecture, as no evidence has been called to support it. This explanation has not been given by the prisoner herself, who is the one person interested to explain it. There is another suggestion which I would put to you. The handkerchief was damp as well as stained, and it might be that the prisoner, as the prosecution has suggested, rinsed her hand under the tap and dried it with the handkerchief.' Darling then discussed the other bloodstains, and continued, 'There is only counsel's conjecture as to how they came onto the tablecloth, and there is no evidence to support this. I am now going to make a remark which I alone can make, and which I should not make under ordinary circumstances. The prisoner in a criminal charge can be called as a witness just like anybody else. It may be that the statements she has made contain all that she knows, [and] that she can tell no more. Bu there are matters where supposition has been offered as explanation in regard to evidence which might have been given. It has been suggested that the prisoner raised her arm, and that this accounts for blood being in a certain direction. Well, the person who can tell us that is the accused herself. There are other points which she might have told us. But you must not convict the prisoner because she does not give evidence, but if there is something which admits of explanation, and that explanation is not given, it must gravely weaken the supposition which has been put forward.'

Speaking very deliberately, Darling concluded his summing-up with a reminder to the jury of their duty 'to return a verdict irrespective of the opinion of other people, and upon the evidence alone before you. If you are not satisfied, if you have reasonable doubts, you must acquit, even if people say afterwards that you ought to have been convinced. If, however, you are satisfied, beyond any reasonable doubt – upon the evidence, not upon what you think might have been – you must return a verdict of Guilty.' Charles Darling's appraisal was irreproachably impartial but it was by no means favourable to Flora. Whether that had any influence on the jury's decision can only, however, be a matter of speculation.

The time was five minutes to three. As the jury retired to determine a verdict, they requested the use of Notley's block plan and the model of the house. They were gone for an hour and twenty minutes; an anxious wait for Flora but an opportunity for those in the public gallery to chat and to while away the time. Then at a quarter past four there was a buzz of excitement as the Sheriff, his chaplain, the Under-

Sheriff and the Judge all took their places. The jury trooped in; Flora was brought up and placed in the dock with a wardress either side of her. The Clerk of the Court, James Read put the fateful question: 'Gentlemen, have you agreed your verdict?'

The foreman replied, 'We have.'

'How say you, gentlemen? Is Flora Fanny Haskell guilty or not guilty?'

'Not guilty, on the ground of insufficient evidence.' Flora's look of worry changed to an expression of gratitude directed at the Jury, before she sank down into her seat and buried her face in her handkerchief. Within a minute or two, however, she was smiling at her brothers, one of whom was joyfully waving his hat. Darling turned to the Jury and said 'You have given considerable time and attention to this case, and I shall order you to be exempt from further jury service for a term of five years.'

Flora, all smiles, was chatting to the wardresses in the dock meanwhile, and as the door was opened and she was free after five months she kissed her brothers and left with them and Alfred Mold. In court, some people cheered, others hissed. Outside the little party was followed by a large crowd as it made its way to the lodging-house on the Bath Road where Mrs Carter had been staying for the duration of the trial. Following afternoon tea at the guest house, the family took Mrs Carter to the railway station for Salisbury, Flora confidently returning the onlookers' gaze. The next morning, Sunday 4 April, Flora took the early train to London with her brothers.

The following Friday, the *Salisbury Times* published a letter from one of Flora's brothers:

SIR. – Will you please allow me, on behalf of my sister, Mrs Haskell, my dear mother and my family, to tender our deep thanks to all those kind Salisbury friends who have stood by us, both sympathetically and financially, through the past terrible five months, now happily terminated.

No-one can realise the suspense, the anxiety, the awful nightmare it has been to us, for in addition to the dreadful charge, we have been aware of the many rumors that have been in circulation to the detriment of my sister's moral character. For these there was no foundation of truth, and subsequent events have proved their falsity. All those who know her have known from the beginning what a mistake has been made and we have always worked with the one idea of regaining the freedom of an innocent woman. The result, of course, has been dearly brought about. A good Councillor and true-hearted friend we have had in Mr. Frank Baker, who has been untiring in his efforts on our behalf; and for the splendid financial aid and public-spirited magnanimity of the Member for Salisbury, Sir Edward Tennant, we shall always feel a deep debt of gratitude; while the hard and painstaking work of Mr. Trethowan and Mr Rayner Goddard, solicitor and counsel, has had the reward it fully deserves.

In conclusion I may say that we are, on the advice of friends, giving my sister a complete rest and change for a few weeks, but presently she hopes to thank all her staunch and kind friends personally. She very keenly feels the loss of her dear "little Teddy" – now far removed from suffering and sorrow, whose earthly remnants are resting in the cold earth beside those of his "Dad" – he was her all in all, for whom she had worked so hard, and of whom the cruel had of fate robbed her on that dark night in October last.

Yours, etc.,

R. Carter (eldest brother)

56 Danby Street,

East Dulwich

April 5th, 1909.[5]

NEWSPAPER PHOTOGRAPHS OF FLORA AND TEDDY

16

'Dangerous realms of speculation': who did kill Teddy Haskell?

THE VERDICT left Flora Haskell a free woman: she walked from the court innocent of the charge of the murder of her only son: innocent in the eyes of the jury, and hence necessarily in the eyes of the world. But the verdict has left the world with the gaping hole of mystery for the last century, and of course the world has, over time, done its best to fill that hole, starting with the view of Chief Inspector Walter Dew, whose claim never to have lost a case is belied by the Haskell case. The jury's decision was not simply one with which he disagreed, but one he met with astonishment: in truth, Dew did not feel he had lost the case, but that the jury had lost it for him.

In his report to the Director of Public Prosecutions dated 29 April 1909, he postulated the theory that Flora alone killed Teddy because he was 'either a hindrance to her getting married to Mold, or to her carrying on intrigues with men'. His explanation of the sequence of events was that Flora put Teddy to bed, and then, when she was confident that her neighbours were abed, she killed him and then planned to call on Mrs Mold (mother of Alfred) for a little while, leaving her front door ajar. She would then return to find her front door open and Teddy with his throat cut, and at that point raise the alarm, 'and then the suggestion would have been that it was another of those mysterious murders of children.' The stolen money could have served as some sort of pretext for the murder, as it was to do in any case.

But then, unbeknown to Flora, Percy called to repay his shilling: Teddy knew he was planning to do

so, but not Flora, and he called just at the wrong moment for her, as, knife in hand, she was sitting in the armchair by the kitchen range and collecting her thoughts after the awful deed. So when he knocked

INSPECTOR DEW'S FINAL REPORT ON THE HASKELL MURDER.

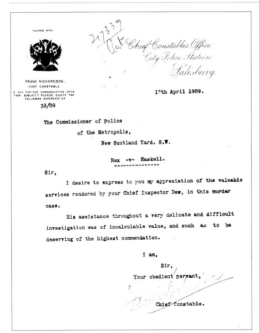
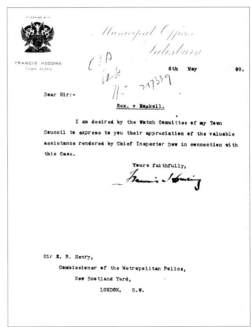

LETTERS OF APPRICIATION SENT BY FRANK RICHARDSON AND FRANCIS HODDING, SALISBURY TOWN CLERK

she had to think quickly of some explanation to keep the salient points of her story in order and verifiable. Where Percy was concerned she only had to think of enough to get him out of the way. Then, in the time it took her to cross from her scullery door to the front door, she had to think of what she would say, consistent with what lay within her house and what she had already told Percy. Other than her reactions to events – including her statements – all was circumstantial evidence, and it was upon this that Goddard had secured Flora's freedom. But, concluded Dew, 'I would respectfully submit that there never was a stronger case of circumstantial evidence, and indeed nothing could be stronger, except the evidence of an eye witness to the perpetration of a crime. I venture to say that it can be well imagined that this enquiry, from the commencement to the finish, was fraught with the utmost difficulties, which were not lessened by the fact that the body was allowed to be disturbed . . . and therefore it is all the more surprising that I was able to collect such a chain of evidence, which in the opinion of almost everybody, was sufficient to secure a more satisfactory verdict.' Frank Froest, Dew's super-intendent, endorsed this view: 'In view of the evidence

and the summing up of Mr Justice Darling, it is more than surprising that the Jury should have acquitted this woman. I venture to submit that throughout this long and most difficult investigation Chief Inspr Dew performed his duty with marked skill and ability.'

The chain of evidence to which Dew refers, and which we now have to consider comprises a number of discrete themes:

- the sequence of events leading to Flora raising the alarm;
- the state of the bedroom and the nature of Teddy's injuries;
- the money;
- the bloodstains on Flora's clothing;
- the bloodstains on the tablecloth and elsewhere;
- the knife and the clearing-up of the house;
- Flora's explanation of events, including the mysterious caller;
- motives for the murder.

The sequence of events up to Flora raising the alarm

According to her first statement, made the day after the murder, Flora had put Teddy to bed at 9.40 or 9.45 p.m.; she went to the lavatory and returned to the kitchen to read for a quarter of an hour before locking the back door in readiness to go out. As she was about to go out of the kitchen in order to leave No. 40 by the front door her nephew Percy knocked at the back door. Before she could turn to answer the door to Percy, she heard movements on the stairs, causing her to go back to the door between the kitchen and the passage where she saw the figure on the staircase and the object was thrown at her. Noticing to her horror that she was left covered in blood, she ran to the back door to tell Percy to run to fetch a doctor. To this account Flora added the arrival of Wyatt with the boots, in her second statement, made on 2 November; but her timing is vague: "It was just after 10 p.m., as near as I can put it", and it was but a brief encounter: "He just gave me the boots at the front door and went away." By the time of her conversations with Mackay leading to his report of 11 February 1909, her estimation of Wyatt's arrival is 10.20; then there is a gap in her recall to 10.30, when she was preparing to go out. According to later conversations, recorded in Mackay's report of 23 March, the time from taking in the boots at 10.20 to the knock on the back door at 10.30 was spent preparing fish for Sunday's breakfast and sitting down reading the paper.

What Flora does not mention, despite her careful accounting of all the time from 2.30 p.m. onwards on the Saturday, is the visit of Gertrude Steer with the jacket. She deposed to calling at the back door of No. 40 en route for the GWR station, where she was due to meet her sister on the 10.03 from Bristol via Warminster. She called at about 9.45 – hence just after Flora had put Teddy to bed. They chatted a few minutes, and Flora volunteered to fetch the money from upstairs, but Gertrude declined to be paid there and then as she did not wish to be late for the train. From No. 40 to the GWR station is a quarter of a mile, and Gertrude would need to have left between 9.50 and 9.55 to be sure of meeting the train, and it thus seems highly unlikely that Teddy died any earlier than 10.00.

Then there is the question of when Wyatt delivered Mrs Manning's boots. Wyatt surmised that he arrived at around 10.20, and estimated his journey time as twelve minutes. Allowing for the time of his departure – 10.05, he could not have arrived earlier

than 10.17. When time is added for him stopping twice in Meadow Road to ask where Mrs Manning lived, and then knocking at her door and waiting, *and* at No. 40 and waiting again until she answered, the estimate of the time of his brief conversation with Flora at 10.20 begins to look optimistic, *i.e.* early. Yet that window of time for Wyatt's exchange – 10.17 to 10.20 – was taken as a given by both prosecution and defence, and taken to be the last time Teddy was known to be alive. The fact that Flora stated the time to be 10.20 in February 1909 can be discounted, because by then she had heard it at the inquest and the magistrates' trial. The window of opportunity was closed – perhaps – by Percy Noble's arrival. At the inquest and at the magistrates' trial, he said he called at No. 40 at "about half-past ten"; at the second trial, his testimony was more precise: 10.28 p.m. At the inquest, Percy was asked how many times he had to knock to get a response – twice, he answered – and how quickly Flora responded. He replied, "Not immediately", to a question put to him twice, about when she came to the door; and she did not come to the door until after the "thump" that Percy heard.

And then Flora raised the alarm. Heard by many – Lily Stretch and Herbert Primmer, the courting couple, Gertrude Skutt on her way home from her mother's, Walter Steer just after he and his family had returned from the GWR station – the time is fixed at just after 10.20 by the testimony of Walter Steer, who noted his family's coming indoors at 10.15, and heard the screams some five minutes later. Similarly, Gertrude Skutt had left her mother's at 17 York Road at 10.20 and had covered no more than a few yards towards her own home at 23 Meadow Road when she saw Percy run out of the passage into York Road and then heard Flora's screams; Herbert Primmer gave the time when he was walking with Lily Stretch as 10.20. Butt and Eccott, the pair at the *Duke of York* reckoned Steer came upon them after 10.15, but by 10.25. And when Sarah Butt went out of her front door at 10.25 to see what was going on there were already people near to 40 Meadow Road. House's testimony – of hearing the clock on the parish church strike the half-hour, and, at once, Flora's scream – may not contribute much, despite the stress laid upon it by the prosecution, as there is no evidence that the scream he heard was Flora's first.

As for the issue of the "strange delay" between Percy Noble's dismissal from No. 40 and Flora's raising the alarm, this is apparently belied by the testimony of Gertrude Skutt, walking from 17 York Road to her home at 23 Meadow Road. As she reached the passage from the backs of 42 and 40 Meadow Road, Percy Noble ran out, and she glanced down the passage. At that point she heard two screams coming from the direction of Meadow Road. Proceeding along the front of 27 York Road to the corner she met Miss Stretch and her young man, and looked up Meadow Road to see Flora on her doorstep. Yet Lily Stretch, somewhat ahead of Mrs Skutt and on the other side of the road, saw Percy crossing the road when she and Primmer were by the South Wilts Dairy Company, at 14 York Road. They crossed the road and proceeded as far as 27 York Road – Mrs Cooper's front door – and at that point heard the scream, while crossing Meadow Road. The couple turned back and saw Flora. There is a clear conflict of evidence; but one amounting to a few seconds only. Long enough for Flora to wash her hands before raising the alarm; or for her to dash upstairs and see what had happened to her son? Wherever the truth lies exactly, the balance of probability favours the Stretch/Primmer account, having, despite odd anomalies and despite the courtroom humour at their expense, more observed detail.

Finally there is the evidence of Samuel Leate, who was called only to the inquest. Unlike the other witnesses out in the street, who either were in York Road or, in the case of House, was not observing the street when the alarm was raised,[1] Leate was walking southwards from Coldharbour Lane into Meadow Road, when he saw a man leave a house on the other side of Meadow Road and striding briskly towards him, followed closely by a woman who, after a few paces stopped, and turned back towards the house, pausing once or twice before reaching her front door. By that time, Leate had reached a point opposite the woman's front door and noted that she was sobbing. He glanced back up the road but the man had

disappeared. By then the woman's crying had become louder, and her neighbours were running to her assistance, as she cried out that someone had killed her Teddy.

This testimony ought to have been a godsend to the defence; but both prosecution and defence dismissed it out of hand; even though Trethowan's briefing to counsel for the second trial stated that 'He has always been understood to be a truthful witness, and that he saw somebody in Meadow Road about the time mentioned by him may be taken for granted.' But for the defence the account stood squarely at odds with Flora's claim never to have left her house, even though it tallied perfectly with the description of the mysterious man, and the assailant jumping down the bottom steps of the staircase and disappearing through the front door. In fact, on the face of it, the main difficulty with Leate's account is in reconciling it with Percy's story about the scene of normality in Flora's kitchen followed directly by the thump as of the assailant jumping down, *if the thump was followed at once by Flora coming in distress to the back door.* For the prosecution the story contradicted the theory that Flora killed her son, and did so quite alone. So both sides dismissed Leate's story without much more ado, chiefly, it seems, because it was uncorroborated.

The most striking reaction to Leate's account was that of Walter Dew, who interviewed Flora on Monday 2 November, as to whether she left the house, following anyone such as the assailant. In her third statement, and the second of that day, Flora flatly denied five specific points put to her about her movements and behaviour derived from Leate's account, and Dew, who disbelieved a great deal else coming from Flora Haskell's lips, chose to accept her word over Leate's. The problem for Dew seems to have been that Leate left it so long before giving his account: 'I asked why he did not give information to Police before late Sunday', wrote Dew on Thursday 4 November, 'although he knew the murder had been committed, and he said, "He forgot all about it."' Commenting on Leate's account in the same report Dew wrote, 'He gave a description similar to what appeared in the newspapers, and which is of no value, because no man was ever described as leaving the house on Saterday [*sic*]. In other words, the information was not corroborated – unless Flora's testimony about a man leaving her house, and her call to stop him is accepted – and was nugatory, because it repeated information in the press, which as of Sunday or Monday had yet to report any account of the murder or to describe the suspect.[2] Dew's final report to the DPP, on 29 April, was even more scathing: 'I satisfied myself that he was an absolute liar. Even the defence did not accept his story.'

Yet his subsequent life history demonstrates Leate to have been anything but mendacious, and, a resident of the St Mark's area of Salisbury, he had no interest in whether or not Flora was guilty of Teddy's murder. The main problem with Leate – as a participant in the form of theatre which was the coroner's inquest – was that he was too scrupulous and too wary to allow himself to be browbeaten into saying anything which he did not mean. He was steadfast in his refrain that if he said something in his police statement, that was his testimony at the inquest, and not, at that much later date, anything which would undermine his statement. The refusal by all sides to take Leate seriously was one of the most peculiar aspects of what turned out to be a very odd case indeed.

And so we come to what Flora said to raise the alarm. Witness after witness, starting with Percy Noble, to whom she said 'Go and see if you can see that man, he's killed my poor Teddy!' reported Flora as saying that her son had been slain, even though not until her fourth statement, of 3 November, does she recall saying any such thing. Even then it is recalled as 'I believe someone has killed my little Teddy', and then only when she had spoken to Steer after he had gone upstairs to see what was wrong. She said, not "Someone has *hurt* my Teddy" or "Someone has *stabbed* my Teddy", but, variously, "Someone has *killed* …", or "…has *murdered* my Teddy." She was saying this almost within seconds of the attack, although within a few moments, she was asking Thomas Rawlins, early to arrive on the scene to tell her what had happened. Doubtless Flora was hoping against hope that her worst fear would be denied rather than confirmed. And almost half an hour later, just before 11.00 p.m., she was asking

Wilks whether it was true that Teddy was dead. Flora's earlier certitude allows for three explanations. One, that she had gone upstairs directly after the assailant had fled the house, and the shock of what she saw induced amnesia. Two, that she was in some way party to the boy's throat being cut and knew for certain he was dead or dying – as the doctors believed and as the prosecution argued. Three, as the defence maintained, the sheer shock of seeing and feeling her son's blood on her own skin through the thin muslin sleeve of her blouse convinced Flora of the worst. And *if* there were just time enough between Flora saying 'All right' to Percy and her opening the back door to him, for her to have pursued a man for a few paces *or* to have gone upstairs, there is unlikely to have been time enough for her to do both. But still less was there time, as the prosecution argued, for Flora to wash her hands, which Percy might well have heard her do, especially if she had had to turn on a tap.

The state of the bedroom and the nature of Teddy's injuries

It was a matter of some chagrin to the investigators that the doctors had cleaned Teddy up and rolled up the bloodstained bedding, placing him on fresh linen so that when Flora saw him at around 11.15 he looked as if he were slumbering, and the room had some sort of an air of normality about it. What is far odder is how tidy the bedroom looked immediately after the murder, when it ought to have looked like a bloodbath, or, to quote Goddard, a shambles. Walter Steer described the bedclothes as being "in perfect order", and again, "The bedclothes were over him and turned back just below his throat." As for the room, "The room generally was in perfect order"; this at a time within minutes of the boy's death, for when he touched Teddy's face, it was "quite warm, like that of a child asleep." Sarah Butt, who followed Steer into the bedroom, said "The clothes seemed in perfect order from what I can remember, and the room was in perfect order." When Wilks described the dead child, he said "He looked absolutely peaceful. The left arm was lying outside the counterpane, the right arm was inside the bed . . . there was no clenching of the hands. The arms were semi-flexed. The left leg was half-flexed and abducted [*i.e.* it was drawn away from being in line with the trunk]. . . The bedclothes were apparently undisturbed and were up to his neck. The room was apparently perfectly in order: nothing was disarranged." Row said "There was no sign of a struggle" and commented that "The general condition of the bedroom was quite tidy." Odder still was that, as Sarah Butt noticed, there was a brass lamp on the landing, on the left as one left the room. It was extinguished and quite cold.

When Teddy was killed, he was despatched swiftly and with force. Wilks testified at the inquest that "The wound had been inflicted with a considerable degree of force with some sharp instrument . . .", and, cross-examined by Trethowan on that very point, he acknowledged that it would have been "easier for a man to inflict the wound than a woman." As well as the cut in his throat, Teddy sustained a nick or abrasion on the back of the fourth finger of his left hand, and the consensus was that he had put his hand up involuntarily as the wound was being inflicted and the hand struck the knife on the follow-through of the fatal cut. Wilks also deposed that he "should have said there was a slight movement of the boy's head at the time the wound was inflicted, but I do not think there had been any movement of the boy's body or the bedclothes after the wound was inflicted." Even so, the overall impression of peace and order about the crime scene *before* the doctors tidied it up for Flora and Mrs Carter's benefit suggests that perhaps the bedclothes had been straightened up and the boy's arm laid neatly over the counterpane.

Teddy Haskell was killed, on the word of three surgeons, by a single cut across the throat from the left side of the windpipe across to the right hand side of the throat, with both the carotid artery and the trachea being severed. Row deposed, at the magistrates' hearing, 'The wound on the finger of the left hand was probably consistent with the hand having involuntarily moved at the time that the wound on the neck was inflicted. The wound on the finger and that on the throat could, I think, have been caused by one movement of the knife.' The wound was shallow on the left side and deeper on the right side. According to Wilks there was a small jag – or

snag – half way along the cut, consistent either with the instrument used being very sharp, but perhaps with a nick part-way along the blade, or the slight movement of the head to which Wilks referred, or, in Pepper's view, simply by the dragging of the blade.

If the cut to the finger happened simultaneously with that to the throat, as Wilks deposed, the inference to be drawn is that the cut took place from left to right, and the left arm was lifted smartly up, the fourth finger catching the edge of the blade as the knife left the throat. The difficulty with this explanation is that as the artery was severed, blood travelled, according to Wilks's testimony at the inquest, about a yard, and it seems strange that none of that blood ended up on the boy's left hand or arm, if it was in the way of the knife after the cut was made. Blood spurted to the left, according to Wilks, to be absorbed by the pillow, and subsequently welled up and trickled to the right. This was an odd deduction given both that it was the right artery that was severed and that there was a great deal more blood on the right pillow than the left. In Trethowan's second briefing to counsel, which draws attention to this, reference was made to a now lost independent forensic report for the defence by one Dr Maurice.[3] Was the prosecution's view framed to account for the distribution of blood to suggest more strongly Flora's presence as the knife was wielded? Row stated that there were no signs of a struggle, and this would account for the tidy state of the bedroom.

As to where the killer stood, Wilks deposed at the magistrates' hearing that they 'must have been standing on the right hand side of the bed [*i.e.* the side away from the wall] and with the left hand on the forehead of the boy and with the right hand have inflicted the wound across and slightly downwards. I should say the person would be standing opposite the head rather above the neck and in front of the chair. In that position the person so standing would be in the line of the blood I have spoken of as coming from the larynx [*i.e.* in an aerosol exhaled with air].' Again, this would seem to implicate Flora, but the presence of blood on the toilet-cover of the chest of drawers and on the knob of the right drawer, as well as that on the right pillow suggests that the killer must have been practically drenched with blood; certainly with more blood than ended up on Flora. As to how the assailant stood, Row said at the second trial that they would have faced the foot of the bed. So the killer steadied Teddy's head and perhaps pushed it down into the pillow to extend the throat with their left hand.

Possibly Teddy came to, briefly at this point, raising his left hand, striking the knife poised to make the fatal cut, which was a single slash, calculated to stop him crying out and to sever a single main blood-vessel so that death would ensue swiftly and mercifully; possibly he raised his arm after the deed was done and it was a matter of chance that his arm escaped the flow of blood. At the time of his death Teddy was not drugged: both Row and Kempe checked the boy's pupils, and they were in the normal state of being dilated. When Walter Steer responded to Flora's plea to see what had happened, the first thing he had to call for was a lamp. The inference to be drawn is that the assailant would have needed some light to see what they were doing, and two hands free to make the incision. That light could have come from a lamp held over Teddy's head, or there may have been enough light from the lamp left on the dressing table as a nightlight if the murderer took care that they were not standing in their own light. Despite the crudity of the instrument used, it was an incision, a cut just deep enough and long enough to achieve a fatal result without showering the room in blood; one of almost surgical skill; a skill unlikely to have been possessed by a laundress. According to Wilks the hand holding the knife would very likely have been covered in blood: before the magistrates he deposed, '[The knife] being so used and gripped, blood would in all probability come onto the back of the hand. It could get inside between the fingers a little and on all the exposed part of the hand.'

As for when the death happened, we know that Flora raised the alarm sometime shortly after 10.20, probably no later than 10.25. Percy Noble had to travel as quickly as he could to the surgery, a distance just over four hundred yards. Even had he walked at four miles an hour the distance would have taken him less than four minutes, and we can therefore assume it took him a couple of minutes. Wilks estimated before the magistrates that his and Row's journey time by bicycle was about a minute; hence they were at the crime scene no later than 10.35 p.m., and possibly by 10.33 p.m. In his briefing to counsel for the defence for the second trial Trethowan estimated the total time elapsed between Percy leaving to fetch the doctor and the pair arriving at No. 40 as ten minutes, and hence 'They arrived, as will be seen, at 10:31, and this again would corroborate Steer's evidence as to time.' Of course, we don't know what time passed between the cut being made and the alarm being raised. Wilks deposed before the magistrates, 'In my opinion, death took place within a minute of the infliction of the wound . . . Death would have been practically instantaneous . . . I should say that death had taken place within a quarter of an hour before I got there. I should say a quarter of an hour would be the maximum. That opinion is based partly on the bubbles of air which were still coming through the blood and partly on account of the condition of the clothing which I saw.'

Hence the earliest time for the murder was 10.20 or possibly 10.16; yet we know Flora was in conversation with Wyatt no earlier than 10.17 and more likely at 10.20 or 10.21, and the consensus was that Teddy was probably still alive at that point. On that premise the time of his death can thus be narrowed down to between 10.21 and 10.25 on the night of October 31. But the alternative is that an intruder had gained entrance to the house and was upstairs – where Flora said to Emma Chivers she heard some movement – either just before or while Flora was at the door with John Wyatt, placing Teddy's death between 10.16 and 10.21. If Wilks's theory, that Teddy died relatively quickly, were correct, that would imply the murder took place toward the end of either period; if Row were correct, and Teddy breathed a few gasps before his last breath, that would imply the murder took place at or soon after the beginning of either period. At any rate, death was recent enough for the body not to have started cooling down, as its warmth was noted by Walter Steer literally a few minutes before the doctors' arrival.

The money

At the second trial, much was made, both by counsel for the prosecution and by the judge, of the sheer implausibility of burglary as being the motive for the crime, on the grounds that not all of the money was taken and that there was no blood anywhere near the drawer that was forced. It was noted also that Flora was an unlikely target for a robbery because she was not possessed of any great means, and in his first report to the DPP on 4 November Walter Dew adds that according to Flora no-one but she, its guardian, Teddy, its owner and Mrs Carter, its donor, knew anything whatsoever about the money. This, of course is an exaggeration, for Emily Thirza Haskell knew about the money, as did Flora's friend Miss Lawrence,[4] and her neighbour Matilda Hawkins at No. 29: who is to say that they were the only others who knew of it? Then there is the question of the man paying Teddy twopence for his name and address, mentioned by Flora to John Cooper and to Frank Richardson on the night of the murder and testified by both at the inquest, on 19 and 21 November and at the Magistrates' hearing on 3 and 5 December. Perhaps there was someone out there – the man seeking lodgings, the man inquiring whether Teddy had brothers and sisters and giving him twopence for his name and address; even though any connection between the two was firmly discounted in court on 3 December. One can conceive of someone – whether with Flora's knowledge and consent or not – being aware, in general terms, of the money, and, not recalling or knowing the precise details either of how much there was or how to reach it. A person in those circumstances might give the drawer where the money was concealed a good yank, breaking the evidently flimsy lock, and grab what came to hand.

One could imagine such a train of events, either earlier in the day on 31 October, or directly before the murder was committed, with Teddy waking up and having his throat cut before he could call out. What seems most peculiar is not so much the minutiae of which tack held the broken lock and so on, but the fact that Flora raised the issue of the money as forcefully and promptly as she did, when, one might have thought, with her child's life either in the balance or stolen outright, a few pounds – equivalent of a few hundred pounds today – would be the last thing on her mind. On Richardson encountering her in the front room of No. 40, Flora

was incoherent with grief, but then, from his testimony to the magistrates ... 'At first I could not seem to make much of her, but eventually she spoke of some money upstairs in a drawer'. One might almost suspect that the robbery were pre-arranged, to provide a pretext for the murder, and something for Flora to be able to say to the police and others, in addition to the stories about the man seeking lodgings and the presumed assailant jumping down the stairs and flinging the knife down.

The bloodstains on Flora's clothing

Taken at face value the bloodstains on Flora's clothing, particularly on her blouse, provide the most damning indictment of her claim to innocence, for the medical and forensic opinion was unequivocal about the means of transmission of the bloodstains upon her blouse, Exhibit No. 28. Pepper counted 28 spots of blood on the body – mainly on the right side – and fifty on the right sleeve, all the way from the wrist to an inch below the yoke. One mark on the sleeve was "tailed off in an upward direction". For any thrown object to have caused the spots on Flora's blouse, in the way that she suggested, there would have to have been a great deal more blood on the floor where the knife was found. On the other hand, a spray of blood on a current of air – such as from the victim's severed windpipe – would cause just such spotting of blood as was observed on Flora's blouse, and the round marks on her skirt, Exhibit No. 27. Kempe, the police surgeon, shown Flora's clothing after she had been relieved of it, agreed that the spots were caused by exhaled air carrying tiny droplets of blood. And while Pepper did not see the bloodstains until November 8 they were observed on Flora's blouse on the night of the murder by witnesses such as Mrs Cooper, Mrs Chivers, Mrs Sweetman and Dr Wilks. Whether Flora dashed up to see her dying child as the assailant was escaping, or whether she was present as the murder took place – either by committing it or as an accessory – the blood spots on her clothing, most tellingly those on her blouse, could prove that she witnessed her son's last gasp. As for Goddard's explanation of the upward mark on her sleeve actually being a downward mark, if Flora raised her arm in alarm as blood dropped from above, the same thing might happen if she were holding her arm aloft with the oil lamp in it to cast light on her son as the wound was inflicted. And were she to have been to one side of the assailant, that might explain why one side only – the right side – was sprinkled with the blood on the boy's dying breaths.

However, blood marks are simply that, and it is their *interpretation* which is of key importance, of which fact Goddard was able to persuade the jurors. Most notably, as Trethowan advised counsel before the second jury trial, the medical witnesses were all called to give evidence for the Prosecution, and they all conferred before the inquest and the magisterial hearing to ensure some uniformity of response. Trethowan went so far as to say that the medical opinion was only that of Professor Pepper, and that the jury needed to be warned in some way that the medical witnesses were not in the true sense independent. For their part the defence team commissioned the City Surveyor, A.C. Bothams, to carry out some experiments on the dispersal of blood from a thrown knife. The experiments were repeated six or seven times. They showed that when a bloody knife was thrown down so that its handle struck a door or door case, blood was thrown from the knife, not onto the door or its lintel (except in one case out of the half-dozen or so trials), but in a shower in all directions away, such as to account for the blood marks on Flora's blouse. Dr Maurice's findings confirmed the results of Bothams' experiments, as well as providing innocent explanations for the bloodstains on Flora's skirt, such as blood from food preparation or from lancing Teddy's stump.

But what, then, of the damp and badly bloodstained handkerchief? It seems unlikely – given the state of her blouse – that if Flora were simply an accessory to the murder, she would have got any blood on her hands. It is almost certain, however, that the assailant did, and that Flora, if helping them to clean up, would have moistened a clean handkerchief in some water from the wash stand and then would have taken it back, not knowing quite how bloody it was, and would have taken it through the kitchen and got blood on the table cloth. She perhaps would have intended to rinse it out but, with someone

at the back door, had no time to dispose of it except by putting it into her skirt pocket. By later on in the evening when she was asked for a handkerchief by Emily Sweetman, she pulled out the bloody handkerchief, again not realising how bloody it was. Perhaps by that time she knew but was past caring, and ready only to commit herself to the care of the "God of all Grace".

Yet again, though, Trethowan's briefing to counsel for the second trial argues that no reliance could be placed on either of the two bloodstained handkerchiefs as evidence of clearing up blood after the murder, as both Flora and Teddy had recent minor injuries, and Flora claimed that both the bloodstained handkerchiefs were used by Teddy to mop up blood from his injured ear, which he had picked at shortly before his death. There are two difficulties with that explanation. Firstly, when Kempe examined the boy's ear on November 3, the injury on his ear had begun to clear up, and had already formed a dry scab, which one presumes was there three days earlier. Secondly, the handkerchief was damp as well as freshly bloody when Flora handed it to Emily Sweetman; so she testified at both trials. The blood could have come, as Flora maintained, from the cut on her nose – even though that had happened on Thursday 29 October, and the dampness from her weeping.

The bloodstains on the tablecloth and elsewhere

There was a clear trail of blood from the bedroom, down the stairs and into the kitchen which on the face of it is inconsistent with the notion of an alleged assailant leaving the house through the front door. So what is one to make of this trail? Wilks noted two or three spots of blood on the floor at the right-hand side of the bed and at the foot of the bed, and a spot of blood on the landing near the banisters. Pepper, at the inquest, reporting his findings from his visit on 8 November, identified the blood on the landing more specifically: 'a large drop, like a blood mark, on the landing at the top of the stairs, on the left of the stair head coming down', and of blood marks on the wallpaper from the other side of the staircase – 'the staircase paper on the left-hand side going up.' There is then a break in the trail as far as the kitchen, but the presence of several spots of blood out as far as the landing, blood marks on the staircase wall, and blood marks on the tablecloth seems to imply some object, laden with blood, being carried into the kitchen – an object such as the bloody and damp handkerchief which Flora proffered to Emily Sweetman when the latter offered to bathe her face. The difficulty with that explanation is that Flora produced the handkerchief from her skirt pocket. At the jury trials Pepper gave his reasons for the marks on the tablecloth not coming from the skirt or the blouse, but from an object carried in the hand. The blouse marks were not smeared, and the marks on the skirt would if transferred to the tablecloth have produced a horizontal mark, parallel to the edge of the cloth. Instead, Pepper opined at the April trial, 'the marks were caused by a duster or handkerchief.' But no such object was found during a search of the premises, and, as we have noted above, the bloodstained handkerchief on Flora's person was inside her skirt pocket

Goddard tried his best to explain away the tablecloth blood marks, by suggesting that they could have resulted from Flora preparing butcher's meat, a crass idea which would never have persuaded a jury which included women, and which in any case took no account of the fact that some at least of the marks must have been on the vertical surface of the tablecloth. But another more likely possibility of which Goddard made much was that of the blood marks in the kitchen being spread by any number of visitors to the house on the night of the murder, and this argument has some validity. The only two people to have had really close contact with the murdered boy's blood were the two medical practitioners, Wilks and Row. Before the magistrates Wilks deposed, 'When I left the bedroom there was no blood on me or on my clothes', and Row stated, 'It was not possible for any blood to have got from my hands or clothes onto a tablecloth on the table in the kitchen.'

However, Walter Steer went up to the bedroom three times before the Police arrived, on the second time going close enough to the bed to touch Teddy's face. He went up again when Richardson and Stephens were there, and a fifth time with water and

cloths for the doctors. He returned with the pail half-full of bloody water and the cloths therein, taking them through to the scullery to wring them out and place them on the window-sill. Sarah Butt followed Steer into the bedroom, to hold up a lamp for him and to do so for the doctors, so was probably there for at least ten minutes. Finally there was Thomas Rawlins, who went into Teddy's bedroom at Flora's bidding to determine what had happened, again when the doctors were there, when he was looking for bloodstains, again when he brought water and a towel for the doctors to wash and dry their hands, and a fourth time when the police were there, when he held aloft a lamp for a short time. On his return from that fourth visit Rawlins walked through the kitchen, and it was not until he came back through the kitchen that he noticed the blood on the cloth. As Trethowan noted in his briefing for the second jury trial: 'Rawlins in his evidence says that he noticed the blood on the table cloth after he had passed it, and the inference can be drawn that as he did not see it when approaching the table on his way to the scullery, it was not then there.' Indeed, this was the cloth on the table at which ten people, including Inspector Stroud, sat down to afternoon tea on Monday 2 November,[5] without, apparently, noticing or commenting on its state.

The knife and the clearing-up of the house

The place where the knife was discovered and the state of the passage between the front door should have provided the litmus tests for the veracity of the central component of Flora Haskell's narrative – namely, someone throwing a bloodstained object at her which turned out to be one of her own knives, and of escaping through her front door.

The knife, at least, seemed to give the lie to Flora's explanation. When it was discovered, having been supposedly thrown down, there were no marks of blood around or near it, consistent with its fall finishing with a jarring impact. Where it lay there was a mark in blood which matched the shape of the blade. In his deposition before the magistrates Wilks stated 'My attention was . . . drawn to a mark on the floor just inside the kitchen door . . . It was a linear mark almost four inches long and was on a piece of linoleum which fitted into the door [case]. It could have been caused by the blade of the knife I have seen resting on it. It was a bloodstain mark. I did not notice any marks of blood near it.' He went on to say that had the knife been thrown down he would have expected to find more than one mark on the floor. Row added 'I saw a mark of blood near the kitchen door on the floor before I went away. It was wet. It was about four inches [long]. If the knife now produced . . . had had blood on it the mark could have been caused by that knife.' One can be fairly confident that the knife Row was shown, Exhibit 20, was the murder weapon and that it was the knife Sergeant Golding picked up, leaving the mark Wilks and Row described. The knife had all the appearance of having been put down, not thrown down, a few minutes before 10.35 when the doctors arrived; but if its fall had been broken by either or both of the kitchen door or Flora's skirt it might have landed gently enough for any blood to puddle below the blade.

As for the assailant leaving by the front door with, one assumes, blood on their clothing and on one hand at least, one might have expected to find a continuation of the bloodstains on the staircase wall paper towards the front of the house. There was, of course, no blood in the passage because it had been mopped up on the morning of 1 November; but the very fact of this occurrence implies that there was something needing mopping up. And that was not all, for Trethowan's case notes reveal that as Mrs Carter was washing the passage, so Flora's friend Miss Lawrence was washing the kitchen floor. We will never know how far in front of the bottom of the staircase any bloodstains extended, but the fact that the floor was mopped from the front door to the threshold of the kitchen implies there was blood in front of the staircase as far forward as the front door, as well as from the foot of the stairs and the threshold of the kitchen where the knife was found. This is part, and perhaps a key element, of the insufficiency of evidence which allowed Flora to walk free. And if the assailant, as Wilks suggested, had blood on the hand that held the knife, the hand with which they had held Teddy's head steady would, if used to open the front door, leave no trace of blood thereon.

Flora's explanation of events, including the mysterious caller

We know Flora Haskell's explanation of the events of the days and hours leading to her son's death, both through the testimonies of her neighbours, and her own statements to the police. At the heart of Flora's defence is the person throwing down the knife and bringing about the bloodstains all over her clothing. That vignette sums up the idea of the other party, a stranger, committing the unthinkable act and of Flora being quite away from the crime scene. The doubts arise, firstly, from the strong possibility that the bloodstains on her clothing, or at least those on the blouse, were the result of her being close to her child as he breathed his last. Secondly, there is the likelihood that the bloody knife was *placed* where it was found. On these two factors alone her defence could have foundered, and all the others, whether in her statements or the testimony of others as to what Flora said at the time could have been taken for mere distractions, beginning with the story of the mysterious caller the night before the murder who is possibly to be associated with the man offering Teddy twopence for his name and address. Both of these come from Flora alone. There are other oddities. Flora claimed to be wearing an apron, and to be able to identify to Superintendent Stephens the one she wore – which had no bloodstains at all, let alone any to match those on the skirt worn underneath. When Flora came to the door to Percy, her hair was partly down, as it might have been if she had been involved in some violent physical activity; but she had not. And then there was the cry of alarm that someone had murdered her Teddy when, if she were altogether innocent, she would not have known that to be the case.

What saved Flora was, on the one hand, the series of alternative explanations for the most apparently damning pieces of evidence. Thus, the falling knife really *did* shower her in blood, and land in such a way as to leave the blood mark that it did; her panicking response was indeed to cry out that Teddy had been murdered, whether rationally she knew it or not; and there is no reason why Flora should not have been wearing an apron on for part of the evening (e.g. to bathe Teddy) and to take it off later. On the other hand, there was the slew of anecdotes and professional observations – ranging from those of Flora buying a comic and some sweets for Teddy, and of telling Gertrude Steer she would be a toff in her new jacket, to those of Wilks and Mackay declaring that there was neither history of mental illness nor of observed insanity militating against her fitness to plead. The clincher was Flora's greeting to her brother directly before her famous observation to Matilda Sheppard. To him she said, 'Oh Dick! Oh Dick! I didn't do it! Do you think I could have done it? Fancy them saying I am insane.' And as Trethowan noted in his briefing for the second jury trial, 'It is therefore scarcely likely that the Prisoner would have said to Mrs. Sheppard almost directly afterwards "If I did it, I don't remember it", unless some sort of leading question were asked her.'

Motives for the murder

When the inquest jury delivered its verdict, they found that Teddy had been murdered, and that Flora had committed the deed; but, they wished to stress, during a moment of temporary insanity. In other words, the jury was thinking of the M'Naghten Rule, by which a defendant can argue their innocence of a crime if they can claim that they were insane at the time of committing the act prompting the criminal charge. There are two "limbs" to the M'Naghten Rule: firstly that one is so deranged that they do not know what they are doing; secondly that they are aware of committing the act but are too deranged to discriminate right from wrong, and hence to know that they are committing a wrongdoing. Either one of these circumstances might have been invoked by Flora's defence; but neither was, and perhaps the fact that Henry Mackay at Devizes had reported repeatedly that she was quite sane enough to plead to the charge may have been a factor in that decision. There is ample evidence of Flora's love for her son; there was also no hint that any strengthening of her ties with Alfred Mold posed any threat to Teddy. She said that if ever she did remarry, she would continue to work to keep her son. And, incidentally, although Flora had recently increased the premium on her son's life insurance, she did not stand to gain from the enhanced payout on that insurance for a year; so

money was not a consideration. Similarly, the notion mooted of her intention to move away and to more commodious surroundings does not bear scrutiny when viewed alongside her actions. It was true Flora looked at a house to rent in Ashley Road, where there would have been more room for drying. Yet this in no way lends credence to the claim that she was seeking somehow to escape to a better life in a more salubrious area of the city. An advertisement placed in the *Salisbury Times* in 1907 by the firm of Case in their capacity of letting agents includes a house in Ashley Road with an enormous back yard, and costing 6s. 0d. per week in rent. The sixpence difference between that rent and what Flora was paying would not even have bought half a pound of butter.

Was there some fear for Teddy's health which might have led Flora to consider saving him from the fate his father had undergone? Flora had spent a great deal of time and effort tending her husband, and, as her brother said, keeping the family together whilst her husband was undergoing a rest cure at Ventnor on the Isle of Wight. But no sooner did he die of pulmonary tuberculosis than her son succumbed to the disease; this time in the hip joint, necessitating an amputation. Her efforts were rewarded when the sickly child was brought back to health; and yet the disease never quite left the boy, as there was ample testimony to ongoing problems. There are references in Alfred Walter Noble's testimonies to the stump bleeding and discharging regularly, and to the need for the mother to lance the site of the wound to release the built-up pus. She often slept with the boy in case he needed comfort or medical attention at night. At the same time Teddy could bear the burden of his ill-health sufficiently lightly to have an active social and sporting life – whether being in and out of his cousins' home next door, or keeping goal in football games, or filing football reports to the local paper. He was a happy child, perhaps even a bit of a handful, a scamp at times; but there was nothing immediately in his state of health to lead Flora to believe she would soon be doing for Teddy what she had had to do for his father.

The one outstanding possibility is that Flora, rightly or wrongly, was concerned for *her own* health and feared for the future for Teddy and herself, if she were not able to keep him, as she stated she always would do, even were she to remarry. The evidence at the time for this hypothesis is slender but not to be discounted. Flora, even without the psychological burdens of a second bereavement and the threat of a severe punishment, was obviously not a strong woman. In court she fainted and succumbed to her emotions repeatedly. Photographic evidence and the newspaper descriptions show she was slightly built and petite. Goddard referred to Flora as 'the poor, frail, weak thing in the dock.' The fact that in prison she put on over a stone in weight is testimony to a hard-lived life on the outside. Although on good terms with her neighbours, Flora kept herself to herself, with Alice Steer describing her as a 'quiet neighbour.' Is it possible that she knew that within herself there already lay the cause of her death, and that her remaining years were marked off? If so that would explain why although she was fond of Mold, she approached the idea of marriage with caution, scepticism even. Flora also seems not to have realised or to have believed, despite the faith in Teddy's future abilities expressed by her brother-in-law, that Teddy would be in any position to make a livelihood for himself. This was so despite her having a brother in the printing trade and neighbours on both sides who were compositors, so Flora had first-hand knowledge that there were careers for which Teddy would in no way have been disqualified by his disability. Instead she believed she would always have to work to keep Teddy. So maybe, *just maybe*, Flora felt that rather than for Teddy to be thrown destitute into the street or the workhouse by her own death, when his own life and health wasn't guaranteed, it would be better for him to be taken now, and were she to be implicated with fatal consequences, that would be to bring something forward that, deep down, she might have suspected was coming to her anyway. But at best, bearing in mind the state of medical knowledge of tuberculosis, this can only be a weak hypothesis.

Conclusion

The prosecution's case, argued cogently and persuasively, was that Flora alone had killed her son. No motive was adduced other than a temporary frenzy. All that counsel for the defence had to do was to show that the other side had not proved *beyond all reasonable doubt* that the available evidence demonstrated Flora's guilt. These were the key tests: *reasonable doubt* and *available evidence*. The evidence to hand was not sufficient to assuage reasonable doubt. Had the charge of murder been along the lines of Flora being an accessory before, during or after the deed, the outcome could have been different and might have been more interesting. In such a scenario, Flora was present when Teddy died, for it is unlikely that the wound that was inflicted could have been done without the crime scene being illuminated. Were Flora to have held up the nightlight which she described in her first statement—the brass lamp left on the dressing table—while standing close to the assailant, that would account for the bloodstains on her blouse and her skirt, and for them being on her right side while her left side was shielded by the assailant. Then, as they departed the scene, she would have time to straighten up the bedclothes and place the lamp safely on the landing beside the stairs.

Assuming, for the moment, that this hypothesis – of Flora being an accessory to the murder – is correct, it would be possible for the murderer to be engaged to despatch Teddy by some less gruesome means—such as suffocation; or possibly there would have been two plans, depending on how deeply asleep Teddy was. The use of the knife would be a fall-back in the event of Teddy waking up or the kind of distractions we know to have happened, with first Wyatt and then Noble coming to the door. If circumstances dictated the adoption of the swifter and more awful path towards death, that would account for Flora's appalled reaction seen by Leate. On this hypothesis Flora had been party to murder, but, confronted with its bloody ghastliness had turned in shock, horror and outrage upon her partner in crime, following him down the street a few paces before returning to her home and raising the alarm. Even if she knew all along about the use of the knife –and knew enough to place it, or perhaps more likely to have it placed, still wet with blood on the kitchen threshold – it is not difficult to imagine Flora remaining calm while the murder took place and in its immediate aftermath. Then, as realisation of the full enormity of what had happened dawned, Flora succumbed to hysteria — a sort of post-traumatic stress disorder — and turned in anguish and remorse upon her partner in crime.

Were this person to have escaped — northwards along Meadow Road, and into Coldharbour Lane or into James Street or into the cul-de-sac opposite, leading via the backs of houses into Marsh Lane — not only would that be consistent with Leate's account, but it would not necessarily conflict with what the other early eyewitnesses — Herbert Primmer, Gertrude Skutt and Lily Stretch — saw. They were walking along York Road, and their attention, like that of Rawlins, Steer and others, was not drawn to the attack until Flora began screaming in panic and despair. By that time the person Leate saw was gone — gone from Meadow Road, probably gone from the Gaol Ground altogether.

The one difficulty with which we are confronted is that of reconciling what Samuel Leate claimed and Percy Noble testified. According to Leate the man emerges from the house which he later identified as 40 Meadow Road, followed by the woman, weeping and crying, and then she turns back whilst he escapes, and she then remains at her doorstep, her cries becoming ever louder as she raises the alarm and is surrounded by her neighbours. Of when this happened we have no precise record. In young Noble's account, his aunt acknowledges his knock at the door with the words called out, "All right"; yet, as mentioned above, he has to knock twice to get an answer and her response is made "Not immediately". Then there is the pushing back of the chair, and directly afterwards the "thump", the screams and then immediately afterwards his aunt coming to the back door to raise the alarm. To reconcile the two narratives, an assumption has to be made regarding Flora's whereabouts at the time Leate testified that he 'did not pay any particular attention to this [Flora standing, weeping in her doorway as the man she had followed disappeared northwards], but walked on until I was half way between York Road and St Paul's Road.' That is, that Flora heard and had time to respond to Percy's knock at her back door, even taking some time to respond.

Leate, meanwhile, sauntering along the southern half of Meadow Road, takes no further notice until Flora starts screaming at the top of her voice; by which time he has walked over two hundred feet, and only then turns round to see what all the commotion is about. Walking at three miles an hour, he has been paying no attention to Flora for about 50 seconds. This would be long enough for Flora, distraught at her front door, on hearing the knock at the back to compose herself enough to tiptoe along the passage and call out 'all right', in an ordinary tone of voice, push the chair in her kitchen to one side, jump and then scream out and begin her act, starting with Percy as her audience. The knife has been laid down, waiting for her to "discover" it on her return from her little trip out for which she had turned the gas down: all Flora would have had to do is to account for the bloodstains on her clothing, for which she promptly invented the story of the man jumping down the stairs and throwing the knife at her. She could loosen her hair with a tug at a couple of hair grips as she came to the back door to answer to whoever was there to make it look as if she had been in some sort of a struggle or tussle. Or perhaps Flora's hair, pinned up all evening, started to come down as she tried to chase after the man. As for Percy claiming to know that the scraping of the chair came from the kitchen, but the thump from the passage, when he is standing outside the door with the blind pulled down over the adjacent window and the gas turned down, it is a wonder the prosecution did not make more of this. And when Flora said to Walter Steer, breathless and in panic, 'Man round the corner' one is compelled to note that she did not say *which* corner; but neither did Steer ask, jumping instead to a conclusion which may well have been the wrong one.

Many factors weakened the Prosecution's case, including the lack of a motive, the alternative explanations for all the circumstantial evidence (however far-fetched these might seem; because they were put to the test), and the sheer implausibility of Flora's involvement judging by her actions and reactions. What gives the lie to the prosecution case that Flora was implicated in the death of her son is the fact that if guilty, she had any number of ways of covering her tracks, the visits of John Wyatt and

Percy Noble notwithstanding. The alternative scenario, that there really was, as Flora claimed, some person who gained access to her property without her knowing deserves all due consideration.

We have seen from our examination of the quarter of an hour from 10.15 p.m. on 31 October just how easy it would be someone to slink quietly away, and if witnesses weren't exactly in the right place at the right time such a person would not be noticed. It would have been just as easy for someone to gain access to 40 Meadow Road, if they picked their moment. There would have been plenty of opportunity during the early evening of 31 October, when according to Flora's first statement, Teddy was out of the house, and so was she, just after 6.00 for a few minutes, leaving the house empty and the back door open, and again, from when she returned until about 6.30, having left both doors unlocked. That would have been time enough for anyone to gain entrance to the property, find the knife, and, not knowing when Flora or someone might return home, perhaps be prepared to secrete themselves in the box room. If that seems too far-fetched and indeed risky, there were good opportunities much later.

Flora was round at the Nobles' at 9.35 to deliver some laundry, and stayed about five minutes: this is from her brother-in-law's evidence, and Flora does not mention the call in her statement, as she does the job of bathing her son before putting him to bed at 9.40 or 9.45. That would have been an opportunity, but a risky one, with Teddy still being up and about, or, if there was any confusion over the timings and hence the order of these two events, at least still awake. The best opportunity to enter No. 40 would have been a little later, when Flora went to the outside lavatory, either just after she put Teddy to bed at around 9.45 p.m., or at 10.00, after Gertrude Steer had left, when she heard the church clock strike.[6] An intruder in the house might well have heard Flora lock the back door just after 10.00. Then they would have to wait until the household was asleep and the streets

were dark before conducting a thorough search for money, with the knife at the ready – or perhaps in this case simply grabbed opportunistically – if anyone came to.

Perhaps that happened; and perhaps the thief took a chance when Flora answered the door to Wyatt, unlocking the front door to do so, but not relocking it. The cue to action would have been Wyatt's call, but by then Teddy was asleep – but not that deeply. If the thief was witnessed by Teddy as he was rifling the broken drawer, he would need to act swiftly and decisively to silence the boy before he could raise the alarm. Perhaps Teddy had unwittingly connived at his fate by accepting twopence for his address; and perhaps, now, before he could utter a cry for his mother, he met his nemesis. As the villain escaped, a dog belonging to Henry and Matilda Hawkins at No. 29 barked furiously and tried its best to clear the fence in pursuit of the stranger. The dog, according to Trethowan's case notes, was quite at ease with the Hawkins's neighbours but disliked strangers, 'and being a "scent" dog, anyone coming up with fresh blood on [their] clothes w[oul]d excite it, and account for its wild behaviour.' Such a turn of events can be explained by the story Flora told the police and the testimonies of others. Even her appeal, that Teddy was already killed, could be explained as her declared anxiety – even, perhaps, a sense of foreboding – about the mysterious caller now being fulfilled.

Who that person was is now unknown, and the fact that this is so can be attributed at least in part to the manner in which the investigation into Teddy's death was carried out by the Police. It was of the form of a game: utterly serious, but a game in which the genuine objective of the enquiry – the identity of the actual killer – was lost. This happened in pursuit of objectives which were chimaerical, because based on hunch and suspicion – namely, the possibility firstly that Mold and secondly Flora might be guilty. The pursuit cost the Police time which they did not have, granting freedom to the villain.

17

Epilogue

RICHARD CARTER, writing on 5 April 1909, said that Flora would be having 'a complete rest and change for a few weeks', but it seems that she never returned to Salisbury. The 1909 directory for the city lists 40 Meadow Road standing empty; that for 1911 shows one Richard W. Allen as the occupant, and in 1912 the house was again listed empty. Meanwhile, elsewhere in the Gaol Ground, life returned to normal and over time people moved on with their lives. Possibly because of the unhappy memories of Teddy's death and the subsequent legal proceedings over many months, perhaps simply as an aspect of mobility in the area and the city, few of those most immediately involved remained long after 1909.

NUMBER 40 (LEFT) AND 42 MEADOW ROAD TAKEN
SHORTLY AFTER THE CRIME, 1908.
© *Timothy W. Frank Walker and Ann Richardson Whittle,
grandchildren of Frank Richardson, Chief Constable.*

So by 1912 those who had moved away included the Manningses and the Nobles either side of No. 40, also the Steers at No. 36, the Rawlinses at No. 26, the Lodges at No. 20 and William Eccott at No. 48. On the other side of the road, the Hayneses at No. 31 moved away, and the Houses moved into their old house from No. 27. Likewise the Skutts moved from No. 23 up to No. 39, on the corner of York Road. The Hawkinses, whose dog had noisily noticed something amiss on the night of the murder, remained at No. 29. John Moxham Cooper had moved on from 14 St Paul's Road, while his mother, Mrs Matilda Cooper remained at 27 York Road. Some did not move far. The Manningses moved to 17 Clifton Road, the Nobles to 84 York Road, the Rawlinses to 19 George Street, the Lodges to 8 George Street and William Eccott to 2 Meadow View, one of a commodious pair of houses at the far end of Avon Terrace. Among others still living where they were at the time of the inquest and trials were the Haydens at 24 Sidney Street, the Butts at 40 York Road[1] and their namesake Edward Butt at 27 George Street. Opposite him at No. 32 was Frederick Stretch, father of Lily, and Emily Sweetman still kept shop for Mrs Saunders. Walter Steer and his family moved to the heart of the city at 43 Bedwin Street; they were directly affected by the Great War with the death of their second son Ernest on 3 July 1918 at Aubigny-en-Artois.

By 1925, only Ernest House was still living in Meadow Road, and at No. 31, with Henry Hawkins his neighbour at No. 29. The Haydens were still living at 24 Sidney Street, joined by the Hayneses at No. 10. The Butts and Emily Sweetman remained at their respective addresses in York Road. Edward Butt had moved from 27 George Street, as had Lily Stretch from No. 32, unsurprisingly as she and Herbert

Primmer had married in the autumn of 1915, and by 1925 they had moved into No. 7 George Street, and Herbert had found occupation on the railways as a platelayer. The Rawlinses and Lodges were still in George Street.

The other witness, the stranger in the Gaol Ground whose evidence given at the coroner's inquest might have made all the difference at the trial was Francis Samuel Leate. A native of Taunton, he came to Salisbury in 1901 and worked for his father, a saddler and harness-maker at 57 Fisherton Street and 4 Butcher Row. Later he moved to the centre of Salisbury, firstly to the Three Swans Yard, Winchester Street, on his own account, repairing sports equipment, then for Wiltons in New Canal in the same line of business. An upright member of the community, Leate was for years a member of the choir at the Congregational Church, and in politics an avowed Liberal. He married in 1912, and died in April 1956 at the age of 71, having retired only two and a half years before

Amongst the other participants in the trial, the two local heroes, William Trethowan and Herbert Wilks did not survive long. Trethowan, a Cornishman, had come to Salisbury to serve his articles in the office of George Nodder, becoming a solicitor and partner in the firm in October 1890, having married his senior partner's daughter in the spring of 1882. Not someone who played a large part in public life he was nevertheless, according to his obituarist in the *Salisbury Times*, 'widely known as a very capable and genial legal advocate. He had a big practice, and his professional services were sought in a wide district around Salisbury. . . He was . . . a sympathetic friend to all deserving causes.' Trethowan was for many years the city's deputy coroner, relinquishing the post in 1911 on his appointment as Coroner for South Wiltshire; he was also a governor of the Infirmary. He died quite suddenly, on Friday 3 January 1913, at the age of 56, having worked until his office closed the previous day, and feeling unwell only when he awoke on the Friday morning. He died before his doctor could arrive, presumably of a heart attack. As the *Salisbury Times* commented, 'His untimely death is mourned by a wide circle of friends in town and country.'

Wilks was the second son of the Revd Theodore Chambers Wilks, Vicar of Woking, and his career included service as a house surgeon at the Infirmary and partnership with Messrs Fawson Lee and Levi Stevenson Luckham, before opening his own surgery. He remained an honorary surgeon at the Infirmary, and was a medical officer at the Salisbury and South Wilts Provident Dispensary. But in 1910 he fell ill, and had to retire from general practice and resign from his appointments. He hoped to take up a post on board ship, where he believed the voyage would aid his recovery. However, before the plan could be put into action his health deteriorated, and he moved into his mother's and sister's home in De Vaux Place and into their care, dying within a few weeks, on 4 June 1911 at the age of 43. His obituarist in the *Salisbury Journal* noted that 'Mr Wilks was a member of the Salisbury Town Council, having for several years sat as one of the representatives of Fisherton Ward; and he was formerly a surgeon in the 1st Wilts Volunteer Rifle Corps. A staunch Conservative, he worked hard for his cause, and for two years held the post of chairman of the Fisherton Conservative Club. He was a keen sportsman, often riding with the Wilton Hounds, and was fond of rod and gun. As an expert swimmer, he was captain of the Salisbury Swimming Club; whilst formerly he was an active supporter of local cricket and football clubs.'

Gilbert Kempe, the Police Surgeon, like Trethowan and Wilks never lived to enjoy retirement. He was born in Shoreham-by-Sea in 1872, the son of a local doctor, Charles Marshall Kempe, and educated at Brighton and Durham, where he gained his doctorate in medicine. An early appointment as house surgeon at the Royal Sussex County Hospital, Brighton, was followed by a spell on a ship of the Castle Line. On his return in 1895, he joined Harcourt Coates's practice, shortly afterwards becoming a partner therein, and in 1899 was appointed a surgeon on the honorary staff at the Infirmary, becoming senior honorary surgeon in 1912. For his service to wounded officers hospitalised at Longford Castle and Wilton House, Kempe was appointed an O.B.E., and during his time in practice in Salisbury he was, in addition to his work for the Police, a consultant to the cottage hospitals at Andover and Shaftesbury. His obituarist in the *Salisbury Journal* wrote 'Both by the general public and by his professional colleagues, Dr Kempe was regarded as among the most brilliant surgeons of the day. He had effected remarkable cures during his career.' Of a piece with his profession, Kempe's major outside interest was his membership of the Elias de Dereham Masonic Lodge. His later life was clouded by illness and bereavement, his wife of 27 years and the mother of his three children dying whilst he was ill with pneumonia and unconscious at the time. He remarried eighteen months later, in January 1930 and shortly afterwards fell ill. After an operation the following December, Kempe passed his final year in a nursing home, dying at the age of 59 in February 1932.

Among the local police, Frank Richardson continued to serve the City as Chief Constable for over twenty years, retiring on 4 October 1929. Born in Gloucester in 1872, the son of a policeman and

FRANK RICHARDSON ON HIS APPOINTMENT AS CHIEF CONSTABLE.
© *Timothy W. Frank Walker and Ann Richardson Whittle, grandchildren of Frank Richardson, Chief Constable.*

with three brothers in various police forces, his progress was rapid, having joined the Gloucestershire force in 1893, and proceeding to Chief Constable of Salisbury only ten years later. The major event in his career was the railway crash of 1906 and it is for his management of that disaster that his name is recalled today. At his retirement, the importance of the Salisbury Police during the Great War was remarked upon, when the presence of the Southern Command HQ transformed the city into a significant military centre. Richardson was also commended for the smooth running of the policing of the several Royal visits during his office. He enjoyed a long retirement, dying in August 1952 in his eighty-first year.

Dew, of course, went on to great things. His next major case involved a Russian named Friedlauski, who had established himself in London under the identity of Conrad Harms in the early 1900s and married in December 1906. His business interests in London collapsed, and he deserted his wife of eight months and decamped to New York. In March 1909 Harms was appointed a clerk in the foreign department of the banking firm of J.S. Bache & Co, where, owing to its lax procedures, he managed to defraud the bank of nearly £1,640. He promptly resigned and returned to London to launder the money and, for good measure, purchase some binoculars and a gold watch from the Crown Emporium Jewellery Company in the Strand. It was the watch that was Harms's undoing. He then travelled to Vienna, pausing only to write from Dover to his erstwhile employers to explain his theft and promising to repay the money at 5% interest as long as neither the police nor the press were involved. At this point Harms's London bank and Scotland Yard were notified, and Dew was assigned to investigate. Dew was not optimistic, as it was clear that Harms was on the continent. Harms, however, soon returned to London as 'Henry Clifford', with a new wife. Meanwhile, Dew had learned of the purchase of the gold watch, and now instructed the shopkeeper to find a way of detaining Harms if ever he showed up again. This he did, on 26 June, to request a refund for his watch, and was asked to return shortly for the proprietor to authorise the refund. On his return he was met by two policemen from Bow Street Station. In prison awaiting trial Harms claimed he was his own cousin and that the similarity in looks notwithstanding – for a photograph of him had been found, and was the basis of his arrest – he maintained it was a case of mistaken identity. But, despite his best efforts to pass himself off as another, including to his first wife, Harms was convicted and sentenced to six years. According to Dew he was 'one of the cleverest swindlers I struck throughout my police career.'

Dew's last and most celebrated case began on 30 June 1910 when his superintendent, Frank Froest called him in to hear the story told by Froest's acquaintances, Mr and Mrs John Nash, that their cousin, Cora Crippen, had been reported as having died in America. They found this suspicious, not least because her name did not appear on any passenger lists consistent with her husband's claim that she had left for America in February, and also that cheques with her signature had been presented in England up until the time of her death on 23 March. Something prompted Dew to take on the case himself, rather than relinquish it to the uniformed branch to enquire into a missing person, only for it to be referred to Scotland Yard if any suspicious circumstances came to light. Dew's enquiries amongst Cora Crippen's friends brought to light a raft of curious items of evidence. These items included a letter of 20 March from Crippen with news of Cora's serious illness while in America, a telegram of 24 March saying she had died in Los Angeles, which fact could not be corroborated from public records, and hasty notes to Cora's friends in the Music Hall Ladies' Guild explaining her departure to visit a sick relative, but not in her handwriting. There were other concerns – Crippen appearing with his secretary, Ethel Le Neve, at the Guild's Benevolent Fund Ball wearing one of Cora's brooches, and Crippen pawning his wife's jewellery.

Dew and a detective sergeant paid an un-announced visit on Crippen on 8 July to explain his concerns, and Crippen gave a statement of about 3,000 words in which he claimed to have made up the entire story about Cora's death, because, he said, she had walked out on him, and he had wanted to avoid the scandal which would have arisen. At that stage he had no suspicions: the idea of arresting Crippen 'did not enter my mind', as he later related, and Dew commented 'From his manner one could only have assumed that he was a much maligned man eager only to clear the matter up by telling the whole truth. I was impressed by the man's demeanour. It was impossible to be otherwise.' A statement from Ethel Le Neve and a search of the premises revealed nothing untoward, but Dew's nagging doubts were confirmed when, without warning, the couple disappeared. Dew now had the opportunity to search Crippen's home unhindered, where, in the cellar, he discovered human remains under the floor, buried in slaked lime which had preserved them rather than the quicklime which would have obliterated them.

A warrant was issued against Crippen and his mistress for the murder of Cora. The couple had left the country, meanwhile, travelling to Brussels as John Robinson, father and teenage son, and then to Antwerp, whence they sailed for Quebec on the SS *Montrose*. Alerted by pictures of Crippen and Le Neve in a continental edition of the *Daily Mail*, the *Montrose*'s captain, Henry Kendall had his wireless operator send a message relaying his 'strong suspicion' that his odd passengers were the fugitive pair. It was the breakthrough that Dew needed and he obtained permission to travel from Liverpool to Quebec on the White Star liner the *Laurentic*, overtaking the *Montrose*, and arriving two days ahead. With two Canadian policemen, Dew was rowed out from Father Point on the St Lawrence River to intercept the *Montrose*, to identify the couple and have them arrested. The evidence against Crippen was overwhelming; that against Le Neve far from it, and the outcome, of his conviction and her acquittal was no surprise to Dew. Crippen appealed against the sentence, but his appeal was turned down by Mr Justice Darling, who had presided over Flora's second trial.

By a strange coincidence on the same day, Dew announced his retirement after nearly twenty-nine years' service, at the age of 47. In his career he had been commended or rewarded by his Commissioner and the judiciary about 130 times, the culmination of which was the exemplary certificate awarded on his retirement on 5 December 1910, showing that no-one had ever lodged a complaint against him. Whilst he received a good pension, of two-thirds his final salary, it was augmented substantially when he brought no fewer than nine libel actions against newspapers during 1911. One of these, the *Daily Chronicle,* had alleged that Crippen had confessed to the murder whilst in Dew's charge, and Dew had revealed all to the press, in blatant contravention of his duty to remain silent on a case under investigation. For this libel Dew was awarded £400, while *Mainly about People* admitted the libel that he had been slow off the mark to shadow Crippen before he had a chance to escape, and paid him an undisclosed sum in damages. Other cases were settled out of court. In retirement, Dew enjoyed gardening, and gave interviews on or wrote for the press on notorious cases past and present, including Agatha Christie's disappearance in 1926, the fatal shooting of PC George Gutteridge in 1927 and the Croydon poisoning mystery of 1929. After his wife's death in 1927, Dew moved to Worthing, where he remarried. He wrote his memoirs, initially as a serialisation in *Thomson's Weekly News* to rebut an erroneous feature article on the Crippen case in the *Daily Mail*, with the book *I caught Crippen* being published in 1938. Dew died aged 84 in December 1947.

The *éminence grise* of the medical witnesses, and the man on whose interpretation of the evidence Dew hoped to secure his conviction, was Professor Augustus Joseph Pepper. Born in 1849, he was destined for a stellar career from the outset, securing an exhibition at University College Hospital, London and gold medals in anatomy, physiology and therapy in the examination for the degree of Bachelor of Medicine, graduating also as a Bachelor of Surgery and gaining gold medals in medicine and its specialist branches of obstetrics and forensics and election to Fellowship of the Royal College of Surgeons, all in 1876. He became a Fellow of University College, where he was surgical registrar and demonstrator in anatomy, before becoming consulting surgeon at St Mary's Hospital, London. He wrote a standard text of the day, *Surgical pathology*, which ran to four editions by 1894, and he was a member of the Harveian Society and of the New York Medico-Legal

Society. As a teacher and pathologist alone Pepper's life's work would be reckoned distinguished, but it was his career as a consultant to the Home Office which brought him to the public's notice. He was appointed Home Office pathologist in the 1890s, and his vast experience can be gauged by the extraordinary diversity of the cases with which he dealt. We have seen at length his interpretative skills in respect of recent trauma in the Haskell case. Less than two years later, with the Crippen case the deployment of his expertise had more to do with forensic archaeology, as was also the case when his discovery of another buried female corpse led to the solving of the Moat Farm mystery and the conviction of another murderer. Pepper also gave evidence in the bizarre Druce case, which turned upon whether or not Thomas Charles Druce of the Baker Street Bazaar was actually the Duke of Portland. The series of cases and the underlying claim was finally thrown out following an exhumation in Highgate Cemetery in 1907. In the words of his obituarist in *The Times*, Pepper 'was largely responsible for the raising of medico-legal work to its present high level in this country.' Retiring in 1919, Pepper died at the age of 86 in December 1935.

Flora's was not the only murder trial in which Rayner Goddard played a part. Whilst on the Western Circuit Goddard prosecuted in a number of murder trials, but few if any of these were of legal or historical significance, as there were by and large no issues regarding identity or matters of evidential interest. But the Haskell Case sealed his growing reputation, and in the words of his biographer he 'continued to ride the Circuit with ever-increasing success.' In those last, golden years before the outbreak of war Goddard had all that one might ask of life, with a family life (for he had three daughters), homes in London and Lulworth Cove, and a career he enjoyed. The Great War reduced the amount of circuit work, but Goddard was busy with work as the honorary secretary of the Barristers' Benevolent Association until 1917 and from 1913 his membership of the Bar Council. Because of his wife's increasing frailty and as a result increasing family responsibilities, Goddard's wartime service was confined to work as a Special Constable, and, from 1917 as a temporary legal assistant for war work at the Board of Trade. That same year saw him appointed Recorder of Poole, which was succeeded by the recorderships of the cities of Bath in 1925 and Plymouth in 1928. Meanwhile, in 1923 he had taken silk, and built up a sound practice in commercial litigation, and 'his earnings were substantial, his publicity generally meagre', according to his biographer. His forays into public life were few and far between, including membership of a Parliamentary Commission to look into a disciplinary controversy in the Police, and an unsuccessful bid for the seat of South Kensington in the General Election of 1929.

By then, his wife had died, and it fell to his middle daughter to run the household for a number of years. In 1932 Goddard was appointed a High Court Judge on the King's Bench Division, where his disciplined management of proceedings lent itself well to the conduct of civil cases, but to a degree of impatience in that of criminal actions. The Court of Appeal was enlarged in 1938, and, with misgivings which in the event were unjustified, Goddard was appointed one of the three new lords justices, spending much of his time, during the war, in the sandbagged cellars of the Law Courts on the Strand. Despite finding the work congenial, Goddard found himself with time on his hands and secured appointment as a supernumerary judge in the King's Bench Division. In addition to these duties, Goddard conducted an inquiry for the Home Office into corporal punishment procedures at the Hereford Juvenile Court, which exonerated the court in the face of claims of improper behaviour.

Then, in July 1944, on the death of Lord Atkin, Goddard reached what would have appeared to be the peak of his career at the age of 67, with his appointment as a Lord of Appeal in Ordinary, taking the title of Baron Goddard of Aldbourne. But eighteen months later, with the retirement from the office Lord Chief Justice of Lord Caldecote on health grounds, it was Goddard rather than the then Attorney-General, Sir Hartley Shawcross, who was appointed to succeed him. In the immediate aftermath of the war, Goddard was faced with a task of Augean proportions to reform the court system, which he achieved by such measures as the establishment of new Crown Courts in Manchester and Liverpool, the scheme to fix dates for trials, and his support for the Denning Committee proposals to reduce a vast backlog of divorce petitions. But it was as a result of his role in the criminal justice system that Goddard became most celebrated, putting the stamp of his opinions upon his office with his maiden speech in the House of Lords in April 1948, commenting on the Criminal Justice Bill.

Thus, he favoured corporal punishment – as a short, sharp shock – over long imprisonment, and he argued for the retention of the death penalty as the ultimate deterrent. This he did, both out of regard for public opinion – expressed as society's abhorrence for the ultimate theft, that of a life – and for the broken lives of the victims' families and friends. So there was a warmth behind the somewhat gruff public persona embodying retributive justice, and that humanity, of which we have ample evidence in his defence of Flora Haskell, was repeated on many occasions. His obituarist in *The Times* reported that 'On innumerable occasions he and his colleagues in the Court of Criminal Appeal set aside sentences of imprisonment and substituted probation orders, especially when young offenders were concerned, where there seemed a chance that they would respond to lenient treatment. His attitude on the Bench was matched by countless acts of unostentatious and almost surreptitious kindness out of court . . . [including] buying new boots for ragged young burglars, and giving many other prisoners money to help them make a fresh start.'

But Goddard is today remembered for his extremely severe summing up at the trial for the murder of a policeman by Christopher Craig and Derek Bentley, for which the former, who pulled the trigger, was given a life sentence and the latter was hanged. While controversy raged until Bentley's conviction was quashed posthumously in 1998, it must be remembered that Goddard was very far from alone in his judgment at the time and for many years afterwards. Goddard resigned in July 1958 at the age of eighty-one, having served the office of Lord Chief Justice for twelve years. But that was by no means the last to be seen of Rayner Goddard. He returned to the Court of Appeal in 1959 for a year to help clear a backlog of cases, and from 1959 until 1963 he sat in the House of Lords, serving on the judicial committee dealing with a number of high-profile cases, and his final contribution to debates in the Lords was his speech in opposition to Lord Arran's bill to decriminalise homosexual acts between consenting adults. He died in May 1971 at the age of 94.

Goddard's main adversary, John Alderson Foote never fulfilled the promise he had once shown. From Charterhouse he went to St John's College, Cambridge, where he took a first in Classics in 1872, and in 1873 gained the Chancellor's Legal Medal and was senior Whewell Scholar in International Law, Foote won a senior studentship in the 1874 Bar Examinations. After being called to the Bar by Lincoln's Inn the following year, he joined the Western Circuit, where he was appointed a revising barrister in 1892, and counsel to the Post Office on the Western Circuit in 1893. Foote was appointed Recorder of the city of Exeter in 1899, and was elected a bencher of Lincoln's Inn in 1905. And there Foote's career stuck. His obituarist in *The Times* wrote that 'Although he could never have been called a great or a subtle lawyer, he had the learning, the gift of lucid expression, and the practical ability which it was thought might bring him to the Bench.' As time passed, so Foote was passed over for promotion, progressing no further than with the office of Commissioner of Assize on the North-Eastern Circuit, in 1913, and in 1915 appointment as counsel to the University of Cambridge. As his obituarist noted sadly, 'it was a pathetic reflection in Foote's later days that the man who was destined by merit, in the opinion of many, for the High Court Bench, was said to have applied for a County Court Judgeship. He lost much of his practice as he grew older and as men of more superficially attractive qualities gained favour.' Within the profession, however, Foote was highly regarded, both for his legal attainments and his character. He died aged 73 in April 1922.

The Treasury's other representative, from the third day of the inquest onwards, was Thomas Henning Parr and, never rising to the higher ranks of the judiciary, ended his career with a strong local connection, reflective of his origins. Parr was born in 1864, the son of the Revd Canon John Parr,

Prebendary of Shipton at Salisbury Cathedral. After Marlborough and Worcester College, Oxford, where he gained a first in classical moderations and a second in *litterae humaniores*, Parr was called to the Bar by the Inner Temple in 1892. Like Foote he joined the Western Circuit and was appointed counsel to the Post Office. From 1914 to 1920 he was acting counsel to the Inland Revenue, and took silk in 1922. A Justice of the Peace for Wiltshire from 1924 onwards he rose to become vice-chairman of the Wiltshire Quarter Sessions. After taking up the post of Chancellor of the Diocese of Portsmouth in 1931, he became a JP for Hampshire, in 1935, and again became vice-chairman of the county Quarter Sessions. He died in March 1937, aged 72.

The judge in the first trial was Sir Edward Ridley. Born in 1843, the second son of a baronet and younger brother to a future Home Secretary, Ridley attended Harrow and Corpus Christi College, Oxford and, like Foote, took a first in classics, in 1866, whence he was elected fellow at All Souls'. After being called to the Bar in 1868 by the Inner Temple, Ridley joined the Northern and North-Eastern Circuits. There his reputation was secured by his role in a case known as Dalton v. Angus, which had (and has) wide-ranging implications in neighbourhood disputes, and ran for four years before being settled in the House of Lords in 1881. Ridley followed in family tradition by gaining, as a Conservative, the Parliamentary seat of South Northumberland in 1878, but held it only until 1880. He was appointed an Official Referee in 1886, bringing, according to his obituarist in *The Times*, 'new life into the Court [of Official Referees], it worked rapidly, economically, and satisfactorily.' During that time, in 1892, Ridley was made a Q.C.; it was also then that he published his blank-verse translation of Lucan's *Pharsalia*, said by his obituarist to be 'better than the original', and equipped with 'notes [which] are a storehouse of literary and political illustration'.

Ridley was appointed a circuit judge in 1897, and his decision in the Divisional Court in the famous West Riding Schools case on religious education was upheld in the House of Lords. His subsequent career was not without incident. Giving judgment on election petitions in 1911 he was harangued by the unsuccessful Liberal candidate at Exeter, and struck by a lump of coal after adjudicating against the Unionist candidate at Hull, where, after his intercession and that of his fellow-judge, the guilty man was jailed only for one week. At the Birmingham Assizes in 1913 he was hit in the face by a stool thrown by a prisoner, and, by then aged 70, had to take sickness leave to recover. Ridley's retirement in 1917 gave him the time to prepare a new edition of the *Pharsalia*, published in 1919, and he died in October 1928 at the age of 85. Of him his obituarist said 'He was, what not all judges have been, a scholar and a gentleman. . . His genuine kindliness of heart and his old-fashioned courtesy were irresistible.'

A man of somewhat sharper intelligence, Charles Darling presided over Flora's second trial. In marked contrast to Ridley's patrician origins, Darling arose from a relatively humble background. He was born in 1849 and was educated privately before working in a solicitor's office when, as we have seen, the death of an uncle brought him the means to train for the Bar, whither he was called in 1874 by the Inner Temple. He joined the Oxford Circuit and took silk in 1885, and was elected Conservative MP for Deptford in 1888. His Parliamentary career lasted until 1897, but in the words of his obituarist in *The Times*, 'the Commons failed to appreciate the bright, scintillating member for Deptford, and even his own side did not do him justice.'

His appointment in 1897 to the Queen's Bench was greeted with astonishment, for despite previous experience as a Commissioner of Assize, his London practice was minuscule, and his circuit briefs were not of the range and depth to betoken any degree of experience. However, his encyclopaedic memory and his grasp of legal principles were solid foundations for his judicial career, and while he gave free play to his wit – indeed may even have chosen the cases he tried in order to do so – he delivered his summings up with all due gravity. One celebrated case on the genuineness of a Romney portrait was tried without a jury, and instead, a panel of experts including Royal Academicians and the Director of the National Gallery of Ireland was amassed to discuss with Darling the merits of the portrait. There were actual Romneys on display for comparison with the disputed picture, and the trial took the form of a *conversazione* amongst connoisseurs and critics. Of him his obituarist wrote 'At Nisi Prius he could handle complicated facts, and was both quick and lucid . . . As a Judge of Assize he was at his best, and in the Court of Criminal Appeal, his good sense and large experience were always useful.'

For a time during the Great War, Darling served as deputy Lord Chief Justice, and was rewarded in 1917 with a place on the Privy Council. Darling retired from the Bench in 1923, and was soon afterwards created Baron Darling of Langham. Membership of the House of Lords was almost a second career, with debates in the House, participation in the work of the Judicial Committee of the Privy Council and chairmanship of two Parliamentary committees in 1925 and 1928. Indeed Darling even returned to the Bench as a volunteer in 1925 and 1928 to cover sickness absences on the part of serving judges. Throughout his legal career and in retirement Darling was a poet and essayist, having eight books published of which one was reprinted four times. His obituarist summed him up thus: 'He had his critics, but he fascinated them; he had his admirers, but he perplexed them. At one moment austere and firm, at another playful to the point of waggishness, he had no predecessor in the long history of the English judiciary whom he could be said to resemble.' Darling died in May 1936; he was aged 86.

The man whose generosity placed Flora's defence in such capable hands was Sir Edward Tennant, Liberal MP for Salisbury between 1906 and 1910. He was born in 1859 to great wealth and, in due course, a baronetcy, and was educated at Eton, Trinity College, Cambridge and the Inner Temple. His career spanned business and public life: on the one hand, a directorship of the Mysore Gold Company and the chairmanship of the Union Bank of Scotland, on the other, assistant private secretary to Sir George Trevelyan at the Scottish Office. In addition, he gave of his time and talents as Lord Lieutenant of Peeblesshire, Lord High Commissioner to the General Assembly of Scotland, and on the committees of the National Defence Association, the

National Service League, the Liberal Colonial Club and the Central Land Association. He also served as a magistrate in Wiltshire, in the Salisbury and Amesbury Petty Sessional Division. In 1911 Tennant was raised to the peerage, taking the title Baron Glenconner of Glen, in Peeblesshire.

Tennant was equally generous with his wealth, of which the author of an appreciation after his death was of the opinion that it was, 'in itself, rather a nuisance to him.' His obituarist in *The Times* wrote that 'he was a man of much generosity, always ready to hold out a helping hand to friends and others in need', to which the anonymous admirer added 'He did not give casually and without thought, but when he had thought and decided to give, as I fancy his instinct generally prompted him to do, he gave with the happiest possible gesture for the recipient.' So his kindness to Flora and the Carter family was entirely in character; other instances noted in his obituary include £1,000 to the board of the Edinburgh Royal Infirmary for radium, and, in 1918, Dryburgh Abbey as a gift to the nation, prefiguring by a matter only of weeks Cecil Chubb's gift of Stonehenge. As a person, Tennant was by nature reserved, but, his admirer noted, 'when interested and in congenial company, his animation was delightful. His fine and well-opened eyes then showed a fire, a gleam of friendliness and humour; and his interest made its full effect, for one quality which no one could ever doubt in him was his sincerity. That radiated from him, and was indeed the essential quality of the whole man.' Tennant's recreations and social networks were extensive, ranging from fishing with Lord Grey of Falloden, to discussing life after death with Sir Oliver Lodge. His obituarist described him as 'a man of many interests and activities and many friends, and will be widely mourned as a kindhearted, upright Scottish landlord, with a sincere and sympathetic regard for the interests and welfare of all those dependent on him, both on his estates and in his business connections.' Lord Glenconner died in November 1920, aged 61.

Of those who served on the coroner's inquest jury, three rendered significant service to the local community. Thomas Bowden Bennett, proprietor of the *Salisbury and Winchester Journal* was a

councillor for the St Mark's Ward in the 1920s. Both Howard Lapham, proprietor of the Magnet ironmongery store at 41 Fisherton Street, and John Sidney Rambridge, goldsmith, jeweller and watch and clockmaker at 9 New Canal were mayors, Lapham in 1919-20, Rambridge in 1931-2. After his mayoralty Rambridge continued to serve St Thomas's Ward as a councillor before becoming, like Lapham, an Alderman of the city. Lapham, perhaps marked by his service on the jury (for it will be recalled for he was one of the three not prepared to sign and seal the verdict of Flora's guilt), became a county magistrate for the Salisbury and Amesbury Petty Sessional Division, giving over twenty-five years' service, until after the Second World War, and after standing down as an Alderman of the city. Among the city magistrates, John Folliott, Robert Harding and Tom Perkins continued to serve on the bench until after the Great War, with Folliott also serving on the local county bench.

Canon Thwaites, on whom Flora had depended for spiritual comfort, in its ancient sense of giving her strength, had, before his incumbency in Fisherton, been curate of St John's Keswick from 1862 to 1865, and Rector of Blaisdon, Gloucestershire from 1865 to 1873. His pastoral work for the parish of Fisherton Anger and the people of Salisbury has been noted in Chapter 2. In addition, as his obituarist in the *Salisbury Journal* noted, 'He fought hard for the voluntary schools and served for a time as a member of the Salisbury School Board. He was one of the original members of the Salisbury Education Committee, and, for a time, Vice-Chairman.' After a lifetime of immensely hard work, he retired to Bournemouth on health grounds in April 1914. The *Salisbury Journal* remarked that 'His retirement . . . was marked by a remarkable gathering, testifying to the deep affection in which Canon Thwaites was held, both by parishioners of St. Paul's and the citizens generally, and advantage of the occasion was taken to present him with a cheque for £400, which was subscribed by several hundred parishioners and friends.' Thwaites was also given a roll top desk by the twenty curates who had served under him. In his new home town he continued his pastorate with domiciliary visiting, and helping on occasion with services at St John's, Boscombe. He died at the age of 80, in April 1919.

Unlike the Haskells and their neighbours in the Gaol Ground, and unlike the various public figures involved in the detection and trial of Flora for murder, the possible murderer – discounting Flora herself – having never been traced, leaves with one exception only the merest spoor. Murder in Victorian and Edwardian Salisbury was very uncommon, particularly the murder of children. However, in 1913 another child murder happened in Castle Street, Salisbury which had remarkable similarities to that of Teddy. Frederick Charles Jefferies was a bookseller and newsagent and his shop was at 9 Castle Street. Here he lived with his wife Annie and their five children Ada, Leonard, Dorothy, Freda and Reginald. The Jefferies family had been involved in the book trade in Salisbury for some years at 25 Endless Street, and Frederick succeeded his father, taking over the running of the business before the turn of the century. He had an excellent reputation for promptness and the business flourished to such a degree as to warrant larger premises. Frederick also had a brother, Sidney Jefferies who, like Flora's brother Richard Carter was employed as a printer's compositor.

On the afternoon of May 24th 1913, in the upstairs bedroom of the shop, Frederick Jefferies murdered his nine year-old daughter Dorothy by cutting her throat with a razor. He carried out the deed whilst his wife worked in the shop directly underneath the bedroom, hearing nothing. Jefferies then walked the short distance to the Police Station in Endless Street where he gave himself up to Sergeant Cutler. He was then taken into custody while Cutler and Dr Armitage, the assistant Police Surgeon, proceeded to the shop where Mrs Jefferies was still busy and completely unaware of what had happened in her home. The scene in the bedroom confirmed the father's statement and on entering they found the little girl lying on the bed with an ugly gash in her throat – a muffler had also been tied lightly over the girl's mouth. A bloodstained razor was found close by the bed and a pool of blood suggested that the murder had been committed while the child was standing and the cut seemed to indicate that she was attacked from behind.

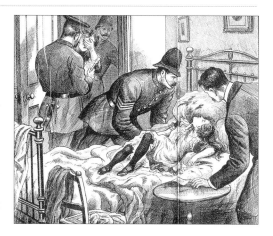

THE MURDER OF DOROTHY JEFFERIES BY HER FATHER IN CASTLE STREET, SALISBURY 1913. SIMILARITIES TO THE HASKELL CASE?
© *ILLUSTRAITED POLICE NEWS*

The main points given by Dr Armitage at the inquest were that the child was found fully dressed on the bed and the razor was found on the floor nearby, bloodstained. In the neck there was a deep cut extending right across the neck which had severed all the soft parts of the front of the vertebral column. On entering the room and seeing the body Armitage formed the opinion that the child had been dead for no longer that half an hour. There were no indications of a struggle and the wound in the neck was a clean cut with no secondary cuts or scratches. It was deeper on the right side than on the left and the right extremity of the wound was at a slightly higher level than the left. The cause of death was haemorrhage combined with shock. At the conclusion of the hearing, the inquest foreman announced 'Our verdict is one of murder against Frederick Charles Jefferies.'

At the trial it was established that Jefferies had been depressed since the death of his mother some months earlier. There was also a strange account regarding Jefferies in which, while on a cycling excursion he had become agitated and exhausted as he tried to ascend Whiteparish Hill. On dismounting from his cycle, he experienced a hallucination in which all the surrounding fields slowly turned red and moved from side to side. After this incident, Jefferies' mental condition at home gradually fell into decline, culminating in the murder of his favourite little daughter, Dorothy. It also transpired at the trial that madness ran in the Jefferies family, resulting in suicide and incarceration in various mental institutes. So it was no surprise when the judge ruled that Frederick Charles Jefferies be detained in a similar establishment. With that, Jefferies and this little-known murder of his daughter were forgotten; but did he take a bigger secret to the grave with him? Was he involved in the murder of Teddy Haskell?

Although we are unable to directly link Frederick Charles Jefferies himself with the murder of Teddy Haskell, there was a distinct coincidence on the 1891 Census. The Carter family living at 20 Meadow Road included a boarder, one Thomas Jefferies. He was then aged 27, he was a dairyman, and had been born in Winterbourne, Wilts. There may have been a family connection, for Mary Carter was a Jeffery before she married, and she had a brother, Thomas, Flora's uncle. Perhaps he may have been the boarder staying at 20 Meadow Road in 1891 and his name may have been recorded as a misspelling; or indeed there may have been some fluidity in the spelling of the name. However, were the spelling of Thomas Jefferies to be correct, we would have a remarkable surname connection involving two child murders – Jefferies in Meadow Road boarding with the Carter family when Flora was 16, and Frederick Charles Jefferies who murdered his young daughter Dorothy in Castle Street.

However, the coincidence would seem to be, unfortunately, just that. The Thomas Jefferies of the 1891 Census tallies with the Thomas Jeffery on the 1871 and 1881 censuses for Winterbourne Earls – both born there in 1863 or 1864. The General Register Office index of births provides confirmation, there being but one Thomas Jeffery being recorded for the Amesbury Registration District, in the second quarter of 1864, and no Thomas Jefferieses. The parish register entry for Thomas Jeffery, recording his baptism at Winterbourne Earls on 8 May 1864 bears this out.

The connection to be established, were the names to have been the same, would be between the presumed Thomas Jefferies and the later murderer Frederick Charles Jefferies, as a candidate for Teddy's murderer. Such a link might be plausible perhaps if they were siblings or cousins, given the

streak of madness in the Jefferies family of the killer of 1913. However, Frederick Charles Jefferies was born in Salisbury, as was his father Henry Jefferies the printer-compositor turned bookseller. His grandfather George Jefferies was a footman and letter carrier born in Milford. If Thomas Jeffery and Frederick Jefferies were related they can have been no closer than third cousins, and Teddy would have been twice removed. Flora would have known Thomas Jeffery, so he is unlikely to have been the mysterious caller on Friday 30 October, or the person offering Teddy coppers. Frederick Jefferies' ghastly decline into insanity and the death of his favourite daughter lay, in 1908, four and a half years in the future, and it is thus only with a century's hindsight that he can be viewed with any suspicion. He would, as a successful businessman, have had no more reason than anyone else to be making curious enquiries around the Gaol Ground at the end of October, but the similarities between the way Teddy Haskell and Dorothy Jefferies were dispatched mean that he cannot be ruled out as a suspect.

There remain two shadowy figures. When Flora and Edwin married in May 1896, one of their witnesses was a certain Sidney Ireland, whose name features in no Salisbury directories after that date. But in November 1908 one Richard Sidney Ireland was charged with assaulting William Cole on 31 October. The assault was so severe that Cole ended up in the Infirmary and was still there three weeks later. In court there was discussion as to how long the case should be adjourned for, given Cole's condition. Trethowan, Ireland's solicitor, was able to tell the court both that his client had always maintained that the assault was entirely accidental, and that the plaintiff had acknowledged that this was so. Cole had, moreover, asked P.C. Tucker to convey that information to Ireland and to say that he would not press charges. That being the case, Ireland told the court through Trethowan that he was quite prepared to recompense Cole for any loss he had suffered because of the injury. Trethowan stressed that it was not Ireland who had approached Cole, but the other way around, and only when Cole said he was not going to take proceedings that Ireland volunteered to recompense him.[2] So we have a Mr

Ireland, possibly associated by acquaintanceship with the Haskell family, involved in severe violence on the day of Teddy's death, willing to offer the man he has injured – deliberately or otherwise – ready money, presumably in some quantity.

Sadly, this too turns out to be a coincidence. Richard Sidney Ireland was a Salisburian, living at 8 Jubilee Terrace, Milford in what was in 1901 the parental home. His father, Frederick, was a carpenter, and had come from Islington, and Richard was then only 15, and a Post Office telegraph messenger. So he was too young to have been witnessing marriages in 1896, though twelve years later quite old enough to get into fights. Perhaps Richard had a brother or an uncle who was Edwin Haskell's best man – but the census returns for the previous twenty years of Frederick and Sarah Ireland's married life offer no such clue, nor do those of the years back to 1851 which shows Frederick as an infant in the household of his parents Frederick and Christina, hailing from London and Salisbury respectively. On the other hand, the census for Meadow Road in 1891 records Sidney Ireland, a tailor and native of Plymtree, Devon, then aged 29 and living at No. 11. He was far likelier to have been the witness to Edwin and Flora's marriage. The reason we hear no more of him is that by 1901 he had moved to Bethnal Green.

The second of these shadowy figures really was elusive, both at the time and subsequently. Among the leads not followed up by the investigators at the time of the inquest and the trials is a man whose name has come to our attention solely through Trethowan's brief for the second trial. Therein he notes: 'It is a curious fact that on the night of the 31st October a man called Ray living in Gas Lane (quite close to Meadow Road) disappeared, and notwithstanding enquiries by the Police it is understood has never been discovered.

'This fact was ascertained in the following way. A man named Miles, a bootmaker, used to have washing done by the Prisoner, and on Alfred Walter Noble calling on him sometime after her arrest for payment of the amount due to the Prisoner, Miles remarked that it was a curious fact that a man named Ray had been missing from Gas Lane since the night

of the murder. He said he had been told this by P.C. Spencer, who had had an appointment with him one night to view one of his houses, and turned up late and explained his delay by stating that the search for this man had detained him. Spencer told Miles that the Police thought there was trouble between Ray and his wife.

'Nothing of this of course was stated by the Prosecution either before the Coroner or before the Magistrates, and great stress was put on the fact that a search was made for some man, and no man could be found, or was known to be missing.'

So we have a man named Ray, a relatively near neighbour of the Haskells, possibly out on the street after a marital dispute, and possibly having an idea of where he might stay locally, at least temporarily, having got wind of Flora putting Mold up when his mother had no room for him.[3] Perhaps this person knew of Teddy's money, as did not a few in the neighbourhood, and had hoped to lay hands on it whilst lodging at No. 40, and, infuriated by Flora's response, determined to find a way of getting hold of the money even if he could not get a bed for a night or two. What adds to the mystery is that Mr Ray features in no contemporary Salisbury directory. Those for 1906 and 1909 record Mrs C. Ray living at No. 3 Gas Lane. By 1911 No. 3 Gas Lane was occupied by one Frederick Bell. In 1912 the only Ray living in the area – indeed the only Ray living in Salisbury – was Mrs E. Ray, of Coldharbour Lane. So was Mrs C. Ray Mr Ray's mother, and listed as head of the household in the same way that Mary Carter was in Meadow Road until she moved into Hayter's Almshouses; and was Mrs E. Ray his deserted wife – or even, widow? We shall probably never know, as the 1901 census return sheds no light on either a C. Ray or an E. Ray who can be associated with the householder of No. 3 Gas Lane in 1908.

With that we return to Flora. As noted before, she never returned to Salisbury, and appears to have remained in south London, and to have reverted to the use of her maiden name. She and Alfred Mold never did marry, possibly because of Mold's perceived responsibility for his mother and siblings. Some of these, as Trethowan's brief to counsel notes, were 'practically imbeciles and unable to earn their

CERTIFIED COPY OF AN ENTRY OF DEATH

GIVEN AT THE **GENERAL REGISTER OFFICE**

Application Number ..... **Y548141** .....

	REGISTRATION DISTRICT					Lambeth			
1920 DEATH in the Sub-district of ..... Stockwell ..... in the ..... County of London									

Columns:– 1 2 3 4 5 6 7 8 9

No.	When and where died	Name and surname	Sex	Age	Occupation	Cause of death	Signature, description and residence of informant	When registered	Signature of registrar
18	Sixth November 1920 20 Willington Road Stockwell	Flora Fanny Carter otherwise Haskell	Female	46 years	Widow of Edwin Haskell a Market Gardener	(1) Phthisis Pulmonalis (2) Exhaustion Certified by O. Gilmore F.R.C.S.	M. E. Carter Sister in law Present at the death 63 Seaforth Road Leeds	Eighth November 1920	G. Fenton Registrar.

CERTIFIED to be a true copy of an entry in the certified copy of a Register of Deaths in the District above mentioned.

Given at the GENERAL REGISTER OFFICE, under the Seal of the said Office, the ..... 14th ..... day of ..... February 2004

DYA 279327

See note overleaf

CAUTION: THERE ARE OFFENCES RELATING TO FALSIFYING OR ALTERING A CERTIFICATE AND USING OR POSSESSING A FALSE CERTIFICATE ©CROWN COPYRIGHT
WARNING: A CERTIFICATE IS NOT EVIDENCE OF IDENTITY.

022317 6276 10/03 SPSL 006237

FLORA FANNY HASKELL EVENTUALLY DIED IN LONDON, 1920.

own living.' The Molds were a feature of Salisbury life in the 1920s, playing a hurdy-gurdy in the streets to earn a few coppers. It is just possible that Mold did marry, for the index to marriages in the General Register Office records the union of Alfred J. Mold to Kate Miles in the autumn of 1925, in Chelsea.

Meanwhile, Flora had already died at 20 Willington Road, Stockwell, on 6 November 1920, aged 46. The cause of death, in the medical usage of the time, was *phthisis pulmonalis* and exhaustion. Flora Haskell, like her nearest and dearest, had succumbed to tuberculosis.

Appendices

Flora Haskell's first statement, read in court at the inquest on Thursday 26th November 1908, and published by The Salisbury Times and South Wilts Gazette, Friday 27th November 1908.

Flora Fanny Haskell, a widow, 34 years of age. My husband died 19th February 1904. His name was Edwin Haskell. He was a lunatic attendant at Fisherton House Asylum. I had only one child, whose name was Edwin Richard Haskell; he was 12 years old on the 19th October.

I have lived in this house – 40, Meadow Road – two years come next Easter [i.e. 1907], and since my husband has been dead I have earned my living by taking in laundry work. My little boy had a diseased hip, and his leg was taken off six years ago the 11th January next [i.e. 11.1.1903].

On Friday evening, about a quarter to nine, a young man came and inquired. When I opened the door he said 'Mrs Haskell?' I believe he said 'You have got lodgings to let.' I said 'Oh, no', and he said 'But I have been recommended to you.' I said 'I never let; it's a thing I never do.' He said 'Could you make it convenient for me to stop one night, as it's so late.' – or 'it's getting late.' I said 'I could not possibly put you up for one night.' He seemed upset, and he said 'It seems strange, as I have been recommended to you.' He said 'Good-night', and went away. He was a man about 35 years of age, medium height and medium build. He was wearing a bowler hat and dark clothes. I believe he was clean shaved, and that is all I can say.

On Saturday, I did my usual housework, and about half-past two I went out with Mrs Mould [sic, i.e. Mold], 2 James Street, to look at an empty house in Ashley Road. The people were moving out the furniture, and Mrs Mold [sic, i.e. Mold] took the house.

I returned about 4 p.m. Before I went out I locked both my doors. The boy was out playing; he came in about half-past four or a quarter to five to tea, and my mother, Mrs Mary Carter, Hayter's Almshouses, Fiseherton Street, came in about five and remained nearly an hour. Then I went to Mr Nicholas' bakehouse, in Wilton Road, and fetched two cakes from there. I locked the front door, and left the back one undone, as I expected my mother to return, the boy being in No. 38, next door, playing with some friends. I was only about three minutes gone up to the bakehouse. I returned home and found that my mother had not come back; then I went out through the front door, leaving that and the back door unlocked. I left a piece of paper on the kitchen table saying that I had gone to the 'Co-op.' I expect I was gone about half-an-hour. I then returned home and found that my mother had not returned.

I then went down into the town, locking both doors behind me. I called at Lipton's, the Home and Colonial, and a fish stall at the Poultry Cross. I returned home about half-past eight as near as I can remember, and I then called my little boy in from next door. Then I went out and took the boy with me.

I went to the little general shop at the corner of Sidney Street. My little boy went to the newsagents to buy a halfpenny paper called The Butterfly. I got back to the house about twenty minutes to nine and my boy returned about a minute afterwards. We both had supper, which consisted of a little ham. I then washed my little boy, and gave him a foot-bath and put him to bed in the upstairs middle bedroom; this would be about twenty minutes or a quarter to ten. Then I came downstairs and went out to the back to the water-closet; then I sat reading in the kitchen for about a quarter of an hour, then I got up and locked the back door, lowered the gas in the kitchen and I was going to open the kitchen door leading to the passage. My little nephew who is about 16 years of age came and knocked at the back door which was locked. As I was going towards the back door I heard someone coming downstairs, and they threw something down at the bottom of the stairs and splashed my sleeve up. When I saw that I said to Percy Noble: 'Rush, Percy, for someone.'

He said 'Where shall I go?' I said 'Go for the doctor.' I do not know why I told him to go for the doctor, only I saw the splashes on my sleeve. I then came through the kitchen from the back door and into the passage and found the front door wide open. I think I called out 'Help! Someone do come to me', when Mr Steer came out of his front door which is No. 36 Meadow Road, and I said 'Oh, Mr Steer do come, someone has been up my stairs. Mr Steer went to the corner and Mrs Steer came in here with me. Several people came in at once and I said 'Do see that my little Teddy is all right', and I believe that Mr Rawlings [sic, i.e. Rawlins] of the South Wilts Dairy also went up. They would not let me go upstairs and I sat in the front room with the door closed, and soon after Dr Wilks and Dr Rowe [sic, i.e. Row] came in and saw me. Dr Wilks said 'What is it, Mrs Haskell?' I said 'I don't know, that's just what I want to know.'

The doctors were upstairs a long time, at least it seemed a long time. Mrs Cooper was in the room with me, and Mrs

Sweetman and Mrs Mold came in. I asked them time after time to tell me what was the matter, but they would not tell me, and said 'Dr Wilks will be down directly.' Dr Wilks came down sometime after, and I heard him say to the women who were sitting with me 'Doesn't she know?' And someone, I don't know who, answered and said 'No, we have not told her.' Dr Wilks then said ' I might as well tell her; she will have to know.' I said 'Do tell me Mr [sic] Wilks' and he said 'Well, Mrs Haskell, I am afraid it's a sad case, someone has taken little Teddy's life,' but he did not say in what way. Dr Rowe was with Dr Wilks when he told me this. The both went away and Dr Wilks came back with a draught for me.

A sergeant of police came, but I do not know whether or not he came before, or whilst Dr Wilks was here. That is all I can say. Perhaps Dr Wilks can give you something more than that.

Before Dr Wilks went the second time I begged of him to let me go upstairs and Dr Wilks said 'She might as well go up, it will do her more good. It might satisfy her.' The sergeant of police and Dr Wilks went up with me and he allowed me to go to the side of the bed and put my hand across his forehead. Then I came downstairs.

When I put my little boy to bed I used a small brass lamp and I left it burning on the dressing table by the window. Mrs Butt, York Road, told me today that she found the lamp on the landing outside the bedroom door, and it was out.

I want to explain that at about quarter past ten I was going round to Mrs Mould's [sic, i.e.Mold's], and I locked the back door, and lowered the kitchen gas, and partly opened the kitchen door leading into the passage so as to go out of the front door, when I heard someone coming down the stairs, when they threw something down which splashed my sleeve, and just at that moment I heard by nephew calling out for me at the back door. There was no light in the passage, and the gas was turned very low in the kitchen. I can't say who it was that came downstairs, but I saw the figure of a man on the bottom stair.

It was before he got on the bottom of the stairs that he dropped, or threw the something, which splashed my sleeve. I cannot tell you what he dropped, and whatever it was I have not been shown it. But whatever it was it did not strike me, but something splashed my sleeve, and I can't tell you what that was. My kitchen is immediately underneath the room in which my little boy was in bed, where I was sitting reading, but I did not hear any sound whatever until I heard the footsteps on the stairs. Whoever it was that came downstairs was wearing boots, but [did] not [have] a heavy tread. It was impossible for me to see anyone's face owing to the gas being turned down. I cannot in any way describe the man who came downstairs, or what he was wearing.

In the same bedroom where my little boy was, in one of the top drawers [of the chest], the one nearest the fireplace, there was eight pounds and two shillings. It was made up of seven sovereigns, two half-sovereigns and a two-shilling piece. It was in between a coloured tablecloth, just under a fold of it. I asked

the sergeant this morning to go and see if the money was alright, and he brought the drawer down to me, and I found that the lock had been forced open, and only three sovereigns and one half-sovereign [were] left. The money belonged to my little boy, and all of it had been given to him by my mother, Mrs Carter, in small sums for about two years, and was being saved up to buy him an artificial leg. This was all the money that was in the house, except [for] a few shillings in the front bedroom upstairs, which belongs to my sister-in-law, who asked me to send her a shilling at a time out of it. All my money I usually carry in my pocket, and I have only the money I earn from week to week.

I saw the money belonging to my little boy safe on Thursday. No-one [else], except my mother and my little boy, knew anything at all about the money.

It was when the sergeant brought down my late husband's watch, which I kept under the pillow upon which he (the boy) was sleeping that I asked him to go and see if the money in the drawer was safe. The sergeant did not bring the drawer down at the time I asked him, when Dr Wilks was here, but about three hours after. I asked him a second time, and that is when he brought it down.

Of course, I have not found the knife that Mr Richardson asked me if I had missed. I could not say where the knife was, as my little boy had it out in the back [yard] on Thursday last. He was sharpening wood, making a 'tip-cat' I think, and I have not seen the knife since. It was a brown-handled knife, and a round handle too, and the blade of the knife was rather pointed at the top. It was a rough knife, and not used for table purposes. It's an odd knife, and I can't say where I got it from in the first place.

The blouse I have spoken of is a pale blue, flowery thing, with white lace yoke. I wore it till about four o'clock this (Sunday) morning when the sergeant asked me to take it off as he would like to take it with him, and he did so just after nine. This is the blouse I wore from half-past two on Saturday until the sergeant asked me for it. I notice that there were blood splashes on my right sleeve, from the elbow downwards, which went through onto the underclothes. What I mean by this is that there is a little blood on the sleeve of my chemise which penetrated through my blouse. With the exception of the bodice which I changed for the blouse, I am wearing the same clothes as I did when the splashes came onto my blouse, and I have not had time to examine to see if there were any marks on these. I was wearing an apron from my waist, but I did not notice any splashes on that.

I have never let lodgings to male or female, and the only male person who has slept in this house is my elder brother, Mr Richard Carter.

The shirt collar, waistcoat and a pair of white cricketing trousers that are upstairs belong to Mr Alfred Mold, who is a steward on the Adriatic, which sails between Southampton and New York, and he has slept in this house twice within the last three months (once about three months ago and last Saturday week), and I do his laundry work for him, which he leaves behind when he is going on a voyage. He left for Southampton a fortnight today, but he did not sail until the following Wednesday. He slept here on those occasions because his mother['s house] was full up.

The missing knife was sometimes kept in the kitchen drawer, and sometimes in the yard, and I should think it was rusty or dirty. It was a knife that would sharpen , because my little boy said to me on Thursday: 'Mother, this knife won't cut much, I'll sharpen it', and I believe he sharpened it on a stone which his dad had in a tool basket in the coal house, but I did not see him sharpen it. I have sharpened it myself, but not lately.

My little boy was insured in the Pearl Life Assurance Company, for about three pounds ten shillings or four pounds. I have had him insured for about three years and paid a penny a week until about twelve weeks ago, when I endorsed his policy and paid an extra penny a week. I shall get no benefit for twelve months from the time when I endorsed it.

I turned the gas up in the kitchen after I had told Percy Noble to go for someone.

I think it was Mrs Cooper who pointed out to me the splashes on my sleeve.

I can't account for there being no blood on the apron, and yet there were blood marks on the blouse. The marks of blood do not commence until about the elbow, downwards. There are no stains only [i.e. except] on the right arm of the blouse sleeve, and I looked at it when the sergeant asked me to take it off.

The knife now shown me is the one that my little Teddy was playing with last Thursday. I have ahd the knife ever since I can remember. I believe his dad brought it home from his work once.

[signed]Flora Fanny Haskell, Nov. 1st 1908. 40 Meadow Road, Salisbury.

Statement made in the presence of Chief Inspector Walter Dew, Captain Hoël Llewellyn, Chief Constable of Wilts. [signed] Frank Richardson, C.C. [signed] Walter Dew, Chief Inspector. 1st November, 1908.

Flora Haskell's second statement, read in court at the inquest on Thursday 26th November 1908, and published by The Salisbury Times and South Wilts Gazette, Friday 27th November 1908.

40, Meadow Road, Salisbury, 2nd November, 1908
Flora Fanny Haskell says:- 'There was something I forgot to tell you yesterday, that a boy came from the Co-op with a pair of boots, that belong to Mr Mannings [sic, i.e. Manning], at 42, Meadow Road. It was just after 10 p.m., as near as I can put it. He just gave me the boots at the front door and went away. This was Saturday evening.

'I did not tell you yesterday that my sister-in-law, Emily Haskell, stayed with me about ten weeks, and left for London a fortnight last Friday [16th October 1908], and is now in Hampstead Workhouse Infirmary.

'On Wednesday last my little boy (deceased) was writing out his name and address on a piece of paper. I asked him what

he was doing, and he said, 'Someone wants it, Mam, at school, he is going to bring me something tomorrow if I take my name and address.' I didn't ask him any questions about it, neither can I say he took it on Thursday. We were quite alone when he told me this.

'I think my mother told you that I went to the drawer where my little boy's money was, on Thursday, to take three shillings to pay Mrs Steer's daughter for the making of a bodice. This is not so; it was to pay her for the trimming. That's all, sir'

[signed] Flora Fanny Haskell

Flora Haskell's third statement, read in court at the inquest on Thursday 26th November 1908, and published by The Salisbury Times and South Wilts Gazette, Friday 27th November 1908.

40, Meadow Road, Salisbury, 2nd November, 1908
Flora Fanny Haskell says, in answer to questions:- 'I opened my kitchen door to go out, and then heard someone coming downstairs, as I have described before. I did not follow the man along the passage, but went across my kitchen to the wash-house and unlocked the back door and told Percy Noble what I have told you. I then came back through the kitchen, along the passage, and into Meadow Road, and when I got there I saw no-one whatever until Mr Steer came. I turned to the left towards Cold Harbour Lane but only went so far as next door, about twice the width of this front room. The Mr Steer came back with me. I screamed very loudly at my back door, and all the time after calling for someone to come. If there had been a man in Meadow Road I must have seen him, but I saw no man on either side of the road. If I had seen a man I should have followed him, but Mr Steer was the very first man I saw in the street. I had not been in the street a minute when Mr Steer came out and met me against Mr Noble's front door and I came back with him into my front passage and stood there about a minute, and then Mrs Butt came, and I came in with her, after walking up and down the passage about twice, calling out, which did not take a minute, and I have never been to the front door since.

'It would not be true if anyone says that I followed a man down Meadow Road between ten and half-past on Saturday night, the 31st ult., and that I walked down as far as about two houses beyond Mr Steer's. I never even went as far as Mr Steer's. It would not be true if anyone says that I walked back to my house after following the man, and stopped once or twice and leaned against the house, and then walked to my own house and stayed outside the front door for a quarter-of-an-hour. This would be quite untrue. It would be quite untrue for anyone to say that I was weeping and wailing quietly when I was in the street. I was screaming and calling at the top of my voice for help.

'It would not be true if anyone said that I followed a man in the direction of Cold Harbour Lane, and said, 'Stop him; he has killed my boy.''

[signed] F.F. Haskell, November 2nd, 1908.

Flora Haskell's fourth statement, read in court at the inquest on Thursday 26th November 1908, and published by The Salisbury Times and South Wilts Gazette, Friday 27th November 1908.

40, Meadow Road, Salisbury, 10 a.m., 3/11/08

On [his] calling at above address Mrs Haskell said to Chief Inspector Dew: 'I should like to speak to you and the other officers alone.' Continuing she said, 'When Mr Steer came down the stairs the first time I went up the stairs – just about three stairs – and met him. He said 'Someone go for the police.' I said, 'What is it, Mr Steer?' I can't quite remember the words he said, but I think he said 'It's too bad,' and would not let me go any further up the stairs. And then I think I went to the front door and said to someone 'Do go for the police, I believe someone has killed my little Teddy.' I think this was the time Mrs Cooper came in, and I believe I said the same words to her. Then Mr Steer went back upstairs. This is all I want to say.'

In answer to my questions as to the blood coming from the little boy's ear, Mrs Haskell said: 'He came home from school, I think it was last Thursday, and I saw the blood on one of his ears. I believe it was the left ear, and I said 'What have you done to your ear, my dear?' He said 'I fell down and knocked it against one of the clothes pegs at school.' That accounts for the blood on the two handkerchiefs you found in the copper last Sunday. He gave one to me on Thursday and I gave him a clean one and the same one I gave him clean on Thursday he gave me on Saturday, and I gave him another clean one which should have been in his pocket. On Saturday I was cleaning up the wash-house and put the two handkerchiefs in the copper. The one you now show me is the one I gave him clean on Saturday. The blood on it must be from his ear. I am sure it is the one I gave him on Saturday. It is one of two his grandmother gave him. I think you will find it is scented. His aunt scented it before she went away a fortnight last Friday, and he carried it for two Sundays in his best coat pocket. I took it out on Saturday morning and gave it to him, now I think of it. His aunt scented two handkerchiefs, one for him and one for me.'

'On Friday the place was quite dry, but he picked it again on Saturday and made it bleed.'

Supt. Stephens showed Mrs Haskell two small handkerchiefs and said, 'I found these in the little boy's jacket pocket on Saturday night.' Mrs Haskell said, 'It's quite likely. He was in the habit of taking handkerchiefs himself. One is mine, and the small blood marks on it is [sic, i.e. are] from a scratch or scar on my nose. I can't say for certain about the other one because his aunt gave him so many different ones.'

[signed] Flora Fanny Haskell. Salisbury. 4th November 1908.

Inspector Dew's first report to the Director of Public Prosecutions: Salisbury, 4 November 1908

With reference to the application of Mr Richardson, Chief Constable of Salisbury (City) for assistance in connection with the murder of Edwin Richard Haskell on the night of the 31st ult.

I beg to report that as directed I proceeded to Salisbury per the 8,30 train on Sunday morning and at once placed myself in communication with Mr Richardson.

The facts of the case are these:-

The deceased boy was 12 years old on the 19th ult and had but one leg, his right leg having been amputated some years ago in consequence of consumption setting in, but he was an intelligent and active youth and found no difficulty in getting about by the aid of a crutch and was universally esteemed.

It seems that he was put to bed by his mother at about twenty minutes to ten on the night of the tragedy and at about twenty minutes after ten Mrs Haskell was heard screaming at her front door and several people declare that they heard her shout 'Someone has killed my Teddy', and 'Someone has murdered my Teddy' and upon the neighbours proceeding to the back bedroom upstairs they found the child dead, with his throat cut.

The mother said that she heard someone coming downstairs and upon opening the kitchen door, at the foot of the stairs he saw the figure of a man go along the passage and out of the front door, but she could not describe him as the passage was in darkness, and she had turned her light down in the kitchen just before.

She also said that as the man came down the stairs he either threw or dropped something which fell on the passage floor against the kitchen and splashed her blouse sleeve.[sic]

Dr Wilkes [i.e. Wilks], who lives near, was sent for and attended with Dr Rowe [i.e. Row] and examined the body, and unfortunately later on washed and moved the body and disarranged all the bed clothes, so that it was impossible on my arrival to see if there had been any blood stained finger impressions etc.

Police also attended shortly after the Doctors had examined [2] the body, and a search was instituted with a view to find the man. Chief Constable Richardson, and Superintendent Stephens, of the Wilts County Constabulary, were also soon on the scene and took charge of the case, and found Mrs Haskell was wearing a light cotton blouse with a number of blood spots on the right sleeve extending from the cuff to the shoulder.

There were also blood spots on the right front of blouse.

Sergeant Golding, who was the first Officer on the scene found at the bottom of the stairs, on the passage against kitchen door, a blood stained table knife which he took charge of, and later Mrs Haskell, who was not shown the knife, was asked if any knives were missing, and a search was made in the kitchen drawer by her mother, Mrs Carter, a Widow, living in the town, in the presence of Mrs Haskell, and they both agreed that a knife was missing. They described it and it was obviously the knife that the Sergeant had picked up.

I would here point out that the knife was never shown to either Mrs Haskell or Mrs Carter until I showed it to Mrs Haskell on the afternoon of Sunday, when she immediately said that the knife belonged to her.

Going back to Saturday night when the Police questioned her as to a missing knife, she went on to explain that the one missing was an old one used for rough purposes and that the last time she saw it was on the previous Thursday, when she said she saw the deceased boy making a tip cat, and sharpen the knife on a whet stone, which subsequently Mrs Haskell told me was in an old tool basket of her late husband's, which was kept in the coal house in the back garden.

Since my arrival on Sunday I have been engaged with the Chief Constable and Superintendent Stephens making inquiries etc with but a few hours rest, and there is still an immense amount of work to do and I therefore do not propose to make a detailed report or fully summarise the statements I have taken at this moment; the statements speak for themselves.

The deceased was found lying on his back ~~near~~ on the side of ~~te~~ the bed away from the wall, his face had a peaceful appearance.

Those first in the room state that the bed clothes were in the [3] same position as if the child had been put to bed and in no way disturbed. The room had an absolutely tidy appearance and there was nothing to indicate that anything whatever had been interfered with, everything apparently being in its proper place.

There was a wound in the throat, a wound on the fourth finger of the left hand about half an inch long, made with a sharp instrument, and situated on the back of the finger, and a small abrasion on the left ear, the last I find having been caused by him falling against a clothes peg at school a few days before.

The wound in the throat, and the cause of death, was made with a sharp instrument. It extended deeply on the right side, severing the common carotid (the larger) artery of the neck. It also severed the larynx. This latter, the Divisional Surgeon states, would prevent any cry being made after the wound was inflicted and death would occur very rapidly from loss of blood.

There were spots of blood on the oil cloth at side and foot of bed and on landing. There were also spots of blood on the front of a chest of drawers standing near head of bed, but the detailed particulars of the marks will be given in a subsequent report.

A small brass lamp, which Mrs Haskell states she left burning in the room was found outside door on landing, out.

Mrs Haskell states that seven sovereigns, two half sovereigns, and a two shilling piece were seen safe in the folds of a table cloth in one of the top drawers of the chest on Thursday last, and after the murder was committed she asked the Sergeant to bring the drawer down to her, which he did, when she said that four sovereigns, one half sovereign and the two shilling piece had disappeared, and she declared that the drawer had been locked, and the key placed in a box on the top of drawers.

When the Officer went to the drawer it was closed in the ordinary way, but on pulling it the drawer came out and the small common lock was hanging on a part of a small screw. There was no apparent forcing of the drawer, and no blood stains on it. The money remaining in the drawer was in the same place that Mrs Haskell says the whole of the £8-2/- was left on previous Thursday.

[4] This money is said to have belonged to the deceased and had been given to him during the past two years by his grandmother to buy him an artificial leg. A watch which Mrs Haskell says she placed under the pillow on which the boy's head was, was quite safe.

On my arrival on Sunday, with the Officers mentioned, and in the presence of the Chief Constable or Wiltshire, Captain Llewellyn, who happened to be in the house I obtained a lengthy statement from Mrs Haskell. The points in this are these:-

(1) Husband died 19th February 1904.

(2) Deceased was the only child.

(3) Had lived at 40 Meadow Road, Fisherton, Salisbury, about two years. (This is the house where the murder was committed, and it is an ordinary one storey house).

(4) She earned her living by doing laundry work at home.

(5) She says that a young man description:- age about 35 years, medium height & build, wearing a bowler hat and dark clothes and believed to be clean shaven, came & enquired of her on Friday evening about quarter to nine, and said addressing her by name, 'I believe you have got lodgings to let' and said he had been recommended to her etc, and she says she can't account for him calling, as he was a total stranger to her. She says she could not recognize him, and refused to take him in.

(6) About quarter to ten on Saturday she went to the Water Closet at back of house, returned and sat reading in kitchen for about a quarter of an hour, then got up and locked the back door, (wash house) lowered the gas in kitchen, and as she was going to open the door leading to the passage to go out to visit a neighbour, her little nephew, Percy Noble, who lives next door (36) came and knocked at her back door, which was locked, and as she was going towards the back door to unlock it, she heard someone coming downstairs, she went back and opened the kitchen door about half way, and then saw the figure of a man, and then the [sic] something was thrown or dropped and splashed her, and when she saw that she went to the wash house door, opened it, and said, to Percy Noble, 'Rush Percy for someone' he said 'Where shall I go' she said 'Go for anyone, go for the Doctor'. She don't [sic] know why she said. 'Go for the Doctor', except that she saw the splashes on her sleeve.

(7) That she then came through the kitchen from the back door, into the passage and found the front door wide open. She thinks she called out 'Help, someone do come to me' and Mr Steer came out of his front door, 36 Meadow Road, and she said to him, 'Oh Mr Steer do come, someone has been up my stairs'. That Mr Steer went to the corner and Mrs Steer came to her, that several people came at once and she said, 'Do see that my little Teddy is alright'

(8) That they would not let her go upstairs and she sat in the front room with the door closed. That soon after Dr Wilkes and Dr Rowe came in and saw her.

(9) That Dr Wilkes said 'What is it Mrs Haskell? And she said 'I don't know, that's just what I want to know'

[5] (10) That she repeatedly asked her neighbours to tell her what was the matter, but they would not.

(11) That Dr Wilkes came in sometime after and she heard him say to the women who were with her 'Doesn't she know? someone said 'No, we have not told her' Dr Wilkes then told her that someone had taken little Teddy's life, but he did, not say in what way.

(12) That the Doctor subsequently allowed her to go into the bedroom, to side of bed and put her band across his (deceased) forehead, she then came straight downstairs.

(13) That there was no light in the passage, and the gas was turned very low in the kitchen, so much so that she could not see the man plainly, only the figure of one, yet she saw splashes on her arm.

(14) That the kitchen in which she was sitting is immediately under the room in which the boy was murdered, but she did not hear any sound whatever until she heard footsteps on the stairs.

(15) That no one except herself, her mother, and the deceased knew about the money.

(16) That she found blood splashes on the arm of her blouse, but did not look to see if there were any on her skirt (taken possession of by me), concerning which I will verbally explain.

(17) That she was wearing an apron over her skirt when the splashes were made.

(18) That the missing knife was kept sometimes in the kitchen drawer, and sometimes in the yard, and she should think it was rusty or dirty.

(19) That the deceased said to her on Thursday that the missing knife would not cut and that he would sharpen it, and she believes he sharpened it on a stone, but she did not see him sharpen it.

That she has sharpened the knife but not lately.

(20) That the boy was insured in the Pearl Life Assurance Company for £3-10/-, but [she] had recently increased the insurance, but will receive no benefit in consequence as sufficient time [manuscript] has not elapsed.

(21) That she turned the gas up after she had told Percy Noble to go for someone.

(22) She thinks it was Mrs Cooper [who] pointed out to her the splashes on her sleeve.

(23) She can't account for no blood being on her apron, yet there were blood marks on the blouse.

(24) That a boy called at her house just after ten on the night of the murder with a pair of boots for a next door neighbourhood.

(25) That the deceased on Wednesday previous to the murder wrote his name and addres on a piece of paper and that he told her that someone at school bad asked him for it, and that he was going to bring something the next day if he took his name and address.

(26) That she on the Thursday previous to the murder took 2/- from the boy's savings in the upstairs drawer to pay for some trimmings.

(27) That on the morning of the 3rd she requested to amend her statement in respect to Mr Steer, and I beg special attention to the greater part of this statement, as it seems an after-thought.

I obtained signed statements at the earliest possible moment from as many persons that [sic, i.e. as] I thought could throw light on the matter and from these it will be seen that Mr Steer contradicts prisoner in many particulars.

He lives at 36 Meadow Road, and was the first on the scene after Percy Noble.

Noble is prisoners nephew and says the light was a good one in Haskell's kitchen. He heard prisoner make a movement as if she was pushing her chair back.

She said to him go, to the top of the passage and. see if you can see that man just gone out, 'He has been and killed my poor Teddy', &c.

Another person almost immediately on the scene was a Mrs Sweetman, of 42 York Road, close to prisoner's address and her statements are of an Important character because a bloodstained handkerchief was handed to Supt Stephens by prisoner's mother. Prisoner says it belonged to the deceased and the blood on it was from a small wound on his ear.

Mrs Sweetman, after prisoner had been arrested volunteered an additional statement in which she says that soon after she went to the house she went to bathe prisoner's forehead with Eau-de-cologne, and in attempting to take a handkerchief out of the hand of prisoner, she found it was bloodstained and damp. She took it from Haskell and placed it on the mantle-piece. Someone remarked 'Be careful', 'This might be used as evidence', but she cannot remember who said this. Mrs Sweetman identifies the handkerchief handed to Supt Stephens as the one that was in Mrs Haskell's hand, and at my request she has places a private mark on this.

A Mr Francis S. Leate, Saddler, 29 St Marks Rd, made a statement that 'He saw a woman leave prisoner's house shortly after 10. p.m. on the night of the murder, she was crying and wailing and following a man down the road, and he heard her [7] say, stop him he has killed my boy. He gave a description similar to what appeared in the newspapers, and which is of no value, because no man was ever described as leaving the house on Saterday [sic].

I asked why he did not give information to Police before late Sunday although he knew the murder had been committed, and, he said, 'He [sic, i.e. I] forgot all about it'.

I saw Mrs Haskell again and questioned her on Leate's statement and she absolutely, (without of course knowing what he had said) contradicted it in every detail.

Mrs Cooper, 27 York Road, two houses from the one in which the murder was committed heard screams and. on running up saw Mrs Haskell standing at her door, and she said 'Oh Mrs Cooper, someone has murdered my Teddy'.

Lily Stretch, a nursemaid in the employ of Colonel Moore, of Salisbury, says that about 10.30. p.m. on the night of the murder she was walking up York Road with her sweetheart, Herbert Primmer, when outside Mrs Cooper's door she heard Mrs Haskell scream, they went back to the corner of Meadow Road and saw Mrs Haskell standing alone in her doorway shouting, 'Someone has killed my little Teddy'. She declared she saw no one except the young lad Noble until she saw the Steers, and that the streets were quiet. Miss Stretch had to pass the top of Meadow Road, not a dozen yards from the fatal house before arriving outside Mrs Cooper's which is at the corner of Meadow Road, so that if Mrs Haskell's story was true she might have been expected to have seen the man run out of the house, because Miss Stretch had only just crossed the road when she heard prisoner screaming at her front door.

Her story is confirmed by Primmer. There are also several statements that I have taken which go to confirm that without even going upstairs to see what was the matter, The prisoner rushed into the street shouting that someone had murdered her Teddy, and yet she herself practically contradicted this.

To my mind the position of the bloodstains on the blouse are consistent with her having cut the boy's throat, and not [8] consistent as being caused in the manner described by her, because I found several blood spots on the oilcloth floor of the bedroom, one on landing at top of stairs, one or two spots and smears on right side of wall hall, coming down stairs, mark of blood outside kitchen door on oilcloth, but an utter absence of splashes on door or wall where she alleges she was standing when the 'Something' was dropped or thrown, and I suggest that that the running blood on [the] knife was practically exhausted before being taken from bedroom.

Referring to the skirt that I took from her on my arrival, I have no hesitation in saying, that there are many bloodspots and splashes thereon, yet prisoner says she was wearing her apron which witnesses contradict,

Having regard to all the circumstances and enquiries made by me, and. in the absence of any real corroboration of Mrs Haskell's statement, I was of the opinion that we should be justified in arresting the mother. At about 10.30. p.m. [on the] 3rd [November] we arrested her at her house, and when told the charge she simply said 'No, No', and when charge was read over she said 'No'.

She appeared before the Court the following day and was remanded until 11th on the understanding that she would then be remanded until the following Friday.

The inquest was opened on 2nd and adjourned till 10. a.m. 11th.

Plans are being prepared, and photographs taken of roads, passages, &c also the interior and exterior of the house itself.

All particulars of blood spots &c have been [manuscript] taken.

There is every appearance that a strenuous fight will be made and some very expert evidence will be required in connection with the marks on blouse, skirt and handkerchiefs, (two bloodstained ones wire found by me in the copper) but the blood on these may have been caused from the boys ear, as I made enquiries at the school he attended and found he had been seen wiping blood from his ear.

Dr Kemp, Police Surgeon, Salisbury, when shown the skirt [9] &c, expressed the opinion that the marks thereon were blood.

A [manuscript note in margin] l beg authority to hand a copy of this report and statements to the Director of Public Prosecutions.

[signed] W. Dew. Chief Inspector. C.I.Dept. New Scotland Yard. A recommended. [manuscript] [signed] F.C. Froest Supt. [manuscript]

Notes

1. The pages are numbered at the foot and in the middle. So new pages are indicated by the page number in square brackets before the first word of text of the new page.

2. Punctuation has been retained from the original, spacing and layout (e.g. absence of first-line indents, right-justification of place and date of report) conform to modern practice.

3. Overtyped corrections have not been indicated.

Inspector Dew's final report to the Director of Public Prosecutions

METROPOLITAN POLICE. CRIMINAL INVESTIGATION DEPARTMENT, NEW SCOTLAND YARD, 29th day of April 1909

[in margin] CENTRAL OFFICER'S SPECIAL REPORT}

SUBJECT Edwin Richard Haskell Murdered at Salisbury.

Mother tried and acquitted. REFERENCE TO PAPERS. 217,339/2.

With reference to the subject named in margin.

I beg to report that at 12,30am 1st November 1908 the Chief Constable, Salisbury City Police, telephoned to the Assistant Commissioner that a boy aged 10 had been murdered in a house in that city at about 9pm 31st October, by a man whose description was given and circulated, and asked that an experienced officer, from this Department, should be sent to assist in the enquiry.

As directed I proceeded to Salisbury, per the 8,30am train on the 1st November, arriving there about ll,30am.

I placed myself in communication with Mr Richardson, the Chief Constable, and from my enquiries ascertained that the boy who had been.murdered was 12 years old, and had but one leg: his right leg having been amputated some years before in consequence of consumption setting in, but he was an intelligent and active youth, and found no difficulty in getting about with the aid of a crutch, and he was universally esteemed.

He lived with his widowed mother Flora Fanny Haskell, who was in poor circumstances, and earned her livelihood by taking in laundry work at 40 Meadow Road, one of a row of 5 roomed houses within the city boundary, a well populated district.

It seems that he was put to bed by his mother, at about twenty minutes to ten on the night of the tragedy, and at 10,30 his mother was heard screaming at her front door, and several persons heard her shouting 'Someone has killed my Teddy', and 'Someone has murdered my Teddy', and upon the neighbours proceeding to the back bedroom upstairs, they found the child dead with his throat cut.

Everyone agreed that the room was in perfect order; that nothing in the room had been disturbed, and that the boy was lying peacefully on his back, there being no indication of the slightest struggle having taken place.

It appears that Doctors Wilks and Rowe, who live closeby, were at once sent for, and upon their arrival found life to have been extinct within a quarter of an hour.

The police were communicated with, & Mrs Haskell's explanation was that she was in her kitchen, and hearing someone coming down the stairs, she opened the kitchen door leading to the passage, and she alleged that a man rushed down the stairs, and as he passed threw something at her, which splashed her, and then he ran out of the front door into the street and disappeared.

An immediate search of the neighbourhood was made, but no one was found.

Upon my arrival I found that unfortunately Dr Wilks had washed the body of the boy, and disarranged all the bedclothes, and later I discovered that the Officer, who was left in charge of the premises, had allowed Mrs (3) Carter, the mother of Mrs Haskell to wash the oil cloth in the passage, and the kitchen.

I made a thorough examination of the premises, and found that the bed and bed clothes were saturated with blood; that several splashes of blood were on the wall paper at head of bed; a few splashes on the chest of drawers, near the bed, some on a cushion, on a chair near head of bed; three or four drops on floor at feet side of bed, near head of child; several on the floor at foot of bed, one at the foot of dressing table nearby, and one on landing just outside bedroom door.

I also found several small spots of blood on the wall, on right hand side coming down stairs, and a long smear of blood just inside kitchen door, at foot of stairs, this last mark being caused by a table knife, which was found lying there, and had a quantity of blood on it, and which was from the first admitted to be the weapon with which the murder had been committed, and one which belonged to Mrs Haskell.

Although I made a very careful search, of the other parts of the premises, I failed to find any other marks of blood, except on 2 small hankerchiefs, which I found amongst some dirty clothes in the copper; they had a quantity of bloodmarks thereon, and also a blouse that Mrs Haskell had been wearing when she gave the alarm, and which was found to have a large number of blood spots on (4) right side, and right sleeve.

I saw Mrs Haskell, and having explained to her that I desired to do all I could to discover the perpetrator of the crime I asked her to tell me, in her own words exactly what had happened, which she did, and this was taken down at the time and signed by her.

This was a very lengthy statement, taking nearly 4 hours, (throughout which she was perfectly calm and collected) the purport off which was briefly as follows;- That she was a widow 34 years of age, her husband having died in 1904; the deceased was her only child, and that since her husband's death she had been earning her living by doing laundry work.

That on the evening before the murder a mysterious man called at her house, and said that he had been recommended to her for lodgings, but that she had declined to accom'm [manuscript] odate him, although he had pressed her to do so; that she told him it was a thing she never did, and that he went away apparently upset.

She went on to describe her movements on the fatal Saturday; One incident being that she went out to find another house to live in. She described most minutely, as to the various shops she had visited, and her movements generally up to about 20 minutes to 9, at which time she said that she and the deceased had some bread & ham; that she then washed him, and at about 20 minutes to (5) ten put him to bed in the upstairs bedroom, immediately over the kitchen.

She said that she then came downstairs, and went into the water closet in the back yard, then returned to the kitchen, and sat reading for about a quarter of an hour; then with the intention of visiting a neighbour she got up and locked the door leading to the yard; lowered the gas in the kitchen and as she was going to open the kitchen door leading to the passage, so as to leave by the front door & gain access to the street her nephew, Percy Noble age 16, who lives next door, came and knocked back door, and that as she was going across the kitchen to answer the door to him she heard someone coming down stairs; that she opened the kitchen door a man rushed downstairs by her and threw something at her, 'And splashed my sleeve up'. She said she then ran to Percy Noble and said, 'Rush Percy for someone'. He said 'Where shall I go [?]'. I said 'Go for anyone, go for the doctor'.

In answer to my question she said she did not know why she told him to go for the Doctor; only that she saw the splashes on her sleeve.

She then described how she came through the kitchen, and found the street door wide open; that she shouted out for help and a Mr Steer, who lived close by, came to her and she told him that someone had been (6) her stairs; that several other people came at once, and she asked them to see if her 'little Teddy' was all right, and that she asked several of them, including the Doctor, to tell her what was the matter, and that later on she was allowed to go up and see the deceased, and place her hands on his forehead.

She said that when she put the boy to bed she left a small brass lamp burning in the bedroom, but when the alarm was given this was found outside the bedroom floor extinguished.

She was unable to give any description whatever of the man who came downstairs, or what he was wearing, saying that the light was too dim.

She complained that in the folds of a table cloth in a drawer, of the chest of drawers in the fatal bedroom, there were 7 sovereigns, 2 half sovereigns, and a 2 shilling piece, which had been given to the deceased by his grandmother to purchase him an artificial leg, and that when she asked a Sergeant of Police to see if it was safe it was found that the lock of the drawer had been forced open, and only 3 sovereigns & one half sovereign were left.

She declares that that was practically all the money in the house, and that she had seen it safe on the previous Thursday, when she had borrowed a small sum from it, and that no-one, except her mother, the deceased and herself knew anything about it. (7) She offered no explanation as to why, when she saw a man run downstairs, she did not go up to see if her boy was safe, or follow the man; nor did she attempt to explain why she jumped to the conclusion that the boy had been murdered.

She said that the deceased boy had had the knife in the back garden, on the Thursday prior to the murder, cutting wood, since which time she had not seen it.

In answer to my questions she said she was wearing an apron at the time the man threw something at her, but on my securing the apron I found no sign of blood on it.

I asked her to take a dark skirt off, which she was wearing, and on making a cursory examination of it I discovered, what proved to be, many splashes or blood.

She explained that the knife was sometimes kept in the kitchen drawer, and sometimes it was lying in the back yard, and she practically admitted that it had been recently sharpened.

On subsequent dates she amended her statements, but I do not think I need trouble about that, for the purposes of this report.

The case struck me as having many difficult and mysterious points about it, and I therefore at once hastened to secure signed statements from about 60 persons and from my enquiries I found that Mr Steer, on the alarm being given, ran into York Road, which is close by, where (8) he saw what he described as 'Two mysterious men' loitering outside the 'Duke of York' public house, one of them he knew by sight; the other was a perfect stranger.

A search was made by the local police for these men, but they could not be found: consequently the conclusion was jumped to that one or the other was either the murderer, or knew something about it, and this theory was encouraged in their minds by the fact that, what was said to be blood stains were found on a gate near to where they were standing, but which was subsequently found to be nothing of the sort.

A man named Leate further complicated the matter by declaring that he had seen a man run out of Mrs Haskell's house about 10,30 on the night of the murder, followed by Mrs Haskell shouting 'Stop him, he has murdered my Teddy' etc;.

This she, not knowing what Leate had said, in answer to questions of mine flatly denied, and later I satisfied myself that he was an absolute liar. Even the defence did not accept his story.

On the Monday evening, following the murder on the Saturday, I discovered the two, so called mysterious men, who turned out to be respectable workmen named Butt and Ewcott [sic], and they were called and gave evidence.

The explanation as to the blood on the handkerchiefs found in the copper was that he (Teddy) had knocked his (9) ear at school, and had wiped it with these handkerchiefs, and my enquiries satisfied me that this was so.

In addition to the points shown, there was a strong rumour in Salisbury that Mrs Haskell was engaged, and anxious to get married to a steward named Mold, and he might have committed the murder, but I found as a matter at fact that he was in New York at the time, and was employed as a steward on R.M.S. 'Adriatic', but a letter found at the house, and one subsequently received by Mrs Haskell, from him, convinced me that the two were on more or less intimate terms, and that marriage had been discussed.

After making exhaustive enquiries in this matter on the Sunday, Monday and Tuesday morning, I was absolutely satisfied that Mrs Haskell herself had committed a premeditated, coldblooded murder, and that her explanation of how the blood spots came on her blouse could not be sustained, and in this I was confirmed by the local police surgeon, to whom I showed the blouse and skirt.

I came to the conclusion that Mrs Haskell found that this poor cripple boy, was either a hindrance to her getting married to Mold, or to her carrying on intrigues with men, and so she determined to get rid of him: that she concocted a story of a man stopping him in the Street a few days before, and asking him for his name & address; that she invented a story of a man calling on her the (10) night previous to the murder, seeking lodgings, and that she actually went so far that day as to look for another house, so as to be prepared to get away from such grim surroundings, after she had committed this terrible deed.

I was of opinion that she was a cool, calculating woman; that she went through her usual performance of shopping on the Saturday, and that after the boy was asleep in bed she satisfied herself that the neighbours on each side of her in bed – for this she undoubtedly did –; that after the boy was asleep she went upstairs and cut his throat, then brought the lamp out of the room, placed it on the landing and proceeded downstairs, and on reaching the bottom was suddenly startled, by hearing someone knocking at her back door; that she became panic-stricken and sat on a chair, just inside the kitchen door, and dropped the knife from her hand on the floor, where it was found; that she then partially recovered from her fright and went into the wash house, probably washed her hands at the sink therein, over which there is a tap (all of which would take but a few seconds) ; then opened the wash house door to her nephew^ [manuscript], Percy Noble [typescript] and commenced screaming and saying that someone had murdered her Teddy, and told him to run for the Doctor,

This latter part is in accordance with Noble's statement.

Strangely enough instead of letting him come into (11) the house, and follow the man, whom she alleged she had seen, she sent him out the back way, quite in the opposite direction, and that she then ran into the street and told everyone she saw that someone had murdered her Teddy, and to some of them she even suggested that it was the man, who had called for lodgings the night before.

I was of opinion that she laid great stress, as to the loss of the money from the drawer in the fatal bedroom: solely for the purpose of suggesting a robbery, and thus accounting for the murder by a man, whom she alleged she had seen leave the house.

In point of fact I never did believe that money had been stolen, as there were no indications of the drawer having been forced in the way one would expect a thief to do.

Subsequent events satisfied me that the woman had at various times pilfered this money herself.

My theory was, having regard to all the points, that after killing the boy Mrs Haskell's intention was to have destroyed the knife etc; leave the house and visit an intimate friend of hers, viz, Mrs Mold: then after some lapse of time return home, find her front door open, raise an alarm, and then the neighbours would have found the murdered boy, and then the suggestion would have been that it was another of those mysterious murders of children.

But, Percy Noble coming unexpectedly to the back (12) door at 10,30pm upset all her plans, and then cool and calculating woman as she revised them as in her statements.

People were about the neighbourhood, at the very moment that it is alleged that the man left the house, yet they saw no one, and at 20 minutes after ten – ten minutes before the alarm was given – a messenger knocked at Mrs Haskell's front door, and left a pair of boots with her for the next door neighbour, whom he had failed to arouse, and he saw no one.

I think it is clear that immediately after this boy left the door Mrs Haskell went & killed her son, and then came the second disturbance in the shape of Percy Noble.

Mrs Haskell never did attempt to explain why, or how a stranger should conceal himself in her small house for the purpose of robbery and murder.

Having come to these conclusions I placed my views before Chief Constable Richardson of the Salisbury City Police, and Superintendent Stephens of the Wiltshire County Constabulary with the result that at 10.30 the same night we arrested Mrs Haskell for the wilful murder of her son, the day prior to the deceased's funeral.

When told the charge she said 'No, no', and that is all she ever did say to Police concerning the matter.

In her possession, singularly enough, was found a (13) purse

containing 8 sovereigns, which she said her mother had given her to mind. Her mother is a poor woman living in Almshouses, but we could not refute the story.

In passing I ought to say that throughout this very difficult enquiry Superintendent Stephens rendered great and valuable assistance to me individually, and to the Chief Constable of Salisbury City.

After Mrs Haskell was remanded the facts, so far as I had collected them, were placed before the Director of Public Prosecutions, and Mr Pepper was requested to examine the blood stains etc, on the blouse and skirt, and both he, Dr Kemp, and the other two Doctors were unanimous in concluding that the blood marks were not caused by a person throwing the fatal knife at Mrs Haskell, as described by her.

The opinion of these gentlemen was, that the blood on the blouse, and some on the skirt was undoubtedly caused by the blood spraying from the wound, on them, and that the stains, especially on her blouse, were actually identical with the blood stains on the wall paper, at head of bed, chest of drawers, and cushion on chair, and that the remainder of stains were caused from blood dripping from a knife held in her hand, as were those on the floor and landing, whilst those on the wall leading downstairs were presumably caused by a blood stained sleeve coming in contact with the paper. (14)

I ought perhaps to explain that the carotid artery was severed, and the windpipe cut, and that the rush of blood from the artery went across the bed, in the opposite direction to which the murderer was standing, and that in the child taking the last gasp there would be a kind of froth and blood sprayed from the windpipe.

On my return to Salisbury, after placing these facts before the Director, I discovered that a Mrs Sweetman, from whom I had obtained a statement, had not disclosed the fact that when she saw Mrs Haskell, a few minutes after she had raised the alarm, she found a damp blood stained han[d]kerchief in Mrs Haskell's hand; later Mrs Haskell suggested that this was also caused by the boy's ear bleeding, but the medical gentlemen would never admit this theory.

It also subsequently transpired that on the night of the murder one of the persons going to the house called the attention of one of the Police Officers to blood smears and spots, on a white table cloth on [the] kitchen table: on the side where a person would pass in going from passage door to scullery, and Mr Pepper was of opinion that this might reasonably be caused, by a person carrying a blood stained han[d]kerchief in their hand, and its catching on the table cloth in passing.

No Officer would admit having been told this, but I found this blood stained table cloth in the kitchen (15) drawer, and it formed an important piece of evidence.

The Coroner's inquest was a protracted one lastin[g] 8 days, with the result that the jury returned a verdict of Wilful Murder against Mrs Haskell, but added that she was insane when she committed the crime.

The Police Court proceedings lasted 6 days, between 40 and 50 witnesses being called, and after she had been committed for trial Mrs Haskell told the Police Matron, that if she (Mrs Haskell) committed the murder she did not remember anything about it.

She was tried before Mr Justice Ridley on the 16th February, and the two following days, and was ably defended by Mr Rayner Goddard, barrister, but the Jury, after a long absence, failed to agree; there being 11 for a verdict of guilty.

She was again tried before Mr Justice Darling on the 1st inst; and two following days, when the Jury returned a verdict of 'Not Guilty'; the foreman saying that they came to that conclusion on the Ground that there was not sufficient evidence.

In conclusion I would respectfully submit that there never was a stronger case of circumstantial eviden[ce] and indeed nothing could be stronger, except the evidence of an eye witness to the perpetration of a crime.

I venture to say that it can well be imagined that this enquiry, from the commencement to the finish, (16) was fraught with the utmost difficulties, which were not lessened by the fact that the body was allowed to be disturbed; that many people were in and out of the house before the arrival of a responsible Officer, and that th[e] floor of the passage in the kitchen was allowed to be washed, by the Officer left in charge of the house, and therefore it is all the more surprising that I was able to collect such a chain of evidence, which in the opinion of almost everybody, was sufficient to secure a more satisfactory verdict.

A [manuscript note in margin] I respectfully beg that this report be submitted to Home Office.

[signed] W. Dew. Chief Inspector. [countersigned] F C Froest [manuscript] Superintendent

Copy [manuscript note in margin] In view of the evidence and the summing up of Mr Justice Darling it is more than surprising that the Jury should have acquitted this woman. I venture to submit that throughout this long and most difficult investigation Chief Inspr Dew performed his duty with marked skill and ability

sgd F C Froest   Superintendent [manuscript addendum] A recommended [manuscript]

Henry Mackay's first report to the Director of Public Prosecutions

H.M. Prison, Devizes. Feby. 11. 09.
The Director of Public Prosecutions, Rex -v- Haskell.
Sir,
I have the honour to submit herewith a report on the mental condition of the above named prisoner.

Before proceeding to deal specifically with the prisoner[']s mental condition, (a) at the date of the commission of the crime, and (b) at the present time, it may be well to make a general statement as to her conduct, and her mental characteristics during the time she has been an inmate of this Prison.

I I have had Mrs Haskell under my observation since her reception, and have had frequent conversations with her during this period. I find her an intelligent, self possessed, and fairly well educated woman. She has conducted herself throughout with perfect propriety, and has occupied herself cheerfully and skilfully in the usual duties that fall to prisoners on remand. She has exhibited no signs of epilepsy, Hysteria, Insanity, nor of any marked neurosis.

She converses readily on the subject of the charge against her and discusses it in an intelligent and reasonable manner. Her mental attitude to this subject is a perfectly natural one. While recognising fully the gravity of her position, she exhibits no violent or unreasonable manifestations of grief – on the contrary she appears on all occasions to have her emotions well under control.

I have been unable to elicit in her personal history any clear record of previous mental derangement.

A statement made by her to me was that she was mentally affected for a period of one week in the year 1903, and that she was then attended by Dr Wilks of Salisbury, was submitted by me to that (2) gentleman for verification. Dr Wilks' reply was to the effect that he had never observed any morbid mental condition in Mrs Haskell.

Nor can I discover from the prisoner herself, any history of insanity, or epilepsy in her family.

She suffers from no physical ailment that might affect her judgement or reason. She has slept well and eaten well. Her general health has been good, and she has gained 13lbs weight.

II Mental condition at the time of the crime.

For evidence on this point I have to rely chiefly on the prisoner's own statements to me.

In several conversations she has given me a detailed account of her acts on the 31st October last, and especially of her proceedings on the evening in question.

She states that on that day she was in her usual health and discharged her ordinary domestic duties as usual.

She can recall no headache, giddiness or abnormal sensations of any kind. She states that she remembers all her acts up to the time when the lad Wyatt brought the parcel of boots for her neighbour, Mrs Manning. She recalls taking this parcel in and estimates the time as about 10.20 pm. But from this time forward, according to her account, there is a lapse in her consciousness, and the next thing she remembers is getting up to go out to buy chocolates about 10.30 p.m. She turned the gas down and was going to the scullery door in response to the knock of her nephew when 'a man passed her and threw a knife at her.'

After this occurrence – she states – her memory is clear as to subsequent events, but as to what happened to her or what she did between 10.20 and 10.30 p.m. she has no recollection.

I have no concern with the question whether or not this

account agrees with the depositions on other occasions.

The point with which I am concerned in connection with this report, is the alleged lapse of consciousness, which coincides, so far as can be ascertained with the probable time at which (3) the crime was committed.

With reference to this point I may premise, that, excluding somnambulism, there are two conditions only known to medical psychology, which, in a person not insane, may give rise to temporary lapses of consciousness, during which apparently purposive, and complex acts may be committed.

Both these states occur in epileptics – one that is known as post-epileptic automatism, and the other is that known as masked, or larval epilepsy.

In my opinion neither of these conditions can be invoked to account for an alleged act of violence, on the part of Mrs Haskell in the present case.

My reasons for this opinion are:-

(a) Mrs Haskell is not, and has not been, so far as any evidence goes, an epileptic.

(b) The acts done in that condition of epileptic, or post-epileptic autoamtism, are invariably reproductions of an act which is an habitual one with the patient, e.g the winding of a watch, or the act of undressing.

(c) Acts of violence done in the condition of masked epilepsy almost invariably bear the stamp of purposeless, and needless ferocity. In the case under question no such exhibition occurred.

For these reasons I am of opinion that the alleged lapse of consciousness on the prisoner's part is not consistent with any mental condition likely to have been present in her case, and I ma unable to obtain from her own statements any evidence or presumption that her mental state at the time of the commission of the crime was other than normal.

III Mental condition of the Prisoner at the present time.

In this matter I am of opinion that the prisoner is in no sense insane, that she is in complete possession of her faculties, and that she is fit to plead to the Indictment.

I have the honour to be &c.

H. Mackay. M.D., M.O. H.M.Prison, Devizes.

Henry Mackay's second report to the Director of Public Prosecutions

H.M. Prison, Devizes, March 26th 1909

Rex –v– Flora Fanny Haskell

Further to my report of February 11th 1909, on the above named prisoner, I have now the honour to report that I have had the prisoner under my observation during the period which has elapsed since that date.

Her bodily health hs been extremely good – she has eaten well, slept well, and gained in weight.

Her demeanour has been quiet, self possessed, and, under the circumstances, cheerful.

Her memory for both distant, and recent events, is good. Her judgment is sound, and her intelligence unimpaired. In the course of a re-examination, directed towards ascertaining the condition of her mental state at the date of the murder, she mentioned that she wished to correct a statement she had previously made to me.

The statement she wished to correct was one to the effect that, as regards the evening in quesiotn, she was unable to recall anything that happened between the arrival of the messenger from the Co-operative Stores with the boots of her next door neighbour, about 10.20 p.m. and the knocking at her back door about 10.30 p.m.

She stated to me on the 24th inst; that 'things have now come back to her' and that she now remembers that after taking in the boots, she prepared fish for the next day's breakfast and after that sat down and read a paper until about 10.30 p.m. and that she got up then to turn down the [2] gas, when she heard the knocking at the back door, and the simultaneous noise she attributed to a man coming down the stair.

As regards the corrected statement (i.e. the record in point of time) I would remark that if it is true, it would in my opinion exclude any possibility of an epileptic seizure accompanied by homicidal violence having occurred in the interval in question. Such a seizure would necessarily be accompanied by unconsciousness, and would cause a blank in the sequence of those events, of which she has now supplied full and connected details.

As regards the Prisoner's mental condition therefore at the time the act was committed, I see no reason to alter the opinion I expressed in my former report.

And as regards her / present mental condition I consider that she is in full possession of her faculties and capable of pleading to the Indictment.

I have the honour to be Sir, Your obedient Servant

H. Mackay, M.D. M.O. H.M. Prison Devizes

The Director of Public Prosecutions, Whitehall

Richard Carter's Testimonial

Richard Carter's Testimonial, published in Lloyd's Weekly News, 8/11/1908 and Salisbury Times and South Wilts Gazette, 13/11/1908.

My sister, I am convinced, is absolutely innocent of this charge. As she says in her letter, she loved Teddy too dearly to think for a moment of taking his life. Little Teddy was an old soldier's son. His father, a Salisbury man, served as a private and non-commissioned officer in the Wiltshire Regiment. For some years he served in India, where we are afraid he contracted the malady which eventually carried him off. Leaving the Army, he obtained a situation at Fisherton House Asylum as an attendant. Whilst he was there he married my sister. That was thirteen years ago.

At that time he was in the Reserve, and when the South African war broke out he obeyed the call, and joined the Veterans' Corps for garrison duty in this country. Later his health began to fail, and he showed signs of falling victim to consumption. His wife battled bravely against this adversity. She did everything she could for him, and while he was undergoing treatment at Ventnor – whither he was sent – she worked hard to keep the home together.

At last, however, he succumbed – that was about five years ago – and my sister was left with little Teddy to care for. But he also caused her great anxiety. About the time of his father's death a disease developed in the right hip, and as a result the leg had to be amputated. For a time Teddy was very sickly. His mother, however, showed the most tender solicitude for him, humoured his every whim, and, in short, strove her utmost to make him a bright child, despite his affliction. He had every attention, including, for a time, the services of a trained nurse. And by-and-bye my sister was delighted to find him getting more robust. To Teddy she was extremely devoted. She gave him everything that she could afford, and was always pleased for him to find recreation with his school mates. Although he had only one leg, he was a very capable footballer, and his mother always took a very great interest in his games. Everyone seemed very fond of Teddy. Everyone had a smile for him as he hobbled along the street. Canon Thwaites, Rector of Fisherton, always displayed great interest in him. Some used to give him odd pence, and at the time of his death he had saved about four shillings.

Eighteen months ago my mother, Mrs Carter, handed the sum of £10 to my sister, which was to be devoted to giving him a start in life. This money, with the boy's own savings, was kept locked up in the chest of drawers in the room which my sister and the boy occupied. (For his mother slept in the same room in order that she might be with him at night. Three weeks ago Mrs Haskell was desirous of buyiung som new clothes for Teddy. She spoke to my mother about it and it was agreed to take the sum of £2 from the money kept in the chest of drawers. That, of course, left £8 4s.

Now, I will give you an account of what happened last Saturday, founded on the statements which have been made to me by various people who will be called to give evidence on my sister's behalf. My sister went out shopping about seven o'clock accompanied by a neighbour. Teddy was left next door with his cousin, Percy Noble. Afterwards he came indoors and read till his mother arrived. When his mother came in she gave him his supper. Then he expressed a desire to go to bed, as he was tired. 'All right, my son, go to bed,' said my sister. She washed him as usual and put him to bed. That would be about half-past nine. In the bedroom she left a small lamp burning on the dressing-table, as was her custom. After putting Teddy to bed my sister went out. She returned in a few minutes.

Shortly afterwards she heard a footstep overhead, but put it down to someone walking about in the next house. At about 10.20 Percy Noble, who had gone into the town, returned and went to

the back door. He tried the door first and then gave two loud knocks on it with his knee. The next moment my sister thought she heard someone coming down the stairs. She ran to the door leading to the passage with the intention of calling up to Teddy. At that moment a man came rushing downstairs, taking the last few stairs with one jump. As he ran past he either threw or dropped something from which blood was streaming onto the floor at her feet. The man ran to the front door and made his escape into the street.

Some time afterwards my mother, at a loss to imagine what could have prompted anyone to kill Teddy, suddenly thought of the money kept in the chest of drawers upstairs. At this time, of course, a police officer was in possession. In his presence my mother exclaimed 'Oh! What about that money?' There was some discussion about it, and then, at my mother's request, the officer went upstairs to see if any of it was missing. He had been previously informed that the key of the drawers was kept in a vase on the mantelpiece. In a few moments he came down, bringing one of the drawers with him. 'There is no need for a key,' he said, displaying the drawer, for it had been wrenched open, the lock being nearly off. On the money being counted, it was found that only £3 10s. of it remained. I fancy the assailant, when disturbed, made a hasty snatch at the money.

After a time my mother noticed that there were a few spots of blood on the right sleeve of the light blouse which my sister was wearing. 'Whatever is this?' said my mother. 'It looks like blood!' My sister then said that the bloodstained article which fell at her feet must in some way have touched her. Of course, I do not know what evidence the police propose to give against my sister. There is, however, one point to which I should like to refer. On Sunday when they searched the house the police took away with them a couple of Teddy's handkerchiefs which bore some bloodstains. These bloodstains admit of a simple explanation. One day towards the end of the week Teddy came into the house holding a handkerchief to his ear. My mother, who was taking tea with Mrs Haskell, said, 'Whatever is the matter, Teddy?' He replied, 'I have only knocked my ear, grandma, and made it bleed.' She said, 'Don't use that dirty handkerchief! Take a clean one.' This he did. Clearing up after tea, my mother put a few soiled articles, including a coarse apron and the two handkerchiefs into the copper.

Now I should like to tell you a curious circumstance which may have an important bearing on this case. On Wednesday Teddy was writing at home. His mother asked him what he as writing. He then said that a man had met him in the street, and asked him his name and where he lived. The boy had told him that he lived alone with his mother. The man gave Teddy twopence. The man said that if he would write his name and address down if he saw him again he would give him something else. Mrs Haskell said, 'You should not do that!' But Teddy replied, 'Oh, he might give me another tuppence!' The mother attached little importance to the incident at the time.

There is another matter I ought to mention. My sister states that on the night prior to the murder a man who appeared to be 'tidily dressed' – that is her description of him – knocked at the door and said, 'Are you Mrs Haskell?' She answered that she was, and asked him his business. He said, 'I want lodgings for the night.' She said, 'Oh, I don't take lodgers.' He said, 'But I have been recommended to you.' My sister again gave him to understand that she did not let lodgings, and shut the door. At this the man seemed much annoyed.

I saw my sister at the police station on Wednesday. After the proceedings at the police court I asked her, point blank, 'Do you know anything about this?' She replie, 'Oh Dick, you know I didn't do it. I would not hurt a hair of his head. Won't they let me see him before they take him away?'

Trethowan's Defence Counsel's Briefing Notes, First Trial, February 1909

All the papers in the matter are [with] Mr Rayner Goddard, the Defence having no funds to enable additional copies to be made.

The Prisoner is a Widow & is about 34 years of age & is charged with the wilful murder of her only child, a cripple boy aged about 12 years on the night of 31st October at a house in Fisherton Anger Salisbury known as No 40 Meadow Road.

There was great affection between Mother & son right up to the time of the latter's death & this will be proved by all the witnesses for the Prosecution who knew the Prisoner.

The evidence against the Prisoner is mainly that of the Doctors who were called in within a very short time of the murder & the evidence of Dr Kempe of Salisbury & Professor Pepper.

The Prisoner has made various statements to the Police which have been put in in evidence. Many of these statements on investigation by the Police have been found to be true.

The bloodmarks & spots found on the Prisoner's blouse & skirt according to Professor Pepper's evidence could not have been caused in the way mentioned by the Prisoner & in going into these marks before the Magistrates Professor Pepper pointed out that some of the spots tailed upwards & some downwards & this he says could not have happened if a knife had been thrown at the Prisoner or down on the ground at her feet but experiments made by Mr Bothams of Salisbury plainly show that both spots of blood in an upward & downward direction could have been caused in this way by the turn of the knife after having struck the kitchen door or the lintel of the door.

[2] It will be seen that the Prisoner is by no means a strong woman & Dr Wilks will admit that the blow which caused the death would be much more easily caused by a man than by a woman.

It was understood that the Doctors' theory at first was that the Prisoner did not actually commit the murder but must have been in the bedroom at the time or else had full cognizance of what was being done & is trying to shield the actual murderer.

In addition to the medical evidence the Prosecution seem to rely on the fact that nobody else was seen coming out or going into the premises at anywhere about the time the murder was committed & that therefore the Prisoner is the only person who could have committed the murder.

Now it is quite clear that two men at all events were at or near the premises at the time of the murder, one being seen by Leate & one by Daniells [i.e.Daniels] both of whom gave their evidence before the Coroner.

The Prosecution before the Magistrates called the witness Lodge, it being suggested that she was the person Daniells saw coming round Mrs Cooper['|s corner. This however is impossible because at the time Mrs Lodge went round the corner Daniells was in the barber's shop in Fisherton St.

No evidence was put forward by the Prosecution to account for the man seen by Leate.

The question of time is important. According to the evidence of Drs Wilks & Row the murder must have taken place at about 10.20.

At just before 10 o[']clock the Prisoner was trying on the coat brought in by Miss Steer & joking with her & was when the clock struck 10 in the W.C.

The witness Wyatt called at 10.20 when the Prisoner opened the door to him & took in a brown paper parcel which she promised to give to her next door neighbour (Mrs Mannings [i.e. Manning]) who had gone to bed the next morning & which parcel was found to have had no blood marks on it when examined by the Police.

It is believed Percy Noble will now say that he was at the scullery door knocking at about 10.20 & the Prisoner got up apparently to answer the door to him & [that was] when she heard the thumping noise at the bottom of the stairs [and] afterwards the scream from Mrs Haskell who came almost immediately to the Scullery door and sent him for a Doctor.

The witness Steer, his wife & mother in law will also say that it was about 10.20 when they heard Mrs Haskell screaming & most of the witnesses for the [3] prosecution seem to support this time.

The only witness who speaks to a later time (viz 10.30) is the witness House. [He states that] He was standing at Slade's shop which is some considerable distance from No 40 Meadow Road talking to Mr Slade when he heard St Paul['|s clock chime the half hour & immediately after heard a scream proceeding from the direction of No 40 Meadow Road [and adds] that on walking towards the house he saw no one in the street (either going towards or coming from the house) but that there were a few people round the door.

From this it may be safely inferred that this was after Mr Steer first appeared on the scene & that he then was either upstairs in the bedroom or else round at the Duke of York looking for a man but the circumstances appear much more likely to support the first of these two inferences.

If these witnesses can be relied upon & the murder was committed at 10.20 Mrs Haskell had no time to wash her hand which must from the evidence given by the Prosecution have been bloodstained.

Another point made a good deal of by the Prosecution was the extraordinary conduct of the Prisoner herself who jumped to the conclusion that her boy was killed & notwithstanding this did not rush upstairs immediately to see what was the matter.

However it is only reasonable to suggest that's when the spots of blood fell on the blouse which is of very thin muslin the blood was felt by her & the conclusion she jumped to after seeing the man & the knife was not unreasonable, neither was it unreasonable that she in her fright rushed for help & her story that after help arrived she tried to go upstairs but was prevented through the kindness of the neighbours is not absolutely denied.

Counsel will be able to ascertain the further points for the defence by reference to Mr Goddard's brief & the papers accompanying to which it is understood he has already had access.

Trethowan's Defence Counsel's Briefing Notes, Second Trial, April 1909

HEREWITH are copy Depositions before the Magistrates, a full note of the state of evidence given at the Inquest on the deceased boy, Copy Statements of witnesses not called before the Magistrates but called at the Inquest, Copy Statement of the Prisoner made to her Solicitors, Copy Statements of witnesses taken before the proceedings by Defendant's Solicitors, Copy Additional evidence filed by the prosecution, copy suggestions made by Dr. Maurice, the various documentary exhibits and plans and photos and three plans prepared for the purposes of the defence.

THE Prisoner is about 34 years of age, and lost her husband, who was first a soldier and afterwards an asylum attendant, from consumption about 6 or 7 years ago.

THERE was only one child of the marriage – the deceased boy – who at the date of his death was about 12 years of age and was a cripple, his right leg having been amputated above the knee owing to tubercular disease, sometime after his father's death.

THE charge against the Prisoner is one of wilful murder of the boy on the night of October 31st last, at the house in which they resided together, No. 40, Meadow Road, Salisbury.

THE Prisoner from the date of her husband's death worked for and maintained herself and this boy, and there is no doubt she lived a respectable life and was respected by everyone with whom she came into contact.

She was always clean and tidy herself, and the boy always seemed happy, well dressed and comfortable, and all the witnesses who were called for the prosecution who knew the parties for any time will speak as to the great affection which existed between Mother and son, and their most intimate neighbours who saw them daily and several times a day will state that they never heard an angry word pass between them.

THE Prisoner earned her living by taking in washing, and though it si understood that the Police will suggest that she hardly earned enough to keep herself and boy alive and that this must occasionally have worried her, the witness Alfred Walter Noble, who will be called by the Prosecution, will state in cross examination that he was in Prisoner's house almost daily and often assisted her with her weekly washing accounts, that she earned from 22/- to 23/- a week and upwards, that the weekly rent of her house was 5/6, and that she obtained her goods (including [2] the soap, soda &c for her washing) from the Co-Operative Stores, in which she was a shareholder, and after deducting her expenses always had sufficient to pay her way and was never worried about money matters.

The Prosecution have all along had a difficulty in suggesting any motive for the alleged crime. It is quite evident that they at first believed that the murder was committed by a man, and they immediately jumped ot the conclusion that the man was Alfred John Mold, who was a Steward on board the Adriatic – a White Star Liner voyaging between Southampton & New York.

THIS opinion no doubt was strengthened by the evidence of the witness, Leate, who states that at about 10:15 to 10:20 he saw a man leave a house, which he believed to be No. 40 Meadow Road & go in the direction of James Street (where Mold's Mother and family then lived) followed by a woman wringing her hands and sobbing quietly.

FURTHER credence was probably attached ot this theory by reason of a rumour that Mold and the Prisoiner were engaged to be married, which rumour however was without any foundation.

THE Police ascertained that Mold had left Salisbury for Southampton on Sunday the 18 th October and sailed for New York on the following Wednesday the 21st., so they of course must have been convinced soon after the murder that he had nothing to do with the actual crime.

Chief Constable Richardson however and Chief Inspector Dew boarded the Adriatic at Plymouth on her return voyage, got Mold just out of his bunk just before midnight and subjected him to a severe cross examination, and even suggested that they were trying to help this poor woman out of her difficulties before they told Mold she was in custody, and they further said that he ought to do his part to assist her as well.

The took a signed statement from Mold, and he offered not to sign on for the next voyage to enabel him to attend the inquest if his evidence was required, and when he was told he would not be required, he promised to call at the Police Station when next in Salisbury for instructions and did so.

HE then asked to read over his statement which the Chief Constable refused to let him do. He wanted however to amend his first statement by saying he had written two letters to the Prisoner prior to or during the voyage he had just finished (instead of one as he had told the Police at Plymouth) and the Chief Constable took down this amendment on a fresh sheet of paper and he signed it. These letters were written by Mold to Prisoner because his Mother was ill at the time he left Salisbury and the Prisoner was looking after the Mother & had written to Mold at Mrs Mold's request as to her health.

THE statement made by Mold has never been seen by the defence, and the prosecution refuse to produce it, but it is quite evident that it could not in any way support the first theory of the prosecution.

IT is a curious fact that on the night of the 31st. October a man called Ray living in Gas Lane (quite close to Meadow Road) disappeared, and notwithstanding enquiries by the Police it is understood has never been discovered.

THIS fact was ascertained in the following way. A man named Miles, a bootmaker, used to have washing done by the Prisoner, and on Alfred Walter Noble calling on him sometime after her arrest for payment of the amount due to the Prisoner, Miles remarked that it was a curious fact that a man named Ray had been missing from Gas Lane since the night of the murder. He said he had been told this by P.C. Spencer, who had had an appointment with him one night to view one of his houses, and turned up late and explained his delay by stating that the search for this man [3] had detained him. Spencer told Miles that the Police thought there was trouble between Ray & his wife.

NOTHING of this of course was stated by the Prosecution either before the Coroner or before the Magistrates, and great stress was put on the fact that a search was made for some man, & no man could be found, or was known to be missing.

ANOTHER motive suggested by the prosecution was that the Prisoner was in monetary difficulties and knew that the money which was being saved up to buy a cork leg for the boy was upstairs in the drawer and having made use of this and knowing it would be found out soon, either by the boy himself or by his Grandmother, Mrs Carter, who had provided the money, she killed the boy to hide the theft.

TO support both these theories, Miss Thirza Haskell was brought down suffering from galloping consumption from a London Workhouse, but on cross examination it will be seen that her evidence was absolutely useless and did not support either theory. The statement of A.W. Noble before set out also disposes of the theory that Prisoner was in monetary troubles.

THE Police no doubt will make a point of the fact that no money (other than that in the drawer) was found in the house, except the 10/- belonging to Mis Thirza Haskell.

THIS is easily explained by the fact that the Prisoner had done her shopping that night and her money for that week's washing would not be paid to her until the Monday morning following, and some or the greater part of it has since been collected by A.W. Noble.

IT will be noticed that in Miss Steer's evidence she stated that the Prisoner said as she was leaving 'My purse is upstairs or I would give it (money for the coat) to you now' The Prisoner however says that she said 'My cash' not my purse (which as a matter of fact she knew to be in the front room), and probably she was referring to the money in the drawer, as it has been admitted

that she took small sums therefrom and replaced them from time to time, and if she had intended taking a small sum to pay Miss Steer meaning to pay it back when her washing money came in on the Monday, it was what anyone might have done under the circumstances.

IT is a curious fact that the 3 statements taken from the Prisoner by the Police under the circumstances detailed in the evidence should have been found by the Police to be so very nearly correct on all points where corroborative evidence could be obtained by them, and some of the slight inaccuracies might very well arise from the way questions were asked and tha answers written down by Chief Constable Richardson.

IT would have been impossible for Prisoner to have made such statements as she did without being closely questioned by the Police and that being so, the words of the questioner would be putdown, and not the actual words of the Prisoner herself. This was bound to have been the case when the Prisoner's answer was monosyllabic.

THERE may be a discrepancy in the Prisoner's statement as to the white apron, which the prosecution seem to have made a great point of. There is no doubt that the Prisoner wore a white apron when she was bathing the deceased in the kitchen that evening, and it is also possible that she took it off before Percy Noble knocked at the door or the noise was heard at the bottom of the stairs, because she had just at that time lowered the gas with the intention of going out to see Mrs Mold to shew her the coat which Miss Steer had just handed to her, & she had previously promised Mrs Mold to look round & see her.

IT is quite possible that she might have been wearing the apron tucked in on one side of her waistband or over her arm, and an examination of the bloodmarks on the blouse and skirt will [4] shew that they are not inconsistent with this theory, except perhaps as to some of the marks on the top of the skirt.

IT will however be seen from the statement which the Prisoner gave to her Solicitors that she believes she took off the apron just before Miss Steer came in, and it was afterwards on the same evening worn by her Mother, Mrs. Carter.

FROM the Prisoner's statement to the police, it would appear that she was wearing an apron that evening, and on the Police asking about this apron, Supt. Stephens went out and fetched it, and produced it to Prisoner, who identified it as her apron, and the one which she had been wearing that evening.

SHE was not however asked as to the time she was wearing the apron, and the sentence was probably inserted in the statement as the result of a mis-understanding between the Prisoner and the Police.

THE contention of the prosecution seems to be that this poor woman who was shewn to have been so devoted to her child had, for some days at least, made up her mind to murder her son, and had told Mrs. Mold, Mrs. Hawkins, Mrs. Carter, Miss Lawrence & A.W. Noble a story of a mythical man calling for lodgings on the 30th. October and who seemed upset because she would not take him in, and also invented the story of the boy writing his name and address on the Wednesday evening prior to his death for someone at school who promised to give him something for it, so that when the boy was murdered suspicion should fall on one of them and not on herself.

If this were so, would it have been probable that the prisoner would have gone about with her neighbours that Saturday evening in a bright, cheery way making the necessary provisions for the Sunday, and have brought a newspaper and sweets for the boy, washed him and provided him with clean clothes, and would have seemed just as usual right up to the time when she was seen by Mrs. Chivers at 9 o'clock, & by Alfd. John Noble at 9:40, and would have joked with Miss Steer just before 10 o'clock within a very short time of the perpetration of the crime and have answered the door to Wyatt in an ordinary way at or near the actual time at which the crime was committed?

A look at the prisoner herself would surely satisfy any unprejudiced person that she could not have arranged the murder with such method without shewing to her most intimate friends & relations something of what was passing in her mind or that something serious was on her mind.

THE woman herself seems frail, is small, and her features are not at all unpleasant, & nothing in her appearance would indicate that it was possible for her to have used the force which undoubtedly was necessary to have cut the boy's throat so cleanly and in such a deliberate way.

Mr Wilks had attended the Prisoner's husband and also attended the boy after his operation, and had known the prisoner and the deceased for some considerable time, and in cross examination he admitted that the wound could have been caused much more easily by a man than by a woman, and it is quite evident from the general tone of his evidence (although he never actually admitted it in so many words) that he considered the act was done by a man and not by a woman.

HE stated that in his opinion the wound was caused by a maniac, and before the Coroner he admitted that he had never found any indication of insanity in the Prisoner.

MR. Wilks was not asked this question before the Magistrates, Prisoner's Solicitor thinking the question too risky, as Mr Wilks had previously watered down before the Magistrates some of his answers given before the Coroner.

THERE is no doubt that Mr. Wilks is favourably disposed towards the Prisoner, but to a great extent he seems to rely more on the opinion of the other Doctors than on his own judgment, & gives one the impression that he is somewhat overawed by Professor Pepper. He never is a strong witness. Dr. Kempe however is, and is somewhat of a partisan always.

THIS weakness on the part of Mr. Wilks was more particularly noticed when he was asked by the Prisoner's Solicitor before the Magistrates (see p. 76 of the depositions) whether if Mrs Haskell lanced the stump of deceased's leg the blood which would flow might not have been the ordinary description of blood such as was found on the exhibits. He first said 'No', because Dr Pepper had said the discharge from the stump would be very

different to ordinary blood. Mr. Wilks however afterwards admitted that it might be ordinary blood, but not before Dr. Kempe whispered to him whilst Mr. Wilks was giving his evidence.

THIS will shew that Mr. Wilks has no reliance in his own judgment.

IT is a curious fact that all the four Doctors had a consultation before the Inquest or magisterial proceedings and their evidence is the result of that consultation.

PROFESSOR Pepper attended the inquest whilst the other Doctors were giving their evidence and suggested to Counsel for the prosecution nearly every question which was put to the other Doctors, and although no objection could be raised to the form of the question asked, yet if the answers given were not exactly in the form which Professor Pepper required, the questions were put again differently until Profr. Pepper appeared to be satisfied.

LOOKING at the meical evidence in this way, it would really appear to be the evidence of Prof. Pepper alone, and the evidence of the other Doctors as to the theoretical matter is not independent evidence at all, and this should be hinted to the jury.

IT is clear from Mr. Wilks' evidence that he did not consider when first called in that the crime could have been committed by the Prisoner, and it is pretty evident from the tone of his evidence that he did not think so afterwards.

HE admitted over and over again that he did not think under the circumstances she could have done it, but he always qualified this by saying 'as an ordinary man'.

BEFORE the Coroner, the Doctors were not quite agreed as to the position of the assailant when the wound was inflicted, Mr. Wilks stating that in his opinion the assailant was standing opposite the head of the boy and between his head and the chest of drawers, and Dr. Row in his evidence agreed as to this position. Dr Kempe stated that the assailant was standing facing towards the foot of the bed and on the right hand side and somewhat behind the wound in the neck, and Professor Pepper stating that the assailant stood on the right hand side probably at the boy's head, and in his opinion the left hand of the assailant was placed on the right temple of the boy pressing the head over to the left side.

BEFORE the Magistrates Dr. Kempe repeated his theory, but Mr. Wilks said the assailant must have been standing on the right hand side of the bed and with the left hand on the forehead of the boy and with the right hand have inflicted the wound across and slightly downwards and that he would be standing opposite the head rather above the neck and in front of the chair, and Drs. Row and Pepper agreed with him in this.

IF the assailant had been standing practically opposite the wound, he must, when inflicting it, have been looking at the boy and across the boy to the wall, nd from the state of the right [6] pillow, a considerable quantity of blood must have spurted on such assailant if in such a position, for blood was found on the toilet cover of the chest of drawers, and on the right hand drawer and its [k]nob.

IT will be seen from the photo of the bedroom that if the

boy's head was on the pillow, the edge of the chair would have been level with the boy's head, and it would seem impossible for any person to be in the position stated by Dr. Kempe unless the chair had been previously moved, which it is admitted is not the fact.

FURTHER, if he were in such a position, it seems an extraordinary fact that there should be blood on the chair cover, and on the wall paper at the back of the chair.

THE body of the assailant if standing in the position mentioned by Dr. Kempe must have been in the line of this blood.

IT seems a curious fact that although all the Doctors agree that the blood must have first spurted to the left, yet there is very little blood on the left pillow, most of it being on the right.

IN connection with this Dr. Maurice's report should be perused.

IT seems certain that the prosecution are not even now satisfied that their evidence is strong enough to obtain a conviction, and the police are still making various enquiries.

AS to motive, they will say there is never any adequate motive for murder, and no onus is on them to prove motive. That the crime, if committed by the mother, might have been done in a moment of madness, and this might account for her leaving all the traces of her guilt where they were found.

IT is quite clear that if the Prisoner committed the crime with the premeditation which the evidence of the Doctors would go to prove, especially the evidence of Mr Wilks, she would also have made some arrangement to dispose of the knife, her blouse and skirt, and the other evidence of guilt.

THE suggestion is however that she was interrupted, but there is absolutely no evidence as to this. The interruption could not have come from the boy Wyatt who brought the parcel to the next door neighbour Mrs. Manning, neither could it have come from Percy Noble.

THE latter simply called at the house to repay 1/- which he had previously borrowed, & it would have been the easiest thing for the Prisoner either to have told Percy Noble she was just going out or to have given him through the kitchen window any necessary answer or to have taken no notice of his knock and remained silent pretending she was out, knowing full well that Percy Noble would have thought she was either out or too busy to attend to him, and which would not have been at all unusual.

BUT for her own action in going to Percy Noble and then rushing into the Street she might have had the whole night to herself to clear away any traces of the bloodmarks, knife &c.

AGAIN the prosecution seem to have made a great point of the fact that when the knife was thrown and the alleged murderer escaped the Prisoner jumped to the conclusion at once that her boy was killed, and notwithstanding that did not rush upstairs to see what had really happened.

IT is submitted however on behalf of the Prisoner that what she did see was sufficient to frighten her, and that she was afraid to go upstairs until she got somebody in the house to help her, and this would seem only reasonable, as the blood falling on her thin muslin blouse was no doubt felt by [?] her through the blouse.

THERE is no doubt that the Prisoner did want to go upstairs to her son as soon as people arrived at the house. She tried to go up when the light had been brought, but Steer met her on the stairs and made her go down, although he denies this. She was advised by other people not to go up, and was practically out of kindness prevented until the Doctor took her up, and she then did what it is submitted no woman could have done had she murdered her child, kissed him on the forehead.

THE statements made by the Prisoner to the Police and to her Solicitors will show clearly what took place on Saturday October 31st. and that at any rate up to the time Miss Steer called on her with the coat to try on & Wyatt called with the parcel there was nothing exceptional in the Prisoner's demeanour or actions.

MRS. Chivers seems to have seen the Defendant between 8 & 9, she thinks about 9, in the town. She was then in her usual spirits, and there was no undue excitement about her and they had a conversation. She also saw the deceased's [i.e. deceased] boy about 9 o'clock.

Alfred John Noble saw the Prisoner at 25 minutes to 10 at his house. She went in with the washing and appears to have stayed about 5 minutes and went back to her house, and Miss Steer must have arrived with the coat almost immediately afterwards and stayed at least five minutes, and it is suggested by the cross examination that she stayed more than five minutes, and that had she done so, she would still have had plenty of time to meet the 10 o'c[lock] train at the Great Western Station (See plan). After Miss Steer left the Prisoner went out to the W.C. & heard 10 o'clock strike whilst there.

THE boy, Wyatt, was at Winchester Street, the other end of Salisbury, at 5 minutes past 10, and went to Meadow Road on his bicycle, arriving at No. 40, Meadow Road at 20 minutes past 10. Prisoner opened the door to him and took in a parcel, which she promised to hand to Mrs. Manning the next day, and this parcel was afterwards found at No. 40, Meadow Road by the police, and was examined for stains of blood, but none were found.

Mr Wilks got to the house at 10:31 and stated that the murder must have been committed within a quarter of an hour before his arrival, and reading his evidence before the Magistrates & before the Coroner, it may be taken that death took place at about 10:20, within a minute of the wound having been inflicted, and therefore at or about the time that Wyatt was knocking at the door.

THE prosecution wished to prove that Wyatt knocked at No. 40, Meadow Road several times & that there was consequent delay in the Prisoner opening the door. The inference that they no doubt wished to convey that Prisoner was then murdering or had just murdered the deceased.

ON cross examination however Wyatt refused to swear that he knocked more than once, and he refused to say that Prisoner did not come to the door immediately.

PRISONER'S statement to her Solicitors shews that she heard the knocks next door, and when her door was knocked, she went immediately to the door and undid it.

PROBABLY the prosecution will now suggest that the murder took place after Wyatt had left, and just prior to the Prisoner coming to the kitchen door to Percy Noble. This cannot be so, because Walter Steer heard Mrs. Haskell scream at 10:20 and rushed out immediately, meeting her just outside her house, and Edward Butt saw Walter Steer outside or opposite the Duke of York Hotel at 10:15 or just after, although Wm. Eccott states it was more like 10:25.

GERTRUDE SKUTT left 17 York Road at 10:20 and would have arrived at the entrance to the passage before 10:21, and this would bear out the time mentioned by Steer, who however was not seen [8] by her, nor was Mrs. Steer nor presumably Eccott or Butt.

ERNEST James House states that he was outside Slade's shop, also shewn on the plan, & heard a woman scream & St. Paul's Clock strike 10:30, & immediately heard Prisoner's scream. On cross examination he states that he was talking to Mr. Slade as to the time. The latter, however states that he did not hear the clock strike 10:30, and remembers no conversation with House about the time. House further states that he walked back to Meadow Road, and when he got to the Prisoner's door, there were a few people round it, but he neither saw Percy Noble, nor Mr. Or Mrs. Steer or Mrs. Chivers.

THE prosecution appear to be relying on House's evidence to prove that the murder took place after the time of Wyatt's call and before 10:30 & they are calling James Asbridge to prove that St. Paul's Church clock which House heard strike was right. Asbridge was not cross examined, but it is understood that he did not wind up this clock on the morning of October 31st.

IT is a part of the case for the prosecution that Steer was first on the scene in Meadow Road, but it is curious that House did not see him either going to or returning from the entrance to the Duke of York and it would appear that Steer must before this have either been into York Road and come back again and was then in the house, or else he had gone to Slade's shop with P.S. Golding after he and Golding had examined the Yard gates of the Duke of York Hotel.

In either case it must have been considerably after Steer first arrived at No. 40, Meadow Road, and House's evidence cannot fix the time of the murder.

The first Policeman on the scene of the crime was Sergt. Golding, and it will be seen from the evidence that his statement does not agree with some of the other witnesses called for the prosecution.

Mr. Steer was then in No. 40, Meadow Road in the bedroom. Steer said when before the Coroner 'I went back into the bedroom & shortly after P.S. Golding arrived. He looked round for a moment & then said 'I must get on the telephone somewhere' & he (Golding) went downstairs & I followed him. At the foot of the stairs my Mother in law Mrs. Chivers said 'Here is the knife' & Golding said 'Don't touch it' & picked it up with a piece of paper'.

Before the Coroner Golding said that he did not see or pick up the knife on his first visit to No. 40, Meadow Road, and did not see it until after he had been to Slade's shop & sent his telephonic message to the Police Station.

AFTER this evidence had been given, it turned out Mr. Steer was right and P.S. Golding was wrong and further that Sergt. Golding when he picked up the knife took it with him to Slade's shop & was seen with it in his hand by Mr. and Mrs. Slade, and Golding asked for a bag in which to wrap it and was handed a brown paper bag without any name on it similar to the bag accompanying the papers.

THIS information was obtained in time to cross examine Chief Constable Richardson at the Inquest, but he stated that he had made investigations and that as far as they went it was not true and that Golding had not found the knife when he went to Slade's.

Mr. Slade saw the report of this cross examination in the newspapers & as he had previously given a statement to the Police to the effect that the knife had been brought to his shop, he at once telephoned to the Chief Constable that he thought of writing to the papers to tell them so, & that he did not intend to be made out to be a liar.

LATER on Chief Constable Richardson & two other Officers saw Slade, and he gave them a second statement confirming his first & commencing 'From what I saw in the papers ———'.

THE Police endeavoured to persuade Slade that he might be wrong about the knife, but he [9] refused to alter his statement and described the knife to the Police in detail and told them he thought he could identify it. He also put a knife in a paper bag and wrapped it up in the same way as Golding did and held it up to Richardson saying 'Do you think I dreamt this?'

COUNSEL will no doubt think it advisable to cross examine both Richardson & Golding as to this, and to ask for production of the statements given by Slade.

IT appears that when Chief Constable Richardson got to No. 40, Meadow Road at about 11 o'clock, Golding told him that he had the knife in his pocket and he was told to keep it there & it was handed over to Richardson between 2 & 3 o'clock on Sunday morning and was then wrapped in brown paper and when he got back to his office he put it in a drawer & locked it up. He afterwards took it out of his drawer and put it with other papers into his bag wrapped up in the brown paper bag, & which bag or brown paper was afterwards said to have been mislaid or lost.

The cross examination of the Chief Constable before the Coroner & Magistrates will shew the extraordinary way in which the Police acted in this matter in obtaining the three statements from the Prisoner.

THE Prisoner though not under arrest was under police surveillance from early Sunday morning and the Chief Constable made a statement to a Magistrate about 8:30 on that morning that she was under suspicion & was believed to have committed the crime.

THE Police now say that these statements were taken from the Prisoner to enable them to look for the man referred to by the Prisoner.

THE nature of the statements themselves and particularly the second statement will shew what sort of questions were put to her.

IT is submitted that the story told by the Prisoner as to a man coming down the stairs and throwing down a knife at the bottom of the stairs when the Prisoner opened the door as detailed in her statements to the Police is not improbable, and that notwithstanding the evidence of the Doctors, for nearly all the blood found on the blouse & skirt was on the right hand side, which would be the side first exposed on her opening the kitchen door.

THE experiment made by Mr. Bothams & already mentioned to Counsel would tend to show that most of the spots shewn on the blouse & skirt could be caused by a knife thrown at the Prisoner & striking the lintel or edge of the door, and the knife would in consequence throw blood both in a downward and upward direction. Apparently Dr. Maurice agrees with this.

THE smudges on the skirt are different, but may be accounted for in the way stated by Dr. Maurice in his report.

IT must however be borne in mind that some of these stains may have been on the skirt for some very considerable time. The skirt was one which had been worn by the Prisoner for nearly two years, and for the last 12 months daily & Profr. Pepper admits in her [i.e.his] evidence that all the blood stains might be months old & he cannot say that they are human blood.

THE Prisoner purchased and cut up her own meat for cooking and it does not seem improbable that some of the smudges and stains might have been caused by blood from fresh meat, or when attending to the stump of the deceased's leg.

BETWEEN the bed and the chest of drawers, there were very few spots of blood. One would surely have expected from the condition of the pillows and bed clothes to have found a considerable amount of blood there, unless such blood had spurted over the murderer.

THE comparatively little blood found on Mrs. Haskell's blouse & skirt & on the floor between the bed and the chest of drawers would not account for the blood which would naturally be [10] expected to have sprayed beyond the bed.

THE only other spots of blood in the room except that on the toilet cover of the chest of drawers, the right hand drawer, on the chair cushion cover & on the wall paper were 9 small spots of blood at the end of the bed on the linoleum marked No. 23.

THESE spots were level with the end of the bed, and it seems a curious place to find them, assuming the murderer was right handed.

ON the linoleum on the landing outside the room & on the wall paper on the right hand side going downstairs there was very little blood. It would seem therefore to follow that if the murder were hurriedly done & the person immediately rushed downstairs, there must have been a considerable quantity of blood on the blade of the knife, on a part at all events of the handle of the knife and between the fingers of the hand which grasped the knife & about the nails of the hand, and this latter would have taken some time to be removed.

NOW it is certain that the Prisoner could not have had very much time to commit the murder and wash her hands between the time of Wyatt's visit and Percy Noble's visit, assuming for the present that the latter knocked at the door at about 10:30 and not 10:20 as shewn by Mr Steer's evidence and that of other witnesses.

FROM Percy Noble's evidence it would appear that when he pushed at the scullery door, the door leading from the scullery to the kitchen was closed, and if the prisoner had just murdered her child when Percy Noble arrived, some blood must have been on her right hand and one would have expected to have hound some mark of blood on the handle of the door leading from the kitchen to the scullery and on the latch of the scullery door itself, but that no trace of blood was found is shewn by the evidence.

NO trace of blood was found on any of the washing utensils in the scullery or on the tap or sink.

IT will be seen from the evidence of the prosecution that there were bloodstains and spots on the white cloth on the kitchen table. The suggestion is that they were caused by the Prisoner's sleeve or other soft material, as she was going through the kitchen towards the scullery.

IT is pretty certain that they could not have bee caused by the sleeve of the blouse worn by the Prisoner that night and could hardly have been caused by the handkerchiefs produced in Court and according to Profr. Pepper's evidence, they could not have been caused by her skirt.

THE other suggestion is that they might have been caused by a towel or duster, but no towel or duster was discovered in the house with blood upon it, although at one time it was suggested that Mrs. Carter, the Prisoner's Mother, had taken something out of the house.

THE suggestion was that some towels or cloths used by the Doctors & carried downstairs by Steer and wrung out by him & placed on the window sill had disappeared, but these towels or cloths were in the scullery the whole time, and on the Police asking Mrs. Carter about them, she told them where to look and the towels were discovered. Mrs. Carter had told the Police before the Inquest where these towels or cloths were, but they no doubt had forgotten the circumstances.

IT must be remembered that people were in the room where the murder was committed before the Police or Doctors arrived on the spot, and even after Sergt. Golding arrived no order was given for people not to go into the room and apparently no such order was given until Chief Constable Richardson arrived on the spot about 11 o'clock.

UP to this time at least Steer, Mrs. Butt, Rawlins, P.S. Golding & the two Doctors had [11] been in & out of the room and some of them more than once, and as will be seen from the evidence Steer and Rawlins at all events went through the kitchen into the scullery, and Rawlins in his evidence says that he noticed the blood on the table cloth after he had passed it, and the inference can be drawn that as he did not see it when approaching the table on his way to the scullery, it was not then there.

MRS. Butt in her evidence says 'I did not see Steer touch the boy. I was behind him. I went up and looked at Teddy. I stood behind Mr Steer at the side of the bed when I looked at him. Mr. Steer was also at the side of the bed.' The distance from the edge of the bed to the chest of drawers is 29 inches & to the mantelpiece 30 inches. If Steer were in front at the side of the bed & Mrs. Butt behind him as stated by her, Steer must have been touching the bed, and leaning over to put his hand on the deceased boy's face, he would probably touch some of the blood without noticing it & might have carried it downstairs to the table cloth.

MR. Wilks in his evidence before the Magistrates (p. 61) says 'I put the bloodstained clothes as far as I remember at the bottom of the bed underneath the other clothes.' Now these clothes were afterwards found under the bed, and it is more than probable that the person who took these clothes out from under the other bed clothes & put them under the bed might have got stains on his or her clothes & might afterwards in going to the kitchen have communicated the smears to the table cloth.

COUNSEL'S attention is drawn to the discrepancies in the evidence as to this tablecloth. Mrs. Sweetman did not mention to the police first when she made her statement, nor to the Prisoner's Solicitor's Clerk when she made her statement to him anything about blood on the table cloth, neither did she mention it when she gave her evidence first before the Coroner. She was however recalled to enable her to give evidence as to these marks, and she then said that she called Supt. Stephens' attention to the marks on the night of the 31st Octr.

THIS whoever Supt. Stephens flatly denied, as will be seen by his evidence before the Coroner & Magistrates.

AGAIN Rawlins never mentioned the marks to the Police when he first made his statement nor yet to the Prisoner's Solicitor's Clerk when he made his statement to him, although this Clerk asked him whether he had seen any other blood marks than those he had described in his statement, and he answered 'No.'

IT is an extraordinary thing that Sergt. Golding who was in & out of the kitchen all night, and who was supposed to have examined everything, makes no mention in his evidence of having seen the blood marks on the table cloth, neither does Chief Constable Richardson.

IT is understood that the table cloth was taken off next day & probably before Chief Inspr. Dew arrived at the house.

GREAT stress was laid by the prosecution on the fact that no blood was discovered on the kitchen door or the lintels, it being evident that if the Prisoner's story was true the knife must have struck something to make the various spots on her clothing.

MR. Bothams' experiments prove that if the handle of the knife struck either the door or the lintel of the door, no blood would necessarily be thrown on such door or lintel, & in making 6 or 7 experiments, only in one case was any blood left on the door itself.

AGAIN the prosecution laid stress on the small amount of blood found on the piece of [12] linoleum leading from the passage into the kitchen.

IT must however be borne in mind that Mrs. Carter, the Prisoner's Mother, washed the passage and this piece of linoleum about 6 o'clock on Sunday morning. She first swept out the place and then got a pail of cold water (the best fluid for removing blood) and a flannel. The patch of blood at the entrance of the kitchen from the passage was then in her opinion about six inches in length. She washed it up as best she could and removed some of the blood, nearly all, but she did not think she got out every mark. She got up as much as she could.

IN addition to this, people were constantly going in and out of the kitchen all that night and the next day, and this must have further tended to obliterate the stain. Golding, however, will say that the stain was bigger when he looked at the linoleum when before the Magistrates than when he first noticed it on the night of the 31st October.

THERE is further Dr. Maurice's theory that the knife in falling was caught by the Prisoner's skirt, and if this were so, a good deal of the blood must have been removed and caused the smears or smudges on the skirt.

WE do not think much reliance can be placed by the prosecution as to the bloodstains on the handkerchiefs, for it is proved conclusively that the boy had a sore on his ear which he had picked, and which had been bleeding during the days just previously to the date of his death, and that Mrs. Haskell had a scar on her nose, which according to the evidence for the prosecution appeared fresh, and this sore and scar would account for the blood on the handkerchiefs.

IF the Prisoner had been guilty, she would never have continued to hold a bloodstained handkerchief in her hand when surrounded by women or have allowed them to take it passively as she did.

ANOTHER reason put forward by the prosecution that the Prisoner has for getting rid of her son was that she wanted to marry A.J. Mold before referred to, and that he was unwilling to marry her unless the boy was put away.

IT will be seen from the evidence that there is really nothing to support this, except a rumour, which was absolutely denied by Mold & the Prisoner, and all her intimate friends and relations, who would be likely to know anything about such a matter if there was any truth in it.

IT is true something was said to the witness A.J. Noble, which was said as a joke & taken by every one hearing it as a joke.

THERE is the evidence of E. Thirza Haskell that she considered Mold wanted to marry Prisoner, but that Prisoner never agreed to it, and Mrs. Mannings' evidence is to the same effect.

MOLD however denies that he ever offered to marry Prisoner or ever had any intention of marrying her, and he states that at present he has to keep his mother & brothers and sisters, several of whom are practically imbeciles and unable to earn their own living.

IN addition to this, Mold was very fond of the deceased's [i.e. deceased] boy & made him quite a playfellow whenever he returned from a voyage and was constantly giving him money, the last 1/- he gave him being to spend at Salisbury Fair, about 10 days before his death.

THE last witness called by the prosecution before the Magistrates was Matilda Sheppard, who described herself as a Police Matron, but who is really a female searcher.

SHE stated that on the night of November 3rd. she searched the Prisoner when in custody and found 7 sovereigns & 2 half sovereigns, & which are the precise gold coins stated by the Prisoner to have been in the bedroom drawer.

NOW the Police & Mrs. Sheppard knew perfectly well that this money belonged to the Prisoner's [13] Mother, Mrs. Carter, and was handed by the latter to the Prisoner to hold for her, as she had to attend the first day's proceedings of the inquest, which took place before the Prisoner was arrested.

CHIEF Constable Richardson was recalled and stated that he had satisfied himself that both purse & money did belong to Mrs. Carter and he afterwards handed them to Mr. William Carter for his Mother.

IT was understood in Court that the prosecution wished to prove that this £8. Was really some portion of the money which had been put on one side to obtain a cork leg for the deceased boy as mentioned on the evidence, & Mrs. Sheppard's evidence caused quit a stir in Court until the real facts were brought out by the further cross examination of Chief Constable Richardson.

IT will be seen that Mrs. Sheppard has since made another statement as to something said by the Prisoner on the evening of Saturday December 5th. After she had been committed for trail & after Canon Thwaites had visited her and left her.

Now prior to Canon Thwaites' visit and prior to Mrs. Sheppard going into the Prisoner, the latter's brother, Richard Carter, had seen her just after her committal, when almost the first words she said to her brother were 'Oh Dick! Oh Dick! I didn't do it! Do you think I could have done it? Fancy them saying I am insane.'

IT is therefore scarcely likely that the Prisoner would have said to Mrs. Sheppard almost directly afterwards 'If I did it, I don't remember it', unless some sort of leading question were asked her.

IT is also curious that Mrs. Sheppard does not remember whether she herself made any reply.

NOW this statement was made on the 5th. December, and on the 30th. December, the Public Prosecutor served the Prisoner's Solicitors with notice of Mrs. Cooper's evidence, so it would appear that up to that time nothing had been heard of Mrs. Sheppard's further evidence, and this further evidence as a matter of fact is dated the 21st. January and was received by the Prisoner's Solicitors on the 22nd.

LEAVING all mention of the proceedings before the Coroner out of the question, the Prisoner had just before she made this alleged statement been before the Magistrates for six long successive days and had been in a state of collapse on very many occasions causing suspensions of the sittings, one of such suspensions having taken place on the morning of the 5th. December for some considerable time and the Doctor was sent for and attended the Prisoner in Court up to the moment of her committal, there being to the last a considerable doubt whether she could stand the strain long enough to enable the proceedings to be terminated on that day.

IT seems to be common knowledge that the three local doctors do not believe that the Prisoner could have committed the murder alone and unaided, their theory being that someone else, presumably committed the murder whilst she was standing by looking on, and that this would account for the small quantity of blood found upon Prisoner's clothing.

THEY further seem to think that this theory is supported by certain facts which have leaked out but which were never brought before the Coroner and the Magistrates.

IT is true that Leate and Daniells [i.e. Daniels] were called before the Coroner, but not before the Prisoner's Solicitor stated that he should make some comment unless they were called. The Coroner then arranged to call them. [14]

LEATE'S evidence is certainly very curious, and will repay a careful study. He has always been understood to be a truthful witness, and that he saw somebody in Meadow Road about the time mentioned by him may be taken for granted.

COUNSEL will see that the evidence given before the Coroner and the statement given to Prisoner['s] Solicitors vary considerably.

IT is clear that the man came out of a house in Meadow Road first and the woman came out within half a minute afterwards, and this would have given the man sufficient time to have got round the corner of James Street or the cul de sac opposite, and this is probably what did happen notwithstanding that Leate says in cross examination 'The man and woman were in sight of me before the man passed.'

IN the newspaper report of the proceedings he said she could have seen the man if he had not in the meantime disappeared.

THERE may be nothing in Leate's story inconsistent with that of the Prisoner, and it is possible that the man Leate saw was the man who rushed out of No. 40, Meadow Road and got round into the cul de sac opposite James Street without being seen by the Prisoner.

NOW when this man however was got into this cul de sac, there was nothing to prevent his getting into the water meadows across to Castle Street, or into the Devizes Road or Stratford Road, quite clear away before any question of search was raised.

IT must be borne in mind that Prisoner in the state she was when she rushed out of the house would be quite as likely to follow the direction in which the man went as not, and it is a little bit surprising that Steer when he saw the Prisoner rushing in the direction of his house should have continued to run in the opposite direction when Mrs. Haskell said 'Man round the corner.'

HE did not even wait to ask which corner. The distance from the Prisoner's front door to the corner of James Street is only 147 feet, which distance a man could easily run in 7 or 8 seconds at the outside, and it would take Mr. Steer, who is by no means an active man, quite that time to get from his kitchen through the door into the scullery, through the scullery into the yard and from the yard through the gate into the passage and along the passage into Meadow Road, and in addition it may be taken for granted that he never heard the first scream, and the man whoever he was had for a start the time which it took the Prisoner to go through the kitchen out to the scullery door to give the alarm to Percy Noble and then return through the kitchen and along the passage to the front door and into the Street.

COUNSEL will remember from his inspection of the premises and neighbourhood how easy it is for anyone to get away if they wanted to.

THE fences themselves are very insecure and are only between 3 & 4 feet high. There are any amount of back yards and passages which would take a person into almost any street he wanted to go without being seen by people in Meadow Road, York Road, Sidney Street, or St. Paul's Road or any adjacent Streets.

THE alleged search for a missing man was a perfect farce. Everybody seemed to be pushing his nose into his neighbour's house without any idea for whom he was looking, and the greater part of the searchers had no description of a man at all, and the others were looking for the witness, Eccott, and he was joining them in the search. [15]

P.C. Cutler was called to prove that he went to the South Western Station and met two excursion trains which stopped at Salisbury and the ordinary mail train, and he did not see anyone answering to the description given by Mrs. Haskell, and it would have been surprising had he done so.

IT will be seen from Daniells' [i.e Daniels'] evidence before the Coroner that he was in the Barber's (Spark's shop shewn on plan) at 10 o'clock, stayed there 10 minutes and walked up Fisherton Street, down St. Paul's Road into Meadow Road, and got to his gate shewn on the plan between 10:15 and 10:20.

HE stood there several seconds looking up Meadow Road towards the direction of No. 40, and he saw someone, whom he is now practically certain was a man, shuffle round the corner by Mrs. Cooper's house at a half trot holding his head down.

HE then went indoors for 3 or 4 minutes, and when he came out all the people were running about and there was a general uproar and he ascertained that Teddy Haskell was dead and told his wife what he had seen.

TO try and explain away this evidence, the prosecution called before the Magistrates Mrs. E.L. Lodge (p. 24), the suggestion being that she was the person whom Daniells saw.

NOW this Mrs. Lodge was seen soon afterwards by Mrs. Daniells, the wife of Edwin Daniells, but she then had no apron on, although she still had the jug in her hand & further Daniells is confident that he was still in the Barber's shop at the time Mrs. Lodge says she went round the corner.

BOTH Leate and Daniells were bound over by the Coroner to attend the Assizes, but were not of course called before the Magistrates.

THEIR evidence will at all events go to prove that there were people about near No. 40, Meadow Rd at or about the time of the murder, notwithstanding that nearly the whole of the witnesses called by the prosecution were called to prove that nobody was in the Streets at the time, and that therefore the Prisoner must have committed the murder.

AS to the money in the drawer upstairs of which £4 : 12 : 0 is now missing, there is no doubt that the appearance of the drawer is consistent with its having been forced open, and this is now admitted by the prosecution.

THE lock is a very cheap flimsy thing, simply fastened to the wood by tin tacks, and although one of these tintacks remains in position and the lock cannot now be replaced over its head, this might easily be caused by the head being knocked out of shape by the wrench. It is understood that the prosecution do not lay any stress on this point.

NO evidence was or could be given as to the original position of the money in the drawer, & the £3 : 10 : 0 found by the Chief Constable was wrapped in a fold of a cloth in the drawer and not visible on first opening of the drawer.

IT is quite probable that the missing money may have been on the top of this cloth, and if this is so, the fact of the money which was not visible being left in the drawer by the thief is perfectly natural.

IT is also probable that the noise caused by the thief in opening the drawer partly awakened the boy and caused him to raise his hand in the way mentioned by the Doctors.

THIS was probably noticed by the man, who may have been known to the boy, and he therefore used the knife impulsively and with the idea of avoiding recognition, or the man may have been disturbed by Wyatt's knock, which also might have caused the boy to move in the act of awakening.

NOW prior to Wyatt's calling, the front door was locked, but Prisoner did not lock the [16] door again after Wyatt knocked, it being her intention to go out that way when she called upon Mrs. Mold.

NOW if the actual murderer had been upstairs at that time he could distinctly have heard all that happened down stairs, and that the Prisoner had not relocked the front door, and could have made up his mind at once that that was his way of escape, and eventually rushed out so hurriedly that he left the door open, and having traces of blood on one hand would naturally use the other one to open the door.

THIS man would have had every opportunity of getting into the house by the back door after Teddy had been put to bed, either when the Prisoner ahd gone into Noble's house or when she was in the W.C. after Miss Steer had visited her, as on both occasions the back door was unlocked.

AS will be seen from Mrs. Chiver's [i.e. Chivers'] evidence Mrs. Haskell is stated to have said that she did hear a noise which at first she thought came from upstairs, but afterwards thought might have been caused by one of the Noble boys nextg door and she thought nothing further of it.

GREAT stress will no doubt be laid on the fact that the knife used was one belonging to the Prisoner or the deceased. It must however be remembered that this knife was a rough one and used mostly by the deceased and was not one of the ordinary kitchen knives and was taken about by the deceased from time to time to the places where he wanted to use it, and nothing is more natural than that the deceased should have had this knife in his bedroom on the evening of the 31st. October.

THE account given by the Prisoner to the Police as to this knife should be noticed, from which it would appear that she had not recently seen the knife, and when she was asked whether she had missed a knife, she and her Mother looked through the knives in the kitchen drawer and both she and her mother said the knife Teddy used was missing and that it was a brown handled knife. It will be seen by Prisoner's first statement that when she was examined first about the knife, it was not shewn to her, although the Police had it in their possession when she first pointed out that it was missing and when they began to take a statement from her.

SHE stated on page 5 of her first statement that she had not found the knife and could not say where it was, and that she had not seen it since the previous Thursday when the deceased was out in the back sharpening wood making a tip-cat, and she gave the correct description of this knife.

IT was not at all certain at this time that Prisoner knew that a knife had been thrown at her. In her statement to the Police she says 'Something was thrown down at the bottom of the stairs and splashed my sleeve.'

SHE did not then know it was a knife, notwithstanding that Steer stated that the Prisoner told him that a knife had been thrown at her. Steer probably used these words because of the knife afterwards being seen.

NOW if the Prisoner had been the murderess she would have known what knife was used to commit the murder and would hardly be likely to describe that knife so carefully and correctly to the Police, knowing where she must, according to the evidence of the prosecution, have left the knife herself.

NOBODY but the Prisoner or her Mother could have identified this knife, and except from the evidence of the Prisoner herself, there would be nothing to shew that the knife belonged to [17] the house.

IN the case of the Police witnesses other than Golding, Chief Constable Richardson is by far the best witness to cross examine to get out all necessary facts. He is a nervous man, and if stuck to will give the answers required. He will try and hedge but soon gets confused.

THE prosecution however must somehow reconcile Percy Noble's evidence with Walter Steer's evidence as to time. It is quite evident that Percy Noble was on the scene first, and it is believed that the prosecution will attempt to support the time mentioned by Percy Noble, otherwise the Prisoner was seen by Steer in the Street at the time Wilks fixes as the time of death, & must have opened the door to Wyatt a minute or so previously.

STEER is supported as to time by his wife, Mrs. Chivers, Edward Butt, Sarah Butt, William Eccott, Herbert Primmer, Gertrude Skutt and Emily Sweatman [i.e. Sweetman].

Mr. Wilks also says he got the message from Percy Noble at 10:30 and this is corroborated by Mr. Row, and Golding arrived at the house at 10:35, and this also goes to shew that Steer's time is the correct time, and not the boy Percy Noble's.

COUNSEL will see the discrepancies between the evidence of Steer, Butt & Eccott as to the occurrence at the Duke of York Gates.

IT may be taken for granted that Percy Noble could not have gone up the Wilton Road & got to Dr. Wilks' house which stands back a considerable distance from the Road and both Doctors could have got their bicycles ready and arrived at Meadow Road in less than 10 minutes. The arrived, as will be seen, at 10:31, and this again would corroborate Steer's evidence as to time.

THE Prosecution themselves seem perfectly aware of this, and that is the reason they pin their faith on House's evidence which they say is supported by the striking of St. Paul's Clock, but it is a curious fact that Slade never heard the striking of the clock & never heard House mention anything about the time, and this can be brought out when attention is called to the fact that Slade has made statements to the Police and has not been called.

FURTHER of course House's evidence is of no value because it probably was not the first scream he heard, and he did not see Steer.

A model of the house has been prepared and will be in Court. It is suggested by the Prosecution that this model shall be put in as a part of Mr. Notley's evidence.

References

Note on abbreviations and conventions: LWN, SJ and ST are abbreviations for, respectively, *Lloyd's Weekly News*, *The Salisbury and Winchester Journal* and *The Salisbury Times and South Wilts Gazette*. TNA refers to the National Archives and is used to prefix call numbers of their documents referred to. Books quoted from are referred at first citations by author, title and page reference and subsequently by title and page reference. Full bibliographic details are given in the list of sources and suggestions for further reading.

Chapter 2

1 ST 17/4/1908, 24/4/1908; advertisement ST 8/11/1908.
2 In 1860, the total of the London and South Western services had amounted to 21 arrivals and 21 departures on weekdays. Source SJ 7/1/1860.
3 ST, editorial, 14/3/1868.
4 SJ, obituary 3/5/1919.
5 The Lent Assizes saw no fewer than 24 prisoners sentenced to death, but eventually only two suffered the extreme penalty: Henry Smith for rape and Timothy Thomas for murder. Henry Wynn was executed for murder following sentence at the Lent Assizes, 1836, and was the first to be buried within the walls of the Gaol. Sources: Wheeler: *Sarum chronology* (1889), p. 50; Dowding: *Statistics of crime from 1801 to 1850* (1855) record for 1836.
6 When gas mains were being laid in the Wilton Road in October 1851, about 20 skeletons were discovered in shallow graves, these being understood to be the remains of those executed at the gallows nearby. Source: Wheeler, *Sarum chronology* (1889) pp. 65-66.
7 Charles would go onto greater things, firstly by repositioning himself in the trade as an antique dealer, and then, from early in the new century, by moving to new premises in the High Street and, later New Street, where he restored the New Inn. He was also involved in local politics: from becoming a councillor for St Paul's ward from 1906, he would go on to be Mayor in 1935. He died in 1945.
8 Plaque on the north side of the bridge.
9 SJ obituary, 23/5/1903.
10 Most notably Belgrave Villas, York Road, which on the 1901 census comprised eight households. TNA RG13/1952, fol. 87 pp.21-2 refers
11 Reeves, M.P. *Round about a pound a week* (1913), ch. 1: The district.
12 *Round about a pound a week*, ch. 3: Housing.
13 *Round about a pound a week*, ch. 3: Housing, appendices A and B.
14 The total wage bill was £1,868 4s 0d; if one assumes this includes 5% employer's pension contribution, the total paid to the force in service was £1,779 4s 9d; divided by 27 = £65 17s 7½d p.a., or 25s 4d per week. Without any deduction the figure is £1 6s 8d. By contrast the Chief Constable received £175 p.a, plus his emoluments as Inspector of the Market, Inspector of Weights, Inspector of Hackney Carriages, etc. Source: City of New Sarum: *Abstract of the Borough Fund accounts for the year ended 31st March 1909.*
15 Farrant, J.P. *The history of Scout Motors of Salisbury, 1902-1921* (undated), p. 6.
16 The house on the north corner is numbered as 39 Meadow Road.
17 Reeves, M.P.*Round about a pound a week* (London: G. Bell, 1913), chapter 1: The district.
18 Reeves: *Round about a pound a week*, Ch. 4: 'Furniture, sleeping accommodation,, equipment for cooking and bathing'.
19 By 1908 Alfred had become a jobbing gardener.

Chapter 3

1 TNA RG13/1952 fol. 91v p. 28 schedule 186, 20 Meadow Road. At some time between 1901 and 1907 Meadow Road was renumbered, from north to south, and 20 Meadow Road became 40.
2 Devizes and Wiltshire Gazette, 12/11/08, states that Richard Carter was 'formerly employed by Mr Lush, who carried on a corn merchant's business in the shop at Warminster now occupied by Mr W.H. Marshman, and went with his employer to Salisbury.'
3 Ibid.
4 ST 6/11/1908
5 Although for statistical purposes in Chapter 2 we have treated the household as being of the Haskells with Mrs Carter as a living-in grandmother.
6 Reeves: *Round about a pound a week*, Ch. 6: 'Budgets'.

7 LWN 8/11/1908, reproduced in full in Appendices, pp.230-2.

8 Dew's report to the DPP, 7/1/1909

Chapter 4

1 By this time the city council also had offices, for the City Engineer, in Endless Street

2 Smith was a solicitor, practising at 53 New Canal, and was also Secretary to the Infirmary and vestry clerk at St Paul's Fisherton Anger and at St Thomas'

3 While Haskins' shops are today a branch of T-Mobile and a shoe shop, Alderman Haskins is today better remembered for his comprehensive accounts of the Corporation's Pictures and plate, and of his definitive account of the city's ancient trade guilds.

4 Godfrey Bowering, Edward Downer, Herbert George, Ernest Kelly, Albert Knee, Bertie Lawrence, Harold Pengelly, Fred Quinton, Tom Say, Bruce Slater, Alfred Wisdom and Albert Withers.

5 Henbest was an accountant and insurance agent, listed at 53 New Canal, hence in the same office as the Coroner. He was the clerk to the Burial Board and assistant secretary to the Infirmary.

6 Edgar Slade, greengrocer, 53 Meadow Road.

Chapter 5

1 John Arthur Beresford, bootmaker, 143 Fisherton Street.

2 Emma Noble died in 1895.

3 Now the King's Head, a Wetherspoon house, at the end of the south side of Bridge Street, Salisbury.

4 The match was at Dean, between Dean Village and St Edmund's Night School, in the Salisbury Minor league, and resulted in a score of 5-0 to St Edmund's, maintaining their position at the top of the league.

5 i.e. 27 York Road, on the north-west corner of York Road and Meadow Road.

6 The passage at the back of Nos. 42 and 40 Meadow Road leads directly into York Road. Of the evidently not very high barriers between the backs of the houses north of No. 40 there were six between the alleyway in York Road and that down the side of No. 2 James Street.

7 The eldest son of Thomas Scamell, builder of the Gaol Ground estate, Edwin Richard Scamell of 5 Nelson Road is listed in directories first as a carpenter, subsequently as a builder.

8 Langmead, together with Thomas Evans of 26 Harcourt Terrace (in 1897), was also the editor of the second of Salisbury's city directories, published in late 1897 and annually thereafter until the mid-1920s, when Salisbury was served, as were the vast majority of English towns and cities by E.R. Kelly's directories known as the buff books.

9 Mrs C Saunders, shopkeeper and grocer, *Brown's Directory of Salisbury and District*, 1912

Chapter 6

1 SJ 21/11/1908, p. 8

2 The adjourned magistrates' hearing.

Chapter 7

1 i.e., one assumes, "anywhere in the county."

Chapter 8

1 i.e. 8 November 1908.

Chapter 9

1 Wednesday 18th, Friday 20th, Saturday 21st

2 ST 4/12/1908.

Chapter 10

1 See Chapter 5 note 6.

2 ST 6/11/1908

3 SJ 7/11/1908

4 LWN 8/11/1908.

5 LWN 6/12/1908 describes the couple simply as Mr and Mrs G. Hawkins, and there were no fewer than four George Hawkinses listed in contemporary local directories. However, given that running charitable appeals is the sort of activity for which public houses are well placed, and the relative nearness of the Malmesbury Arms to the scene of the crime, it seems likely that 'Mr and Mrs G. Hawkins' were the publican and his wife.

6 LWN 29/11/1908

7 LWN 6/12/1908.

8 Funds were so tight, even at the time the jury trial opened, that, as noted in the first of Trethowan's briefs to counsel in February 1909, 'All the papers in this matter are with Mr Rayner Goddard, the Defence having no funds to enable additional copies to be made.'

9 One of the most curious aspects of the investigative and legal processes, given the amount of hearsay evidence aired in court, is the fact that Canon Thwaites was never interviewed about his exchanges with Flora, let alone called as a witness. Dew himself, in his report to the Director of Public Prosecutions dated 31 Dec 1908, said that 'under no circumstances [was anyone] to approach the Rev. gentleman referred to.' There is no clerical privilege in English law, and in any case Thwaites appears to have broken the seal of the confession in what he divulged to Tucker and Stroud on 5 December. And while Dew took statements from Tucker and Stroud, and repeatedly urged action on Richardson's part, nothing appears to have been done by the time that Dew was reporting to Froest early in January, nor subsequently. Dew's sense of punctiliousness seems to have been matched by that of the Salisbury police.

10 Renamed from 1975 Turner Peacock.

Chapter 12

1 The Devizes and Wiltshire Advertiser report describes the weather as 'disagreeable', the contemporary review of the week's weather in The Times reports a strong westerly airflow bringing showers and longer outbreaks of rain.

Chapter 14

1 The text which follows is not a full *verbatim* transcript, being taken primarily from contemporary press accounts, which differ widely in the weight given to witnesses' testimonies, counsels' arguments and the judge's summing-up. The main source for Goddard's closing address in this account has been the *Salisbury Times and South Wilts Gazette*, which gives the fullest account, and accurately conveys the flavour of Goddard's oratory even when that is not reproduced word-for-word. The *Devizes and Wiltshire Advertiser*, though presenting a far briefer rendering of Goddard's speech, has at various points a number of key phrases which seemed to us so characteristic of his style of oratory that they have been incorporated into the transcript.

2 There was a possibility, mooted at the time, that an attempt had been made to nobble the jury, but no action was taken to investigate the claim. The fact that one of the jury was Robert Henry Jefferies, who may or may not have been a relative of Flora's on her mother's side of the family, serves only to heighten the sense of intrigue.

Chapter 15

1 The Times, 30/5/1936.

2 ST 2/4/1909.

3 "The court was crowded this morning to a state of discomfort, but not a tithe of those who endeavoured to gain admission were able to do so." – SJ, 2/4/1909.

4 ST 2/4/09; Mackay, H., *Report to the Director of Public Prosecutions* 26/3/1909. His earlier report, 11/2/1909, recorded that she had gained 13lb in weight.

5 Receipts on the two briefs to counsel show that Alfred Schuster was paid £3 3s. 0d. on 17 February 1909, after the first jury trial, and that Goddard was paid £23 2s. 0d., including £2 2s. 0d. for a 'conference', on 31 March 1909, just before the second jury trial. The accounts were rendered in guineas.

Chapter 16

1 He was chatting to Edgar Slade outside the latter's shop, 53 Meadow Road, over 50 yards south of the junction with York Road. He never noticed Percy Noble, so was not alerted to the situation until he heard Flora's screams.

2 Dew's report states that Leate made his statement late on Sunday, 1 November, while Richardson testified (see p.150) that Leate visited the City Police Station on Monday morning, 2 November.

3 Dr Maurice is not identified in Trethowan's brief to counsel, but there was in Marlborough, thirty miles north of Salisbury, a medical dynasty of Maurices which began with a partnership in 1792. By 1907 there were three Maurices in general practice in Marlborough, any one of whom could have been the author of the report. There is to this day a member of the family practising in Marlborough.

4 Not definitively identified, but she may have been Dulcie Lawrence, who in 1901 was a maidservant in the household of Emma and Francis Deverell, siblings, of 17 Devizes Road; Francis was the manager of a steam laundry. In 1908 Dulcie would have been 32 or 33.

5 Trethowan's case notes.

6 Trethowan's brief to counsel, 31 March 1909, p. 7.

Chapter 17

1 Of whom it had been Sarah who had followed Steer up the stairs at 40 Meadow Road.

2 ST 20/11/1908 p 7 col. 5 "An adjournment"

3 Mrs Mold lived in James Street, off Meadow Road and only about 150 yards from the houses in Gas Lane

Bibliography

Primary and Contemporary Sources

Archival Resources

National Archives

ASSI 21: Assizes: Western Circuit Crown Minute Books, including

ASSI 21/80:- Assize Courts: *Diaries for the two jury trials of Flora Haskell*, February and April 1908.

ASSI 26: Assizes: Western Circuit Criminal Depositions and Case Papers, including Salisbury Coroner's Court: *Verdict certificate against Flora Haskell*, 27/11/1908; Magistrates' Hearing: *Rex v Haskell: charge sheet and depositions of witnesses*, 30/11/1908-5/12/1908.

MEPO2/7823: Metropolitan Police Files:-

Dew, W.: *Reports to the Director of Public Prosecutions*, 4/11/1908, 12/11/1908, 24/11/1908 [typescripts], 28/11/1908 [manuscript], 26/12/1908, 31/12/1908 [manuscript], 7/1/1909, 8/2/1909, 1/3/1909, 29/4/1909 [typescripts].

Hailstone, A.: *Report to the Director of Public Prosecutions*, 1/11/1908 [typescript].

Hodding, F.: *Letter of thanks to the Commissioner of the Metropolitan Police*, 6/5/1909. [typescript].

Mackay, H.: *Reports to the Director of Public Prosecutions*, 11/2/1909, 26/3/1909. [typescript].

Richardson, F.: *Telegram sent to the Commissioner of the Metropolitan Police*, 1/11/1908. [manuscript].

Richardson, F.: *Letter of thanks to the Commissioner of the Metropolitan Police*, 17/4/1909. [typescript].

HO107, RG9, RG10, RG11 and RG12: *Census enumerators' returns*, June 1841, April 1851 – April 1891.

RG13: *Census enumerators' returns: Salisbury Enumeration District 13 [and elsewhere in Salisbury and Devizes]*, April 1901.

Private Collection: Mrs Ann Whittle: Richardson, E.F.: *Photograph album of the crime scene and other interior and exterior views of 40 Meadow Road, and of Meadow Road and other locations in Railway Town, Fisherton, Salisbury.* November 1908.

Private Collection: Mr H. Brock Trethowan: Goddard, R.: *notes on the Magisterial hearing, 30/11/1908-5/12/1908.* [November-December 1908]. [manuscript in exercise-book].

Messrs Nodder and Trethowan, Salisbury: *Rex v. Haskell: wilful murder, Wilts Winter Assizes, Devizes, 12th February 1909: brief for the defence.* [receipted] 17/2/1909. [manuscript].

Messrs Nodder and Trethowan, Salisbury: *Rex on the prosecution of Flora Fanny Haskell: wilful murder, Wilts Winter Assizes, 1st April 1909: brief for the defence on the re-trial of this case.* [receipted] 31/3/1909. [typescript].

Trethowan, W.J. *Case notes on the first jury trial, February 1909, comprising glosses to the press reports from the Devizes and Wiltshire Advertiser and the Salisbury Times and South Wilts Gazette, and names of people with information of value to the defence case.* [1909]. [manuscript and letterpress paste-downs in exercise book].

Directories, Railway Timetables, Official Reportage

Brown and Co.: *Directory of Salisbury and district. 9th ed. (-12th ed.)* Brown and Co., 1906-1912.

Great Western Railway: *Timetables of the Great Western Railway, January, February, March and April 1902.* Ian Allan, 1969 (reprint of original edition).

London and South Western Railway: *Timetables, 7th June to 30th September 1914.* Ian Allan, 1967 (reprint of original edition, Waterlow, 1914).

Kelly, E: *Post Office directory of Wiltshire, 1848.* E. Kelly, 1848.

Kelly's Directories: *Kelly's directory of Salisbury and neighbourhood, 1927 (-1959).* Kelly's Directories, 1927-1959

Kelly's Directories Ltd: *Kelly's directory of Wiltshire, 1895 (-1939).* Kelly's Directories, 1895-1939.

Langmead and Evans: *Directory of Salisbury and district.* Langmead and Evans, 1897.

Mundy, F. *and Co.: A directory of the city of Salisbury and surrounding districts.* F. Mundy, 1891.

New Sarum, City of: *Abstract of the Borough Fund accounts for the year ended 31st March 1909.* [Salisbury City Council, 1909].

Salisbury Chamber of Commerce: *Directory of Salisbury and*

the neighbourhood. Bennett Bros, 1925.

Maps

Ordnance Survey: *Wiltshire Sheets LXVI.11 and LXVI.15*, editions of 1881, 1901, 1925. Scale 1:2,500.

National Grid Plans SU 1330 NE, SU 1330 SE, SU 1430 NW, SU 1430 SW, editions of 1953. Scale 1:1,250.

Newspapers and periodicals

Daily Graphic, November 1908; daily.

Daily Mirror, November 1908; daily.

Devizes and Wiltshire Advertiser, November 1908-April 1909 and 29/5/1913 (murder of Dorothy Jefferies); weekly.

Devizes and Wiltshire Gazette, November 1908-April 1909; weekly.

Hansard: "Business of the House [of Commons], etc. 25th February 1909" (in *Parliamentary debates: Commons, 5th Series, Vol. 1, January-March 1909*. Eyre and Spottiswoode, 1909).

Illustrated Police News, November-December 1908; weekly.

Lloyd's Weekly News, November 1908; weekly.

News of the World, November-December 1908; weekly.

Salisbury and Winchester Journal, November 1908-April 1909 and as referenced in the text; weekly.

Salisbury Times and South Wilts Gazette, November 1908-April 1909 and as referenced in the text; weekly.

The Times, November 1908-April 1909 and as referenced in the text; daily.

Weekly Dispatch, November-December 1908; weekly.

Wiltshire County Mirror and Express, November 1908-April 1909; twice weekly.

A note on primary sources. The main source for the proceedings of the inquest, the magisterial hearing and the two jury trials is the reportage in local and national newspapers. Outside the High Court, there is no official, *verbatim* transcript of legal hearings, nor of depositions save those taken at inquests, which are normally sealed for many years and retained in county record offices. The survival of inquest reports is not guaranteed, and in the case of the inquest into the death of Teddy Haskell, we have been unable to discover any material in the Wiltshire and Swindon Record Office. It is therefore a matter of great good fortune that the depositions taken at the magisterial hearing and the certificate of the verdict from the inquest survive in The National Archives. The main sources throughout have been *The Salisbury Times and South Wilts Gazette* and the *Devizes and Wiltshire Gazette* studied in tandem, with expansions provided mainly by readings from *The Devizes and Wiltshire Advertiser*. (Please see also Chapter 14 note 1). The *Salisbury and Winchester Journal* has been most useful for providing some background information on the legal proceedings. It will be clear from the foregoing that whilst the record we have, and that which is presented to the reader, is as close as it is now possible to reach to the words spoken in court, it is of necessity a reconstruction.

Secondary sources and further reading

Baker, A.: *History beneath our feet: a guide to the Devizes Road and London Road Cemeteries.* Salisbury District Council, [1993].

Bresler, F. *Lord Goddard: a biography of Rayner Goddard, Lord Chief Justice of England; with a foreword by Lord Denning.* London: Harrap, 1977.

Chandler, J.H.: *Endless Street: a history of Salisbury and its people.* Rev. ed. Hobnob Press, 1987.

Coe, D.: *Salisbury Electric Light and Supply Company.* South Wiltshire Industrial Archaeology Society, 2008. (SWIAS Historical Monograph 19).

Connell, P. *Walter Dew: the man who caught Crippen.* Stroud: Tempus Books, 2006.

Cossor, W.E.: *Historical notes relating to St Clement's and St Paul's churches,* [Fisherton], compiled by W.E. and R.H. Cossor. 2nd ed. [The authors], 1931. – [typescript; copy in Salisbury Library].

Crittall, E., editor: *A history of Wiltshire, vol. 6: (the Borough of Wilton, the Borough of Old Salisbury, the City of New Salisbury, the Hundred of Underditch).* Oxford University Press [for] the University of London Institute of Historical Research, 1962. (The Victoria history of the counties of England).

Dowding, W.: *Statistics of crime from 1801 to 1850, compiled by the Governor of the County Gaol,* [Fisherton]. F.A. Blake, 1855.

Farrant, J.P.: *The history of Scout Motors Limited, of Salisbury, (1902-1921).* Salisbury and South Wiltshire Group for Industrial Archaeology, [1967].

Hart, P.: *Salisbury and Wilton street names.* [The author], 2002. – [typescript copies in Salisbury Library and the Wiltshire and Swindon History Centre].

Hartman, M.S.: *Victorian murderesses: a true history of thirteen respectable French and English women accused of unspeakable crimes.* Robson Books, 1977.

Kingston, C.: *Dramatic days at the Old Bailey.* Stanley Paul, [1923].

Lyle, D.P.: *Forensics for dummies.* Wiley Publishing, 2004.

Maidment, A.: *I remember, I remember: the story of my boyhood in Salisbury.* Baverstock Books, 1990.

Newburn, T. and others: *Handbook of criminal investigation, by Tim Newburn, Tom Williamson [and] Alan Wright.* Willan Publishing, 2007.

Newman, R. and Howells, J.: *Salisbury past.* Phillimore, 2001.

Northy, T.J.: *The popular history of Old and New Sarum.*

Wiltshire County Mirror and Express, 1897.

Oxford Dictionary of National Biography – for biography of Lord Goddard; available on-line.

Petherick, W.: *Criminal profile: into the mind of the killer*. Reader's Digest, 2005.

Purvis, B.: *Salisbury: the changing city*. Breedon Books, 2003.

Reeves, M.P. *Round about a pound a week*. G. Bell, 1913.

'Religious forces in Salisbury' (in *Supplement to the Daily Graphic*, 16 December 1908) – contains reference to Canon Thwaites' ministry in Salisbury.

Salisbury, South Wilts and Blackmore Museum: *The festival book of Salisbury, published to commemorate the jubilee of the Museum, 1864-1914*; ed. F. Stevens. Bennett Bros, [printers], 1914.

'The twelve greatest detectives of the world: the true story of their most famous cases; this week: Inspector Dew, the man who caught Crippen' (in *The Saturday Post*, 29 January 1916).

Summerscale, K.: *The suspicions of Mr Whicher, or The murder at Road Hill House*. Bloomsbury, 2008.

Walker, T.W.F.: *Ernest Frank Richardson, previously Chief Constable of Salisbury*: [report forming part of a family history archive dossier]. [The author], 2000. [typescript]. [copies in Wiltshire and Swindon Record Office and in Salisbury Library Ephemera Collection, ref. SAL.346].

Watts, J.H.: *Salisbury Gasworks: the Salisbury Gas Light and Coke Company*. South Wiltshire Industrial Archaeology Society, 1991. (SWIAS Historical Monograph 12).

Wheeler, W.A.: *Sarum chronology: a brief record of the most salient events in the history of Salisbury*. Brown, 1889.

Who was who – biographical sketches of Darling, Foote, Lord Glenconner (Sir Edward Tennant) Lord Goddard, Pepper, Ridley; available on-line.

Index

A page reference in *italic* type indicates an illustration.

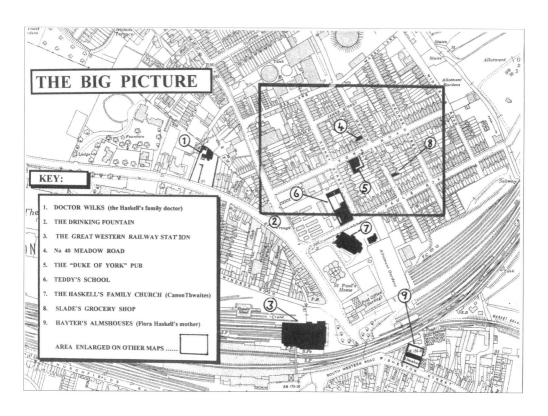

THE BIG PICTURE

KEY:

1. DOCTOR WILKS (the Haskell's family doctor)
2. THE DRINKING FOUNTAIN
3. THE GREAT WESTERN RAILWAY STATION
4. No 40 MEADOW ROAD
5. THE "DUKE OF YORK" PUB
6. TEDDY'S SCHOOL
7. THE HASKELL'S FAMILY CHURCH (Canon Thwaites)
8. SLADE'S GROCERY SHOP
9. HAYTER'S ALMSHOUSES (Flora Haskell's mother)

AREA ENLARGED ON OTHER MAPS ......

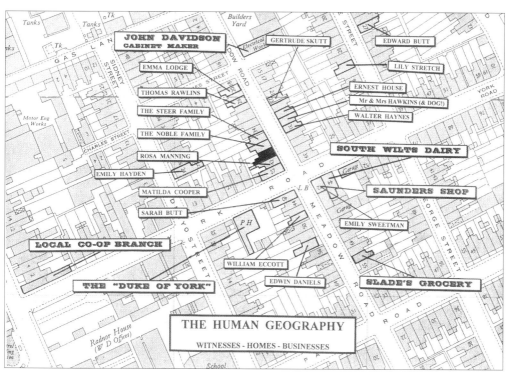

JOHN DAVIDSON CABINET MAKER

GERTRUDE SKUTT

EDWARD BUTT

EMMA LODGE

LILY STRETCH

THOMAS RAWLINS

ERNEST HOUSE

Mr & Mrs HAWKINS (& DOG!)

THE STEER FAMILY

WALTER HAYNES

THE NOBLE FAMILY

SOUTH WILTS DAIRY

ROSA MANNING

EMILY HAYDEN

MATILDA COOPER

SAUNDERS SHOP

SARAH BUTT

EMILY SWEETMAN

LOCAL CO-OP BRANCH

WILLIAM ECCOTT

THE "DUKE OF YORK"

EDWIN DANIELS

SLADE'S GROCERY

THE HUMAN GEOGRAPHY

WITNESSES - HOMES - BUSINESSES

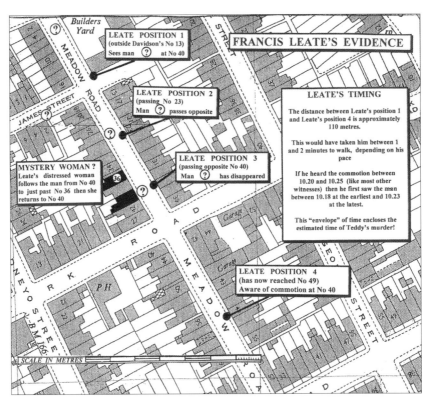

FRANCIS LEATE'S EVIDENCE

Builders Yard

LEATE POSITION 1
(outside Davidson's No 13)
Sees man (?) at No 40

LEATE POSITION 2
(passing No 23)
Man (?) passes opposite

MYSTERY WOMAN ?
Leate's distressed woman follows the man from No 40 to just past No 36 then she returns to No 40

LEATE POSITION 3
(passing opposite No 40)
Man (?) has disappeared

LEATE'S TIMING

The distance between Leate's position 1 and Leate's position 4 is approximately 110 metres.

This would have taken him between 1 and 2 minutes to walk, depending on his pace

If he heard the commotion between 10.20 and 10.25 (like most other witnesses) then he first saw the man between 10.18 at the earliest and 10.23 at the latest.

This "envelope" of time encloses the estimated time of Teddy's murder!

LEATE POSITION 4
(has now reached No 49)
Aware of commotion at No 40

SCALE IN METRES

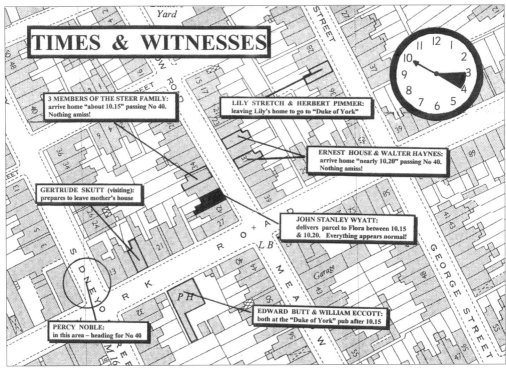

TIMES & WITNESSES

Yard

3 MEMBERS OF THE STEER FAMILY:
arrive home "about 10.15" passing No 40.
Nothing amiss!

LILY STRETCH & HERBERT PIMMER:
leaving Lily's home to go to "Duke of York"

ERNEST HOUSE & WALTER HAYNES:
arrive home "nearly 10.20" passing No 40.
Nothing amiss!

GERTRUDE SKUTT (visiting):
prepares to leave mother's house

JOHN STANLEY WYATT:
delivers parcel to Flora between 10.15 & 10.20. Everything appears normal!

PERCY NOBLE:
in this area – heading for No 40

EDWARD BUTT & WILLIAM ECCOTT:
both at the "Duke of York" pub after 10.15

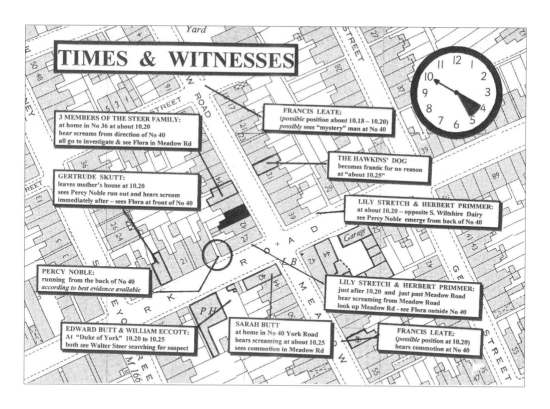

TIMES & WITNESSES

FRANCIS LEATE:
(*possible* position about 10.18 – 10.20)
possibly sees "mystery" man at No 40

3 MEMBERS OF THE STEER FAMILY:
at home in No 36 at about 10.20
hear screams from direction of No 40
all go to investigate & see Flora in Meadow Rd

THE HAWKINS' DOG
becomes frantic for no reason
at "about 10.25"

GERTRUDE SKUTT:
leaves mother's house at 10.20
sees Percy Noble run out and hears scream
immediately after – sees Flora at front of No 40

LILY STRETCH & HERBERT PRIMMER:
at about 10.20 – opposite S. Wiltshire Dairy
see Percy Noble emerge from back of No 40

PERCY NOBLE:
running from the back of No 40
according to best evidence available

LILY STRETCH & HERBERT PRIMMER:
just after 10.20 and just past Meadow Road
hear screaming from Meadow Road
look up Meadow Rd - see Flora outside No 40

EDWARD BUTT & WILLIAM ECCOTT:
At "Duke of York" 10.20 to 10.25
both see Walter Steer searching for suspect

SARAH BUTT:
at home in No 40 York Road
hears screaming at about 10.25
sees commotion in Meadow Rd

FRANCIS LEATE:
(*possible* position at 10.20)
hears commotion at No 40

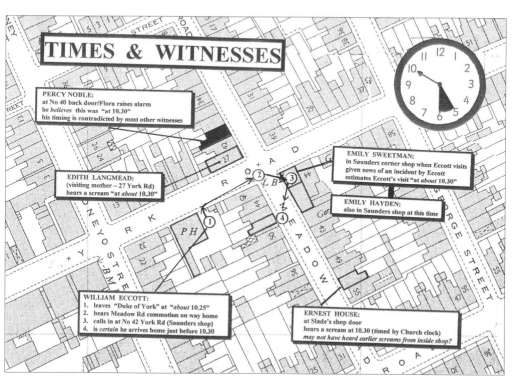

TIMES & WITNESSES

PERCY NOBLE:
at No 40 back door/Flora raises alarm
he *believes* this was "at 10.30"
his timing is contradicted by most other witnesses

EDITH LANGMEAD:
(visiting mother – 27 York Rd)
hears a scream "at *about* 10.30"

EMILY SWEETMAN:
in Saunders corner shop when Eccott visits
given news of an incident by Eccott
estimates Eccott's visit "at *about* 10.30"

EMILY HAYDEN:
also in Saunders shop at this time

WILLIAM ECCOTT:
1. leaves "Duke of York" at "*about* 10.25"
2. hears Meadow Rd commotion on way home
3. calls in at No 42 York Rd (Saunders shop)
4. is *certain* he arrives home just before 10.30

ERNEST HOUSE:
at Slade's shop door
hears a scream at 10.30 (timed by Church clock)
may not have heard earlier screams from inside shop?

Hobnob Press publishes books about Wiltshire and neighbouring counties, including histories of towns and villages, walking guides and academic texts. It also publishes *Sarum Chronicle*, an annual journal about the history of Salisbury and its district, and **Sarum Studies**, a series of monographs about the Salisbury area. For full details visit **www.hobnobpress.co.uk** or write for a catalogue to
Hobnob Press, PO Box 1838, East Knoyle, Salisbury SP3 6FA